Assemble the Social Web with
zembly

Assemble the Social Web with zembly

GAIL ANDERSON AND PAUL ANDERSON

WITH TODD FAST AND CHRIS WEBSTER

PRENTICE HALL

Upper Saddle River, NJ • Boston • Indianapolis • San Francisco
New York • Toronto • Montreal • London • Munich • Paris • Madrid
Capetown • Sydney • Tokyo • Singapore • Mexico City

Many of the designations used by manufacturers and sellers to distinguish their products are claimed as trademarks. Where those designations appear in this book, and the publisher was aware of a trademark claim, the designations have been printed with initial capital letters or in all capitals.

Sun Microsystems, Inc. has intellectual property rights relating to implementations of the technology described in this publication. In particular, and without limitation, these intellectual property rights may include one or more U.S. patents, foreign patents, or pending applications.

Sun, Sun Microsystems, the Sun logo, J2ME, J2EE, Java Card, and all Sun and Java based trademarks and logos are trademarks or registered trademarks of Sun Microsystems, Inc., in the United States and other countries. UNIX is a registered trademark in the United States and other countries, exclusively licensed through X/Open Company, Ltd. THIS PUBLICATION IS PROVIDED "AS IS" WITHOUT WARRANTY OF ANY KIND, EITHER EXPRESS OR IMPLIED, INCLUDING, BUT NOT LIMITED TO, THE IMPLIED WARRANTIES OF MERCHANTABILITY, FITNESS FOR A PARTICULAR PURPOSE, OR NON-INFRINGEMENT. THIS PUBLICATION COULD INCLUDE TECHNICAL INACCURACIES OR TYPOGRAPHICAL ERRORS. CHANGES ARE PERIODICALLY ADDED TO THE INFORMATION HEREIN; THESE CHANGES WILL BE INCORPORATED IN NEW EDITIONS OF THE PUBLICATION. SUN MICROSYSTEMS, INC. MAY MAKE IMPROVEMENTS AND/OR CHANGES IN THE PRODUCT(S) AND/OR THE PROGRAM(S) DESCRIBED IN THIS PUBLICATION AT ANY TIME.

The authors and publisher have taken care in the preparation of this book, but make no expressed or implied warranty of any kind and assume no responsibility for errors or omissions. No liability is assumed for incidental or consequential damages in connection with or arising out of the use of the information or programs contained herein.

The publisher offers excellent discounts on this book when ordered in quantity for bulk purchases or special sales, which may include electronic versions and/or custom covers and content particular to your business, training goals, marketing focus, and branding interests. For more information, please contact: U.S. Corporate and Government Sales, (800) 382-3419, corpsales@pearsontechgroup.com.

For sales outside the United States please contact: International Sales, international@pearsoned.com.

Library of Congress Control Number: 2008941460

Copyright © 2009 Sun Microsystems, Inc.

4150 Network Circle, Santa Clara, California 95054 U.S.A.

All rights reserved.

Printed in the United States of America. This publication is protected by copyright, and permission must be obtained from the publisher prior to any prohibited reproduction, storage in a retrieval system, or transmission in any form or by any means, electronic, mechanical, photocopying, recording, or likewise. For information regarding permissions, write to: Pearson Education, Inc., Rights and Contracts Department, 501 Boylston Street, Suite 900, Boston, MA 02116, Fax: (617) 671-3447.

ISBN-13: 978-0-13-714431-0
ISBN-10:   0-13-714431-8

Text printed in the United States on recycled paper at Courier in Stoughton, Massachusetts.
First printing December 2008

Contents

Preface   *xiii*

Acknowledgments   *xvii*

Chapter 1   What Is zembly?   1

     1.1   Social Programming   2

     1.2   zembly's Environment   4

     1.3   zembly's Audience   6

     1.4   Publishing and Scaling with zembly   7

     1.5   Monetizing with zembly   8

     1.6   Coming to zembly Soon   8

           Meebo   8

           OpenSocial   8

           Scripting Languages   9

           A Final Thought   9

Chapter 2   zembly Basics   11

           What You Will Learn   12

           Examples in This Chapter   12

     2.1   Exploring the Samples   13

           Using Clone   15

           Widget Actions   16

           Tags on zembly   16

           AmazonProductSearchWidget—Widget Preview   17

           Embedding AmazonProductSearchWidget   18

           Sharing Your Widgets with Clearspring   19

- 2.2 About You—Your Home Page 20
  - Your Profile 21
  - People—Adding Contacts 22
- 2.3 Your Keychain and Service Providers 24
- 2.4 Creating Your First Service: LoanPaymentService 25
  - Specifying Parameters in a Service 27
  - Error Handling 29
  - Testing LoanPaymentService 30
  - Capturing Example Return Data 30
  - Saving Drafts 31
  - Using the JavaScript Editor 31
  - Publishing LoanPaymentService 32
  - Calling LoanPaymentService 32
- 2.5 Creating Your First Widget: LoanPaymentWidget 34
  - Uploading an Image 36
  - Including Library Prototype JS 37
  - Building LoanPaymentWidget 38
  - Using CSS for Styling 38
  - Calling LoanPaymentService in Your Widget 39
  - Previewing and Publishing 41
  - Embedding LoanPaymentWidget 42
- 2.6 Drafts, Versions, and Timelines 42
  - Edit History 42
  - Viewing Versions 44
  - Online/Offline Status 44
- 2.7 Putting It All Together—Using the WeatherBug API 45
  - Using Your Keychain 46
  - Building WeatherBugService 47
  - Using E4X and JavaScript 48
  - Calling WeatherBugService 50
  - Building WeatherBugWidget 51

Chapter 3   Building Flickr Widgets   55

- What You Will Learn 55
- Examples in This Chapter 56

3.1 Using Flickr 56
3.2 Building a Slide Show Widget 57
Looking at the Source 59
Using CSS Styles 59
Working with JavaScript 61
Sharing Your Widget 66
Embedding Your Widget in a Web Page 67

3.3 Building a Service for Your Flickr Photos 67
Getting a Flickr Application Key 68
Creating Service FlickrPeopleService 68
Using Find & Use to Add JavaScript 69
Testing and Publishing 71

3.4 Creating a Flickr User Slide Show Widget 71
Specifying Widget Parameters When You Embed 72
Creating Widget MyFlickrRandomSlideshow 73
Reusing JavaScript Code 74

Chapter 4   Building Zillow Widgets   79
What You Will Learn 79
Examples in This Chapter 80

4.1 Using Zillow 80
4.2 Building a Zillow Service 82
Obtaining a Zillow API Key 82
Zillow Property IDs 82
Building a Zillow-based Service with Parameters 83
Using E4X and JavaScript 84

4.3 Building a Zillow Widget 88
Creating RecentSalesWidget 89
Embedding RecentSalesWidget 92

4.4 Building a Google Maps Mashup 92
Exploring Google Maps API 93
Designing Widget RecentSalesMashup 94
Creating Widget RecentSalesMashup 95

Chapter 5 Facebook Basics 101

What You Will Learn 101
Examples in This Chapter 102
The New Facebook Design 102

5.1 About Facebook 103

What Is a Facebook Application? 103
Canvas Page 104
The Facebook User 105
Friends 105
Your Profile 105
Applications and Application Settings 106
Profile Boxes 108
Left-Hand Column 109
Application Tabs 110
Application Access 111
Email and Notices 112
Story Types and News Feed Templates 112
Profile Publisher 113
Application Info Sections 114

5.2 Creating a Facebook Application 114

Facebook Application Wizard 115
Core Services and Widgets 120

5.3 Loan Calculator—Your First Facebook Application 121

Deleting Home and Creating a New Widget 121
Editing Widget Home (NewWidget) 122
Uploading Resource Image 123
Including Library Prototype JS 124
Previewing and Publishing Widget Home 124
Configuring Home 124
Running Your Application in Facebook 125
Facebook Application Defaults 126
Enhancing Your Application on Facebook 127
Making Your Application Accessible 129

5.4 zembly and Facebook—A Closer Look 130

Exploring the Facebook APIs 131
Facebook Code Testing Tools 133

Application Context and Permissions   134
Controlling the Allow Access Process   136

5.5 BuddyPics—Using FBML and FBJS   137
FBML Overview   138
The BuddyPics Application   139
Adding Content to Your Profile   141
Building the BuddyPics Facebook Application   141
Creating Dynamic Content with FBML   142
BuddyPics Home Widget (FBML)   143
Service GetFriendInfo   153
Testing a Facebook Service   155
Service UpdateProfileBox   157
Summary of Differences with FBML Widgets   158
The HTML Alternative   160
What's Next   160

Chapter 6   Facebook Integration   161
What You Will Learn   162
Examples in This Chapter   162

6.1 Capital Punishment—A Challenging Facebook Application   162
Cloning the Facebook Application   164
The Capital Punishment Home Widget   164
Service UpdateProfileBox   181
Publishing Feed Stories   182
Sending Challenge Invitations   186
Application FriendChooser   191

6.2 Using the Facebook Data Store and FQL   191
Facebook Data Store Model   192
Data Model for Capital Punishment   193
Facebook Data Store Admin Tool   193
Service CreateDataStore   196
Service SaveScore   198
Using FQL with DataStoreAdmin   199
Services FBMLGetMyScores and FBMLGetFriendScores   201
Service DeleteScore   204
Widget SeeScores   205

- 6.3 Mood Pix—Leveraging Facebook Integration 208
  - Go To Application 209
  - About Mood Pix 209
  - Widget Home 214
  - Service FeedHandlerService 218
  - Application Info Section 219
  - Mood Pix Application Tab 223
  - Profile Publisher 224
  - Widget SendMoodPix 227
  - Mood Pix Widgets and Services—The Rest of the Story 231
- 6.4 Facebook Connect—Looking Forward 231
  - Running the zemblyConnectDemo Widget 232
  - fbConnectDemo2 and fbConnectDemo3 Widgets 234

Chapter 7 Working with Dapper 237

What You Will Learn 237
Examples in This Chapter 238

- 7.1 Getting Content with Dapper 238
- 7.2 Photo Search Widget 239
  - Creating the flickrPhotoSearch Dapp 240
  - Creating a Dapper-Based Service 243
  - Creating a Dapper-Based Widget 244
- 7.3 London Tube Widget 248
  - Creating the London Tube Dapp 250
  - Creating Service LondonTubeJourneyPlanner 252
  - Parameter Escape Value 253
  - Creating LondonTubeWidget 254
- 7.4 MLB Scores Widget 258
  - Building the mlbupdate Dapp 259
  - Creating Service mlbscores 262
  - Creating mlbScoresWidget 263
- 7.5 Creating a Feed Reader 265
  - Building a Feed-Based Dapp 267
  - Building Service GambitsfromGailFeed 268
  - Building GambitsSummaryWidget 268

Chapter 8   Widget Gallery   273

What You Will Learn   273
Examples in This Chapter   274

8.1   LiveWeatherBugWidget   274
Using E4X to Build LiveWeatherBugService   276
Building LiveWeatherBugWidget   279
Embedding LiveWeatherBugWidget   283

8.2   LiveWeatherMapWidget   284
Modifying LiveWeatherBugService   285
Building LiveWeatherMapWidget   286
Embedding LiveWeatherMapWidget   289

8.3   LondonTubeMapWidget   289
Building LondonTubeMapWidget   291
Adding Geocode Data for Stations   292
Using CSS for the Map Widget   293
Building Mashup LondonTubeMapWidget   294
Embedding LondonTubeMapWidget   298

8.4   Yahoo! Pipes   298
Creating a Pipe   300
Fetch Feed Source   300
Union Operator   301
Filter Operator   302
Sort Operator   303
Saving and Publishing Your Pipe   304
Building Widget zemblyrumblings   304
Doing More with Yahoo! Pipes   307

Chapter 9   Building for the iPhone   309

What You Will Learn   309
Examples in This Chapter   310

9.1   Targeting the iPhone   310
iPhone Applications   311
A Closer Look at the iPhone   311
The iUI Library   313

- 9.2 iLoanPayment Widget   314
  - Running iLoanPayment on Your iPhone   315
  - Adding an Icon to Home Screen   317
  - Including the iUI and Prototype Libraries   318
  - Widgets on the iPhone Dashboard   318
  - Building the iLoanPayment Widget   319
- 9.3 iLiveWeather Widget   322
  - Building the iLiveWeather Widget   324
  - iLiveWeather CSS Code   325
  - iLiveWeather JavaScript Code   327
- 9.4 iCapitalPunishment Widget   331
  - Building the iCapitalPunishment Widget   333
  - iCapitalPunishment CSS Code   334
  - iCapitalPunishment JavaScript Code   335
- 9.5 Facebook Integration—iPhoneHome Widget   337
  - Executing a Facebook Application Widget   339
  - Facebook Session Authorization   339
  - Building the iPhoneHome Widget   341
  - Building the iPhoneHome Services   348
- 9.6 iLondonTube Widget   348
  - iLondonTube Resources   350
  - Building the iLondonTube Widget   351
- 9.7 iCandy—Samples from Apple   356
  - iLeaves Widget   356
  - iButtons Widget   359

Index   363

Preface

There once was an engineer named Todd who had a vision of creating the programmable web. He wrote a white paper describing his ideas and the social climate for making his vision a reality. As the participation in social networking continued to grow (and, as we have noted in Chapter 5, continues to grow each month by big numbers), the motivation for implementing such a widget-building, application-building environment becomes easier and easier to justify.

This book comes out on the leading edge of **zembly**'s existence. The environment we document and describe today will no doubt change, but for you pioneers of social network programming, it will only get richer, easier, and more rewarding (maybe even financially rewarding).

The biggest challenge we face in writing a book like this is keeping current with **zembly**. As **zembly** evolves it will improve incrementally and continuously. One of the great advantages in offering a web-based tool is that new "versions" happen often and are not tied to lengthy production cycles that traditional development tools use. To keep current, we point readers to **zembly** itself (`zembly.com`), its blog (`blog.zembly.com`), and wiki (`wiki.zembly.com`). These resource points will go a long way in keeping you up to date with new **zembly** features that are rolling out, even as we finish up this manuscript.

About the Audience

This book is aimed at **zembly** users of all technical levels. We hope not only to help you use **zembly** effectively, but to provide examples that will get you up to speed quickly. We anticipate that **zembly** users will represent a whole range of technologists. You might be classically trained software engineers or what we call *casual technologists*; that is, users who are comfortable on the web, dabble a bit in HTML, CSS, or JavaScript, and see the internet as a tool to be exploited. You might be a professional social network game developer or a home-grown blogger ready to expand your widgetry. You might even be a community organizer ready to reach out to untapped audiences for your cause célèbre.

JavaScript Programming

As we write about the programmable web, the next logical question might be "What language do I use to program this programmable web?" The short answer is JavaScript. If you're an experienced JavaScript, HTML, and CSS coder, you will be very comfortable constructing services, widgets, and applications on **zembly**. But what if you've never used JavaScript before? Maybe you know Java, or C/C++ or even C#. Or, perhaps you have a background in scripting languages, including Perl, Python, Ruby, or PHP. Fear not; at least one of the author's first exposures to JavaScript programming occurred while working on this project.

To help get you up to speed with JavaScript, consult the web for tutorials at www.w3schools.com. Here's a few tips to get you started.

- JavaScript tutorials are at www.w3schools.com/js.
- HTML tutorials are at www.w3schools.com/html.
- CSS tutorials are at www.w3schools.com/css.
- David Flanagan's *JavaScript, The Definitive Guide* is an excellent reference to have at your desk.
- Begin by cloning and building upon already-published widgets, services, and applications. Not only can you learn from previously written JavaScript, CSS, and HTML code found in these examples, but you can use these as starting points to build your own artifacts.
- Consider using the Prototype JavaScript library. This library is available for your **zembly** widgets and provides some nice JavaScript programming help. Prototype tutorials and references are at www.prototypejs.org/learn.
- **zembly** provides widget templates that let you easily build and configure widgets. You just might be able to build a widget with no programming at all using templates!
- Use the **zembly** forum to ask questions. The forum (forum.zembly.com), is not only a place to ask questions of other **zembly** users, but it also provides a place to report bugs or anomalous behavior.

About the Examples

Use **zembly**'s Search mechanism to find all of the examples presented in this book. Because the examples are live, deployed services and widgets, you will always find the most current, published version on **zembly**. Provide the search term **zembly-book** and click **Search**, as shown here in Figure 1.

Preface xv

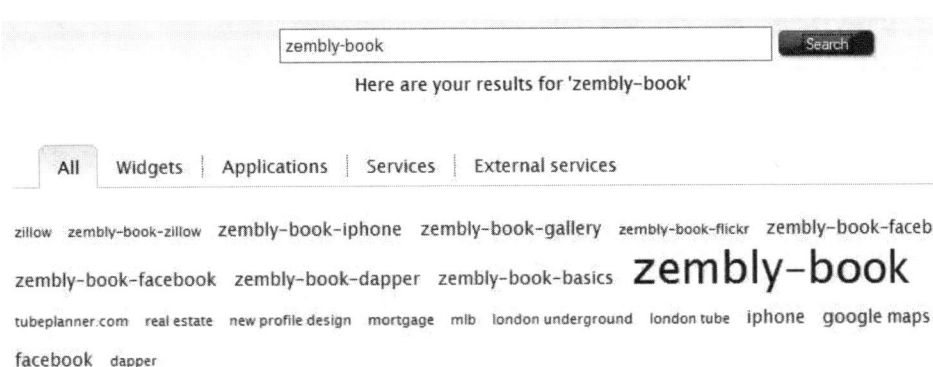

Figure 1. Finding all of the examples presented in this book

Notational Conventions

We've applied a rather light hand with font conventions in an attempt to keep the page uncluttered. Here are the conventions we follow.

Element	Font and Example
zembly UI controls	**Publish**, **Create something!**, **Add a new parameter**
URLs	zembly.com
inline code elements	`result.user.nsid`
code blocks and listings	`if (result.user) { . . . }`
widget names	LoanPaymentWidget
service names	LoanPaymentService
application names	CapitalPunishment
key combinations	Ctrl+Alt+F, Ctrl+Space
user input	specify minimum **1** and maximum **20**

Acknowledgments

zembly is a collaborative web site, and as such, this book is a collaborative project. Many people offered feedback, kept us in the loop, and provided technical gems.

We'd first like to thank Greg Doench, our editor at Prentice Hall, for supporting this project and helping us with logistics in publishing the manuscript. Octavian Tanase and Prakash Narayan first introduced us to the idea of writing a book on zembly. Prakash then spearheaded the project. Todd Fast and Chris Webster, the architects behind zembly, provided us with technical expertise. Todd also created the initial cover design. Myrna Rivera continues to promote the book both within and outside Sun Microsystems.

In writing a technical book, there always seems to be one person who shines through and selflessly provides technical help beyond expectations. Jiri Kopsa (Jirka) has been that "go to guy" for us on this project. He responded quickly to questions, fixed problems so that our development efforts could move forward, and provided detailed explanations on how things work. He followed through on outstanding issues and offered suggestions on approaches to solving problems. He also provided feedback on the manuscript, especially on the material dealing with Facebook applications.

We recruited many people (friends, relatives, and colleagues) to test widgets and Facebook applications. These people all provided feedback either in programming suggestions or user interface improvements. We'd like to thank Sara Anderson, Kellen Anderson, Scott Campbell, Gerry Brown, Victoria Hilpert, Conny Hilpert, Todd McClintock, Barbara Castro, Ryan Kennedy, and Mark Kahn, who all tested our applications and helped make them better.

We were fortunate to have people read drafts of the manuscript. Paul Fussell, Yutaka Hosoai, Ningyi Ma, Alex Choy, Sherry Barkodar, Earlence Fernandes, and Gerry Brown provided feedback and made suggestions that improved the manuscript.

Finally, we'd like to thank Elizabeth Ryan and the Pearson production staff for their support and Michael Thurston for a detailed reading with invaluable suggestions.

Gail and Paul Anderson
Anderson Software Group, Inc.
December 2008

1 What Is zembly?

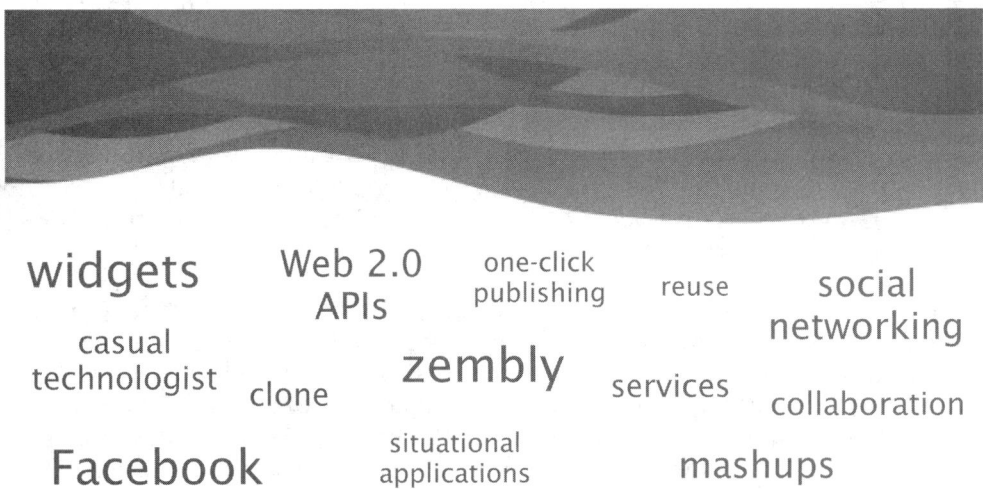

Imagine writing web applications where your own creativity is the only limiting factor. The challenge becomes thinking up that killer application, not implementing it. No matter where you get your material (from web site content, API calls, or simply hooking one data stream to another), you can fashion that cool, customized widget or full-blown social application. If you can imagine it, you can build it. And if you can build it, you can deploy and scale it, too.

zembly is the first step to realizing this goal. Imagine a "programmable web," where the browser is your development environment and your colleagues are thousands of perhaps unknown but similarly-minded developers. In the **zembly** environment, developing social applications in itself becomes social. Developers create building blocks that can be shared and reused. The rich variety of web APIs out there (the Web 2.0 promise) populates your palette and lets you construct widgets and applications that suit your immediate needs.

This book shows you how to use **zembly** to further this goal. You'll learn how to create services and widgets and deploy applications with a one-touch Publish button (no deployment descriptors required). But before you start with menus and tabs, news feeds and contacts, let's discuss what **zembly** is and how it fits into the big picture of web development.

1.1 Social Programming

zembly is all about building social applications in a social networking environment. **zembly** is not only the world's first Facebook application development environment, but OpenSocial and Meebo application development are just around the corner. What you're doing with **zembly** is *social programming*. That is, developing applications with other people using social networking-type features. Not only can you reuse pieces and parts that other people have previously built to construct new applications, you collaborate with your "contacts" (friends and colleagues). You see what your colleagues are working on via news feeds. You keep up with what they publish and even with changes they make.

zembly's environment is browser-based. This means that activities such as editing, testing services, previewing widgets, documenting chunks of your application, and deploying all happen within your browser, potentially with the collaboration of other developers. By inviting and collaborating with others, you can reuse what they have built to create your own services and widgets. You can also "clone" **zembly** pieces. This lets you build your own version that you can modify to fit your particular situation.

All this makes developing web applications easier. If the barrier for building social applications is lowered, you open the door for more participants to fuel the "long-tail" of social application development. When less expert knowledge is required from developers, you let them create "situational applications." These types of applications are often narrowly focused and can be thrown away or retooled as situations change. When the cost to enter the fray is negligible, more people will join and enrich the field for everyone else. With **zembly**, you can move beyond developing large applications for thousands of users that need care and maintenance. You can target a small group (less than a hundred, say) who share a common interest addressed by a very specialized application. This collaboration and reuse feeds on itself. The more people who develop with **zembly**, the richer its environment becomes. And, the more useful **zembly** becomes, the easier it is to create (perhaps only incrementally different) applications. More developers then flock to **zembly**.

Let's look at an example of collaboration on **zembly**. One of **zembly**'s engineers, Jiri Kopsa, created an iPhone-friendly Facebook application called Pixelife. (To try this out, search for the application on **zembly** as shown in Figure 1.1.)

Social Programming 3

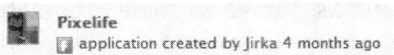

Figure 1.1 Using zembly's Search mechanism to find Facebook application Pixelife

Pixelife is a fun iPhone web application that lets you create pixel-based designs using the iPhone touch screen. Figure 1.2 shows a screen shot of this application. (Okay, so we may not have the next Picasso here.)

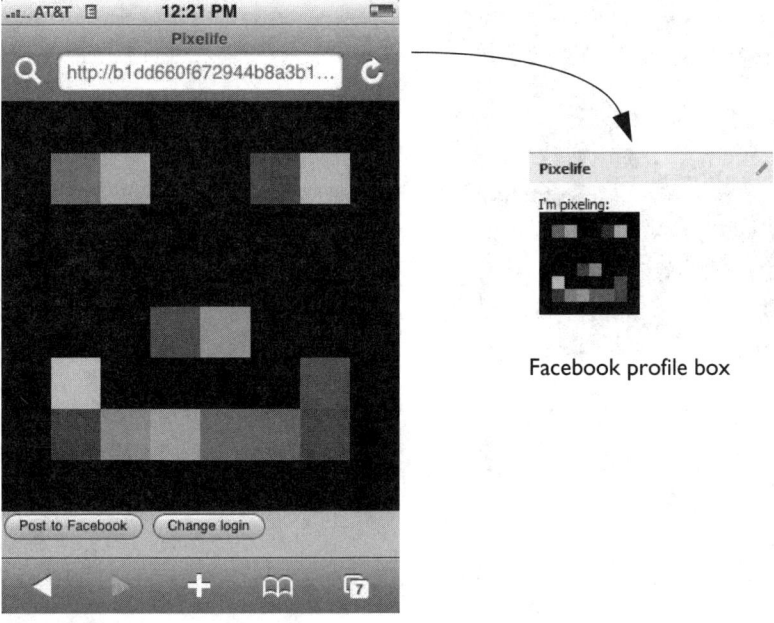

Figure 1.2 Be an artist (or scribbler) with iPhone-friendly Pixelife Facebook application

Along comes another developer named Yutaka Hosoai, who builds a brand-new Facebook application called Guess Who. This application displays a randomly selected friend's profile picture completely blacked out. You have a limited time to guess whose picture you're looking at. You see more and more of the picture as you remove the black pixels obscuring your friend's face as shown in Figure 1.3. Guess Who adds motivation: if you don't guess your friend's name within the allotted time period, a dire notice informs your friend that you don't know their name.

As you might have guessed, Yutaka uses the same code (cloned from Pixelife) to uncover the profile picture in small pixel-based chunks. Yutaka was able to build the Guess Who application very quickly because of the following reasons.

- You can build the basic Facebook application structure in zembly in about two minutes.
- zembly's collaboration and code reuse let you pull together and assemble pieces developed by others.

Figure 1.3 Guess Who is a zembly-based Facebook application that tests your ability to recognize friends' profile pictures

1.2 zembly's Environment

zembly looks at the entire web as an API and attempts to bring together disparate sources of data and functionality. zembly's platform is the web and its goal is to make the programmable web environment more consistent for the developer. This approach not only gives developers a richness, but makes it possible to build applications based on different APIs: Twitter, Yahoo!, and Google Maps, to name a few. Note that each API is different in how you invoke services and how you learn about them. **zembly** provides a level of consistency because it manages platform-specific API keys, provides a consistent calling interface, and provides a consistent link to API documentation. Through the **zembly** Find & Use facility, you can search for available services and platform-specific adapters from all **zembly** sources, including services written and published by other developers.

One of **zembly**'s long term goals is to help developers architect applications across multiple platforms. It helps you break up applications into reusable pieces (generally services and widgets). **zembly** offers common tools that help modularize your applications by providing a common model or abstraction for different environments like Facebook, Meebo, and MySpace, for example. The reality is that those different platforms are actually very heterogeneous, even within OpenSocial (a common API for social applications). The OpenSocial environment is fractured and each platform has its own extensions and capabilities. **zembly** lets you easily reuse common code and helps you isolate the differences among the platforms.

You can, of course, use platform-specific API calls. If you decide, for instance, that the Facebook data store API is appropriate for your storage mechanism, you can program directly to the Facebook API.

Let's look at another example. The myPicks U.S. Election 2008 application (see Figure 1.4), designed by Pramati and built with **zembly**, is a social networking application that works in both MySpace and Facebook. This application lets you voice your opinions on the 2008 U.S. presidential campaigns and discuss issues surrounding the election. After installing this application on your Facebook or MySpace profile, you can do the following.

- Participate in a poll indicating how you will vote in the presidential election.

- Provide your opinion on issues being debated by the candidates.

- State what you believe are the views of your friends. You can also invite your friends to play, guess their views on various issues, and give them an opportunity to agree, disagree, or comment on the issues.

Figure 1.4 Application myPicks U.S. Election 2008 runs on both MySpace and Facebook

Why is this application significant? First, myPicks U.S. Election 2008 aggregates data between Facebook and MySpace users of the game.

But there is a second significant point here. Pramati developed myPicks U.S. Election quickly so the application would be relevant during the rapidly changing politics of the campaign. Note that this application has a built-in shelf-life, since its relevancy disappears after November 4. (The predecessor application developed by Pramati focused on the Beijing Olympics—also an application with a built-in ending time.) Clearly, if building a compelling social application quickly is not possible, these "situational applications" would not exist.

1.3 zembly's Audience

So, who exactly is the target audience for **zembly**? If the previously stated goal is to make application development easy (or at least easier), then part of the realization of that lofty premise is to attract application builders who might not really think of themselves as traditional software developers. Indeed, one group of **zembly** application builders could be termed "Casual Technologists." This is a group of developers who are comfortable with the web, use Facebook or MySpace every day, use Twitter or instant messaging, but may not be classically-trained engineers. These casual technologists are comfortable manipulating flickr data and searching for interesting photos, for example. With this in mind, the next step might be to write a flickr-based slide show widget. (And we show you how. See "Creating a Flickr User Slide Show Widget" on page 71.) **zembly** aims to accommodate both the professional application builder and the casual technologist.

What skills do application builders need to use **zembly**? The development environment of **zembly** is based on scripting languages. Currently, **zembly** developers use HTML for markup, CSS for styling, and JavaScript for program logic. Facebook appli-

implementing the OpenSocial APIs are interoperable with any social network system that supports them, including features on sites such as Hi5, MySpace, orkut, Netlog, Sonico, Friendster, Ning and Yahoo!.

zembly anticipates supporting OpenSocial target sites soon (myPicks U.S. Elections 2008 already runs on both MySpace and Facebook platforms).

Scripting Languages

zembly is planning to target other scripting languages besides JavaScript. Target languages include PHP, Ruby, and Python. Scripting languages are important in **zembly**, because they simplify the programming environment. With scripting, you don't have to worry about compilation and linking, deployment, or other software building-related tasks.

A Final Thought

zembly Axiom

*The more people who use **zembly**, the better **zembly** becomes. And that's good for everyone!*

2 zembly Basics

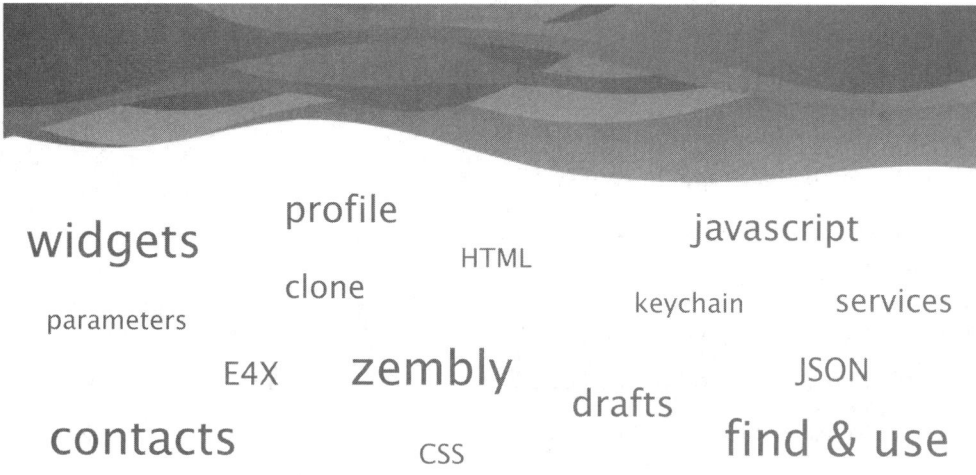

Welcome to **zembly**.

zembly lets you build services, widgets, and web applications and publicly deploy them. The philosophy behind **zembly** is to encourage you to build upon previously published services and widgets, to discover what other **zembly** users are building, and to socialize the building process by collaborating with your **zembly** contacts. As **zembly** matures, it will allow you to build widgets, services, mashups, and social applications targeting the many social networks present on the web. This chapter is aimed at those who are just getting started with **zembly**, giving you a glimpse into the future of building the web.

zembly is a social network. It encourages you to build your own contacts and collaborations. Those of you who work on group projects will appreciate the easy collaboration in code development, and by extension, idea sharing. The ultimate goal for **zembly** is to make the threshold very low for building and deploying a widget or mashup that others can drop into a web page (such as a blog or Facebook profile page). Combining social networking, collaborative development, and sharing a collection of published services and widgets, **zembly** facilitates each step that results in a published, deployed, and fully accessible and easily importable widget, service, or application.

This chapter will help you get started. It assumes that you are a registered zembly user.

What You Will Learn

- How the zembly site is organized
- The types of things you can build with zembly
- What you'll find on the Samples page
- How to embed a widget in your web page
- How to view or edit your Profile page
- All about the zembly Keychain
- How to find zembly service providers
- How to create, test, and publish a service
- How to create, test, and publish a widget
- How to include a library with your JavaScript code
- How to manipulate drafts, versions, and the timeline
- How to create a service and widget that calls an external service

Examples in This Chapter

All examples in this chapter are tagged **zembly-book-basics**. To search for them, select **Search** at the top of any zembly page. Supply the search term **zembly-book-basics** and click the search icon as shown in Figure 2.1.

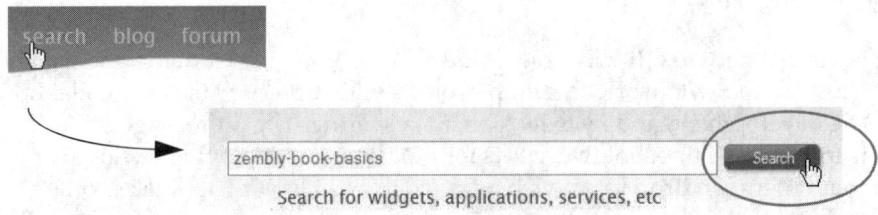

Figure 2.1 Searching for the examples in this chapter

The search results lists the widgets and services discussed in this chapter.

2.1 Exploring the Samples

Let's start with the **zembly** Samples section, which lists applications (Facebook and OpenSocial), widgets (blue badge), and services (orange badge). To see **zembly**'s samples, select **samples** from the top dashboard, as shown in Figure 2.2.

Figure 2.2 The **zembly** samples help you get started

The sample Facebook applications include CapitalPunishment, which is presented in Chapter 6 (see "Capital Punishment—A Challenging Facebook Application" on page 162). The sample services run on the **zembly** server and generally call other services out on the web to do things. Right now[1] the sample services include

- **AmazonProductSearch**—lets you search Amazon's product catalogs and retrieve detailed product information, including prices, images, etc.
- **FlickrPhotoSearchService**—calls the flickr picture search service.
- **GoogleGeocodeSampleService**—enables you to search a ZIP code for a given address.
- **HelloWorld**—takes your name and says hello.
- **WeatherTodayService**—retrieves weather for a specific U.S. zip code.
- **YahooTripSearchService**—enables your applications to use a Yahoo! API to search for public trip plans that were created with Yahoo!.
- **YouTubeSampleService**—lists information about videos that have a specified tag.
- **ZillowSampleService**—finds a property given an address. The returned information includes the address for the property or properties, the Zillow Property ID (ZPID), the current Zestimate, the date the Zestimate was computed, a valuation range, and the Zestimate ranking for the property within its ZIP code.

---

1. **zembly** will add more samples to this page, so check back often.

- **zventsSearchService**—search for events that are happening around a given U.S. location.

The Sample section also includes a list of widgets. Widgets provide a user-friendly object that you can embed in a web page. All of the above services have corresponding widgets. To view a widget's page, click its name in the Samples section. For example, if you select **HelloWorldWidget**, zembly takes you to its page so you can see how it was built. To view its source, select the **View** tab as shown in Figure 2.3.

Figure 2.3 Exploring the HelloWorldWidget development page

Further down the page zembly shows you how to embed the widget in a page by providing the code you can select, copy, and paste. Figure 2.4 shows the code window to embed widget HelloWorldWidget (Share This Widget).

Share This Widget

Use this code to embed this widget in a Web page, like your blog, wiki, or other website.
Make sure to fill in the real values where you see [value]!

```
<iframe
   src="http://dde7e989aa2a4122aef8a6e53f29e9fb.zembly.com/things/dde7e989aa2
```

Figure 2.4 Embedding (sharing) a widget

For example, you can create a web page and call the HelloWorldWidget using the following code:

```
<iframe
   src="http://dde7e989aa2a4122aef8a6e53f29e9fb.zembly.com/things/
   dde7e989aa2a4122aef8a6e53f29e9fb;iframe" frameborder="0">
</iframe>
```

You can then open this file in your web browser, which calls the HelloWorldWidget. This widget displays a box and provides an input field to supply a name. A call is made to the HelloWorld service to display the name provided by the user, as shown in Figure 2.5.

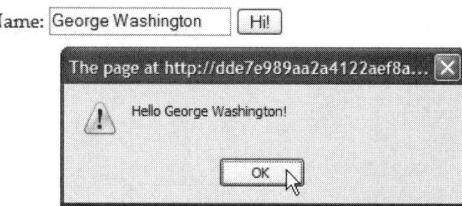

Figure 2.5 Embedding and running the HelloWorldWidget in a web page

Using Clone

You can clone any application, widget, or service on **zembly**. This means that you create a copy for yourself. Once you clone a thing on **zembly**, you own it and you can then modify it. **zembly** encourages you to clone artifacts that you like; it is both a great learning tool and more importantly, you can build something innovative based on the work someone else has already done. This makes **zembly** users more productive. To clone a widget, select **Clone this widget** on its development page, as shown in Figure 2.6.

Furthermore, when you clone something on **zembly**, the score of the original widget (or service or application) increases to reflect the cloning. Scores also change when people rate **zembly** "Things" or favorite them.

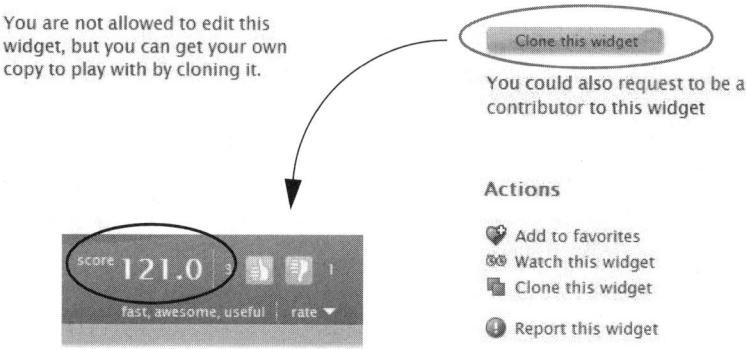

Figure 2.6 Cloning a widget increases its score

Widget Actions

Widgets (this applies to services and applications as well) list actions on their page. Besides cloning, you can add a widget to your list of favorites, report a widget, or watch a widget. When you mark something as a favorite, you have an easily accessible "bookmark" as shown in Figure 2.7.

Figure 2.7 Your Favorites give you a convenient bookmark

When you watch something, **zembly** lets you know when its owner publishes a new version.

Tags on zembly

Use **zembly** tags to label your widgets, services, and applications to help others find Things through the **zembly** search mechanism, as shown in Figure 2.8.

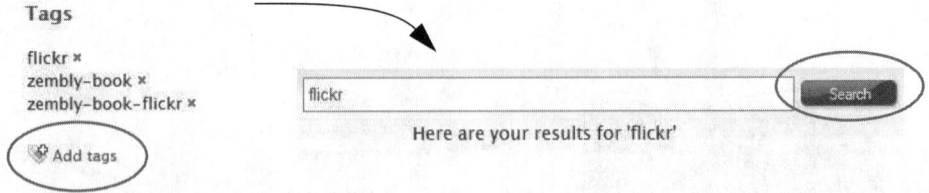

Figure 2.8 Tags let you find widgets, services, and applications through searching

AmazonProductSearchWidget—Widget Preview

Let's explore the AmazonProductSearchWidget. From the Samples page, select AmazonProductSearchWidget. zembly takes you to this widget's page. You'll see a box area with the instructions **Click here to preview this widget**. When you click the box, the widget runs in a preview window. You can increase the size of the preview window by selecting the corner (or edges) and dragging until the preview window is the size you want, as shown in Figure 2.9.

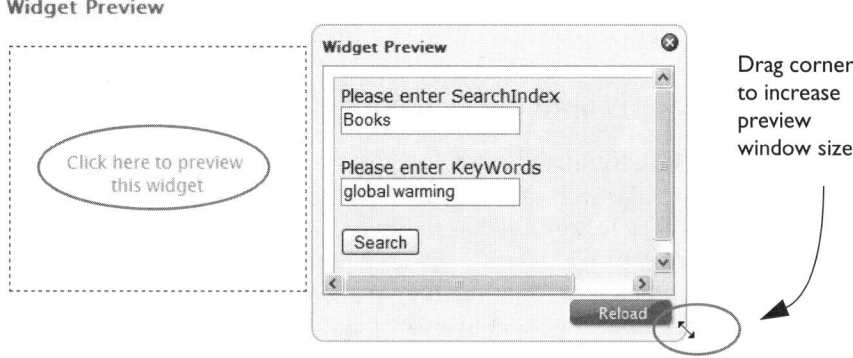

Figure 2.9 Previewing a widget and adjusting the preview window size

Provide product search index and keywords and click Search. Figure 2.10 shows the result after searching for keyword "zembly" in search index "Books."

Figure 2.10 Previewing the AmazonProductSearchWidget

Widget code includes (X)HTML (for rendering), CSS (for styling), and JavaScript for program logic and calls to external services. When you make a service call, results typically come back in XML or JSON format. Exactly what the data represents depends on the service and the format it uses. For example, with XML you may see results that are RSS 2.0, or ATOM. As it turns out, the Amazon service that AmazonProductSearchWidget calls returns data in XML format. The external web service will specify how to interpret the data that is returned.

You are encouraged to look at the XHTML, CSS, and JavaScript code for this widget (click View as shown in Figure 2.3 on page 14). This chapter will delve into building widgets soon, but first let's show you how to use this widget in a web page.

Embedding AmazonProductSearchWidget

The AmazonProductSearchWidget has sharing enabled. This means you can export the widget to many popular web sites and pages by simply selecting the logo that corresponds to the target site. zembly has partnered with Clearspring to provide sharing and tracking of your widgets (see www.clearspring.com). We show you how to enable sharing in Chapter 3 (see "Sharing Your Widget" on page 66). However, let's first show you how to embed a widget in a web page.

Since sharing is enabled for AmazonProductSearchWidget, select **Embed** from the list of options as shown in Figure 2.11. The share window now displays option Other Sites. Select **Other Sites** and you'll see the window with the JavaScript code you need to invoke the widget from an arbitrary HTML page.

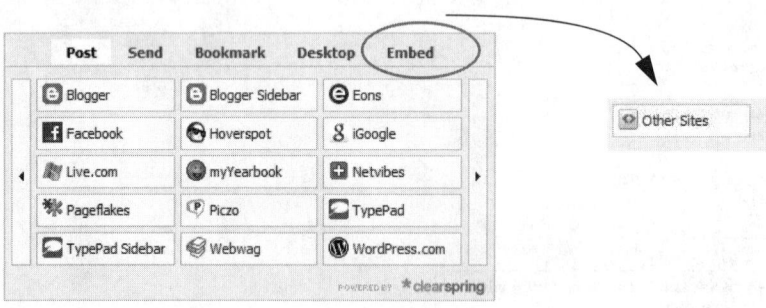

Figure 2.11 Embedding AmazonProductSearchWidget in a web page

Cut and paste this code into the HTML editor of your choice and open it in your browser. You can add other rendering code as shown in Listing 2.1. Here is the source for the HTML file used to run this widget in a browser.

Listing 2.1 AmazonProductSearchWidget HTML file

```
<h2 style='margin-left:10px; margin-bottom: 0px'>Let's search Amazon!</h2>
<script type="text/javascript"
src="http://widgets.clearspring.com/o/49249714e57f0b59/4924d27e70974fe2/
4924971425b85ee0/cafd08e6/widget.js">
</script>
```

After creating the HTML file, open it in your browser. Enter a product search index and one or more keywords, then click **Search**. Figure 2.12 shows the browser output.

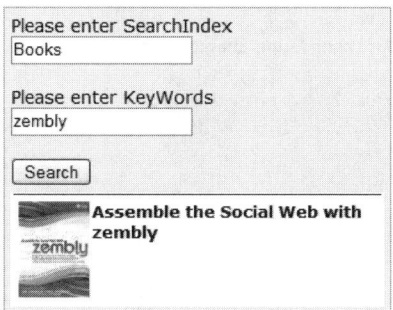

Figure 2.12 AmazonProductSearchWidget running in a browser

Sharing Your Widgets with Clearspring

Besides embedding widgets in pages, you can also share widgets by adding them to any number of popular sites, such as your iGoogle Home page (see www.google.com/ig). You don't have to be the widget's owner. Click **Post** from the list of options and then select **iGoogle** from the option icons in the grid (see Figure 2.11). Now click **Open** in the Add to your iGoogle page display, as shown in Figure 2.13

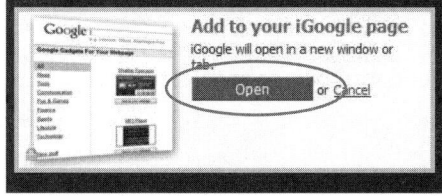

Figure 2.13 Adding AmazonProductSearchWidget to your iGoogle home page

20   Chapter 2   zembly Basics

After clicking **Open**, you'll be redirected to Google and asked to confirm. Click the big blue **Add to Google** button, as shown in Figure 2.14. You will now see your iGoogle home paged updated with the widget inside.

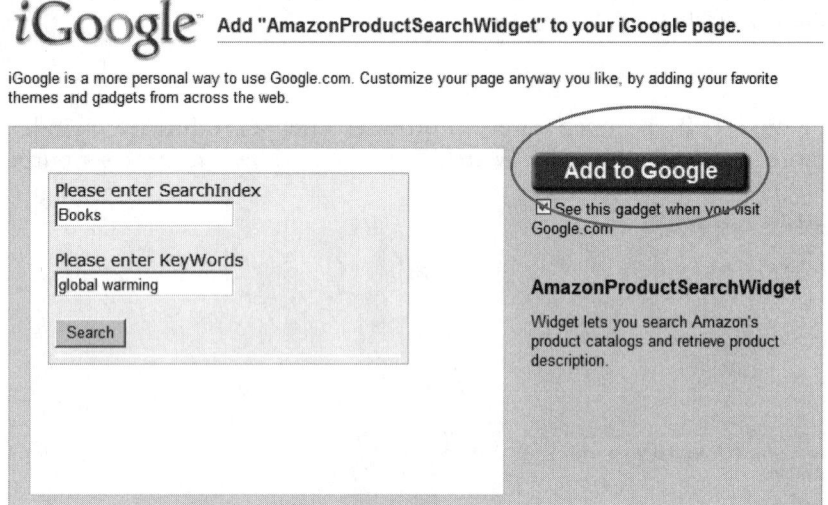

Figure 2.14 Adding AmazonProductSearchWidget to your iGoogle home page

2.2 About You—Your Home Page

zembly is about people like you who participate in building and publishing widgets, services, and other objects. The **You** tab takes you to your home page. This is the starting point for the work you do on **zembly**. Figure 2.15 shows your home page with the top-level tabs and the right-side navigation area. From the right-side navigation area you can

- edit or view your profile,
- manage your Keychain (a list of API keys for web services),
- view your favorite **zembly** things (widgets, services, or applications).

From the **Things** tab, you can

- see your work in progress,
- see all the things you own,
- select one of your things to edit.

About You—Your Home Page

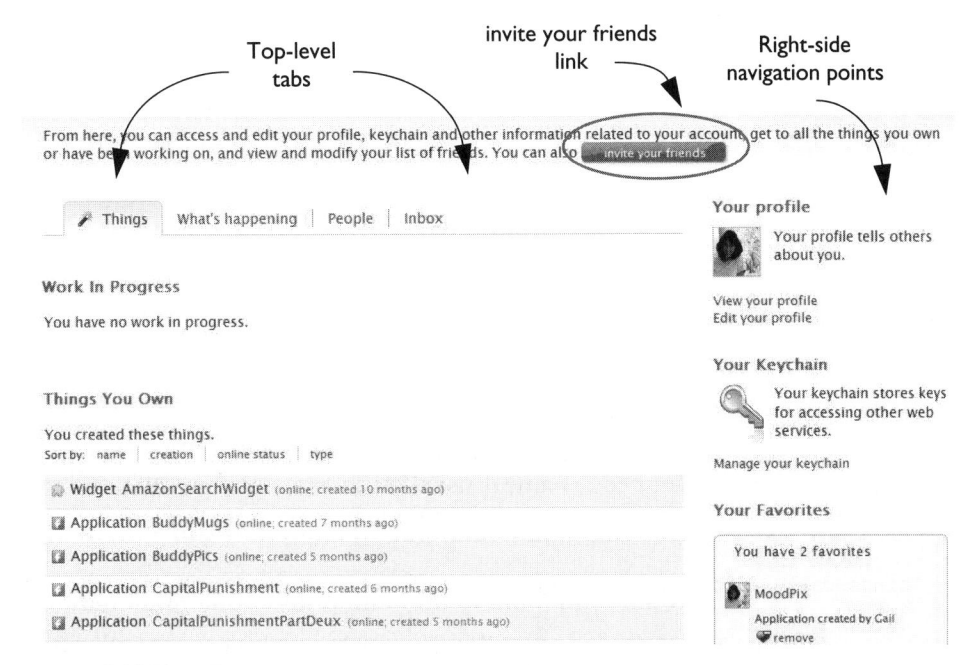

Figure 2.15 Your home page is your starting point

From the **What's happening** tab, you can see what others are doing (reported in the news feed).

From the **People** tab, you can

- view your contacts (other **zembly** users that you have added to your profile),
- search **zembly** for additional contacts.

From the **Inbox** tab, you can

- see messages others have sent you,
- see requests to collaborate that others have sent you.

And the **invite your friends** button lets you bring your friends into the world of **zembly**.

Your Profile

Let's start with your profile. Your profile tells other people about you. Click **View your profile**, as shown in Figure 2.16. Your profile includes a picture, your description, your contacts, a list of all the things you own, and a time line that shows what you've been doing.

Your profile

Your profile tells others about you.

View your profile
Edit your profile

Figure 2.16 You can Edit or View your profile

You can set your screen name and code name. (You can only set your code name once.) The code name is used to group widgets, services, and applications that you contribute. For example, if your code name is **user1234** then people can call one of your published services (say "myservice") from a widget using something like

```
Things.callService("user1234.myservice")
```

Your screen name is a conversationally nice thing you want other people to call you.

People—Adding Contacts

Your contacts are people whom you invite to collaborate with you on creating widgets, services, or applications. Contacts are visible on your profile page. You can also view and search for contacts under the People tab on your home page as shown in Figure 2.17.

About You—Your Home Page 23

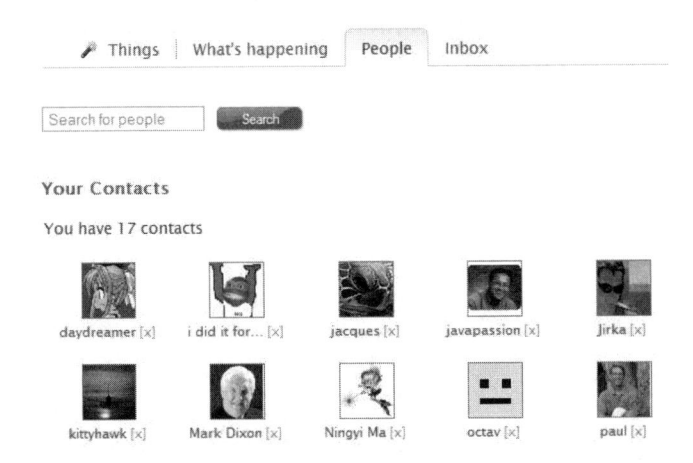

Figure 2.17 Viewing contacts under People

zembly encourages collaboration when creating and editing services and widgets. Before you can request someone to collaborate with you on a project, you must add them as a contact. You add them by viewing their profile page and selecting the **Add as Contact** button. Alternatively, search for them from the **People** tab. Type a word in the search box and hit Search. To add a person to your contacts, simply click the **Add to contacts** link below the person's name, as shown in Figure 2.18. If a person is already a contact, you'll see a message saying so.

Figure 2.18 Adding contacts

Once you add contacts, you can then read what they've recently done through the news feed and add them as a contributor to one or more things that you own. To view the News Feed, select the **What's happening** tab as shown in Figure 2.19.

> Things | **What's happening** | People
>
> **Your News Feed**
>
> **Today**
> - Ryan removed New User from contacts   6 hours ago
> - Jirka published a new version of the trivialni widget, "*Mam tady hotovo*"   8 hours ago
> - Jirka published a new version of the trivialni widget, "*Hotovo*"   8 hours ago

Figure 2.19 Your News Feed reports what your contacts are doing

2.3 Your Keychain and Service Providers

Under your home page (click **You** at the top of any page) you'll find your Keychain (click **Manage your keychain** on your home page, as shown in Figure 2.20). Your Keychain is a list of keys that are associated with select service providers. Service providers have *adapters* on the **zembly** site. Adapters are wrapper services deployed in the **zembly** container that provide access to one or more of the Service Provider's API calls. Adapters make using your key a simple matter of specifying your Keychain—**zembly** extracts the appropriate key for the specific adapter seamlessly behind the scenes.

> **Your Keychain**
>
> Your keychain stores keys for accessing other web services.
>
> (Manage your keychain)

Figure 2.20 Accessing your Keychain

When you access your Keychain, **zembly** lists all of the service providers that have adapters. For each service provider that you want to use in a service, specify your key. Note that you need to obtain the key on your own first. The process is slightly different for each service provider, but is usually quick. Service providers typically email you a confirmation. Once you have a key, you enter it into your Keychain using the **Add key** link (as shown in Figure 2.21).

Your Keychain is a very important and necessary part of building the web. You want to keep your keys handy, but you also want them private. **zembly** does this all for you. When other people call your published services, **zembly** uses your key (from your Keychain), but its value remains private.

You can see a list of adapters available by clicking the service's **Check out the services offered by** link. For example, you can see the services offered by Amazon AWS by clicking the link, as shown (circled) in Figure 2.21.

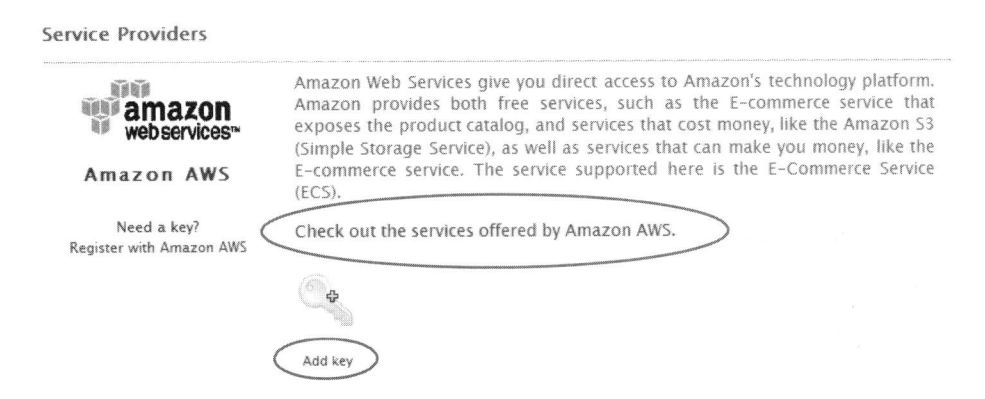

Figure 2.21 Building your Keychain for service providers

When you follow this link, you'll see the service adapters currently deployed within the **zembly** container, as shown in Figure 2.22.

You can further explore each service adapter by following its link to the detailed documentation page. Here, you'll find the service's parameters, error codes, and other pertinent information, which frequently includes external links to the provider's online documentation. "Putting It All Together—Using the WeatherBug API" on page 45 steps you through the process of building a service using one of **zembly**'s external service providers.

2.4 Creating Your First Service: LoanPaymentService

Using some of the posted samples as guidelines, let's create a new service. You won't call an external service here; instead, you'll build one using JavaScript. A familiar example is a service that calculates one's monthly mortgage payment based on principal, interest rate, and length of loan (years).

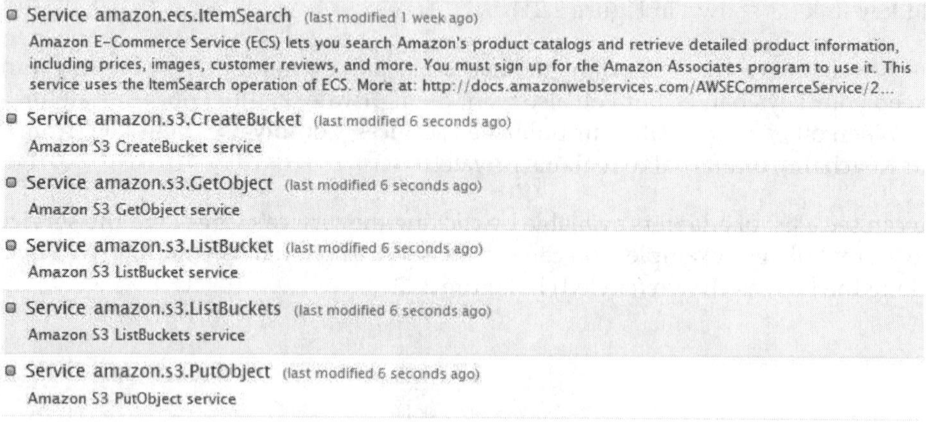

26   Chapter 2   zembly Basics

- **Service amazon.ecs.ItemSearch** (last modified 1 week ago)
  Amazon E-Commerce Service (ECS) lets you search Amazon's product catalogs and retrieve detailed product information, including prices, images, customer reviews, and more. You must sign up for the Amazon Associates program to use it. This service uses the ItemSearch operation of ECS. More at: http://docs.amazonwebservices.com/AWSECommerceService/2...

- **Service amazon.s3.CreateBucket** (last modified 6 seconds ago)
  Amazon S3 CreateBucket service

- **Service amazon.s3.GetObject** (last modified 6 seconds ago)
  Amazon S3 GetObject service

- **Service amazon.s3.ListBucket** (last modified 6 seconds ago)
  Amazon S3 ListBucket service

- **Service amazon.s3.ListBuckets** (last modified 6 seconds ago)
  Amazon S3 ListBuckets service

- **Service amazon.s3.PutObject** (last modified 6 seconds ago)
  Amazon S3 PutObject service

Figure 2.22 Amazon services include Simple Storage Service and E-Commerce Service (ECS)

Here's a summary of the steps you'll follow.

1. Create a new service. Give it a name and a description.
2. Add parameters to the service (optional).
3. Provide JavaScript code that returns data to the caller.
4. Add any error types (optional).
5. Test drive your service and modify as necessary.
6. Capture example return data (optional).
7. Publish your service.

Let's start. To create a service, click [Create something!] at the top of the page and select **Service** as shown in Figure 2.23. You'll see a new page that asks you to provide a description of the service. The default service name is NewService, which you should change to something meaningful. Many times, service names end in "Service," but this is not a requirement. Call the service **LoanPaymentService**.

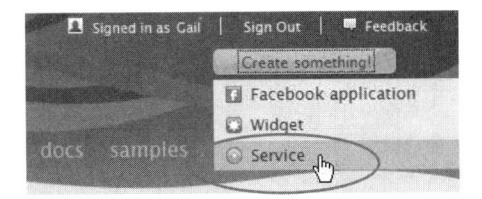

Figure 2.23 Creating a Service

This service requires three input parameters and returns a single numerical result. Error handling for input validation is handled completely by zembly; we discuss this further in the next section. Here's the JavaScript that provides the service.

Listing 2.2 LoanPaymentService (JavaScript)

```
// LoanPaymentService
// Input parameters are all NUMBERs and all Required

var principal = Parameters.principal;
var interest = Parameters.interest;
var interest_rate = interest / 1200;
var years = Parameters.years;

//Perform the calculation
var months = years * 12;
var x = Math.pow(1 + interest_rate, months);
var payment = (principal * x * interest_rate)/(x-1);

return payment.toFixed(2);
```

Specifying Parameters in a Service

When you create a web service, you tell the service interaction page about the parameters for your service. To add parameters, click **Add a new parameter** in the Call - Parameters window. You specify a parameter's characteristics in a dialog box.

When you add a new parameter you choose its type. By using the appropriate type, you take advantage of zembly's built-in parameter validation. Table 2.1 lists the types supported.

TABLE 2.1 Parameter Types for Services

Type	Additional Fields	Examples
Binary	-	`1101`
Boolean	-	`true, false`
Email	-	`info@buildtheweb.org`
JSON	-	`{"firstName":"John", "lastName":"Smith"}`
Key	Keyset Provider	(Depends on provider)
Number (integer, real, or floating point)	Min Value, Max Value	`55, 25.3`
String	Max Length, Escape value	`any string <= Max Length`
URI	-	`http://www.asgteach.com`
XML	-	`<firstName>John</firstName> <lastName>Smith</lastName>`

For this service, specify three parameters (principal, interest, and years). Make them all **required** and Type **Number**. With Number you also specify the minimum and maximum values. For principal use minimum **10** and maximum **2** million (2,000,000). For interest specify minimum **1** and maximum **20**. Finally, for years use minimum **1** and maximum **99**. Figure 2.24 shows the Parameter Editor for parameter years.

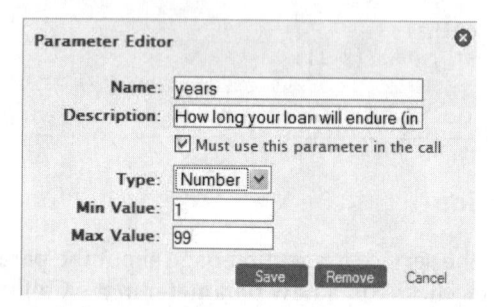

Figure 2.24 Creating and editing a web service parameter

Programming Tip

If your service expects numbers for input, be sure to specify **Number** *for the parameter type. The built-in parameter validation will verify the correct type and provide range checking as well. Figure 2.27 on page 30 provides an example result for out of range input.*

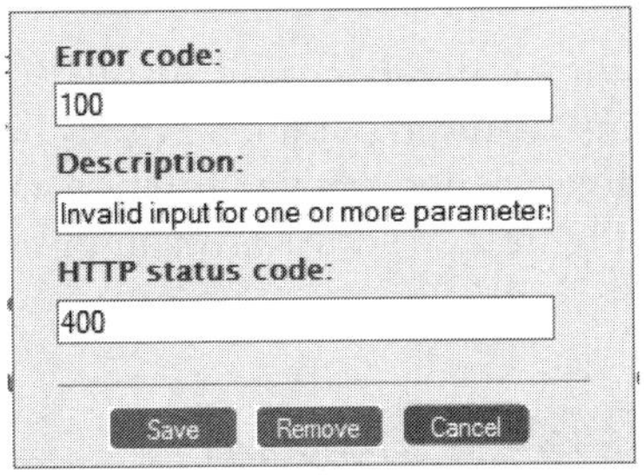

Figure 2.25 Creating and editing web service error codes

Note that if you make a parameter required, **zembly** flags an error if the caller doesn't provide a value. If you want the parameter to be optional, uncheck **Must use this parameter in the call**.

Once you've specified the parameters, you can access them in JavaScript. For example, you access the LoanPaymentService `principal` parameter with `Parameters.principal`.

zembly Tip

It's a good practice to provide a description for parameters as shown in Figure 2.24. The description will then appear in your service's documentation page. It will also appear when you add code to call the service through **zembly***'s Find & Use feature (see "Calling LoanPaymentService in Your Widget" on page 39).*

Error Handling

When you detect a problem in your service, error codes can communicate status to the caller. You specify error codes in the service's Error Codes section. To add an error code, click **Add a new error type**. Figure 2.25 shows the dialog box that lets you specify a new error type. (You may also edit error codes that you have already defined.)

The error code, description, and HTTP status code all appear on your web service's documentation page. Note that you don't need to define an error code for the LoanPaymentService, since all error handling is performed by the built-in parameter validation.

Testing LoanPaymentService

Once you've built a service, you'll want to test it. Use the Call tab located next to the source editor window. You must provide values for any required parameters and click **Test drive now**. This calls the service with the parameter values you've provided and displays any results (or error codes) in the window. Figure 2.26 shows an example with a successful test.

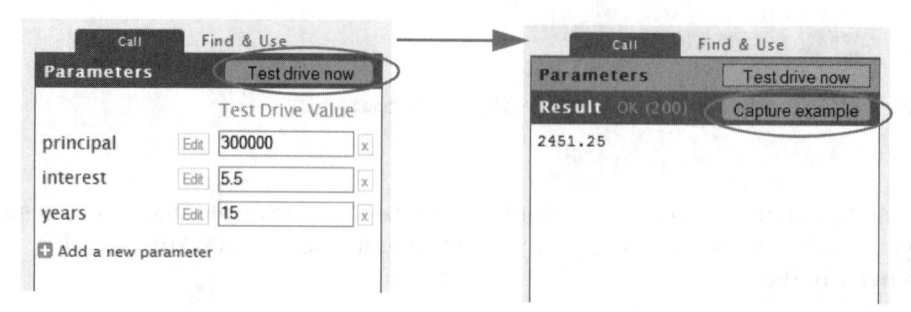

Figure 2.26 Testing a service

Figure 2.27 shows the built-in parameter validation when you provide a value outside the range for parameter years.

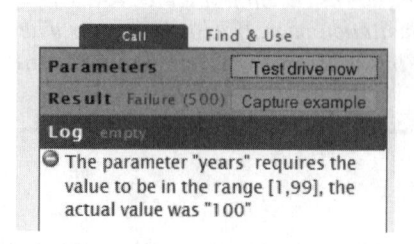

Figure 2.27 zembly's parameter validation

Capturing Example Return Data

To help others use your service, you can capture the return data after testing your service. Simply click the **Capture example** button (as shown in Figure 2.26). zembly creates a new heading on your service's documentation page and displays the output. This helps users, especially if the return data contains specific formatting (such as XML or JSON data). Figure 2.28 shows an example for LoanPaymentService.

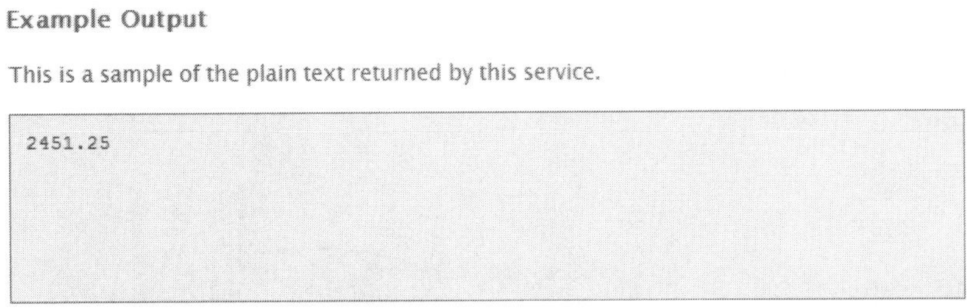

Example Output

This is a sample of the plain text returned by this service.

```
2451.25
```

Figure 2.28 You can display sample output on your service's documentation page

Saving Drafts

Each time you edit your code and test drive the service, your current code is automatically saved in a draft for you. zembly displays a small bar to indicate the current draft (the bars are displayed on the right with the most recent modification saved on top of the stack).

You can force a saved draft by clicking the Save Code icon at the bottom of the editor (or typing Ctrl+Alt+S). You can return to any previously saved draft or published version simply by clicking the bar. Also, you can see the timestamp and draft or version number by holding the cursor over the bar. See "Drafts, Versions, and Timelines" on page 42 for a more detailed discussion.

Using the JavaScript Editor

The JavaScript editor color codes key words, comments, and objects. The editor includes icon commands in the lower right window (as shown in Figure 2.29) to save your draft (Ctrl+Alt+S), toggle full screen editing (Ctrl+1), format code (Ctrl+Alt+F), undo editing (Ctrl+Z), redo editing (Ctrl+Y), or create a code snippet (Ctrl+Shift+N). You can also invoke code completion with Ctrl+Space.

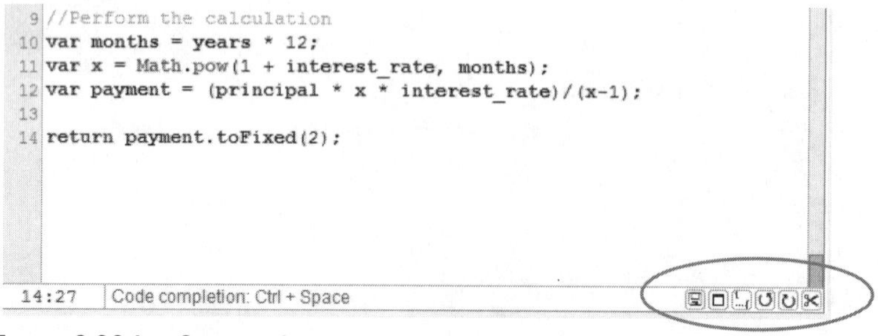

```
 9  //Perform the calculation
10  var months = years * 12;
11  var x = Math.pow(1 + interest_rate, months);
12  var payment = (principal * x * interest_rate)/(x-1);
13
14  return payment.toFixed(2);
```

Figure 2.29 JavaScript editor command icons

Publishing LoanPaymentService

Click the **Publish** button to publish your service. This is the magic step that **zembly** provides to make services and widgets available to others. When you publish your service, **zembly** creates a deployable web service and deploys it in its own managed container. As you modify your service, **zembly** keeps track of drafts (unpublished edits) and versions (published edits). With each version you are encouraged to specify how the new version has improved (why it is cool).

Calling LoanPaymentService

Once you've tested and published your service, you'll want to call it from another service or widget. The page provides the code you need to call the service from another service, from a widget, or through the browser. However, the easiest way to call your service is to use **zembly**'s Find & Use feature which automatically adds the code as a template in the editor. The Find & Use feature is context sensitive, so it will import the correct code depending on whether you're currently developing a widget or service. In addition, with Find & Use you'll see documentation about the service and its parameters.

Use the following (JavaScript) code to call your service from another service. **zembly** generates the comments for each parameter from the documentation you provide.

zembly Tip

Note that this example calls the service using code name ganderson. *When you create your own service,* **zembly** *uses your code name, which is unique to you.*

```
var result = Things.ganderson.LoanPaymentService({
    principal: 0, // The principal of the loan (in dollars)
    interest: 0, // The interest rate (per cent) (e.g., 6.5)
```

```
        years: 0 // How long your loan will endure (in years)
});
```

Use the following template (JavaScript) code to call your service from a widget.

```
    Things.callService("ganderson.LoanPaymentService",
{
    principal: 0, // The principal of the loan (in dollars)
    interest: 0, // The interest rate (per cent) (e.g., 6.5)
    years: 0 // How long your loan will endure (in years)
},
{
    onSuccess: function(data) {
        Log.write(data);
    },
    onFailure: function(error) {
        Log.write("Error: " + error.code + " : " + error.message);
    }
});
```

Programming Tip

The statement `Log.write(data)` *writes messages to the JavaScript debugger Firebug if it's installed. If not,* ***zembly*** *loads Firebug lite to get you started (use F12 to bring it up). Logging is enabled by default when you preview drafts and disabled for published versions. You can keep your* `Log.write()` *statements in the code. They will go to null (unless you enable debugging of published versions with the debug query parameter).*

A third way to call a service is to cut and paste the URL provided on the service page into the address line of your browser. Pasting the URL in your browser address line calls the service from HTTP. You must specify the parameter values in place of each [value] marker. Here is the LoanPaymentService URL with values replacing [value] in the URL.

```
http://zembly.com/things/2ef3f34205c84fca9b0d91c538fc6a5b;exec
    ?principal=232000&interest=4.5&years=15
```

zembly Tip

Note that you must delete the brackets when you specify the actual value for each parameter. However, if you accidentally leave in the brackets (in this example), the built-in parameter validation returns an error.

Figure 2.30 shows the browser window after calling the LoanPaymentService.

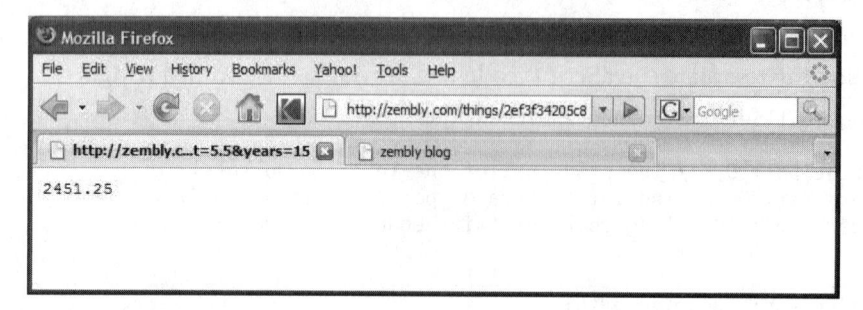

Figure 2.30 Calling a service with HTTP using its URL in the browser

2.5 Creating Your First Widget: LoanPaymentWidget

Now it's time to build a widget that uses the previously built LoanPaymentService. Here's a summary of the steps you'll follow to build a widget.

1. Create a new widget. Give it a name and a description.
2. Upload any resources, such as images (optional).
3. Include any libraries your widget uses.
4. Provide the HTML, CSS, and JavaScript code.
5. Use **Find & Use** to call zembly services from your widget.
6. Preview and publish.
7. Embed in a web page.

At the top of the page, select [Create something!] and then select **Widget**. zembly pops up a secondary dialog that lets you either select a template for your widget or simply create a blank widget. Select **Create a blank widget** as shown in Figure 2.31.

Figure 2.31 Creating a blank widget

zembly Tip

*Widget templates are a recent addition to **zembly**. Templates let you choose a configurable starting point for building widgets. You navigate and find the template widget that's closest to what you want to build and click* **Choose this template**. *At this point the widget's code is visible but not editable. Use the form in the Configure tab to change the widget's look or behavior. If the customizations available do not cover your needs, you can edit the code by selecting button* **Switch to edit mode**. *Then, you can change anything you want in the CSS, Java-Script, and HTML source code, as well as libraries, resources, and so on. We encourage you to experiment with the various template categories before building a widget from scratch. For this example, however, you will start with a "blank" widget.*

When you create a widget, you have the opportunity to supply three different files. You can also add images (which you'll do in this example) and include libraries in a separate step. You'll use (X)HTML for page markup, CSS for style specifications, and JavaScript for program logic. Figure 2.32 shows LoanPaymentWidget, the target widget that you'll build, running in a browser.

This widget includes an image, three input text fields with labels arranged in a table, a Calculate Payment button, and an output field that displays the result returned from the service.

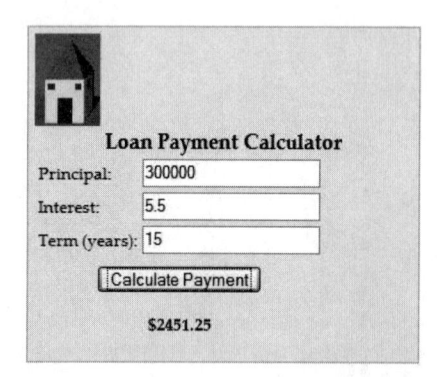

Figure 2.32 LoanPaymentWidget running in a browser

Uploading an Image

To include an image with your widget, you upload it to **zembly**'s servers. To upload the image, click **Browse** in the Resources dialog. Navigate and select an image from your file system. After you click **Upload**, the image appears in the Resources window, as shown in Figure 2.33. Now click on the image to add it to your widget as an `<img>` tag.

> **zembly Tip**
>
> *The easiest way to do this is to preview the already-built LoanPaymentWidget. First, specify LoanPaymentWidget in the **zembly** Search window and click on LoanPaymentWidget in the results list. While the widget is running in the preview area, right-click the image and save it to your local machine. You can then upload the image as described above.*

Creating Your First Widget: LoanPaymentWidget   37

Figure 2.33 Uploading images to add to your widget

After selecting the image, the HTML code includes an `<img>` tag as follows. (Select the **(X)HTML** tab.)

    <img src="${res('house.jpg')}">

You'll move the `<img>` tag inside the outermost `<div>`, as shown in Listing 2.3.

Including Library Prototype JS

From the Resources tab, select **Libraries** at the bottom. Select **Prototype** from the list of libraries, as shown in Figure 2.34. Prototype is a general-purpose JavaScript library that includes functions (such as enhanced array iteration) and syntax shortcuts for DOM elements.

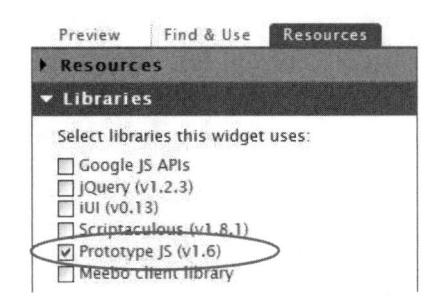

Figure 2.34 Including the Prototype JavaScript library in your widget

Building LoanPaymentWidget

Listing 2.3 shows the HTML code for this widget. The input elements are organized within a table element to create symmetrical spacing. The `<div>` tag with `id="resultDiv"` holds the results returned from the LoanPaymentService; the `<div>` tag with `id="errorDiv"` holds any returned error messages.

Listing 2.3 LoanPaymentWidget (HTML)

```
<div id="loanDiv" class="widget">
   <img src="${res('house.jpg')}">
   <div id="headingDiv" class="heading">
   Loan Payment Calculator
   </div>
   <table>
      <tr><td>Principal:</td>
         <td>
         <input id="principal" type="text" size="20" value="300000">
         </td></tr>
      <tr><td>Interest:</td>
         <td>
         <input id="interest" type="text" size="20" value="6.0">
         </td></tr>
      <tr><td>Term (years):</td>
         <td>
         <input id="years" type="text" size="20" value="30">
         </td></tr>
      <tr><td colspan="2">
         <div id="calcdiv" class="calc">
         <button id="calcButton">Calculate Payment</button>
         </div>
         </td></tr>
      <tr><td colspan="2">
         <div id="resultDiv" class="results">
         </div>
         <div id="errorDiv" class="errorResults">
         </div>
         </td></tr>
   </table>
</div>
```

Using CSS for Styling

The widget's CSS file provides style sheets for the widget. Note that there is a separate style for `results` and `errorResults`. Here is the CSS code.

Listing 2.4 LoanPaymentWidget (CSS)

```
div.widget {
   background-color: #e6e6ff;
   border: 1px solid #aaaaff;
   padding: 5px 5px 5px 5px;
   font-size: 0.8em;
}
div.heading {
   font-size: 1.3em;
   font-weight: bold;
   text-align: center;
}
div.calc {
   margin: 5px;
   text-align: center;
}
div.results {
   margin: 5px 2px 2px 2px;
   padding: 1px 2px 2px 2px;
   font-weight: bold;
   text-align: center;
}
div.errorResults {
   margin: 5px 2px 2px 2px;
   padding: 1px 2px 2px 2px;
   font-weight: bold;
   color: #C61C1C;
   text-align: center;
}
```

Calling LoanPaymentService in Your Widget

zembly makes it easy for you to add code to call services in your widget (this works when building services, too). Open the JavaScript editor for your widget (click the JavaScript tab in the editor zone). Then select the **Find & Use** tab in the window to the right of the editor zone. You'll see a Search window. Type in LoanPaymentService and click **Search**.

Chapter 2 zembly Basics

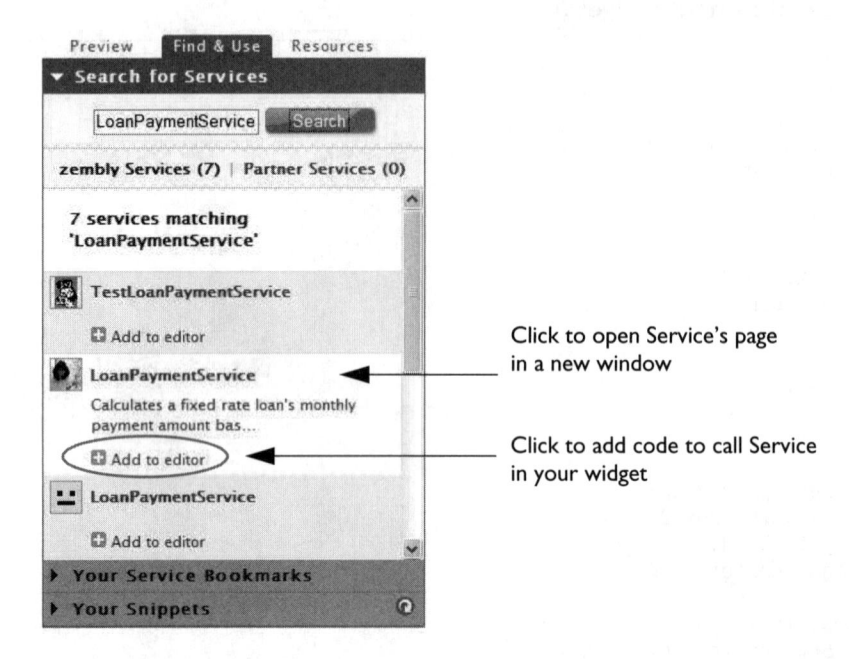

Figure 2.35 Find & Use Search for Services lets you easily add code to your widget

Figure 2.35 shows the results (quite a few, as it turns out). Using the avatars as a clue, find the LoanPaymentService near the start of the list. If you click its description, **zembly** opens the LoanPaymentService page in a new window. You can then study its documentation (or code). To add code to call the service to your widget, simply click **Add to editor** in the search results window. This will give you the correct calling template as a starting point. You can then edit the JavaScript to specify the parameter values and add the coding logic for your widget.

Listing 2.5 shows the JavaScript that calls LoanPaymentService using the three input values. Prototype's Event.observe function connects the calcButton click event to the handler.

After obtaining the principal, interest, and years input from the user, you pass these parameters to the LoanPaymentService. The return value is in data, which you prepend with a dollar sign ($) (for a successful payment result) or error, which returns an error code (error.code) and message (error.message). You insert the payment or the error information into the page's HTML markup.

```
$("resultDiv").innerHTML = [insert payment html here];
$("errorDiv").innerHTML = [insert error html here];
```

Because style `errorDiv` defines its text color as red as shown below (and in Listing 2.4 on page 39), error messages appear in red and normal return results are in black.

```
div.errorResults {
   margin: 5px 2px 2px 2px;
   padding: 1px 2px 2px 2px;
   font-weight: bold;
   color: #C61C1C;
   text-align: center;
}
```

The Prototype shortcut notation uses `$("element_id")` instead of the more verbose `document.getElementById("element_id")`.

Listing 2.5 LoanPaymentWidget (JavaScript)

```
Event.observe($("calcButton"), 'click', function() {
   var principal = $("principal").value;
   var interest = $("interest").value;
   var years = $("years").value;

   Things.callService("ganderson.LoanPaymentService",
   {
      "principal": principal, // The principal of the loan (in dollars)
      "interest": interest, // The interest rate (per cent) (e.g., 6.5)
      "years": years // How long your loan will endure (in years)
   },
   {  onSuccess: function(data) {
            var resultsHtml = "$" + data;
            $("resultDiv").innerHTML = resultsHtml;
            $("errorDiv").innerHTML = "";

      },
      onFailure: function(error) {
            $("errorDiv").innerHTML = error.code + ": " + error.message
               + ".<br/>";
            $("resultDiv").innerHTML = "";
         }
      });
});
```

Previewing and Publishing

Test your widget using the Preview tab or the Preview widget box. When you're satisfied that the widget is working, publish your widget by selecting the Publish button. After you publish a widget, you can embed it in any web page.

Embedding LoanPaymentWidget

This widget is embedded in a web page with the following HTML source.

```
<iframe width=400 height=280
   src="http://94f52847744e493b944aed46cf255e63.zembly.com/things/
       94f52847744e493b944aed46cf255e63;iframe" frameborder="0">
</iframe>
```

You copy/paste the source from the widget's documentation page (under Share This Widget). Here, we've supplied height and width attributes to adjust the size of the iframe tag area.

---
zembly Tip

You can add width and height attributes to the iframe tag as shown above to make the widget larger than the default iframe size.

2.6 Drafts, Versions, and Timelines

When editing a service or widget, **zembly** records the changes you make as intermediate drafts. **zembly** automatically saves a new draft every time you make a change, such as adding a parameter or editing the code. A draft is a clone of the entire state of your service or widget. A draft comes to an end when you publish a service or widget. You can see which version you are looking at or editing below your object's title, as shown in Figure 2.36.

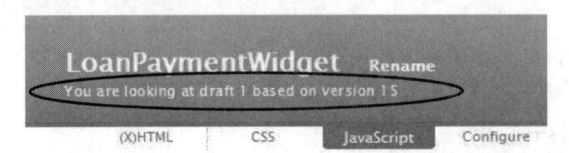

Figure 2.36 Draft and version number of object's current edit session

Edit History

A stack on the right side of the edit zone (small boxes) shows the history of your published versions and drafts, as shown in Figure 2.37. The oldest versions are on the bottom of the stack and, if you hover the mouse over a box, you can see when **zembly** saved the draft (light box) or the published version (dark box).

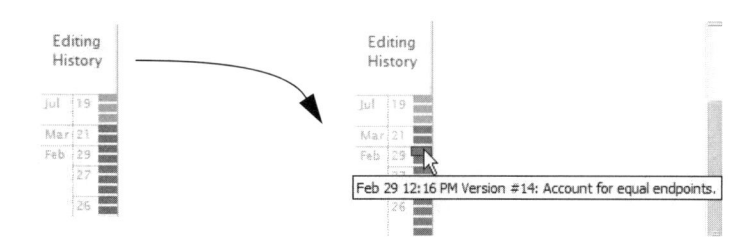

Figure 2.37 Edit history is a stack of published versions and drafts

If you look quickly when you make a change to the service or widget, or when you click around on the page after making a change, you'll see a new box being added to the top of the stack, as shown in Figure 2.38.

Figure 2.38 Saving a new draft

When you click on one of the boxes, the current changes are saved (as a new draft) and the old draft or version you clicked on is loaded. This lets you move back and forth within your edit history seamlessly. Once you begin editing by changing something, **zembly** creates a new draft based on the draft you changed.

Any changes you make are related to your current draft, which is the thing you're working on before you've published. You can keep multiple drafts for any length of time. You only create a new version of a service or widget when you publish. Then your edit history for the draft is wiped out (along with the current draft, which converts to a published version). At this point, you start over and any changes are saved as new drafts based on the latest published version.

You can also remove all current drafts of a service or widget if you don't want to keep any of the changes saved for your code. Select **Erase and start over**, as shown in Figure 2.39. **zembly** confirms the action before removing the drafts.

Figure 2.39 Erase and start over removes all saved drafts

Viewing Versions

The timeline lets you look at older versions of widgets or services as shown in Figure 2.40.

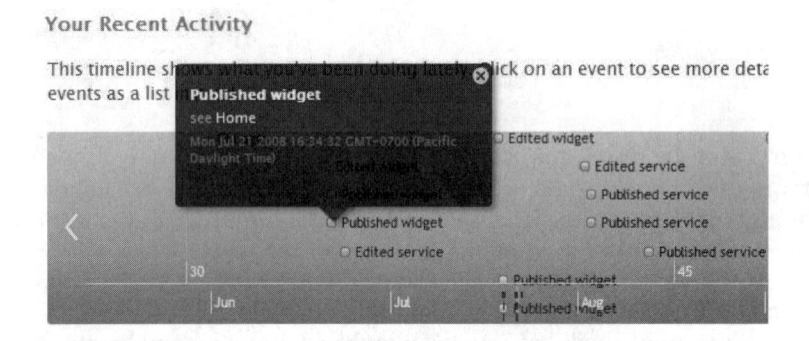

Figure 2.40 Finding a previous version of a published object

When you click on one of the points on the timeline, zembly reloads the page with that version.

Online/Offline Status

You can bring a published service or widget offline by toggling its online/offline status indicator as shown in Figure 2.41. Currently, this affects all published versions of the item. In the future, you will be able to specify individual versions for offline publishing.

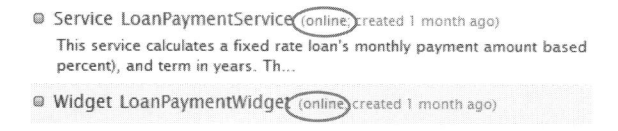

Figure 2.41 Online/offline toggle for a service or widget

2.7 Putting It All Together—Using the WeatherBug API

You'll now build a service and widget that uses the WeatherBug API. (Note that **zembly** already provides a sample service and widget for the WeatherBug API. However, in this section you'll build your own.) Here's a summary of the steps you'll follow to build this service and widget.

> **zembly Tip**
>
> *As with all the examples throughout the book, you are encouraged to clone the examples (find them using the **zembly** search mechanism). We provide the steps here so that you can easily build services and widgets on your own.*

Steps to create the WeatherBugService

1. Obtain a WeatherBug API key (from WeatherBug) and add it to your **zembly** Keychain.
2. Create a new service to access the WeatherBug API.
3. Add a parameter to the service.
4. Using **Find & Use**, add the JavaScript code to call the WeatherBug API.
5. Format the return data.
6. Test and publish the service.

Steps to create the WeatherBugWidget

1. Create a new blank widget.
2. Provide HTML for formatting.

3. Using **Find & Use**, add the call your WeatherBug service.
4. Include the Prototype library.
5. Add JavaScript code.
6. Preview and publish the widget.
7. Embed it in a web page.

Let's begin. The WeatherBug API is included in the list of services you can access from **zembly**. These services have been wrapped as adapters by the **zembly** structure, giving you easy access to WeatherBug's API.

Using Your Keychain

To start, access your Keychain (click **Manage your Keychain** from your home page). This displays the service providers currently supported on **zembly**. Scroll down to the WeatherBug's listing, as shown in Figure 2.42.

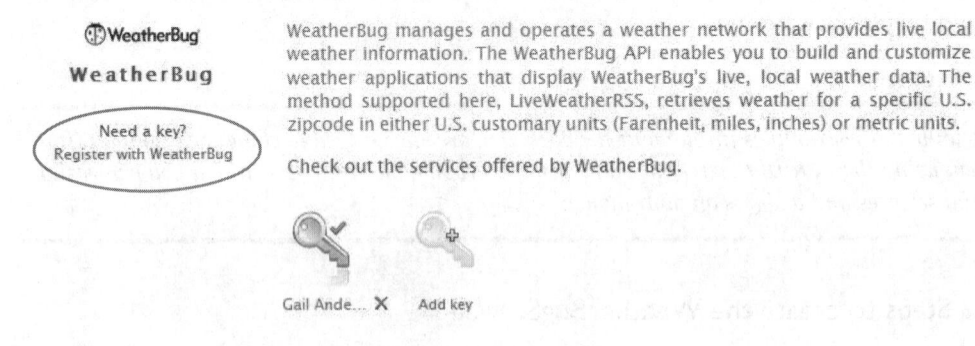

Figure 2.42 Accessing WeatherBug's registration page

The first step is to register with the WeatherBug service to obtain a key. You do this directly with WeatherBug. (Click **Register with WeatherBug** to get started.) After several email confirmations, WeatherBug will send you a key. When you add the WeatherBug API key to your keychain, **zembly** prompts for your name. (Each API site has its own requirements for what constitutes a legal API key.) Your name is stored with the key in your private keychain data.

zembly knows this key is associated with the WeatherBug API. When you access the WeatherBug API using `Owner.keychain`, the WeatherBug key is used in exactly the correct format required by WeatherBug. Also, when other people use a service you build, they access the service using your key. Your key is protected since it is wrapped in the Keychain mechanism.

Building WeatherBugService

Now that you have a WeatherBug key, you can build a service. From your Keychain page, scroll down to the WeatherBug listing and click **Check out the services offered by WeatherBug**. This directs you to the list of services; currently LiveWeatherRSS is the only one. Now click on **WeatherBug.LiveWeatherRSS** and zembly directs you to the LiveWeatherRSS page, as shown in Figure 2.43.

The WeatherBug.LiveWeatherRSS information page describes how to call the adapter and use its data. Besides the description, the page provides information on the parameters and error codes and a text box tells you how to call the adapter from a service.

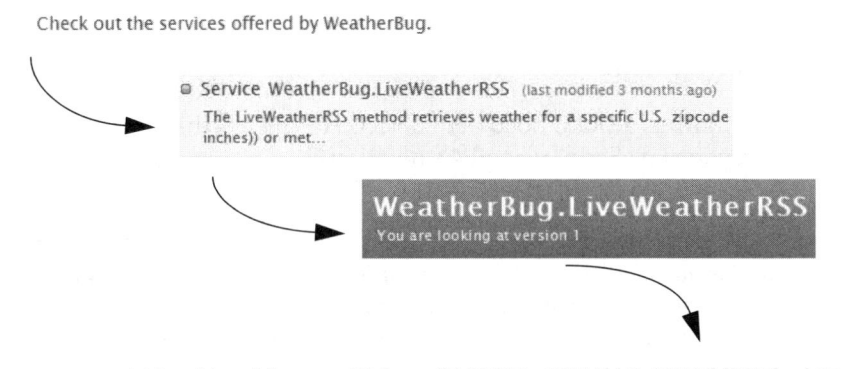

Figure 2.43 Drilling down to check out the services offered by WeatherBug

Here's the code template to access the LiveWeatherRSS adapter.

```
var result = Things.WeatherBug.LiveWeatherRSS({
    zipcode: "", // 5-digit ZipCode, U.S. cities only
    // unittype: "", // Optional. Default value is 1. Values are 0
    // (US customary units) or 1 (metric units - kms, degrees Celsius, etc).
    keys: Owner.keychain
});
```

What Are Things?

zembly provides the Things *object in the environment. It represents all artifacts (services, widgets, and applications) that are potentially accessible. Group* WeatherBug *specifies the publishing owner. Currently LiveWeatherRSS is the only service available under this group.*

The LiveWeatherRSS API call takes three parameters: the target zip code, the unit type (this is optional, but it defaults to '1' which means metric units), and keys. When you build this service, you'll supply values for unit type and keys and allow the user to supply the target zip code.

Now, let's build the service. Click [Create something!] at the top of the page and choose **Service** from the drop down menu. For this service, you'll have a single parameter (the target zip code). The unit type defaults to "1" (metric units) but you'll specify U.S. units (such as Fahrenheit and inches) which is "0". For the keys data use `Owner.keychain`, which pulls your WeatherBug-specific API key. You write this service using JavaScript. The LiveWeatherRSS service returns XML. You'll extract just the data you want and return the results to the caller in JSON.

Using E4X and JavaScript

zembly returns XML data as a DOM document object. This means that you can access the object directly in your JavaScript using E4X notation.

zembly Tip

*Although E4X support is not standard in all browsers, it is supported in the **zembly** environment. Therefore, you can use E4X without sacrificing portability in the services you build. However, for maximum portability, avoid using E4X in widgets. (This is why this service returns results in JSON.)*

Listing 2.6 shows a sample of the XML response from WeatherBug. Let's show you how to access the various nodes using JavaScript and E4X.

Listing 2.6 Sample XML Response from WeatherBug

```
<rss version="2.0">
   <channel>
      <title>Observations from Encinitas, CA - USA</title>
      <link>...</link>
      <description> . . . (contains HTML code) . . . </description>
         . . . omitted data . . .
   </channel>
</rss>
```

Because the data is already returned as a DOM document object, you access node title using (for example),

```
data.channel.title
```

Putting It All Together—Using the WeatherBug API   49

As discussed earlier, you provide a single parameter ("zipcode"), which is a String, it's required, and is escaped, as shown in Figure 2.44.

zembly Tip

Only a limited subset of characters are allowed in URLs. Escaping means that any special characters such as space, quotation marks, or the ampersand sign are encoded and then unencoded within the service. Typically characters must be encoded because they have a special meaning within a URL (such as ; ? or =) or there is a possibility of misinterpretation (such as space or #).

Figure 2.44 Editing a parameter

To add the code you need to call the adapter to the editor, select the **Find & Use** tab in the box to the right of the editor. Specify **LiveWeatherRSS** and click **Search**. zembly returns the matching services. Click **Add to editor** and zembly adds the code you need to the editor, as shown in Figure 2.45.

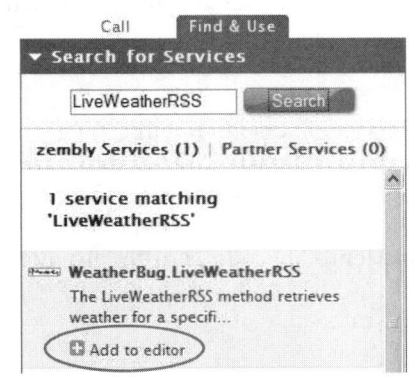

Figure 2.45 Find & Use lets you search for services and add code to the editor

Listing 2.7 shows the JavaScript source for WeatherBugService. Function Log.write allows you to write information to a log file that you can view in the Call window to the right of the editor. Select **Log** at the bottom of the Call window to view. Here, function Log.write(typeof data) writes "xml" to the log file.

Using the E4X notation, the WeatherBugService extracts the data for the title, description, and link to pass to the caller. This is the data you'll work with when you create a widget that uses this service.

Listing 2.7 WeatherBugService (JavaScript)

```
var data = Things.WeatherBug.LiveWeatherRSS({
   "zipcode": Parameters.zipcode, // 5-digit ZipCode, U.S. cities only
   "unittype": "0",
   "keys": Owner.keychain
});

//log type of the result object (XML object)
Log.write(typeof data); // writes "xml"

//You can use E4X notation to access the elements and attributes
//inside this object directly

var result = new Object();

result.title = ""+data.channel.item.title;
result.description = ""+data.channel.item.description;
result.link = ""+data.channel.link;

// Returns JSON
return result;
```

As you build the service, you can test drive it and look at the results that are returned.

Calling WeatherBugService

The next step is to build a widget that uses this service. The point of building a widget is to create a user-friendly snippet of code that others can paste directly into a web page. This widget should provide nice formatting of the data returned by WeatherBugService. Before leaving the WeatherBugService page, you'll see that it tells you how to call this service from a widget. Here is the template code **zembly** provides.

```
    Things.callService("ganderson.WeatherBugService",
     {
         zipcode: "" // 5-digit ZipCode, U.S. cities only
     },
     {
```

Putting It All Together—Using the WeatherBug API 51

```
    onSuccess: function(data) {
        Log.write(data);
    },
    onFailure: function(error) {
        Log.write("Error: " + error.code + " : " + error.message);
    }
});
```

When you build your widget, you'll use this code to call the service. Let's take a brief look at the response you get when you make a successful call to a service (the `onSuccess` handler). The code within `Things.callService` examines the response and gives you a pointer to the `data` object directly (as the first argument).

- If the service returns an object (if the response content type is *application/json*), then `data` is a JavaScript object. The WeatherBugService returns JSON data to the calling widget.

- If the service returns an XML document (if the response content type is *application/xml*), then `data` is a DOM object.

- If the service returns a plain string, number, boolean or date, then the `data` object will have its string representation. The LoanPaymentService returns a number, which will have its string representation in the calling widget.

Note that the `onFailure` handler accesses the `error` object.

Building WeatherBugWidget

From the top of the page, click **Create something!** and select **Widget** from the drop down menu. Choose **Create a blank widget**. The widget page lets you rename the widget, provide a description, and specify HTML, CSS, and JavaScript code. The HTML code should provide an input field for the zip code and a button to click and grab the weather data. You'll also need a named `<div>` tag to display the results. (This is `id="weatherBugResults"` in Listing 2.8 below.)

Here is the HTML code for the WeatherBugWidget.

Listing 2.8 WeatherBugWidget (HTML)

```
<div id="weatherBugWidget">
    Please enter a ZipCode to search WeatherBug service: <br/>
    <input id="zipcode" type="text" value="92024" />
    <br/>
    <button id="weatherButton">Get Weather</button>
    <br/><hr/><br/>
    <div id="weatherBugResults"></div>
</div>
```

Sample JSON Output

Before you look at the JavaScript code for this widget, let's look at the data that the service returns. Listing 2.9 shows sample JSON output (property `description` has been shortened). The result object is embedded in curly braces { } and each property is identified in quotation marks followed by a colon and its value. Properties are separated with commas.

Because the data arrives to the caller as a JavaScript object, you do not need to perform any parsing. For example, the `title` property is accessed using (for example)

```
data.title
```

Listing 2.9 Sample JSON Output

```
{
   "title": "Live Conditions from Encinitas,  CA - USA",
   "description":
"<img src=\"http://deskwx.weatherbug.com/images/Forecast/icons/cond026.gif\"
      border=\"0\" alt=\"Current Conditions\"/>

   ( . . . data omitted . . . )

   <br />",
   "link":
   "http://weather.weatherbug.com/CA/Encinitas
weather.html?ZCode=Z5546&Units=0&stat=ENCNT"
}
```

WeatherBugWidget JavaScript

This widget doesn't specify any CSS. Listing 2.10 shows the JavaScript code for this widget. Note that each property in the returned data object (`data`) is accessed directly using JavaScript notation. Since the data in property `description` is straight HTML, you can use that directly in the HTML markup.

> **zembly Tip**
>
> *The JavaScript code in Listing 2.10 relies on the Prototype Library. Be sure to select Prototype from the list of libraries under the Resources/Libraries tab.*

Listing 2.10 WeatherBugWidget (JavaScript)

```
// WeatherBugWidget (WBW)
// Register a listener for the "weatherButton" with Prototype Event.observe
```

Putting It All Together—Using the WeatherBug API

```
Event.observe($("weatherButton"), 'click', function() {
   var zipcode = $("zipcode").value;
   // call service and pass zipcode
   Things.callService("ganderson.WeatherBugService", {
      zipcode: zipcode},
      {
      onSuccess: function(data) {
         // format the return data and inject into page markup
         var resultsHtml = "<b>" + data.title + "</b><br/>" +
            data.description + "<br/><b><a href=" + data.link +
            ">weather details</a></b><br/> " ;
         $("weatherBugResults").innerHTML = resultsHtml;
      },
      onFailure: function(error) {alert(error.code);}
   });
});
```

Each time you edit the widget, you can test it directly on the widget page. Once you're finished editing, publish it. zembly provides the code you use to run the widget in a browser. You can configure the iframe by specifying height and width attributes. Here is the HTML source.

Listing 2.11 Sample HTML source to call the WeatherBugWidget

```
<iframe width=500 height="350"
   src="http://0eb6e21170b8405ca2658cec54fc5005.zembly.com/things/
0eb6e21170b8405ca2658cec54fc5005;iframe" frameborder="0">
</iframe>
```

Figure 2.46 shows sample output from running the above HTML.

zembly Tip

See "LiveWeatherBugWidget" on page 274 and "LiveWeatherMapWidget" on page 284 for enhancements to this widget.

54   Chapter 2   zembly Basics

```
Please enter a ZipCode to search WeatherBug service:
[92024]
[Get Weather]
_____

Observations from Encinitas, CA - USA
   (○)   Sunny
Temperature: 60.5 °F
Humidity: 41 %   Wind Speed: 3 mph NE   Pressure: 30.02 "
Dew Point: 37? °F   Gusts: mph ENE   Rain Today: 0.00 "

weather details
```

Figure 2.46 WeatherBugWidget running in a browser

3 Building Flickr Widgets

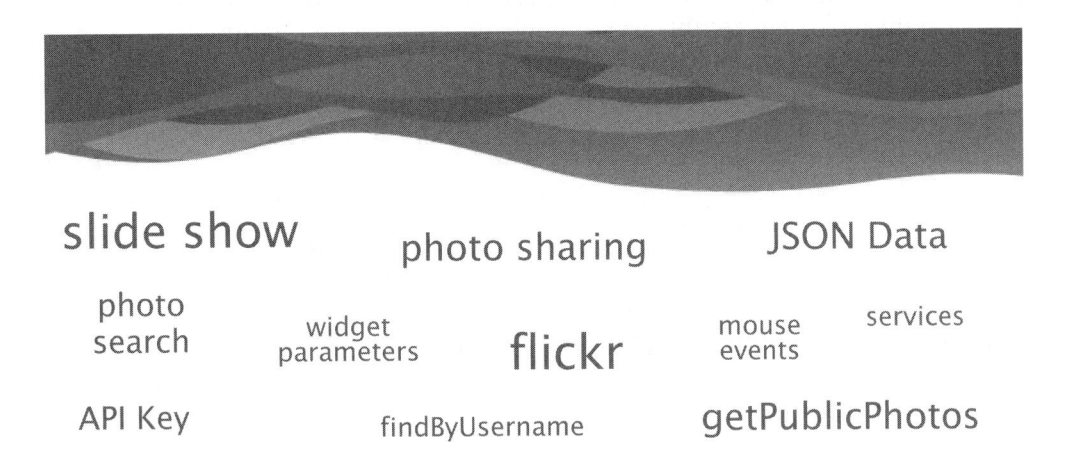

slide show   photo sharing   JSON Data

photo search   widget parameters   flickr   mouse events   services

API Key   findByUsername   getPublicPhotos

Flickr is a an online social, photo management, and photo sharing site where people post their favorite photos, tag them, and make them available for friends, groups, or the world to see. Flickr has an API that enables you to write programs that present public Flickr data, such as photos, tags, profiles, or groups, the way you want. Flickr users can tag images, provide titles, and organize images in creative ways. This chapter explores several widgets and services you can build based on data retrieved from Flickr services. Along the way, you'll see some useful CSS styles, powerful JavaScript, and service results in JSON that will help you build your own cool and fancy widgets.

What You Will Learn

- Introducing the Flickr API services
- Flickr basics: photo tags, constructing photo source URLs, photo titles
- Building a Flickr-based widget
- Accessing JSON data in JavaScript
- Using CSS styles to control your widget's appearance
- Building a photo slide show with JavaScript

- Building a Flickr-based service
- Passing arguments to your widget

Examples in This Chapter

All examples in this chapter are tagged **zembly-book-flickr**. To search for them, select **Search** at the top of any **zembly** page. Supply the search term **zembly-book-flickr** and click the search icon as shown in Figure 3.1.

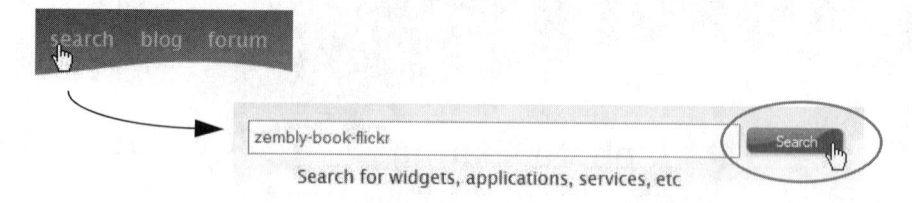

Figure 3.1 Searching for the examples in this chapter

3.1 Using Flickr

Flickr has an API that enables you to completely manage Flickr data, such as adding and deleting photos, searching for photos by tags, getting a list of recent activity on making comments or manipulating photos, managing your profile or contacts, getting a list of favorite photos, managing and searching groups, and getting a list of recent interesting photos. In short, **zembly** has over 100 adapters for the Flickr API. Here is a short sample of several adapters. For the complete list, go to your home page and select **Manage your keychain**, then click **Check out the services offered by Flickr**.

- **flickr.interestingness.getList**—returns the list of interesting photos for the most recent day or for a user-specified date. For more information, see http://www.flickr.com/services/api/flickr.interestingness.getList.html. See http://www.flickr.com/services/api/misc.urls.html for information on how to construct image URLs.
- **flickr.people.findByUsername**—returns a user's NSID, given the username.
- **flickr.people.getInfo**—get information about a user.
- **flickr.people.getPublicPhotos**—Get a list of public photos for a given user. For more information, see http://www.flickr.com/services/api/flickr.people.get-PublicPhotos.html.

- **flickr.photos.addTags**—add tags to a photo.
- **flickr.photos.comments.addComment**—add comments to a photo as the currently authenticated user.
- **flickr.photos.geo.getLocation**—get the geo data (latitude, longitude, and accuracy level) for a photo.
- **flickr.photos.search**—return a list of photos matching some criteria. Only photos visible to the calling user will be returned. To return private or semi-private photos, the caller must be authenticated with read permissions and have permission to view the photos. Unauthenticated calls return only public photos. For more information, see `http://www.flickr.com/services/api/flickr.photos.search.html`.
- **flickr.photosets.getList**—return the photosets belonging to the specified user.
- **flickr.photosets.getPhotos**—get the list of photos in a set.

In this chapter, we'll look at widgets and services that use the `flickr.photos.search`, `flickr.people.getPublicPhotos`, and `flickr.people.findByUsername` adapters.

3.2 Building a Slide Show Widget

The **zembly** Samples section includes a widget that creates a slide show based on photos returned from Flickr's photo search service. Once the photos are displayed in a preview list, you can select them for the slide show. You can then auto play the slide show or step through the photos manually.

The widget you build in this section will do exactly that; however, you'll use CSS style sheets and JavaScript to improve the user experience. Specifically, you'll display the photo as soon as you add it to the slide show, let users know when a photo is in focus by listening for mouseover and mouseout events, and constrict the height of a photo to make the widget size consistent. As you read over the JavaScript and CSS styles, you'll learn how to implement these features.

As you gain experience building widgets with **zembly**, you'll see that coding skills with JavaScript, CSS styling, and HTML help you build more sophisticated applications. With that in mind, we hope to share several JavaScript coding pearls that will provide you with a solid base for building widgets. Perhaps the best advice is to encourage using CSS so that styles are not intermixed with HTML or embedded in HTML code generated by your JavaScript. These Flickr-based widgets illustrate this technique effectively.

Figure 3.2 shows the FlickrSlideShow widget running in a browser. An input field provides one or more tags to influence Flickr's list of photos returned. Here the tag "green purple" returns photos with these colors. The Search button invokes the search.

Once the search returns results, the widget builds its preview list—the array of ten small photos at the bottom of the widget. Note that when the widget first comes up, there is no photo in the slide show area.

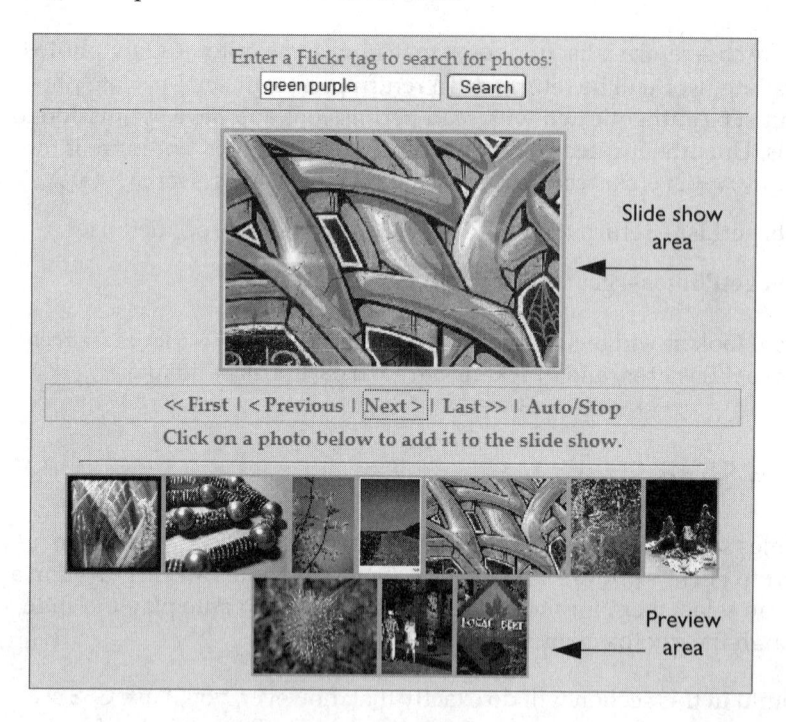

Figure 3.2 FlickrSlideShow widget running in a browser

Now the user interaction takes place. If you move the mouse over any of the preview photos it becomes temporarily faded and returns to its normal brightness as you move the mouse away from the image. These are the "mouseover" and "mouseout" events alluded to earlier. Furthermore, clicking on a preview photo makes it appear in the slide show area, letting the user know that the photo was successfully added to the slide show. You can add photos in any order and even add photos more than once. It's also possible to add photos to the slide show after you start the slide show auto play.

Finally, you can control the slide show. The First, Next, Previous, and Last links display the respective photo. The Auto/Stop link starts and stops the slide show. Let's now show you how to build this widget.

Here is a summary of the steps to build this widget. (For detailed discussion of the steps to create a widget, see "Creating Your First Widget: LoanPaymentWidget" on page 34.)

1. Create a new blank widget. Rename it and provide a description.
2. Include the Prototype library.
3. Provide the HTML, CSS, and JavaScript code.
4. Use **Find & Use** to call zembly services from your widget.
5. Preview and publish.
6. Configure your widget.
7. Embed in a web page.

Looking at the Source

Listing 3.1 is the HTML code for the Flickr slide show widget. The main div tag contains the instruction text, input field, and Search button that invokes the Flickr service call. A second div tag (id="FlickrSearchResults") serves as a place holder for displaying the results.

Listing 3.1 Widget FlickrSlideShow (HTML)

```
<div id="FlickrSlideShowWidget">
    Enter a Flickr tag to search for photos: <br/>
    <input id="name" type="text" value="Blue Green" />
    <button id="searchButton">Search</button><br/><hr/>
    <div id="FlickrSearchResults"></div>
</div>
```

Using CSS Styles

CSS styles are powerful because you can create styles that belong to arbitrary HTML tags. Listing 3.2 shows the CSS styles for the FlickrSlideShow widget. You see styles defined for div tags FlickrSlideShowWidget and FlickrSearchResults (these tags are defined in Listing 3.1).

FlickrSlideShowWidget is the main div tag. Its contents are centered, the text color is gray (#666666), the background is light gray (#e1e1e1), and it has a 1px border with a 5px padding.

You also see CSS styles defined for tags not defined in Listing 3.1. These added tags are generated in the JavaScript code. However, to keep the main tenet of our coding style, you still write styles for these generated `div` tags in the CSS section of your widget.

The preview area holds a list of up to 10 photos. Tag `previewpic` limits the height of the preview photo to 75px and places a 2px border around each picture. The slide show area (tag `slideshowpic`) is larger. Here the image height is 180px and `max-width` limits the width to 530px to prevent very long photos from spilling outside the bounds of the widget.

Tag `slidecontrols` define the links that control the slide show area. The style specifies a border, padding and bold font. The four additional styles for `slidecontrols` specify how its links (tag a) are styled. No text decoration (such as underlining) is used and the color for links and visited links does not change. However, when a user hovers over a link, the background color and text color change. These styles help provide user feedback as the mouse moves.

Listing 3.2 Widget FlickrSlideShow (CSS)

```
#FlickrSlideShowWidget {
    text-align: center;
    color: #666666;
    background: #e1e1e1;
    border: 1px solid;
    padding: 5px;
}

#FlickrSearchResults {
    padding: 5px;
}

#instructDiv {
    font-weight: bold;
}

#previewpic {
    height: 75px;
    border: 2px solid rgb(180,180,180);
}

#slideshowpic {
    height: 180px;
    max-width: 530px;
    border: 3px solid rgb(180,180,180);
    padding: 2px;
    margin-bottom: 10px;
}

#slideshowDiv {
    height:200px;
```

```
}
#slidecontrols {
   border: 1px solid rgb(180,180,180);
   padding: 3px;
   font-weight: bold;
}

#slidecontrols a { text-decoration: none; }
#slidecontrols a:link { color: #666666; }
#slidecontrols a:visited { color: #666666; }
#slidecontrols a:hover { background-color: #333; color: #ccc;
   border-color: #000 #ccc #ccc #000; }
```

Working with JavaScript

The JavaScript for this widget is divided into four parts for display convenience only. Parts 1 and 2 consist of JavaScript support functions. Parts 3 and 4 contain the processing logic for building the picture preview array and generating the HTML markup to display the slide show. If you're rusty with JavaScript or haven't coded that much in JavaScript, this is your chance to roll up your sleeves and dig into some code.

This widget uses the Prototype JavaScript library. From the Resources tab, select **Libraries** (at the bottom) and include **Prototype** from the list of libraries, as shown in Figure 3.3.

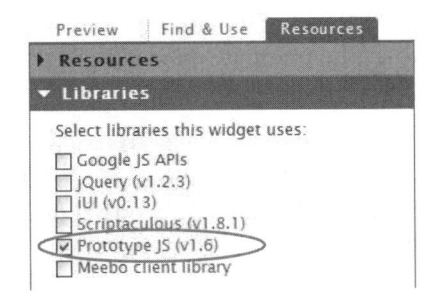

Figure 3.3 Adding the Prototype library to your widget

Array `FlickrPicArray` holds the URL of each photo that the user adds to the slide show. Function `addtoSlideShow` simply pushes the photo's URL onto the array. Function `setPicture` makes the photo appear in the slide show area of the widget dynamically by modifying element `flickrSlideShow` src attribute. Function `updateSlideShow` selects the next photo to display.

Listing 3.3 Widget FlickrSlideShow (JavaScript)—Part 1

```
var CurPic = 0;
var ShowTimer = 1500;
var AutoRunFlag = false;
var run;

var FlickrPicArray;

function addtoSlideShow(pic) {
   FlickrPicArray.push(pic);
   // show the picture when you add it
   setPicture(FlickrPicArray.length - 1);
}

function updateSlideShow(direction) {
   CurPic = CurPic + direction;
   if (CurPic > FlickrPicArray.length - 1) CurPic = 0;
   if (CurPic < 0) CurPic = FlickrPicArray.length - 1;
   setPicture(CurPic);
}

function setPicture(picIndex) {
   document.flickrSlideShow.src = FlickrPicArray[picIndex];
   CurPic = picIndex;
}
```

In Listing 3.4, functions showMouseOver and showMouseOut manipulate the opacity of an object (one of the image tags in the preview area). As the user moves the mouse over the image, the photo becomes less opaque. Likewise, the photo is restored to its normal opacity when the user moves the mouse out of the image.

Function autoSlideShow is a toggle for turning on and off the automatic slide show. The call to setInterval invokes updateSlideShow every ShowTimer milliseconds (1500), which displays the next photo every 1.5 seconds. If the slide show is already running, the function clears the timer, stopping the slide show.

Listing 3.4 Widget FlickrSlideShow (JavaScript)—Part 2

```
function showMouseOver(picName) {
   var object = document.getElementsByName(picName)[0].style;
   object.opacity = .50;
}

function showMouseOut(picName) {
   var object = document.getElementsByName(picName)[0].style;
   object.opacity = 1;
}
```

```
function autoSlideShow() {
   if (AutoRunFlag == true) {
      AutoRunFlag = false;
      window.clearInterval(run);
   } else {
      AutoRunFlag = true;
      run = setInterval("updateSlideShow(1)", ShowTimer);
   }
}
```

When the user clicks the Search button, the JavaScript calls the `searchButton 'click'` event listener, as shown in Listing 3.5. This function calls the `FlickrPhotoSearchService` (in **zembly**'s Samples) with the user-provided tags and builds the preview list with Flickr photo URLs. The returned JSON data can be accessed as a JavaScript object. Listing 3.5 uses Prototype's enumerable each function to build the preview list. (The following code snippet shows the structure of Prototype's each function.)

```
Flickrdata.photos.photo.each(function(photo,i) {
    // use photo to access each element
    // use i to get at the index number
});
```

zembly Tip

Search for services you need with the Find & Use tab to the right of the JavaScript editor, as shown in Figure 3.4. You can then go directly to the service's page on **zembly** *(click its name) or add the code to the editor (as shown circled below). We discuss the Find & Use mechanism in more detail in "Using Find & Use to Add JavaScript" on page 69.*

Figure 3.4 Searching for services with Find & Use

Listing 3.5 Widget FlickrSlideShow (JavaScript)—Part 3

```
Event.observe($("searchButton"), 'click', function() {

   FlickrPicArray = new Array ();
   var tags = $("name").value;

   Things.callService("scriblx.FlickrPhotoSearchService", {
      flickrTag:tags}, {
      onSuccess:
         function(data) {

            var Flickrdata = data;

            var previewlist = "";
            Flickrdata.photos.photo.each(function(photo,i) {
               var picurl = "http://farm" + photo.farm + ".static.flickr.com/"
                  + photo.server + "/"
                  + photo.id + "_"
                  + photo.secret + "_m.jpg";

               previewlist += "<img id=\"previewpic\" name=\"pic" + i +
                  "\" src=" + picurl +
                  " onClick=\"javascript:addtoSlideShow('"+
                  picurl +"')\"" +
                  " onMouseover=\"javascript:showMouseOver('pic" + i + "')\"" +
                  " onMouseout=\"javascript:showMouseOut('pic" + i + "')\""
                  + ">";
            });
```

Let's digress now to look at a sample of the data returned from this call to Flickr, as shown in Listing 3.6.

The JSON notation [ ] defines an array of data that is accessible with JavaScript array syntax (the first index is 0). For example, here is how you access the owner ("76488215@N00") and title ("My Garden") of the first photo.

```
// Flickrdata is the JavaScript object returned
var owner = Flickrdata.photos.photo[0].owner;
var title = Flickrdata.photos.photo[0].title;
```

In this widget, Prototype's enumerable each function (in Listing 3.5) lets you use a shorthand notation (photo) to construct the Flickr photo source URL, storing the source URL in variable picurl, as follows.

```
            var picurl = "http://farm" + photo.farm +
                     ".static.flickr.com/" +
                     photo.server + "/" +
                     photo.id + "_" +
                     photo.secret + "_m.jpg";
```

(See http://www.flickr.com/services/api/misc.urls.html for information on how to construct image URLs.)

Programming Tip

Note that the photo source URL ends with a size suffix "_m.jpg". This suffix limits the image size to 240 pixels on the longest side. Other size suffix choices are listed on the Flickr Services Photo Source URL documentation page.

The JavaScript code (still in Listing 3.5 on page 64) then generates the preview list, which is HTML code to display each photo using an img tag. Each img tag listens for three events: onClick (the image is added to the slide show and displayed in the slide show viewing area), onMouseover (the image becomes translucent), and onMouseout (the image returns to normal opacity).

Programming Tip

Once again, it's important to emphasize that you should define style information for generated div tags in CSS code (#previewpic, for example) where you can easily modify its style if you need to.

Here is sample JSON data from the call to the Flickr service.

Listing 3.6 Sample JSON Data

```
{"photos":{"page":1,"perpage":10,"total":"94",
"photo":[
   {"isfriend":0,
   "ispublic":1,
   "title":"My Garden",
   "server":"2168",
   "secret":"28abce21de",
   "owner":"76488215@N00",
   "id":"2246048748",
   "farm":3,
   "isfamily":0},

   {"isfriend":0,
   "ispublic":1,
   "title":"All coiled up Necklace",
   "server":"2309",
   "secret":"122e8f4f0b",
   "owner":"20873486@N05",
   "id":"2068299120",
   "farm":3,
   "isfamily":0},
```

```
   . . . data for photos 3-10 omitted . . .
   ],
"pages":10},"stat":"ok"}
```

Listing 3.7 shows the code that generates HTML for the `FlickrSearchResults` div tag. Here you generate several div tags that have their respective id attribute set. This lets you specify styles separately in the CSS style sheet. Tags with id `slideshowDiv`, `slideshowpic`, `slidecontrols`, and `instructDiv` all have separately defined styles (found in the CSS code in Listing 3.2 on page 60).

If the service call has an error (condition `onFailure`), you generate an error message for the `FlickrSearchResults` div tag.

Listing 3.7 Widget FlickrSlideShow (JavaScript)—Part 4

```
            var resultsHtml =
" <div id=\"slideshowDiv\"> " +
"<img id=\"slideshowpic\" src=\"\" name=\"flickrSlideShow\" "+
" alt=\"Click on a photo below to add it to the slide show.\"> </div> " +
" <div id=\"slidecontrols\"> " +
" <a href=\"javascript:setPicture(0)\"><< First </a> " +
" | <a href=\"javascript:updateSlideShow(-1)\">< Previous </a> " +
" | <a href=\"javascript:updateSlideShow(1)\">Next > </a> " +
" | <a href=\"javascript:setPicture(FlickrPicArray.length -1 )\">" +
"Last >></a> " +
" | <a href=\"javascript:autoSlideShow()\">Auto/Stop</a> " +
" </div> " +
" <div id=\"instructDiv\"> " +
"Click on a photo below to add it to the slide show." +
"</div> <hr width=\"90%\"/> " + previewlist ;

            $("FlickrSearchResults").innerHTML = resultsHtml;
         },
      onFailure:
         function(error){
            var resultsHtml =
               "An error occurred accessing FlickrPhotoSearchService.</br>" +
               "Error: " + error.code;
            $("FlickrSearchResults").innerHTML = resultsHtml;
         }
      }
   );
});
```

Sharing Your Widget

Once you build a widget, you'll want to share it. To this end, **zembly** has partnered with Clearspring (`www.clearspring.com`) to provide sharing and tracking of your widgets. On the widget's edit page under Share This Widget, select **Setup sharing and tracking**. In order to initiate tracking, you must first register with Clearspring. To post this widget on another site, simply select the target and zembly steps you through the particulars of your target. Figure 3.5 shows some of the target sites where you can post your widget.

Figure 3.5 Sharing your widget with Clearspring

Embedding Your Widget in a Web Page

To embed your widget on an arbitrary web page, select **Embed** as shown in Figure 3.5. Now click **Other Sites**. zembly displays the code you can use.

Listing 3.8 Embedding the Widget

```
<script type="text/javascript"
   src="http://widgets.clearspring.com/o/4923804f5526689a/492387b4ed26cdf2/
   4923804f7b99ec70/6e39c739/widget.js">
</script>
```

3.3 Building a Service for Your Flickr Photos

Suppose you have a personal home page, a blog, or other web page in which you'd like to embed a widget that randomly displays your most recent Flickr photos. You don't want to provide any input; you simply want to embed the widget code in your page. When visitors view your page, they'll see a random selection of your Flickr photos. In this section (and the next), you'll build such a widget. Now that you've worked a bit with Flickr services, you're already familiar with the sorts of data that Flickr services provide. The first step is to build a service that provides the Flickr data you want.

Here is a summary of the steps required to build this service.

1. Obtain a Flickr API key (from Flickr) and add it to your **zembly** Keychain.
2. Create a new service to access the Flickr API. Provide a name and a description of the service.
3. Add a parameter to the service.
4. Using **Find & Use**, add the JavaScript code to call the Flickr API adapters you'll use.
5. Test and publish the service.

Getting a Flickr Application Key

In the previous widget example, you used a Flickr service from **zembly**'s Samples section. For this widget, however, you'll access the Flickr adapters `flickr.people.findByUsername` and `flickr.people.getPublicPhotos` to grab your own photos (or those of any arbitrary Flickr user if you'd like). For this, you'll need a Flickr Application Key. Go to Flickr's web site at `http://www.flickr.com/services/` to get started. You'll find a Terms of Service document, API documentation, and a link to apply for an API key. The process should be quick and painless.

Once you have a Flickr API key, add it to your **zembly** managed keychain (see "Your Keychain and Service Providers" on page 24). Now you're ready to create a new Flickr service.

Creating Service FlickrPeopleService

zembly provides an adapter that will get public photos from a Flickr user's account. Adapter `flickr.people.getPublicPhotos` takes a Flickr user id, several optional parameters, and an API key. However, most people know their flickr user names (screen names), not their user ids. To make access more user friendly, you'll create a service that takes a flickr *screen name* and returns a list of that user's public photos. This service, then, will make two calls to Flickr's API: `flickr.people.findByUsername` to determine the user id and then `flickr.people.getPublicPhotos` to get the list of photos.

Now let's create the service. On **zembly**, select **Create something!** as shown in Figure 3.6 and provide the name **FlickrPeopleService**. This service will have one parameter, `username`, a required String.

Figure 3.6 Creating a service on zembly

Using Find & Use to Add JavaScript

As you write your service, you'll want access to the documentation of the services (or adapters) that you'll be calling. Select the **Find & Use** tab in the test drive zone to the right of the editor. Provide the search term **flickr.people.findByUsername** and click **Search** as shown in Figure 3.7. zembly returns the matching services. You can either add the code to call the service right away (click **Add to editor**) or click the service's name and zembly opens a pop up window with additional information.

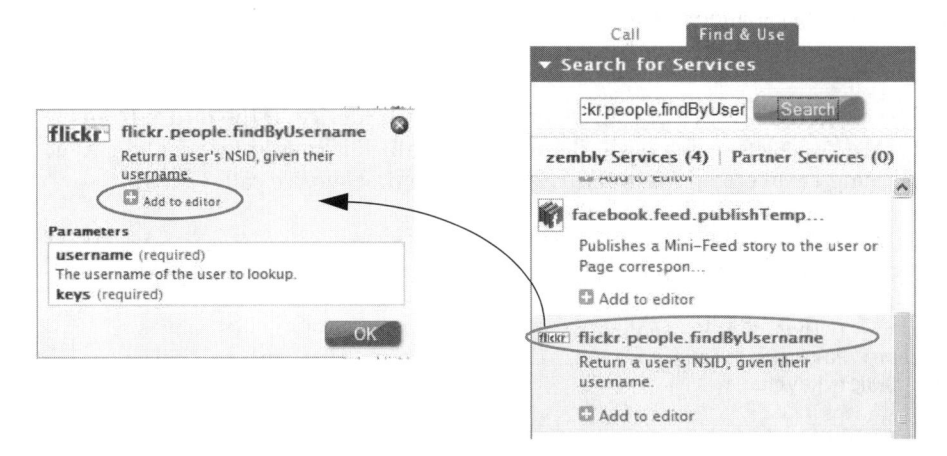

Figure 3.7 Using Find & Use search mechanism

Now you can click **Add to editor** (if you didn't earlier), to automatically add template code to call the adapter from your service as shown in Figure 3.7.

zembly Tip

The Find & Use tab will let you call the services you need without going back and forth between your current session and the documentation you need to call these services.

After you click **Add to editor** for adapter `flickr.people.findByUsername`, use Find & Use to search for and similarly add service `flickr.people.getPublicPhotos` to the editor.

Service FlickrPeopleService has a parameter (`username`). Select **Add a new parameter**, specify **username** for Name, and Type **String**. Check both **Must use this parameter in the call** and **Escape value**. Click **Save**, as shown in Figure 3.8.

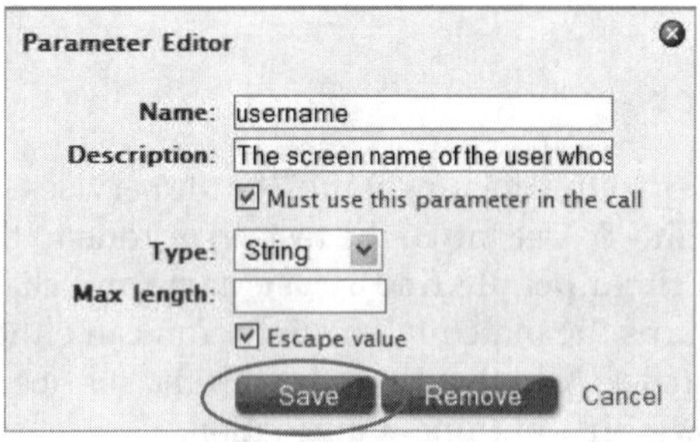

Figure 3.8 Adding parameter username

Listing 3.9 shows the JavaScript source for FlickrPeopleService. If the return from `flickr.people.findByUsername` is valid, the service calls Flickr adapter `people.getPublicPhotos` using `result.user.nsid` returned from the first service call. There are several optional parameters that we don't include here.

Listing 3.9 FlickrPeopleService

```
var result = Things.flickr.people.findByUsername({
   username: Parameters.username, // The username of the user to lookup.
   keys: Owner.keychain
});
//return result;

if (result.user) {

   var uid = result.user.nsid;
   result = Things.flickr.people.getPublicPhotos({
   user_id:uid,
   keys:Owner.keychain});
}
return result;
```

Testing and Publishing

Uncomment the first `return result`, supply a screen name argument, and click **Test drive now** from the Call tab. You can look at the format of the return data to determine how to extract the user id, as shown in Figure 3.9.

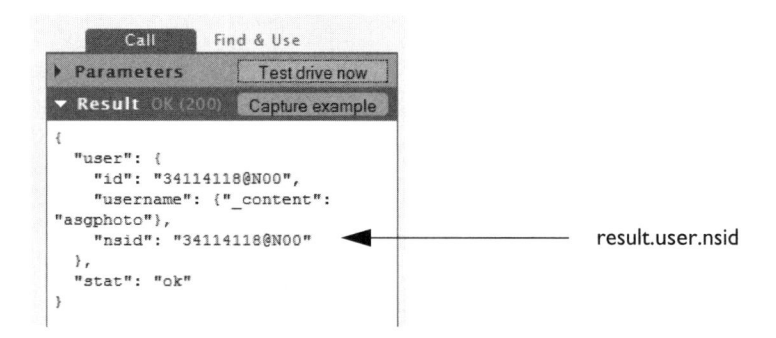

```
Call          Find & Use
▶ Parameters        Test drive now
▼ Result OK (200)   Capture example
{
  "user": {
    "id": "34114118@N00",
    "username": {"_content":
"asgphoto"},
    "nsid": "34114118@N00"    ◀──── result.user.nsid
  },
  "stat": "ok"
}
```

Figure 3.9 Using **Test drive now** to look at return data

Now re-comment the first return statement so that the service makes the second adapter call. Go ahead and test the service again (provide your own Flickr user name to test it). The JSON results will display in the Call window. Listing 3.6 on page 65 shows sample JSON data (the format is the same for this call). Note that zembly extracts your Flickr API key from `Owner.keychain` for you. Once you publish this service, you're ready to create the slide show widget.

3.4 Creating a Flickr User Slide Show Widget

Figure 3.10 shows MyFlickrRandomSlideshow widget running in a browser. Note that no input fields or buttons activate this widget; it just runs. Also, there is no obvious mechanism to provide any input. However, as you will see, there is a mechanism to do so; it's just a bit hidden.

Here's a summary of the steps you'll follow to build this widget.

1. Create a new blank widget.
2. Add parameter `flickrname`.
3. Include the Prototype library.
4. Provide HTML and CSS for formatting.
5. Add JavaScript code; use **Find & Use** to call your new FlickrPeopleService service.

Figure 3.10 MyFlickrRandomSlideshow widget running in a browser

6. Preview and publish the widget.
7. Embed it in a web page using the your Flickr screen name parameter.

Specifying Widget Parameters When You Embed

Before you begin, look at the code you need to embed this widget in a browser, as shown in Listing 3.10. The code should look familiar to you, except for the added `flickrname` parameter and value pair, as follows.

```
&flickrname=asgphoto
```

Listing 3.10 Embed this Widget

```
<iframe width=330 height=300
   src="http://1dbb12b5bd1f4a69b44a177851d366a1.zembly.com/things/
   1dbb12b5bd1f4a69b44a177851d366a1;iframe&flickrname=asgphoto">
</iframe>
```

Embedded within the iframe `src` attribute, the Flickr screen name information becomes available inside the iframe window. You can access this information by parsing `window.location.search` in the document's JavaScript code. Or, (more easily) you can add a parameter to your widget and access the parameter using `Parameters.flickrname`.

What does all this mean? When you publish your widget, you want other people to use it in their web pages. To make the widget general, but not require users to provide their Flickr screen name interactively, users "hard-wire" their Flickr name in the embedded iframe tag as shown in Listing 3.10. Users have to do this only once at the point that they're including the iframe tag in their own web page.

Creating Widget MyFlickrRandomSlideshow

Go ahead and create a new (blank) widget using zembly and rename it **MyFlickrRandomSlideshow**. In the Preview box to the right of the editor window, select **Add a new parameter**, as shown in Figure 3.11. Specify name **flickrname**, uncheck option **Must use this parameter** (make it optional), and click **Save**.

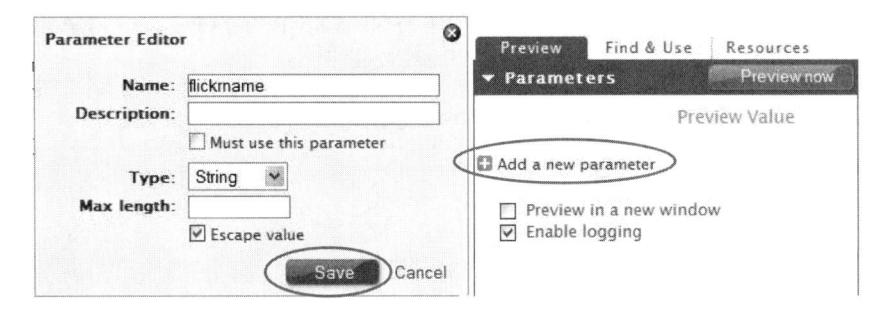

Figure 3.11 Adding a parameter to widget MyFlickrRandomSlideshow

You access the parameter in JavaScript using `Parameters.flickrname`. It is not an error if the caller does not supply a parameter value (since the parameter is optional). Therefore, you'll have to check for a value in the widget's code.

This widget uses the Prototype JavaScript library. From the Resources tab, select **Libraries** (at the bottom) and choose **Prototype** from the list of libraries, as shown in Figure 3.3 on page 61.

As you examine the code for this widget, much of it will be familiar to you, since it's similar to the FlickrSlideshow widget you've already seen.

Listing 3.11 shows the HTML for MyFlickrRandomSlideshow. Note that there are two `div` tags with `id` attributes. As before, you will provide CSS styles for these tags.

Listing 3.11 Widget MyFlickrRandomSlideshow (HTML)

```
<div id="FlickrSlideShowWidget">
   <div id="FlickrPhotoResults"></div>
</div>
```

Listing 3.12 shows the CSS code. Besides `FlickrSlideShowWidget` and `FlickrPhotoResults`, there are styles for `slideshowpic` (the style for the `img` tag), `pictitle` (the photo title's style), and `slideshowdiv` (the image view area).

Listing 3.12 Widget MyFlickrRandomSlideshow (CSS)

```css
#FlickrSlideShowWidget {
   text-align: center;
   color: #666666;
   background: #e1e1e1;
   border: 1px solid;
   padding: 5px;
}

#FlickrPhotoResults {
   padding: 5px;
}

#slideshowpic {
   height: 200px;
   max-width: 265px;
   border: 3px solid rgb(180,180,180);
   padding: 2px;
   margin-bottom: 10px;
}

#pictitle {
   font: 65% Verdana, sans-serif;
}

#slideshowDiv {
   height:250px;
}
```

Reusing JavaScript Code

The FlickrSlideShowWidget shown earlier in this chapter builds an array with picture URLs. The widget's JavaScript code traverses the array and displays each photo one after the other, controlling the order and pace with function `autoSlideShow`. The widget also builds a "preview" list to display small versions of the photo that the user adds to the slide show array.

In this version, you don't use a preview list at all. The code that loops through the results returned from the service call puts each photo in the `FlickrPicArray` and adds the photo's title as well. It also specifies a listener for the `onClick` event, which stops and restarts the slide show. When the slide show stops, the photo is "dimmed." This lets the user know the slide show is no longer running. A subsequent click restarts the slide show (and returns the photo to its normal brightness level).

You'll also see the code that extracts the provided Flickr screen name (that you'll pass to the service built in the previous section).

Listing 3.13 shows Part 1 of the JavaScript code containing several support functions. Function `randomSlideShow` sets the slide show picture by selecting the `FlickrPicArray`'s index number randomly.

Listing 3.13 Widget MyFlickrRandomSlideshow (JavaScript)—Part 1

```javascript
var CurPic;
var ShowTimer = 4000;
var AutoRunFlag = false;
var run;

var FlickrPicArray;

function addtoSlideShow(pic) {
   FlickrPicArray.push(pic);
}

function randomSlideShow() {
   CurPic = Math.floor((Math.random() * FlickrPicArray.length));
   setPicture(CurPic);
}

function setPicture(picIndex) {
   document.flickrSlideShow.src = FlickrPicArray[picIndex].picurl;
   $("pictitle").innerHTML = FlickrPicArray[picIndex].title;
   CurPic = picIndex;
}
```

Listing 3.14 shows Part 2 of the JavaScript code. Function `autoSlideShow` toggles the state of the slide show. To stop the slide show, it clears the window's timer and calls `showDim` to makes the image dim. To restart the slide show, it returns the image's brightness to normal and starts a new timer.

Function `getScreenName` extracts the (optional) `flickrname` parameter value. The built-in function `unescape` removes escape characters from the user id.

Programming Tip

If the user does not supply a `flickrname=value` *parameter value pair, function getScreen-Name returns a known valid flickr screen name.*

Listing 3.14 Widget MyFlickrRandomSlideshow (JavaScript)—Part 2

```
function autoSlideShow() {
   if (AutoRunFlag == true) {
      AutoRunFlag = false;
      window.clearInterval(run);
      showDim();
   } else {
      AutoRunFlag = true;
      showBright();
      run = setInterval("randomSlideShow()", ShowTimer);
   }
}

function showDim() {
   var object = document.getElementsByName("flickrSlideShow")[0].style;
   object.opacity = .55;
}

function showBright() {
   var object = document.getElementsByName("flickrSlideShow")[0].style;
   object.opacity = 1;
}

function getScreenName() {
   var screen = Parameters.flickrname;
   if (screen == null) screen = "asgphoto";
   return screen;
}
```

Listing 3.15 (Part 3) calls `FlickrPeopleService` and processes the results. (**Find & Use** will supply the template code for calling this service from your widget.) This function is invoked when the page is loaded (the window 'load' event) and is not dependent on a user action such as clicking a button. Since the (JSON) results are returned as a JavaScript object, you can access them using normal JavaScript syntax.

The Prototype enumerable each function constructs each photo's source URL as well as the photo's title and adds object `flickrpic` to `FlickrPicArray`. Note that the photo URL source includes the suffix "`_m.jpg`", which loads a smaller image size. This is appropriate for the widget's size and helps display the photos smoothly.

Programming Tip

Object `flickrpic` *has two fields:* `picurl`, *the photo's URL source from flickr, and* `title`, *the photo's title. When you make* `flickrpic` *an object, you can encapsulate both fields and pass the single object to function* `addtoSlideShow`.

The `onSuccess` handler builds the generated HTML markup that gets inserted into the document. The `img` tag appears inside a `div` tag. The `src` attribute is empty, but will have data when function `setPicture` is invoked.

After the HTML is generated, you insert the generated HTML in the page's markup and start the slide show.

If a call to `FlickrPeopleService` returns an error, the error message includes the iframe's query string. An invalid Flickr screen name is a likely error source.

Listing 3.15 Widget MyFlickrRandomSlideshow (JavaScript)—Part 3

```
Event.observe(window, 'load', function() {
   FlickrPicArray = new Array ();
   var screenname = getScreenName();
   Things.callService(
      "ganderson.FlickrPeopleService", {username: escape(screenname)},{
   onSuccess:
      function(data) {
         var Flickrdata = data;
         CurPic = 0;
         Flickrdata.photos.photo.each(function(photo) {
            var flickrpic = {};
            flickrpic.picurl = "http://farm" + photo.farm +
                  ".static.flickr.com/" +
                  photo.server + "/" +
                  photo.id + "_" +
                  photo.secret + "_m.jpg";
            flickrpic.title = photo.title;
            addtoSlideShow(flickrpic);
         });
         var resultsHtml =
            " <div id=\"slideshowDiv\"> <img id=\"slideshowpic\" " +
            "src=\"\" name=\"flickrSlideShow\" "+
            " onClick=\"javascript:autoSlideShow()\"" +
            " title=\"Click the photo to start/stop the slide show.\"" +
            " alt=\"Waiting for your photo from flickr.\"> " +
            " <div id=\"pictitle\"> </div> " + "</div> ";
         $("FlickrPhotoResults").innerHTML = resultsHtml;
         autoSlideShow();
      },
   onFailure:
      function(error) {
```

```
            var resultsHtml = "There was a problem with the call to Flickr."
                <br/>" + "Check your flickerid value: " +
                window.location.search + "<br/>" + error.code;
            $("FlickrPhotoResults").innerHTML = resultsHtml;
        }
    });
});
```

4 Building Zillow Widgets

mashups   citystatezip   longitude   property comparisons

latitude   XML   **Zillow**   widgets   Google Maps

map markers   JSON   zestimate

Even if you're not in the real estate business, Zillow (http://www.zillow.com) is a useful source for investigating property values in the U.S. Zillow provides housing data for home owners, prospective home owners, home sellers, and agents. Zillow has several adapter services on **zembly** that you can use to build useful services and widgets.

Building widgets is all about displaying your data in the best way possible. The Google Maps API lets you take your Zillow-generated data and display it on a Google map.

What You Will Learn

- Introducing the Zillow API services
- Building a Zillow-based service
- Zillow Basics: zpids, Zestimate, principal, comparables
- Using E4X to extract data in JavaScript
- Building a Zillow-based widget
- Introducing the Google Maps API

- Google Map basics: initialization, GLatLng, marker icons, markers, zoom level
- Building a mashup with Zillow and Google Maps

Examples in This Chapter

All examples in this chapter are tagged **zembly-book-zillow**. To search for them, select **Search** at the top of any **zembly** page. Supply the search term **zembly-book-zillow** and click the search icon as shown in Figure 4.1.

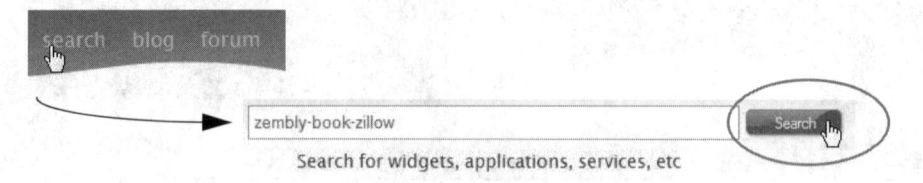

Figure 4.1 Searching for the examples in this chapter

4.1 Using Zillow

Zillow is an interactive real estate service that enables you to obtain an estimate of what a home is worth, list a home for sale, add photos and information about the home, and more. You can gather publicly available information, such as comparable home values and taxes, and homes are displayed on a map with information readily available as pop-up windows and charts. The Zillow APIs let you access much of this information from your applications. Using the APIs that **zembly** supports, you can get a Zillow reference ID for a property by specifying its address, get an estimate of a property's value (a Zestimate), get a chart showing historical changes in value for either a property or a region, get a list of comparable recent sales for a property, get full information on a property (deep search results), and get full information on comparable sales (deep comps). Here are the API service calls from Zillow that have adapters on **zembly**.

- **zillow.homevaluation.GetChart**—returns a URL for an image file displaying historical Zestimates for a property specified by Zillow property ID. This chart shows percentage or dollar value change, and you can constrain the size of the image. The historical data covers periods of 1, 5, or 10 years.
- **zillow.homevaluation.GetComps**—returns a list of comparable recent sales for a property. The results include the address, the Zillow property ID, and the Zestimate for the comparable properties and the principal property.

- **zillow.homevaluation.GetDemographics**—returns a set of demographic data which includes a URL linking to the corresponding demographics pages at Zillow.com, census information organized into affordability, homes, real estate and people categories, who lives here, and what's unique about the people.

- **zillow.homevaluation.GetRegionChart**—returns a URL for an image file displaying historical Zestimates for a region specified by city, state, and/or zipcode. This chart shows percentage or dollar value change, and you can constrain the size of the image. The historical data covers periods of 1, 5, or 10 years.

- **zillow.homevaluation.GetRegionChildren**—for a specified region, returns a list of subregions which includes subregion type, region IDs, region names, URL to corresponding Zillow page (only for cities and neighborhoods), latitudes and longitudes. A region can be specified at various levels of the region hierarchy. Allowable region types are country, state, county, and city. Country and county are optional parameters unless they are the region to be specified. An optional child-type parameter can also be specified to return subregions of a specific type.

- **zillow.homevaluation.GetSearchResults**—locates a property from an address. The returned information includes the address for the property or properties, the Zillow Property ID (zpid), the current Zestimate, the date the Zestimate was computed, a valuation range, and the Zestimate ranking for the property within its ZIP code. If no exact address match for a property is found, a match for nearby properties is returned.

- **zillow.homevaluation.GetZestimate**—for a specified Zillow property identifier (zpid), returns the most recent property Zestimate, the date the Zestimate was computed, the valuation range, the Zestimate ranking within the property's ZIP code, the full property address and geographic location (latitude/longitude), and a set of identifiers that uniquely represent the region (ZIP code, city, county, and state) of the property. If a request is made for a property that has no Zestimate, an error code is returned (502 if a property is found, but there is no Zestimate).

- **zillow.propertydetails.GetDeepComps**—returns a list of comparable recent sales for a property. The results include the address, the Zillow property identifier, and the Zestimate for the comparable properties and the principal property, as well as extensive property data for the comparable properties.

- **zillow.propertydetails.GetDeepSearchResults**—locates a property from an address. The returned information includes the address for the property or properties, the Zillow Property ID (zpid), the current Zestimate, the date the Zestimate was computed, a valuation range, and the Zestimate ranking for the property within its ZIP code. If no exact address match for a property is found, a match for nearby properties is returned. This deep search also provides detailed property data like lot size, year built, bath/beds, last sale details, and so on.

In these next sections, you will see how to build a custom widget (a "mashup") that takes data from Zillow and presents it using Google Maps.

4.2 Building a Zillow Service

In this section, you'll build a Zillow-based service. Here is a summary of the steps you'll follow to build this service.

1. Obtain a Zillow API key (from Zillow) and add it to your **zembly** Keychain.
2. Create a new service to access the Zillow API. Provide a name and a description of the service.
3. Add two parameters to the service (address and citystatezip).
4. With **Find & Use**, add the JavaScript code to call the Zillow API adapters you'll use.
5. Extract the XML data and build a JSON return object.
6. Test and publish the service.

Obtaining a Zillow API Key

In order to build your own Zillow-based service, you must first obtain the Zillow-specific API key from Zillow (see their web site at http://www.zillow.com/howto/api/API-Overview.htm) and add it to your keychain. (The section "Using Your Keychain" on page 46 contains information on the **zembly** Keychain mechanism.)

Zillow Property IDs

Suppose you want to build a widget based on Zillow that displays a home's value, along with five comparable values of nearby homes. Your first step is to figure out which Zillow APIs to call and build a service that returns the data that interests you. The next step is to build a widget to provide the user interface you want, as well as present the data in a pleasing way to your users.

In order to obtain comparable home value data, you must first obtain Zillow's zpid (Zillow property ID) for the target property. Calling zillow.homevaluation.Get-SearchResults will return (among other data) the zpid. Once you have the zpid you can then call either zillow.propertydetails.GetDeepComps or zillow.homevaluation.GetComps.

Building a Zillow-based Service with Parameters

With an idea of which Zillow adapters to call, select **Create something!** from the top of the **zembly** page and choose **Service** from the menu as shown in Figure 4.2. Provide a meaningful name (such as RecentSalesService).

Figure 4.2 Creating a service

In order to call `zillow.homevaluation.GetSearchResults` you'll provide two parameters: the address and the citystatezip (any combination that includes at least one of city, state, or zip code for the target property). Change the name parameter to address; it should be required, escaped, and its type is String. Add the second parameter; its name is citystatezip, it is required and escaped, and its type is String. Figure 4.3 shows the **zembly** Parameter Editor.

Figure 4.3 Adding parameter `citystatezip`

The third argument, your Zillow API key, is extracted by the **zembly** Keychain mechanism using `Owner.keychain`. Here is the JavaScript that makes this call.

```
var result = Things.zillow.homevaluation.GetSearchResults({
    address: Parameters.address,
    citystatezip: Parameters.citystatezip,
    keys: Owner.keychain
    });
return result;
```

84　Chapter 4　Building Zillow Widgets

You can examine the returned data (result) using the test drive window, as shown in Figure 4.4.

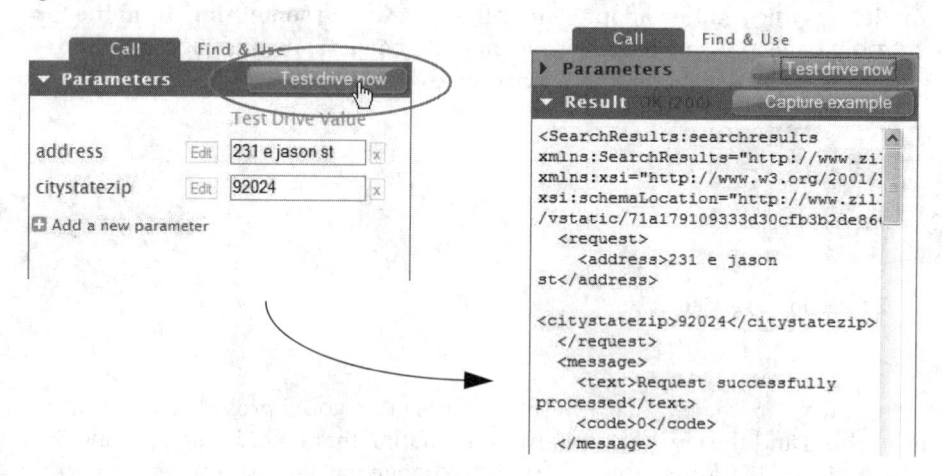

Figure 4.4 Using **Test drive now** to examine returned data

> **zembly Tip**
>
> You can also use the **Capture example** feature in the Call window to more easily examine the data. You'll want to extract the zpid data, as shown in the result sample displayed in Listing 4.1.

Using E4X and JavaScript

E4X is short for ECMAScript for XML. It is a standard extension to JavaScript designed specifically to process XML data. Unfortunately, it is not universally supported, but you can use it in **zembly** services since **zembly** JavaScript includes E4X support.

Listing 4.1 displays a portion of the returned result (XML) from the `zillow.homevaluation.GetSearchResults` web service call.

Listing 4.1 Sample XML Output from `zillow.homevaluation.GetSearchResults`

```
<?xml version="1.0" encoding="utf-8" ?>
<SearchResults:searchresults . . . >
   <request>
   . . .
   </request>
   <message>
```

```
        . . .
    </message>
    <response>
        <results>
            <result>
                <zpid>48749425</zpid>
                . . .
                <address>
                    <street>2114 Bigelow Ave N</street>
                    <zipcode>98109</zipcode>
                    <city>Seattle</city>
                    <state>WA</state>
                    <latitude>47.637924</latitude>
                    <longitude>-122.347929</longitude>
                </address>
                . . .
            </result>
        </results>
    </response>
</SearchResults:searchresults>
```

To process the returned data, first convert it to an XML object using the following JavaScript. You can then extract the information that you need using dot notation for each XML tag level.

```
var searchresults = new XML(result);
var zpid = searchresults.response.results.result.zpid;
```

With E4X you can also define placeholder variables that make your code less verbose. For example, define variable address as follows.

```
var address = searchresults.response.results.result.address;
```

Now to extract the property's address, use

```
var html_addr = address.street + "<br/>" + address.city + ", "
    + address.state + " " + address.zipcode;
```

There's more you can do with E4X, which we'll show you later in this chapter. In this service, you want to check the returned code for errors and extract the zpid. With the zpid, you can now call zillow.propertydetails.GetDeepComps passing your API key (Owner.keychain), the zpid, and the comparison count (5). You'll use E4X to extract part of the GetDeepComps data to pass to the service's caller.

Listing 4.2 shows Part 1 of the JavaScript code for RecentSalesService. You first make a call to zillow.homevaluation.GetSearchResults to obtain the property's zpid. Next you call zillow.propertydetails.GetDeepComps to get the comparables' data (stored in result).

Listing 4.2 RecentSalesService (JavaScript)—Part 1

```
var result = Things.zillow.homevaluation.GetSearchResults({
   address: Parameters.address,
   citystatezip: Parameters.citystatezip,
   keys: Owner.keychain
   });
var searchresults = new XML(result);
var returncode = searchresults.message.code;
if (returncode != 0) { //error
   Log.write(searchresults.message.text);
   throw returncode;
}

var zpid = searchresults.response.results.result.zpid;

result = Things.zillow.propertydetails.GetDeepComps({
   keys: Owner.keychain,
   zpid: zpid,
   count: "5"
   });
```

Listing 4.3 shows Part 2 of the JavaScript code for RecentSalesService. Here you see how to use E4X to extract the data and to create the `zillowresult` object which holds the returned data.

Variable `zillowresult` is an object with two properties: `principal` and `compsinfo`. These in turn are also objects, whose properties are set with the data from the XML object zdata. You build the `zillowresult.compsinfo` object looping through the XML data in `zdata.response.properties.comparables.comp` and building a `compdata` object. After all the data is extracted, compdata is pushed onto `CompsArray`. Finally, `CompsArray` is installed into the `compsinfo` property of the `zillowresult` return object.

Listing 4.3 RecentSalesService (JavaScript)—Part 2

```
// Build the return data and put in zillowresult
var zdata = new XML(result);

var CompsArray = new Array();
var zillowresult = new Object();
zillowresult.principal = { };
zillowresult.compsinfo = { };

// Get the principal data first
var target = zdata.response.properties.principal;

zillowresult.principal.homedetails = target.links.homedetails + "";
zillowresult.principal.address = target.address.street + "";
zillowresult.principal.zestimate = target.zestimate.amount + "";
```

```
zillowresult.principal.latitude = target.address.latitude + "";
zillowresult.principal.longitude = target.address.longitude + "";
zillowresult.principal.finishedSqFt = target.finishedSqFt + "";
zillowresult.principal.bedrooms = target.bedrooms + "";
zillowresult.principal.bathrooms = target.bathrooms + "";

// Build the data for the comparables and put in CompsArray
var comps = zdata.response.properties.comparables.comp;
for (var i = 0; i < Number(zdata.request.count); i++) {
  var compdata = { };
  compdata.homedetails = comps[i].links.homedetails + "";
  compdata.address = comps[i].address.street + "";
  compdata.lastSoldPrice = comps[i].lastSoldPrice + "";
  compdata.finishedSqFt = comps[i].finishedSqFt + "";
  compdata.bedrooms = comps[i].bedrooms + "";
  compdata.bathrooms = comps[i].bathrooms + "";
  compdata.latitude = comps[i].address.latitude + "";
  compdata.longitude = comps[i].address.longitude + "";
  CompsArray.push(compdata);
}
zillowresult.compsinfo = CompsArray;
return zillowresult;
```

By returning a JSON object, the calling widget can easily access the data using JavaScript notation. Furthermore, if you decide to add more properties to `zillowresult` in the future, any calling widgets won't break if there's added properties in the return object. Your service is thus backwards compatible.

Before building the Zillow widget, let's examine the data that RecentSalesService returns. Listing 4.4 shows sample output returned in object `zillowresult`.

Listing 4.4 Sample JSON Data from RecentSalesService

```
{
  "principal": {
    "zestimate": "1296500",
    "address": "2114 Bigelow Ave N",
    "finishedSqFt": "3290",
    "bathrooms": "3.0",
    "longitude": "-122.347929",
    "bedrooms": "4",
    "latitude": "47.637924",
    "homedetails": "http://www.zillow.com/HomeDetails.htm?city=Seattle&
    state=WA&zprop=48749425&s_cid=Pa-Cp-X1-CLz1cd710sc24k_pbmwz&
    partner=X1-CLz1cd710sc24k_pbmwz"
  },
  "compsinfo": [
    {
      "address": "2323 Bigelow Ave N",
      "lastSoldPrice": "1240000",
```

```
        "finishedSqFt": "2300",
        "bathrooms": "3.0",
        "longitude": "-122.34849",
        "bedrooms": "3",
        "latitude": "47.63975",
        "homedetails": "http://www.zillow.com/HomeDetails.htm?city=Seattle&
    state=WA&zprop=48879046&s_cid=Pa-Cp-X1-CLz1cd710sc24k_pbmwz&
    partner=X1-CLz1cd710sc24k_pbmwz"
      },
      {. . .},
      {. . .},
      {. . .},
      {. . .}
   ]
}
```

The response is in two parts. The first part provides data on the principal property (the property whose address corresponds to parameter zpid). The second part provides data on the five comparable properties (in the compsinfo array). (Only the first comparable data is shown.)

4.3 Building a Zillow Widget

Figure 4.5 shows the completed widget running in a browser. To build this widget, include a Zillow logo button and two input fields for the address and the city, state, and/or zip code. A search button invokes the service. Everything below the horizontal line is generated from data returned by the call to RecentSalesService.

The data on the principal property (Property) appears first followed by the data on the comparable properties (Houses Nearby). Links to more detailed information takes you to the Zillow.com web site.

Here is a summary of the steps you'll follow to build this widget.

1. Create a new blank widget.
2. Provide HTML for formatting.
3. Include the Prototype Library.
4. Add JavaScript code; use **Find & Use** to call RecentSalesService.
5. Preview and publish the widget.
6. Embed it in a web page.

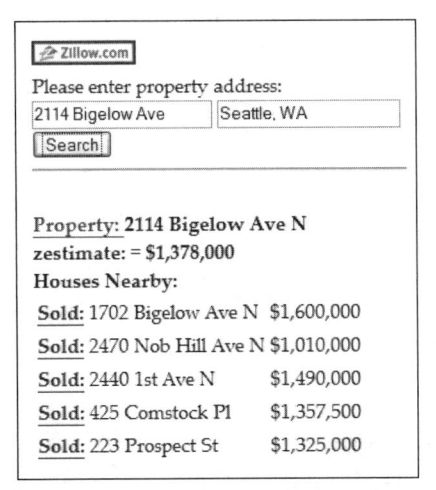

Figure 4.5 Recent sales widget running in a browser

Creating RecentSalesWidget

From the zembly site, click **Create something!** at the top of the page and choose **Widget** from the menu. Provide a name (RecentSalesWidget) and a description.

Listing 4.5 shows the HTML code for the RecentSalesWidget. Tag <a> implements the Zillow logo button. Tag <input> with attribute id set lets you grab the input in the JavaScript implementation code. There is default text for both input fields. Tag <button> with attribute id set lets you invoke a JavaScript function to process the request. Finally, tag <div> with attribute id set to recentSalesResults provides a placeholder for the HTML code generated in the JavaScript.

Listing 4.5 RecentSalesWidget (HTML)

```
<div id="recentSalesWidget">
   <a href="http://www.zillow.com" ><img
      src="http://www.zillow.com/static/logos/zillowtiny1.gif" width="80"
      height="15" alt="Real Estate Valuations" /></a>
   Please enter property address: <br/>
   <input id="address" type="text" value="2114 Bigelow Ave" />
   <input id="citystatezip" type="text" value="Seattle, WA" />
   <br/>
   <button id="searchButton">Search</button>
   <br/><hr/><br/>
   <div id="recentSalesResults"></div>
</div>
```

This widget uses the Prototype JavaScript library. From the Resources tab, select **Libraries** (at the bottom) and choose **Prototype** from the list of libraries, as shown in Figure 4.6.

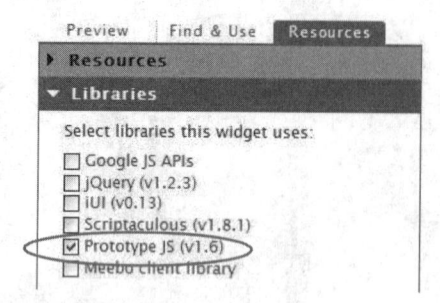

Figure 4.6 Adding the Prototype library to your widget

Listing 4.6 shows Part 1 of the JavaScript code for RecentSalesWidget. Since this widget displays large (monetary) numbers, you need a way to format them with comma delimiters. Function `CommaFormatted` places a comma delimiter after every third digit.

Listing 4.6 RecentSalesWidget (JavaScript)—Part 1

```
function CommaFormatted(amount)
{
   var delimiter = ","; // replace comma if desired
   var n = new String(amount);
   var a = [];
   while(n.length > 3)
   {
      var nn = n.substr(n.length-3);
      a.unshift(nn);
      n = n.substr(0,n.length-3);
   }
   if(n.length > 0) { a.unshift(n); }
   n = a.join(delimiter);
   return n;
}
```

Listing 4.7 shows Part 2 of the JavaScript code for RecentSalesWidget. The `'click'` event listener triggered by button `searchButton` invokes the main processing function in this script.

Listing 4.7 RecentSalesWidget (JavaScript)—Part 2

```
Event.observe($("searchButton"), 'click', function() {
   var address = $("address").value;
   var citystatezip = $("citystatezip").value;

   Things.callService("panderson.RecentSalesService", {
      address:address,
      citystatezip:citystatezip},
      {
      onSuccess:
         function(data) {
            var p = data.principal;
            var c = data.compsinfo;

            var resultsHtml = "<b><a href= " + p.homedetails
               + ">Property: </a><b/> " ;
            resultsHtml += p.address + "<br/> " ;
            resultsHtml += "<b>zestimate: = </b>" + "$"
               + CommaFormatted(p.zestimate) + "<br/> " ;
            resultsHtml += "<b>Houses Nearby:</b>" + "<br/> "
               + "<table>" ;
            for (i = 0; i < c.length; i++) {
               resultsHtml += "<tr><td><b><a href= " + c[i].homedetails +
                  ">Sold: </a><b/></td> " ;
               resultsHtml += "<td>" + c[i].address +
                  "</td><td style=\"text-align: right;\">$" +
                  CommaFormatted(c[i].lastSoldPrice) + "</td></tr> ";
            }
            resultsHtml += "</table>";
            $("recentSalesResults").innerHTML = resultsHtml;
         },
      onFailure:
         function(error){
            resultsHtml = "<i>There was a problem with the search."
               + "<br/>Please double-check the address for errors.</i>";
            $("recentSalesResults").innerHTML = resultsHtml;
         }
      }
   );
});
```

You set the address and citystatezip parameters from the input fields, which you then pass to the previously deployed RecentSalesService. You process the return, which is either successful (onSuccess) or not (onFailure).

With a successful return, you access the results in data and generate the HTML for the principal property.

To access the five comparable properties, iterate through the elements in `compsinfo` using array notation and build an HTML `<table>` construct. After the HTML is generated, you insert it into the page's HTML markup.

With a failure, you supply a helpful error message urging the user to recheck the input parameters.

Embedding RecentSalesWidget

The last step (and to experiment a bit with the look of the widget) is to embed it in a web page. Here is the code that produces the widget sized like the screen shot shown in Figure 4.5 on page 89.

Listing 4.8 RecentSalesWidget.html

```
<iframe width=370 height=380
   src="http://97f29d4afad64b32a2fa90fc504680c8.zembly.com/things/
   97f29d4afad64b32a2fa90fc504680c8;iframe">
</iframe>
```

4.4 Building a Google Maps Mashup

The RecentSalesWidget (Figure 4.5 on page 89) is a good example of extracting data from a service and building an easy-to-use widget that gives users a lot of useful information. Furthermore, the links enable users to further explore interesting properties at the Zillow web site. The table arrangement gives a nice, compact display of the comparable properties and their respective selling prices.

However, wouldn't it be more compelling to create a widget that provides a map showing not only the principal property, but the comparables as well? While Zillow includes a mapping mechanism on its site, it does not (currently) provide access to mapping services through its API.

The Zillow data is quite complete. Not only do you have addresses for all of the properties, but you also have each property's longitude and latitude coordinate values (geocodes). This is exactly what you need to map these properties with Google Maps.

In this section you'll build a widget that displays Zillow housing information using Google Maps. Here is a summary of the steps you'll follow to build this widget.

1. Create a new widget. Give it a name and a description.
2. Sign up for a Google Maps API Key. Include your widget artifact number with `zembly.com` on the Google Maps sign up page.

3. Provide the HTML and JavaScript code; use **Find & Use** to add the JavaScript code to call the RecentSalesService.
4. Include the Prototype library.
5. Preview and publish.
6. Embed in a web page.

Exploring Google Maps API

In order to use the Google mapping services, you'll have to access Google Maps directly. This is only slightly inconvenient; instead of using zembly's keychain mechanism you provide your Google API key directly when you load the Google Map API. (You'll apply for your Google Maps API key after you've actually created your widget. Detailed instructions are on page 95.)

After loading the API, you initialize a map, tell it where to put its center, and give it a zoom level. You can then add markers to the map. Of course, one of the parameters to creating a marker is its location, that is, the geocode coordinates (or point), which Zillow provides.

Listing 4.9 shows the code to load the Google Maps API. You include this code in the HTML source of your widget.

Listing 4.9 Code snippet to load the Google Maps API

```
<script src="http://maps.google.com/maps?file=api&amp;v=2&amp;key=Google Key"
    type="text/javascript">
</script>
```

Note that you must provide your Google Maps API key as part of the `<script>` tag's src attribute. Once the library is loaded you can initialize a map, as shown in Listing 4.10. String `"map_canvas"` refers to a named `<div>` tag you'll define in the HTML code. The parameters lat and lng are the latitude and longitude of the map's center point. You'll use the geocode from the property's address returned by Zillow for this.

Listing 4.10 Code snippet to initialize a Google map object

```
function init_map(lat, lng) {
   if (GBrowserIsCompatible()) {
      map = new GMap2(document.getElementById("map_canvas"));
      map.setCenter(new GLatLng(lat, lng), 14);
   }
}
```

Method `map.setCenter` sets the map's center point. It requires a GLatLng coordinate (a point defined by its latitude and longitude) and a zoom level. The zoom level for normal map mode goes from 0 (the whole world) to 19 (you can see individual buildings).

> **Programming Tip**
>
> *Method `setCenter` must be called before you can perform any other operations on the map. If the map does not appear to be what you expect, check that the values for the center coordinate are correct. If you expect to map an area in the U.S., an incorrect latitude may send you to Canada or Chile. An incorrect longitude might send you to China or Russia.*

Once these two setup steps are complete, you have a basic map. There are no controls (such as zoom in and zoom out), but you can move the map within the viewport with the mouse. You can also add markers to the properly initialized map. We show you how to add map controls in Listing 4.12 on page 97.

Google Maps provides a good introductory tutorial for accessing the Google Maps API at http://code.google.com/apis/maps/documentation/introduction.html. It also has additional documentation at http://code.google.com/apis/maps/documentation/.

Designing Widget RecentSalesMashup

Figure 4.7 shows the RecentSalesMashup widget running in a browser. While it's similar to the RecentSalesWidget, you see that it displays a map with markers for the comparable properties. Yellow markers indicate properties whose sale price is lower than the principal property and red markers indicate properties whose sale price is higher than the principal property. A green marker indicates the principal property. (In Figure 4.7, the green marker is obscured behind a pop-up information window associated with one of the yellow markers.)

When clicked, each marker produces a pop-up information window that displays the property's address, the price at which it sold (or the Zestimate for the principal property), and some basic property characteristics: square footage and number of bedrooms and bathrooms. The address is also a link to more home details on Zillow's web site.

The map includes two Google map control objects. A map type object controls the type of map Google displays: Map (normal, shown), Satellite, or Hybrid. The second object includes directional controls to move the map and a zoom control to zoom in or out.

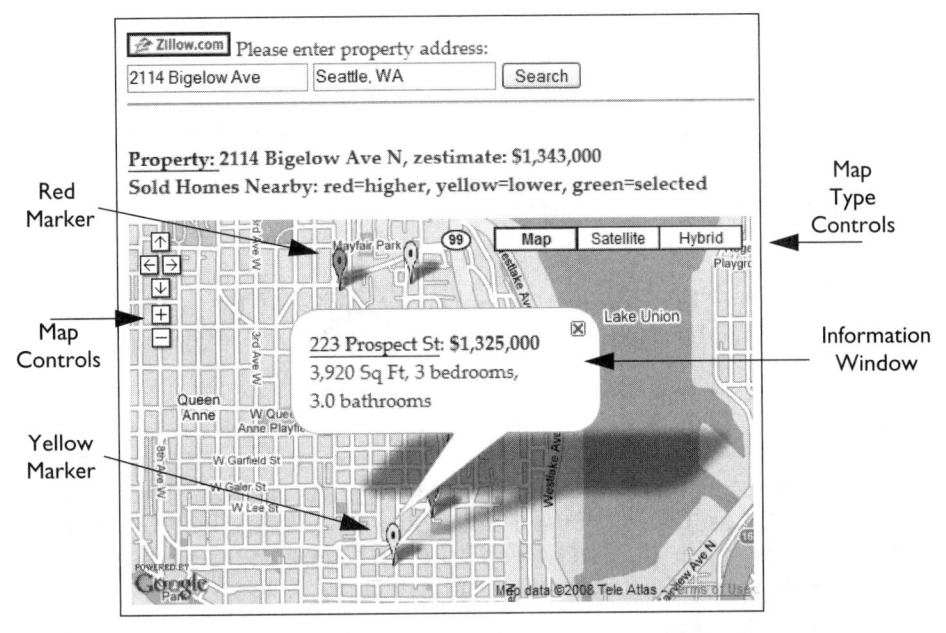

Figure 4.7 Using Google Maps to display results from Zillow

Creating Widget RecentSalesMashup

It's time to create the widget. From the top of the zembly page, select **Create something!** and choose **Widget** from the menu. Provide the name **RecentSalesMashup** and a description.

You'll need a Google Maps API key. Visit `http://code.google.com/apis/maps/signup.html` to sign up and obtain a generated key *after* you've created your widget. (The key is displayed immediately for you. Copy and paste it into the widget HTML editor on zembly.)

Google Maps Tip

Google requires that your Google Maps API key be matched to the web site URL. Use your widget's artifact number with `zembly.com` *when signing up for your Google Maps API key, as shown in Figure 4.8.*

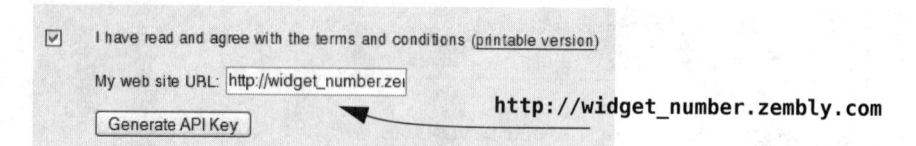

Figure 4.8 Specify widget_number.zembly.com for your web site URL

Listing 4.11 shows the HTML source. (Replace your Google API Key as indicated below.) You'll note that the HTML code is very similar to the already-created RecentSalesWidget.

First, load the Google Maps API code with the `<script>` tag. The `<body>` tag attribute event `onunload` calls function `GUnload`, which releases resources used by object `GMap2`. The `<div>` tag with `id` attribute set to `"recentSalesWidget"` is unchanged from the RecentSalesWidget. Near the end of the listing, you see a `<div>` tag with `id` set to `"map_canvas"`. The `init_map` function (shown below in Listing 4.12) references this object. This sets the size of the map's container (viewport).

Listing 4.11 RecentSalesMashup (HTML)

```
<script src="http://maps.google.com/maps?file=api&amp;v=2&amp;key=Your Google Key"
type="text/javascript"></script>
<body onunload="GUnload()">
    <div id="widgetDiv">
        <div id="recentSalesWidget">
            <a href="http://www.zillow.com" ><img
                src="http://www.zillow.com/static/logos/zillowtiny1.gif"
                width="80" height="15" alt="Real Estate Valuations" /></a>

            Please enter property address: <br/>
            <input id="address" type="text" value="2114 Bigelow Ave" />
            <input id="citystatezip" type="text" value="Seattle, WA" />
            <button id="searchButton">Search</button>
            <br/><hr/><br/>
            <div id="recentSalesResults"></div>
        </div>
        <div id="map_canvas" style="width: 500px; height: 300px"></div>
    </div>
</body>
```

This widget uses the Prototype JavaScript library. From the Resources tab, select **Libraries** (at the bottom) and choose **Prototype** from the list of libraries, as shown in Figure 4.6 on page 90.

Listing 4.12 shows Part 1 of the JavaScript code. It includes the support variables for Google Maps and the custom markers, as well as three support functions: CommaFormatted (you have already seen this code), init_map, and add_marker.

Function init_map initializes object GMap2 with the geocode values from the principal property and sets the zoom level. It adds a small map object to control zoom level and compass movement, and a second object to control the map type (map, hybrid, or satellite). Function add_marker builds a custom marker. Parameters lat (latitude) and lng (longitude) create a Google Map point. Parameter amount is the property's selling price or Zestimate—you use its value to determine the color of the marker. Object markerOptions stores the marker's icon characteristics using pre-built images from the Google Maps site and standard icons (GIcon).

Method GEvent.addListener makes the specified marker a listener for the mouse click event. The event handler opens a HTML information pop-up window and displays the HTML markup from parameter htmlstr. Once the marker is completely initialized, you add it to the map with the addOverlay function.

Listing 4.12 RecentSalesMashup (JavaScript)—Part I

```
// Support variables for Google Maps and custom markers
var map;
var yellowIcon = new GIcon(G_DEFAULT_ICON);
yellowIcon.image =
    "http://www.google.com/intl/en_us/mapfiles/ms/micons/yellow-dot.png";
var greenIcon = new GIcon(G_DEFAULT_ICON);
greenIcon.image =
    "http://www.google.com/intl/en_us/mapfiles/ms/micons/green-dot.png";
var redIcon = new GIcon(G_DEFAULT_ICON);
redIcon.image =
    "http://www.google.com/intl/en_us/mapfiles/ms/micons/red-dot.png";
var target_amount = 0;

function CommaFormatted(amount) {
    . . . See Listing 4.6 on page 90 for omitted code . . .
}

function init_map(lat, lng) {
    if (GBrowserIsCompatible()) {
        map = new GMap2(document.getElementById("map_canvas"));
        map.addControl(new GSmallMapControl());
        map.addControl(new GMapTypeControl());
        map.setCenter(new GLatLng(lat, lng), 14);
    }
}

function add_marker(lat, lng, amount, htmlstr) {
    if (amount > target_amount) {
        markerOptions = { icon:redIcon };
```

```
    }
    else if (amount < target_amount) {
       markerOptions = { icon:yellowIcon };
    }
    else { // equal
       markerOptions ={ icon:greenIcon };
    }
    var point = new GLatLng(lat, lng);
    var marker = new GMarker(point, markerOptions);

    GEvent.addListener(marker, "click", function() {
       marker.openInfoWindowHtml(htmlstr);
    });
    map.addOverlay(marker);
}
```

Listing 4.13 shows Part 2 of the JavaScript code. The structure is very similar to the RecentSalesWidget you previously built, except that you make calls to init_map and add_marker to display the Zillow information on the Google map.

You first extract the latitude and longitude of the principal property and use this to initialize the map. Variable target_amount holds the principal property's Zestimate dollar figure. You use this to determine a marker's color as explained earlier.

Programming Tip

Note that you must call function Number to correctly convert p.zestimate *(a String) to a numeric value.*

```
    target_amount = Number(p.zestimate);
```

If the amounts are not converted to numbers, the comparison operators (> and <) compare Strings instead of numbers, yielding incorrect results. One million, for example, will be less than, say 800,000.

Variable htmlstr holds the HTML markup that the information window displays when the user clicks the marker. You build this string by extracting the home detail links, the property's address, its amount, square footage, and number of bedrooms and bathrooms. When you call add_marker, pass this string along with the coordinate values and the Zestimate amount.

```
    add_marker(plat, plng, target_amount, htmlstr);
```

After the marker for the principal property is built, you extract the data for each comparable property. First you build htmlstr and call add_marker with the property's coordinate values, its last sold price (converting the price to a number of course), and the generated htmlstr.

```
        add_marker(c[i].latitude, c[i].longitude,
              Number(c[i].lastSoldPrice), htmlstr);
```

Remember that the value of `Number(c[i].lastSoldPrice)` determines the color of the new marker.

Listing 4.13 RecentSalesMashup (JavaScript)—Part 2

```
Event.observe($("searchButton"), 'click', function() {
   var address = $("address").value;
   var citystatezip = $("citystatezip").value;

   Things.callService("panderson.RecentSalesService", {
      address:address,
      citystatezip:citystatezip},
      {
      onSuccess:
         function(data) {
            var p = data.principal;
            var c = data.compsinfo;
            var plat = p.latitude;
            var plng = p.longitude;
            target_amount = Number(p.zestimate);
            init_map(plat, plng);
            var htmlstr = "<a href=" + p.homedetails + ">" +
               p.address + "</a>: " + "<b>$" +
               CommaFormatted(target_amount) + "</b><br/>" ;
            htmlstr += CommaFormatted(p.finishedSqFt) + " Sq Ft, " ;
            htmlstr += p.bedrooms + " bedrooms,<br/>" + p.bathrooms
               + " bathrooms" ;
            add_marker(plat, plng, target_amount, htmlstr);
            var resultsHtml = "<b><a href= " + p.homedetails
               + ">Property: </a></b> " ;
            resultsHtml += p.address + ", " ;
            resultsHtml += "<b>zestimate: </b>$"
               + CommaFormatted(p.zestimate) + "<br/> " ;
            resultsHtml += "<b>Sold Homes Nearby: red=higher, " +
               "yellow=lower, green=selected</b><p>";

            for (var i = 0; i < c.length; i++) {
               var htmlstr = "<a href=" + c[i].homedetails + ">" +
                  c[i].address + "</a>: " + "<b>$" +
                  CommaFormatted(c[i].lastSoldPrice) + "</b><br/>" ;
               htmlstr += CommaFormatted(c[i].finishedSqFt) + " Sq Ft, " ;
               htmlstr += c[i].bedrooms + " bedrooms,<br/>" +
                  c[i].bathrooms + " bathrooms" ;
               add_marker(c[i].latitude, c[i].longitude,
                     Number(c[i].lastSoldPrice), htmlstr);
            }
            $("recentSalesResults").innerHTML = resultsHtml;
         },
      onFailure:
```

```
            function(error){
                GUnload();
                $("map_canvas").innerHTML = '';
                resultsHtml = "<i>There was a problem with the search.<br/>" +
                    "Please double-check the address for errors.</i><br/>";
                $("recentSalesResults").innerHTML = resultsHtml;
            }
        });
});
```

5 Facebook Basics

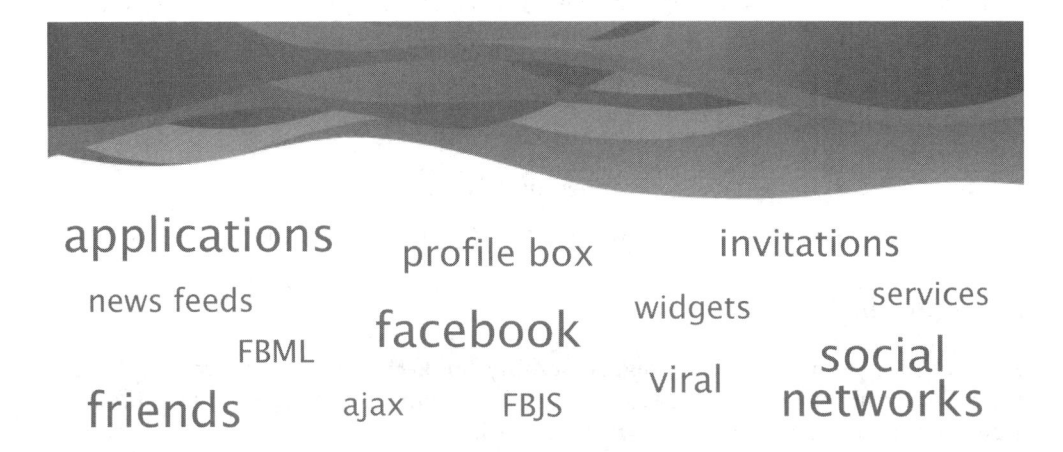

applications   profile box   invitations
news feeds   widgets   services
         FBML   facebook
friends   ajax   FBJS   viral   social
                                      networks

zembly includes support for Facebook application development. After all, the web is not just made up of widgets and services. To help fulfill **zembly**'s goal of "building the web," you can use **zembly** to build and deploy Facebook applications. What is Facebook and why should you care? Facebook is simply the 800-pound gorilla of social networking sites—it cannot be ignored. Section 5.1 gives you an overview of Facebook, but the short answer gets down to numbers: 100 million[1] active users—and counting.

In this chapter, you'll learn about Facebook and how Facebook enables third-party applications to hook into Facebook's social network. With **zembly** taking care of the authorization and API key details for you, as well as hosting your application, you'll see that you can easily develop and deploy a Facebook application. In no time, you can create a potentially viral Facebook phenomenon.

What You Will Learn

- Creating a Facebook application with **zembly**

---

1. Facebook, Facebook.com, September 2008. (This number changes every month!)

- All about Facebook users, Facebook profile pages, and users' friends
- Adding the Facebook Developer application
- Writing a Facebook application Home widget
- Previewing Facebook widgets and services
- Enhancing your Facebook application with descriptions, icons, logos, and screen shots
- Controlling developer mode and private installation settings
- Finding Facebook developer documentation
- Making Facebook API calls and generating dynamic FBML
- Coding in Facebook Markup Language (FBML) and Facebook JavaScript (FBJS)

Examples in This Chapter

All examples in this chapter are tagged **zembly-book-facebook**. To search for them, select **Search** at the top of any zembly page. Supply the search term **zembly-book-facebook** and click **Search** as shown in Figure 5.1.

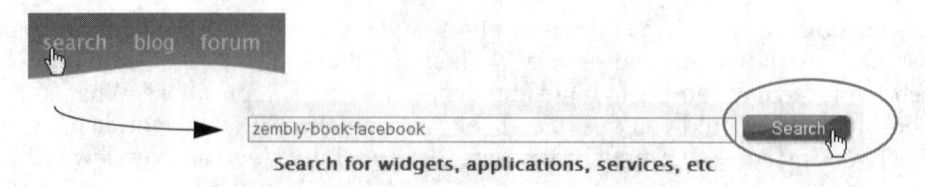

Figure 5.1 Searching for the examples in this chapter

The search results lists the Facebook applications discussed in this chapter.

The New Facebook Design

In July 2008 Facebook launched a revamped profile design with new or modified integration points. For zembly developers, much of the behind-the-scenes authorization is performed for you, and basic widget behavior is unaffected. However, to maximize the integration of your application with the new Facebook profile features, you will necessarily make some changes to your widgets and services. We discuss the new Facebook profile look and feel in this chapter. You will find detailed coding examples that leverage the new Facebook integration points in the next chapter (see Chapter 6 "Facebook Integration" on page 161).

5.1 About Facebook

Facebook (`http://www.facebook.com/`) is a social networking site. Founded in early 2004, Facebook has grown to over 100 million participants and continues to grow. Originally hosting only college students, anyone 13 and older can now join. Once you sign up, you can interact with other Facebook members through friendship relationships, networks, groups, applications, and pages. Facebook allows you to configure and display your profile, upload and tag photos, and create photo albums. You can "poke" friends, send virtual gifts to friends, write on friends' "walls," and send notices and invitations. Invitations can challenge friends to play games, invite them to join groups, or request participation in events. The options are almost limitless, but the emphasis is on participation and networking.

In 2007 Facebook opened up its platform, enabling third parties to create applications that hook into core Facebook features. Once your applications are no longer in "developer mode," users can invoke them like any of the core applications that Facebook provides. And, when an application has at least five users, developers can submit it to the Facebook application directory, making it readily available to any Facebook user. The huge install base of Facebook users has prompted many individuals and companies to wade into the potential lucrative world of third-party Facebook applications.

Before you jump in and create your first Facebook application, let's look at some of the Facebook artifacts you can leverage in your application. Using several example applications throughout this chapter and the next chapter, we show you how to implement all of these integration points in a Facebook application. For now, let's look at these features from the user's point of view.

Facebook Tip

Facebook provides many "integration points" for an application developer. As Facebook users become more comfortable with the new Facebook profile design and application options, your application will look and feel more like a native Facebook application when you take advantage of as many integration options that make sense for your application. Then, users decide how they want to interact with your application. Ultimately, you increase your chances for acquiring new users and maintaining current users if you hook into as many integration points as possible.

What Is a Facebook Application?

So far, you've built plenty of widgets and services using zembly. A Facebook application, however, is a bit more complicated. Every Facebook application is a collection of widgets and services that work together to implement your application: widgets interact with Facebook users and services hook into the Facebook infrastructure (or even call outside web services). Third-party Facebook applications do not reside on Facebook, but Facebook provides the integration points that allow users to access them. Table 5.1 lists the Facebook artifacts you'll use with your applications. The table includes a short description and a reference to the section that discusses each feature in more detail in the following sections.

TABLE 5.1 Summary of Facebook Features and Integration Points

Feature	Quick Take	More Detail
Canvas Page	An application's main interface with the user	"Canvas Page" below
User	The person who is logged into Facebook running your application	"The Facebook User" on page 105
Friends	List of Facebook users the user has a "friend" relationship with	"Friends" on page 105
User Profile	A user's personal data and interactions subject to privacy settings	"Your Profile" on page 105
Applications	Built-in and third-party programs executed within the Facebook environment	"Applications and Application Settings" on page 106
Profile Boxes	Application-generated displays reflecting the user's actions	"Profile Boxes" on page 108
Left-hand Column	Profile area that holds "main" profile boxes	"Left-Hand Column" on page 109
Application Tabs	Optional application-specific tab on user's profile	"Application Tabs" on page 110
Application Access	Dialog in which users grant Applications access to profile information	"Application Access" on page 111
Email and Notices	User actions that generate email, notices, or invitations	"Email and Notices" on page 112
News Feed	Posted time-stamped information generated by applications	"Story Types and News Feed Templates" on page 112
Profile Publisher	Allows users to create content for their own Wall or friends' Wall	"Profile Publisher" on page 113
Application Info Sections	Information about the user that can appear under Info tab on profile	"Application Info Sections" on page 114

Canvas Page

The canvas page is your application's main interface with the user. For example, when you view or upload photos on Facebook, you're interacting with the Facebook photo application on its canvas page. Actions you take here can affect your profile or result in notices sent to friends.

A widget implements the main actions of your application. Similar to other widgets you've built with **zembly**, you can define the look and feel using standard HTML with JavaScript for program logic. You can also use Facebook's own Facebook markup language (FBML) with Facebook JavaScript (FBJS) for program logic. Both HTML and FBML use CSS and for styling. We'll show you how to develop applications using both widget types.

The Facebook User

The Facebook user is the person who is logged into Facebook running your application. Facebook automatically provides information about the user to the application, such as the user's Facebook user ID, the user's name, and the user's list of friends (subject to privacy settings from both the user and the user's friends). Additional user information becomes available only after the user has explicitly granted the application access, usually through the "Allow Access" dialog (see "Application Access" on page 111).

Friends

Facebook automatically provides a list of the user's friends (whether or not the user has "logged into" the application) to all applications. An application can also retrieve information about these friends (with the user's permission). The information retrieved is subject to the user's ability to see this data. Friend profile information includes the friend's current status, the About Me profile section, activities, affiliations, current location, education history, name, interests, music and movies the friend likes, favorite quotes, religion, politics, work history, and a plethora of other personal information. Much of the information besides the friend's name is optional and may be blank. The BuddyPics application (see "BuddyPics—Using FBML and FBJS" on page 137) shows how to obtain and display a user's friend information.

Your Profile

Your profile is an accumulation of personal data, interactions with friends, and interactions with the applications you use. By using an application, you can add content to your profile page (in the left-hand column), within the Boxes tab, or under an application-specific tab. You can also add information to your personal data found under the Info tab if the application offers this. Figure 5.2 shows a portion of a Facebook user's profile.

106 Chapter 5 Facebook Basics

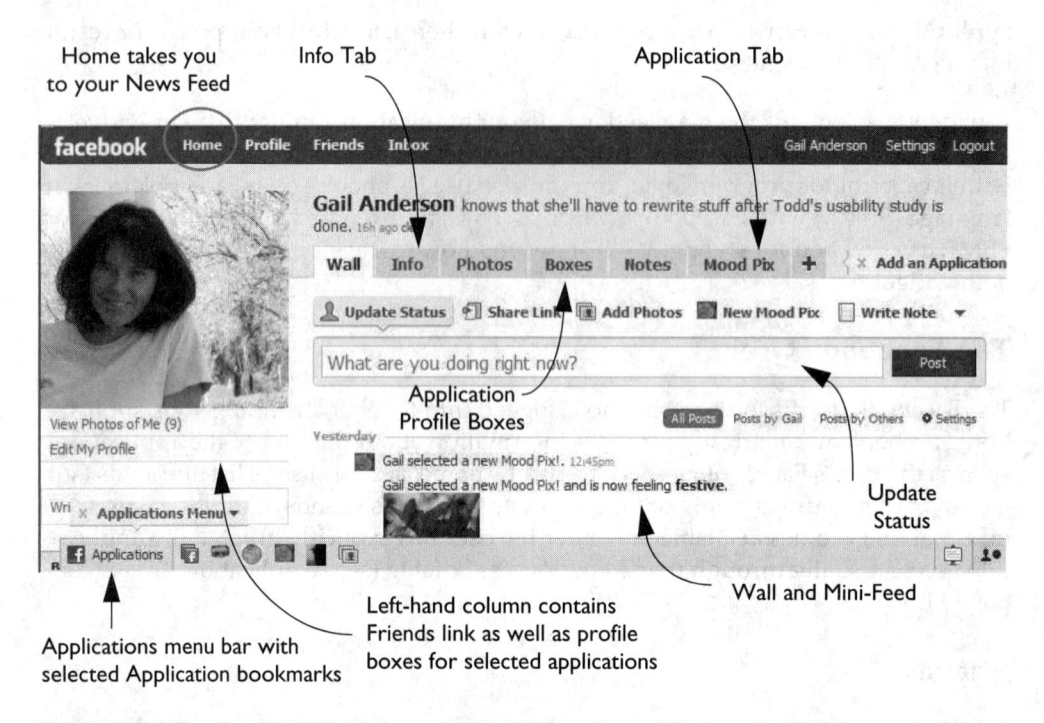

Figure 5.2 A Facebook profile

Your profile tells the world about you. Who the world is depends on who you let view your profile: just your friends, people in your network, or the whole world. The top chrome provides access to your Home link (circled above), Profile, Friends, and Inbox. The Home link displays your News Feed (stories about your friends). The Friends link shows your friends and the Inbox lets you view and send requests, notifications, and messages. The Settings link (on the right) lets you control your account, privacy settings, application settings, and what types of stories you'd like to see. The Applications menu bar (moved to the bottom of the page) lets you configure and run applications.

Applications and Application Settings

The Applications menu bar (shown in Figure 5.3) lets you run applications by selecting an application icon. Or, when you click the Applications menu, a complete list of your applications appears. You can reorder them so that the ones you want show up on the menu bar.

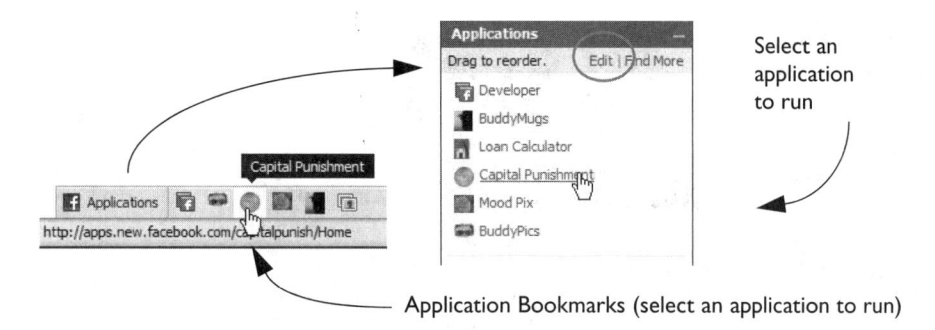

Figure 5.3 The Applications Menu Bar lets you select applications to run

The Edit link (circled in Figure 5.3) navigates to the Applications page where you configure your applications (Edit), go to the About page (About) or remove the application bookmark (Remove). This page, shown in Figure 5.4, displays application settings according to selected criteria, such as Bookmarks or Added to Profile. In addition, the "Browse more applications" button takes you to the Facebook Application Directory where you can search for new applications you might like.

Figure 5.4 Configuring your applications

Figure 5.5 shows a sample Edit Settings menu for application BuddyPics that appears when you click Edit opposite the application (circled in Figure 5.4). A user can grant application access in several areas.

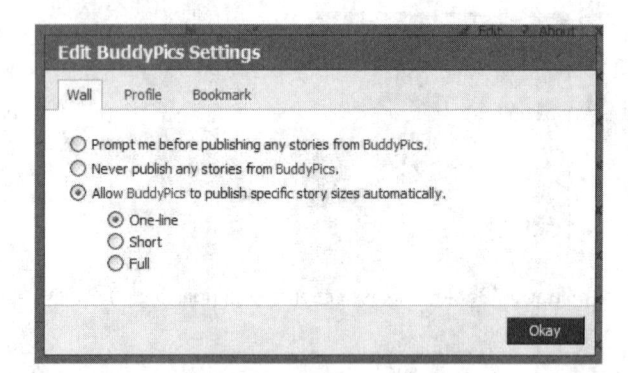

Figure 5.5 Editing an application's settings

- **Wall**—Applications can publish stories that appear on your wall. (The new profile design merges a user's news feed and wall posts.) This tab lets you select three levels of permission pertaining to publishing stories and the types of stories (one line, short, or full) that you permit the application to publish.

- **Profile**—Applications can generate content that appears under your Boxes tab or in the main profile left-hand column. This setting lets you specify where an application can generate profile boxes. If the application generates content for the Info tab, you will also see an option that lets you add or remove Info content. You can also specify privacy levels separately for each application.

- **Bookmark**—Bookmark your favorite applications to easily invoke them from the Application menu as shown in Figure 5.3. You can rearrange the bookmarks so that your most-used applications appear first.

- **Additional permissions**—Specify whether or not an application can send you emails and whether an application can access your data even when you're not using the application. To edit these settings, select Additional Permissions from the Applications page, as shown in Figure 5.4.

Profile Boxes

In the early days of Facebook, there were two profile columns: wide and narrow. Now these standard profile boxes automatically appear under the Boxes tab. An application generates profile boxes to help you express something about how you interact with it. For example, the Capital Punishment application (see "Capital Punishment—A Challenging Facebook Application" on page 162) creates a profile box that shows a color-coded map of the world's capitals a user has correctly identified. The user can recreate this map by running the application and updating the profile box with a new score.

Figure 5.6 shows a sample profile box for the Capital Punishment application. When you select the pencil icon, a menu appears that lets you move the box to the Wall tab (left-column area) or remove it.

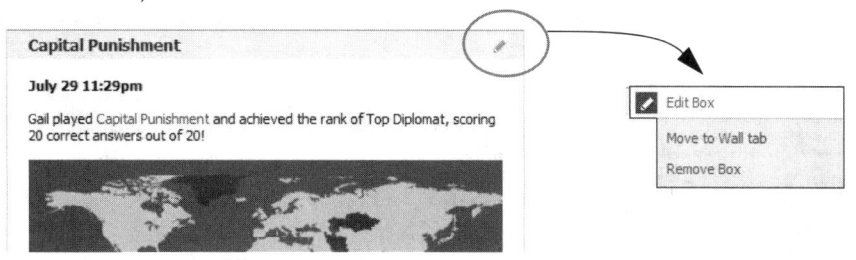

Figure 5.6 Profile Boxes appear under the Boxes tab

Profile boxes do not appear until a user has clicked the Add to Profile button (if provided by the application) or edited the application options through the Applications page. Figure 5.7 shows both the Add to Profile and Add to Info buttons for the Mood Pix application. (See "Mood Pix—Leveraging Facebook Integration" on page 208.)

Figure 5.7 Add to Profile and Add to Info buttons

Left-Hand Column

Alternatively, if an application generates profile markup that targets the main profile page, a user can display the application profile box in the left-hand column. This area is restricted to 200 pixels wide by 250 pixels high but is directly visible on the profile. Figure 5.8 shows example left-hand column profile boxes. When you select the pencil icon, a menu appears that lets you move the box to the Boxes tab or remove it.

> **Facebook Tip**
>
> *Application authors decide whether to generate separate markup appropriate for the left-hand column. To do this, use the* `profile_main` *parameter when calling adapter* `Things.facebook.profile.setFBML`. *See, for example, Listing 6.10 on page 182, "Service UpdateProfileBox (JavaScript)—Capital Punishment".*

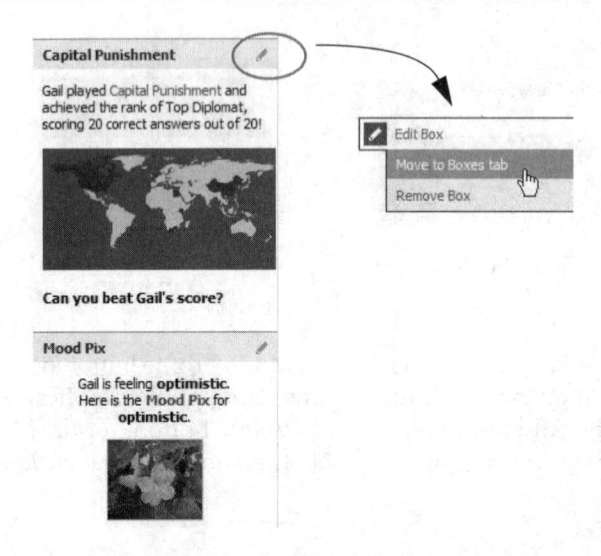

Figure 5.8 Left-hand profile (main) application boxes

Application Tabs

Applications can also include a widget that generates markup for an application-specific tab. Then, users can choose to add a new tab for your application. This means the application is easily accessible for a user and more visible to others who visit the user's profile. Application Tabs use a restricted version of FBML. Figure 5.9 shows adding a custom tab for the Mood Pix application.

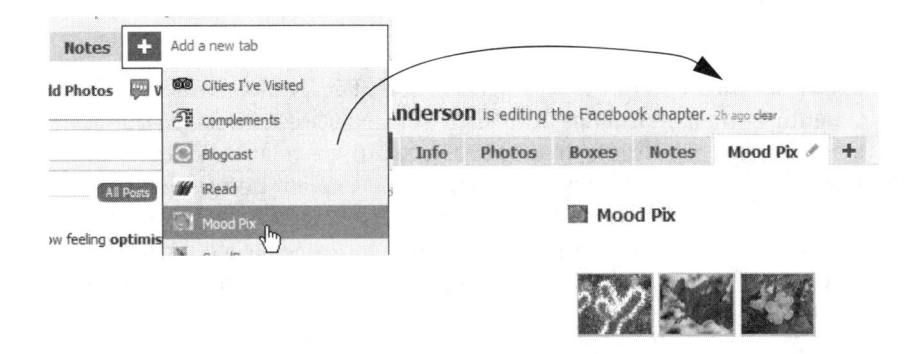

Figure 5.9 Adding custom tabs to your profile with application tabs

Application Access

Users typically allow applications access to their user data through the Allow Access dialog, as shown in Figure 5.10. The Allow Access dialog includes a link to the application's Terms of Service widget (circled below).

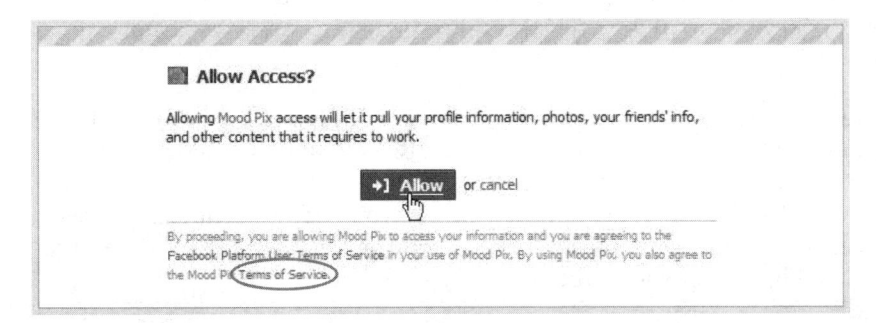

Figure 5.10 Applications ask users for permission when logging in is required by the application

Facebook Tip

While most applications require users to grant access (login), this is not a universal requirement. For example, the Loan Calculator application presented in this chapter does not require users to login.

Email and Notices

Your application can generate email messages and notices to friends, to other users who have added the application, or to the logged in user. Facebook is sensitive about applications generating "spam" and has built-in governors to restrict the frequency and number of messages. These limits are not absolute but are relative to an application's installed user base and activity levels. You must get explicit permission from users to send them email; explicit permission is not needed for notices or requests. For example, Capital Punishment sends "challenge" notices to users' selected friends, inviting them to play the game. Mood Pix sends notices to friends when a user sends them a Mood Pix message.

Story Types and News Feed Templates

While an application's profile box is a one-shot posting area on the user's profile page, a news feed is a stream of information that shows how a user has interacted with an application over time. For example, the Capital Punishment application creates news stories in two situations. First, when a user challenges one or more friends, the application creates a story listing friends who have been challenged. Second, users can publish a story with their score and the countries whose capitals they correctly identified. Stories don't wipe out previously published stories (like profile box updates do), but instead push new date and time-stamped items onto the user's news stream. These stories will show up in the user's Mini-Feed with the most recent story appearing first.

Facebook defines three story types: one-line, short, and full. A fully-integrated application provides all three types. (You can select a different story size after the story is published or you can delete a story completely.) Figure 5.11 shows an example story generated by the Facebook Photo application when you add new photos. The selection dialog (shown) lets you change a story size, edit privacy settings, or delete the post altogether. Figure 5.11 shows the short story version.

Figure 5.11 Story options let you select the story size that appears on your profile

Stories are also published to friends' News Feeds. To view your News Feed on Facebook, click the Home link (as indicated in Figure 5.2 on page 106). The News Feed shows stories involving your friends. You can customize your News Feed by telling Facebook the type of stories you want to view, as well as the friends you're interested in (or not interested in) when reading stories.

When you create a story within a Facebook application, there is no guarantee that it will show up in a particular user's news feed. If a user has many active friends, your news feed story competes with other news feed stories. It will more likely appear on friends' news feeds that have less competition for other stories or a "closer" relationship with the user. And, like email and notices, Facebook regulates which news feed stories actually show up in a friend's news feed.

Facebook specifies that news feed stories should originate from actions performed by users engaged in the application.

Profile Publisher

You can also setup your Facebook application to provide instant publishing. Then, users create stories that appears on their own Wall, or go to a friends' profile and create stories appropriate for publishing to a friend's Wall. For example, the Mood Pix application lets you select a new mood when publishing to your own Wall or send a mood pix when publishing to a friend's Wall. Figure 5.12 shows how to add the Publisher option for Mood Pix and the interface for publishing to your own Wall.

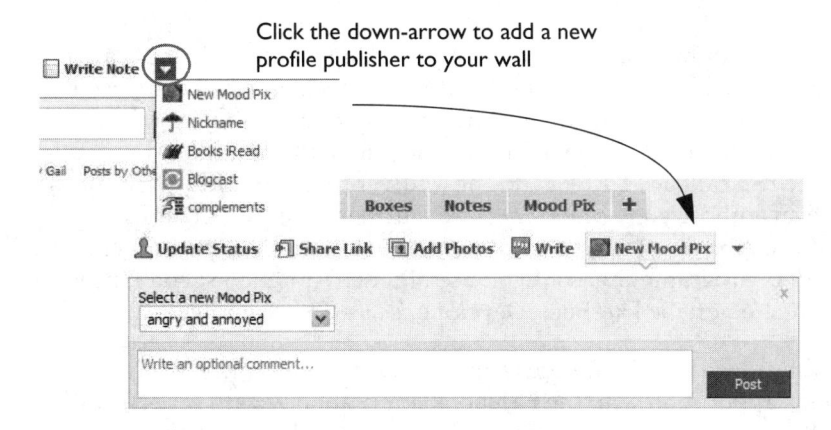

Figure 5.12 The Publisher lets you create stories directly on your Wall or a friend's Wall

Application Info Sections

In the tabbed profile, the Info tab shows information about a Facebook user, including education or employment information, contact information, and so forth. Info data is optional; a flexible interface lets you edit and display personal data.

Applications can provide application Info sections that appear under the Info tab. This gives users the option of displaying information about themselves generated by using your application. For the Mood Pix application, the Info section includes the user's favorite Mood Pix (set by interacting with the application). You can also add favorites to the Mood Pix Info section by editing the Info section directly.

An application's Info section won't appear within the user's Info tab until the user has clicked the Add to Info button using the application or edited the application options through the Applications menu. Figure 5.7 on page 109 shows the Add to Info and Add to Profile buttons that let you add information to these sections.

5.2 Creating a Facebook Application

With this little tour of Facebook under your belt, you'll now create a Facebook application with **zembly**. The process of creating an application involves interacting with both **zembly** and Facebook, but **zembly** orchestrates the process. The first time through might seem overwhelming, but don't worry—the process is quick and painless.

If you've previously thought about jumping in and writing a Facebook application and have actually stepped into the water and gotten a bit wet, you may have been discouraged by the amount of Facebook architecture knowledge required to create even the simplest application. Not only do you need to acquire API and secret keys, but you must also specify a callback URL (a URL on a server that will host your application) and acquire an authorized Facebook session. Furthermore, you must specify configuration information for your application. Facebook documentation is generally slanted towards PHP programming, so if you use other environments, you'll need to filter the documentation on the Facebook Developer's site to fit your needs.

Thankfully, **zembly** addresses all of these issues. In just a few minutes you can create your first Facebook application with the Facebook application wizard on **zembly**. In this section you'll step through the wizard to create a Loan Calculator Facebook application. You'll use the LoanPaymentWidget you created in Chapter 2 (see "Creating Your First Widget: LoanPaymentWidget" on page 34) as the basis for this application. This exercise not only shows you how to create a Facebook application, but also shows you that all you really need is a standard **zembly** widget to get started.

Facebook Application Wizard

Let's begin. From zembly, select **Create something!** and choose **Facebook application** from the drop down menu.

---
zembly Tip

---
zembly *will soon offer application templates for new Facebook applications. Similar to creating new widgets, you select from among template categories (such as quizzes, gifts, or surveys) and then choose a specific template. Of course, you can always create your own Facebook application from scratch by selecting Create a blank Facebook application.*

---

zembly brings up a new Facebook application page. Rename your application to **LoanCalculator** and click **Save**, as shown in Figure 5.13.

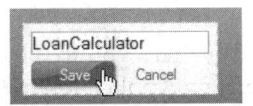

Figure 5.13 Renaming the application LoanCalculator

zembly now guides you through the process of setting up the application on Facebook. Click **Create application on facebook.com**, as shown in Figure 5.14.

Figure 5.14 Creating the application on Facebook.com

zembly takes you through a six-step wizard that interacts with Facebook from within zembly. This wizard helps you set up the parts of your Facebook application that zembly needs to manage. Let's go through this, step by step.

Step 1 of 6: Log into Facebook

If you're already logged into Facebook (you'll see your home page) you can click **Next** on zembly and proceed to Step 2. Otherwise, login using your Facebook email and password and click **Next** on zembly when you're finished.

Step 2 of 6: Install the Facebook Developers Application

The Facebook Developer application lets you create and manage Facebook applications on Facebook.com. Although you can manage most of your application from this site, zembly needs the Developer application installed to proceed with creation.

If you don't have the Developer application installed, zembly takes you to the Allow Access page for the Facebook Developer application. Install the Developer application now and click **Next** on zembly when you're done.

If you already have the Developer application installed, zembly takes you to the Developer application within Facebook. You'll see the Set Up New Application button on the Developer page. Click **Next** on zembly.

Step 3 of 6: Set up a new application

Once you've added the Developer application, click button **Set Up New Application** on the Facebook Developer page (if necessary). Then click **Next** to proceed.

Step 4 of 6: Enter application details

In the Facebook frame, you'll see the Facebook New Application page. Facebook needs some information: the Application Name and Canvas Page URL. Supply **Loan Calculator** for the name, click the check box that indicates you have read and agree to the terms of the Facebook Platform, and expand the **Optional Fields**, as shown in Figure 5.15.

Facebook Tip

Do not click the Submit button on the Facebook page yet (you're not quite done).

After you expand the Optional Fields, you'll have access to one more (*important!*) field you need to fill in, the Canvas Page URL.

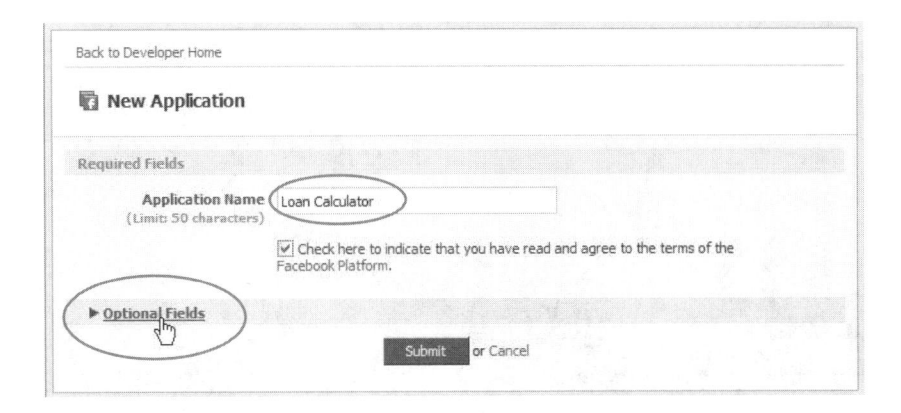

Figure 5.15 Setting up the new application within the Facebook window

As shown in Figure 5.16, provide a Canvas Page URL name for your application on Facebook. Make sure the name is all lowercase letters and at least seven characters long. As you type in a name, Facebook tells you if the name is available. (Note that you'll need to pick a name other than `loancalculate`, which is not available.)

zembly Tip

The Canvas Page URL name must be all lowercase letters, underscores, or dashes. Do not include spaces, numbers, or other special characters. Facebook converts uppercase letters to lowercase without telling you, making the connection between zembly *and Facebook incorrect. If you use any unacceptable characters, Facebook only provides feedback after you click the Submit button. (Available means the name is available only, not that it is legal!)*

You do not need to fill in any of the other fields! After you've provided an available and acceptable name, click **Submit**, as shown at the bottom of Figure 5.16.

118   Chapter 5   Facebook Basics

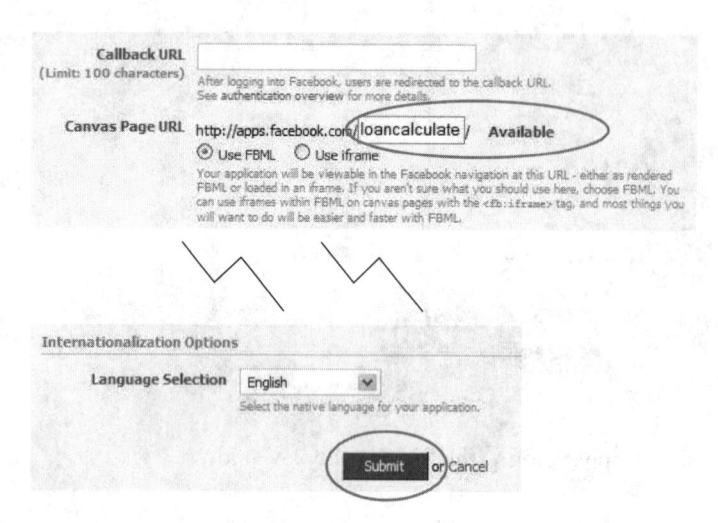

Figure 5.16 Providing the Canvas Page URL and submitting the application to Facebook

When you submit the application to Facebook, the Developer application displays your application within Facebook (as shown at the bottom of Figure 5.17). Click **Next** on zembly.

Step 5 of 6: Copy API Keys

Copy and paste the API and secret keys from the Facebook page to zembly's text fields, as shown in Figure 5.17. Click **Next** on zembly when you are finished.

Step 5 of 6 Copy API keys

Well done! You got a spot on facebook.com. Now copy and paste your API Key and Secret from the facebook.com page to the fields below.

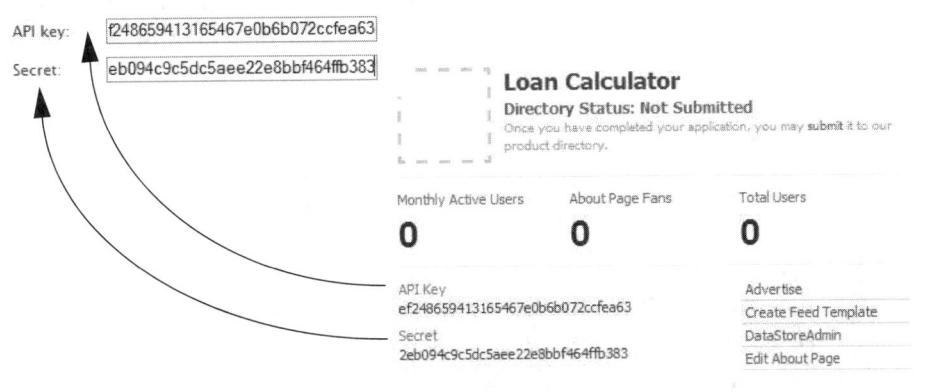

API key: f248659413165467e0b6b072ccfea63

Secret: eb094c9c5dc5aee22e8bbf464ffb383

Figure 5.17 Copying the Facebook API Keys to zembly

Step 6 of 6: You're done!

When you see the message "Congratulations! You're all set." click **Done** on zembly, as shown in Figure 5.18.

Figure 5.18 The last step is to click Done

zembly Tip

*At this point, you have a functional Facebook application that generates profile box contents. Below the Edit window under Actions, click **View application**, and you can run your new application on Facebook.*

Core Services and Widgets

Figure 5.19 shows the core services and widgets of your Facebook application. And, by default, the Home widget, your application's main widget, is locked (indicated by the lock badge), meaning that it requires users to allow access to execute. You'll see that several of the widgets and services are assigned specific roles within the Facebook framework. You can change any of these settings and, of course, modify the widget and service templates that **zembly** provides for you. You'll see how to do this in the next section.

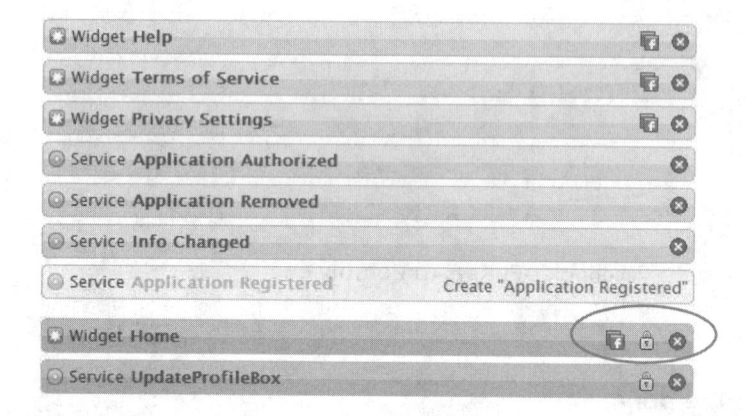

Figure 5.19 Default services and widgets within your Facebook application

If you look inside the Home widget (simply click it), you'll see that it uses FBML code for page rendering and FBJS for program logic. The other option is HTML for rendering and JavaScript for logic. Which should you use? On the one hand, FBML and FBJS give you a stronger Facebook "look and feel," are quite powerful, and give you easy access to many Facebook features. Indeed, **zembly** widgets default to FBML. On the other hand, HTML and JavaScript are more familiar and portable. If you think you might target other social networks then the portability of HTML and JavaScript may be important. This chapter presents Facebook widgets developed both ways.

Facebook Tip

For your widgets, you can choose HTML (with JavaScript) or FBML (with FBJS) on a case by case basis. A typical Facebook application consists of a main widget (Home) and auxiliary widgets that implement specific behaviors. In Capital Punishment, for example, (see "Capital Punishment—A Challenging Facebook Application" on page 162), the Home widget uses HTML and JavaScript, but the widgets that let you challenge friends and see friends' scores and rankings use FBML and FBJS.

5.3 Loan Calculator—Your First Facebook Application

Figure 5.19 lists the default widgets and services that zembly creates for you in a Facebook application. Users execute the Home widget when they "go to" your application. Because Facebook's FBML is specifically crafted to take advantage of special Facebook features, zembly provides an FBML template by default for your Home widget. For this first application, however, you'll use the same HTML, CSS, and JavaScript that you already know (and love).

Here's a summary of the steps you'll follow to build the Loan Calculator application from the base application widgets and services that zembly provides.

1. Delete the default FBML Home widget.
2. Create a new (HTML) widget. zembly calls it NewWidget by default.
3. Rename NewWidget to Home.
4. Copy and paste the HTML, CSS, and JavaScript from LoanPaymentWidget.
5. Upload image house.jpg into your widget's Resources directory.
6. Include the Prototype JavaScript library.
7. Preview and publish widget Home.
8. Configure Home as the "go to application" link.
9. Run your application on Facebook.

Deleting Home and Creating a New Widget

In order to use HTML for the Home widget, you'll delete the default FBML Home widget first and then create a new widget. From the LoanCalculator application page, delete widget Home. Click the circular **X** opposite Home as shown in Figure 5.19 on page 120. zembly pops up a confirmation dialog (Figure 5.20). Click **Yes**.

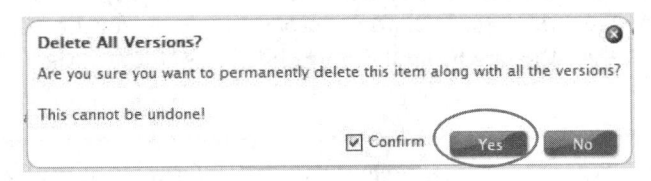

Figure 5.20 Delete item confirmation dialog

Now you're ready to create a new Home widget. Click **Create something!** and select **Widget** as shown in Figure 5.21. Be sure to specify Widget so you'll get the HTML flavor—not Widget (FBML). zembly creates HTML widget NewWidget.

zembly Tip

Make sure you select the Widget option that is inside application LoanCalculator. The drop down menu displays In LoanCalculator in its option list, as shown in Figure 5.21.

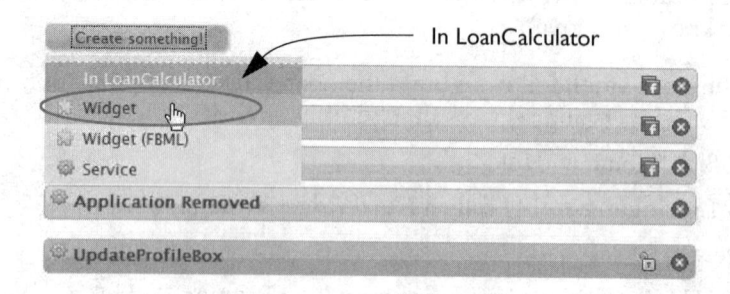

Figure 5.21 Creating Widget in LoanCalculator

Note that using LoanPaymentWidget as a base for your application shows you that the core functionality of a Facebook application can be implemented from a simple **zembly** widget.

Editing Widget Home (NewWidget)

From the LoanCalculator application page on **zembly**, select widget NewWidget so that you can edit it. You'll see a widget editing page that provides standard features for building any widget on **zembly**. Rename NewWidget to Home. Click **Rename** next to the widget name, provide the new name, and click **Save**.

In a separate window, open up the LoanPaymentWidget you built in "Creating Your First Widget: LoanPaymentWidget" on page 34. Copy and paste the code for the HTML, CSS, and the JavaScript into the LoanCalculator application's Home widget.

zembly Tip

*If you built this widget previously, use your own LoanPaymentWidget. Otherwise, search for LoanPaymentWidget using **zembly**'s search box and select it from the result list, as shown in Figure 5.22.*

Loan Calculator—Your First Facebook Application   123

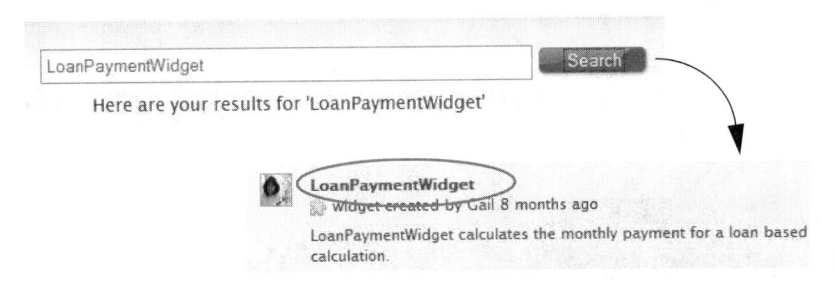

Figure 5.22 Searching for LoanPaymentWidget

Uploading Resource Image

LoanPaymentWidget uses an image. To incorporate the image with the Home widget, locate and then upload the image under Resources.

zembly Tip

Here's an easy way to do this. Return to the LoanPaymentWidget page and preview LoanPaymentWidget. While the widget is running in the preview area, right-click the image and save it to your local machine (see Figure 5.23). You can then upload the image (see "Uploading an Image" on page 36).

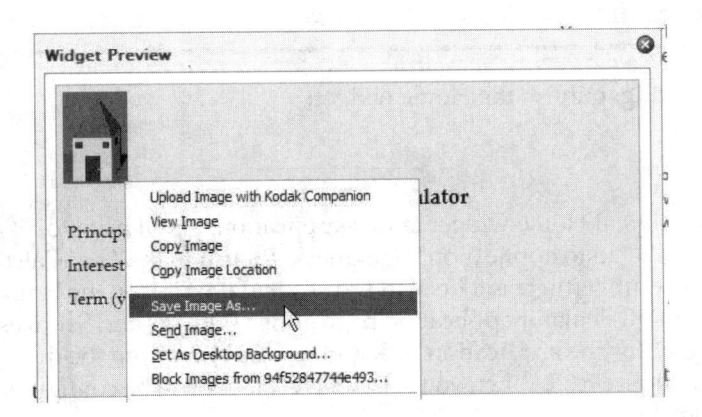

Figure 5.23 Grabbing an image from the Widget Preview window

Including Library Prototype JS

The LoanCalculator Home widget uses the Prototype JavaScript library. From the Resources tab, select **Libraries** (at the bottom) and choose Prototype from the list of libraries, as shown in Figure 5.24.

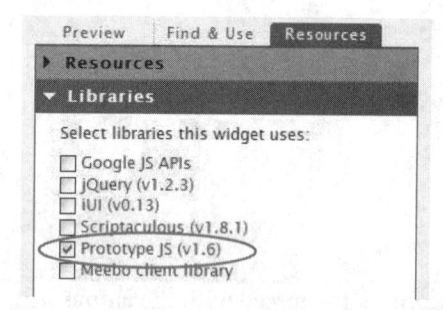

Figure 5.24 Adding Prototype JS library to your widget

Previewing and Publishing Widget Home

You can preview the Home widget before publishing it.

---
zembly Tip

Since the Home widget for LoanCalculator makes no calls to the Facebook platform, you don't need to acquire a Facebook session in order to preview the widget.

When you are finished testing, publish the Home widget.

Configuring Home

Because you deleted the original Home widget in this application, you'll need to reconfigure the application's "go to application" bookmark. Return to the LoanCalculator application page on zembly (there is a **back to LoanCalculator** link on the Home widget page). From the LoanCalculator application page under Widgets and Services, click **Please select a widget for the application link** and select **Home** from the drop down menu, as shown in Figure 5.25. When you select **Save**, Home will be configured for the "go to application" link.

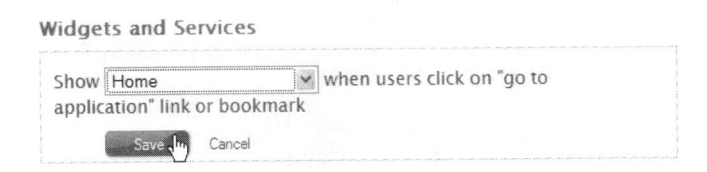

Figure 5.25 Configuring Home for the "go to application" bookmark

zembly Tip

Note that the HTML Home widget is unlocked (the yellow lock icon is open). The Loan Calculator Home widget doesn't require user permission to run. It makes no Facebook API calls that require a Facebook session. If you lock a widget, **zembly** *brackets your widget code so that users must grant access to the application, allowing* **zembly** *to acquire a Facebook session.*

Running Your Application in Facebook

You'll now run the application in Facebook. From the LoanCalculator application page on zembly, page down below the edit window and select the yellow **View about page** button, as shown in Figure 5.26. This takes you to LoanCalculator's About Page on Facebook. (Note that the page lacks an image and description, which you'll remedy soon.) On the Facebook About Page, click the blue **Go to Application** button.

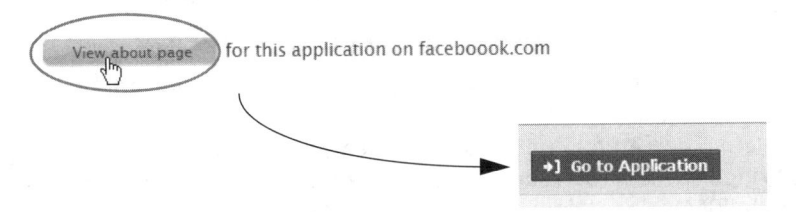

Figure 5.26 Using an application from the About page

Facebook invokes URL `http://apps.facebook.com/{your_canvas_page_url}/Home`, which is a proxy for the Loan Calculator application's Home widget on zembly. Figure 5.27 shows this application running on Facebook.

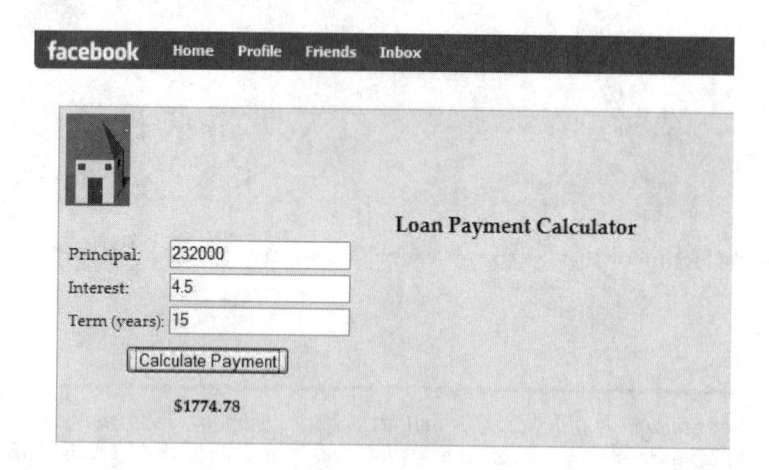

Figure 5.27 Loan Payment running on Facebook

Facebook Application Defaults

Before you build more involved and engaging Facebook applications, let's look at some of the basic widgets and services *zembly* provides for you.

Facebook displays a link to the Terms of Service widget from the Allow Access dialog. This lets users examine your Terms of Service before giving access to their account information. Edit the Terms of Service widget to provide the Terms of Service you want for your application.

The Help widget displays instructions or other background information about your application. You can provide a link to the Help widget from your Home widget using the relative URL ./Help. The Capital Punishment Home widget shows how to provide a link to the Help widget with HTML and the Mood Pix Home widget shows how to provide the link with FBML.

Applications can generate content for a user's profile box (displayed either under the Boxes tab or directly on the main profile page). Users can choose whether or not your profile box is actually displayed, where it's displayed (main profile or tab), and the order it appears relative to other applications' profile boxes. You update an application's profile box by calling service UpdateProfileBox included with your application. Applications BuddyPics, Capital Punishment, and Mood Pix all implement versions of service UpdateProfileBox to generate content for both the "main" profile box and the Boxes tab profile box.

Note that each of these widgets and services are templates. That is, they contain minimal text and you are expected to edit them to fit your application's requirements. You can modify any of these widgets and services by clicking their links and zembly takes you to a standard widget or service editing page.

Enhancing Your Application on Facebook

You can enhance your application to make it more appealing to potential users. There are several ways to do this.

Add a description to the About Page

Potential users go to an application's About Page to learn more about an application. The description should tell them in as few words as possible what your application does and why it might be useful, fun, or interesting to them.

To add a description, click **edit application's about page** under the application's Configuration heading on zembly. zembly takes you to Facebook where you can edit your application's settings (see Figure 5.28). Click **Edit** following the Application Information and add a description. When you're finished editing, click **Submit** (and Facebook will automatically provide the dialog for uploading a picture, as described in the next section).

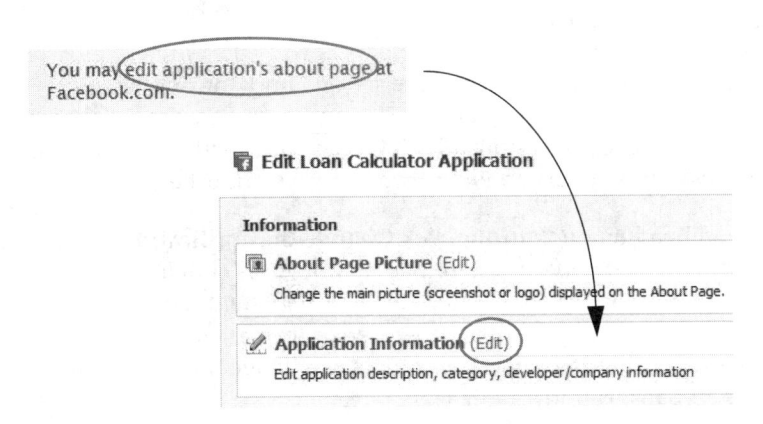

Figure 5.28 Adding a description to the application's About Page

Add a screen shot or other picture to the About Page

A logo or screen shot of your application running in Facebook helps people identify the type of application they're looking at.

From Facebook, select **Step 2: Picture** and follow the instructions to upload a picture to your application's About Page, as shown in Figure 5.29.

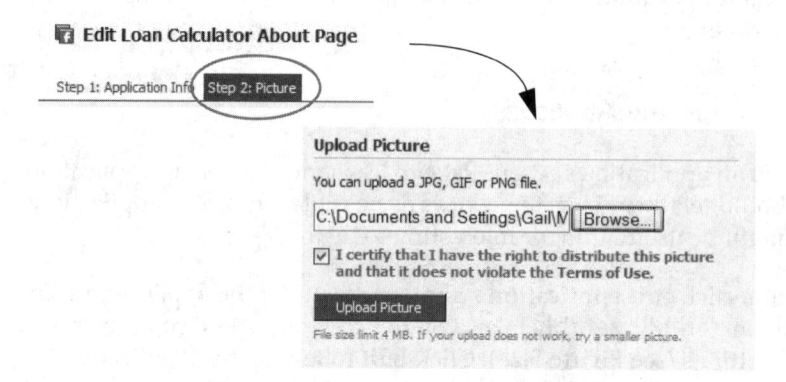

Figure 5.29 Uploading an image for the application's About Page on Facebook

Add an icon to your application

If you don't add an icon to your application, people see an annoying and terribly unhelpful blank box whenever your application is referenced on Facebook. Facebook uses icons on your canvas page, on the application's About page, with menu bar bookmarks, with profile boxes, and wherever a News Feed story is published.

Under the Configuration heading on zembly, click **Change the application icon**, which takes you to Facebook so that you can upload an image, as shown in Figure 5.30. The preferred format is a 16 x 16 GIF file. Facebook will resize and convert an icon image if you upload a file with another size or format. When you're finished, refresh the icon on zembly. It's a good idea to use an image that is visually simple with a transparent background.

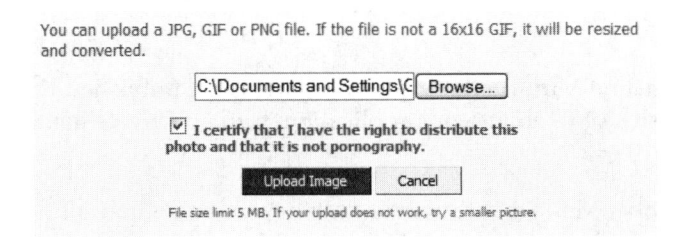

Figure 5.30 Uploading an image for an application icon on Facebook

Add a logo to your application

An application's logo shows up in two places. It appears on your application's information page inside the Facebook Developer. The Developer lets you manage and configure all of your applications on Facebook. You're the only one who will see the logo here. The second place the logo appears is in the Facebook Application Directory. (Figure 5.32 on page 130 shows the Capital Punishment listing in the Facebook Application Directory.)

To add a logo, go to your application's page from the Facebook Developer and follow the instructions to upload an image.

Make the application's profile box interesting

Graphics or images in the profile box always help create interest. In BuddyPics, for example, the profile box displays six random friends' profile pictures. In Capital Punishment, the profile box includes a color-coded world map.

Generate feed stories for your application

Feed stories help publicize who is using your application and how they're interacting with it. Both Capital Punishment and Mood Pix show you how to create feed stories.

Making Your Application Accessible

When you initially create your Facebook application, both the Developer Mode and Private Installation are enabled. Developer Mode restricts the people who can access your application to the application's developers. You can add people to the list of developers for your application to provide a controlled environment for testing.

When you're ready to let non-developers add your application, turn off Developer Mode.

Private Installation means that no Mini-Feed or News Feed items are published. When you're ready to publish stories about your application, turn off Private Installation.

You can turn off both Developer Mode and Private Installation using your application's page on **zembly**. Click the button that says **Make it public** as shown in Figure 5.31.

Figure 5.31 Making your application publicly accessible

The last step to promote your application is to publish it in Facebook's Application Directory. You must apply through Facebook and have at least five users. Consult the Facebook Developer application to perform this step. Figure 5.32 shows the directory listing for Capital Punishment.

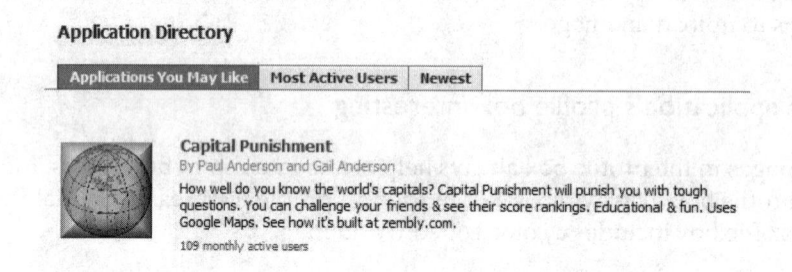

Figure 5.32 Adding your application to the Facebook Application Directory so people can find it

5.4 zembly and Facebook—A Closer Look

The Loan Calculator application is a great way to gain confidence when you create and modify your first Facebook application. But it lacks a key feature. Loan Calculator doesn't use the Facebook platform to engage you or your friends. When you build an application that hooks into the Facebook platform, you build services that call the

Facebook adaptors on **zembly**. Your widgets will let users interact with the Facebook platform. Let's look at some of the resources you can use to make coding easier.

Exploring the Facebook APIs

To truly leverage the Facebook platform, you'll need to make calls to the Facebook API. You can learn about the Facebook APIs through several paths.

- During code development you can use the **zembly** JavaScript editor's code completion (type CTRL-space) to explore Facebook API calls from **zembly**. For example, typing `Things.facebook.friends.` followed by CTRL-space pops up a list of possible API methods. Select a method and hit Enter (or click when selected) to add the code snippet that performs the call, as shown in Figure 5.33.

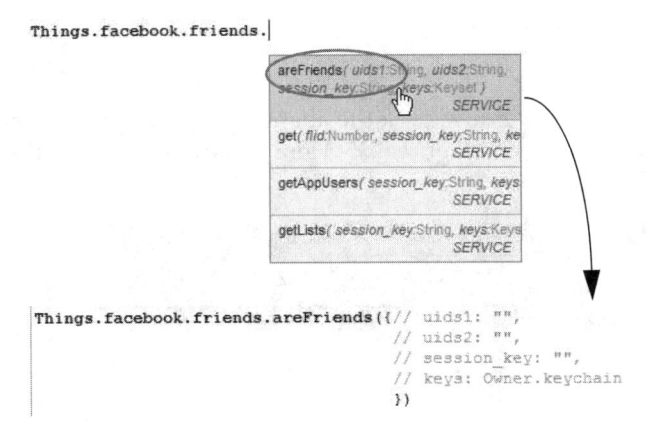

```
Things.facebook.friends.
             areFriends( uids1:String, uids2:String,
             session_key:String, keys:Keyset )
                                       SERVICE
             get( fid:Number, session_key:String, ke
                                       SERVICE
             getAppUsers( session_key:String, keys
                                       SERVICE
             getLists( session_key:String, keys:Keys
                                       SERVICE

Things.facebook.friends.areFriends({// uids1: "",
                                    // uids2: "",
                                    // session_key: "",
                                    // keys: Owner.keychain
                                    })
```

Figure 5.33 Type CTRL-space to activate code completion and select to add code

- **zembly**'s Find & Use lets you search for services. Select the **Find & Use** tab to the right of the **zembly** editor. Here we specify `facebook.friends` and click **Search**. **zembly** returns a list of possible adapters. Now you can either add the code snippet that calls the adapter directly to your code (select **Add to editor**) or request a pop up documentation window as shown in Figure 5.34 (select the adapter name).

132   Chapter 5   Facebook Basics

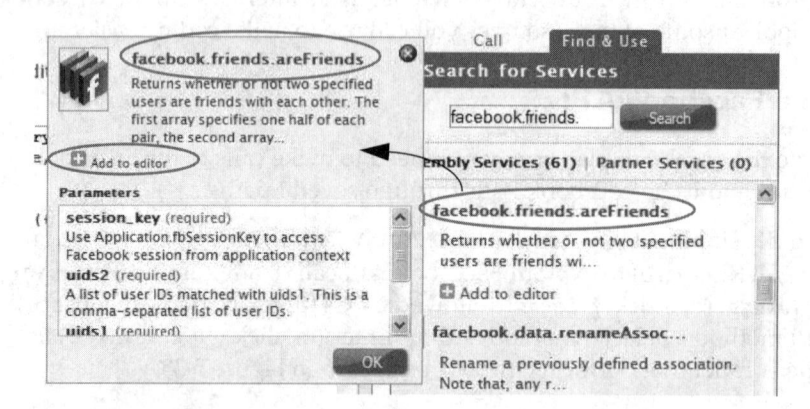

Figure 5.34 Searching for services with Find & Use

Within the pop up documentation window, click the adapter name to navigate to the adapter page in zembly, as shown in Figure 5.35. Here you can read about the API method in more detail.

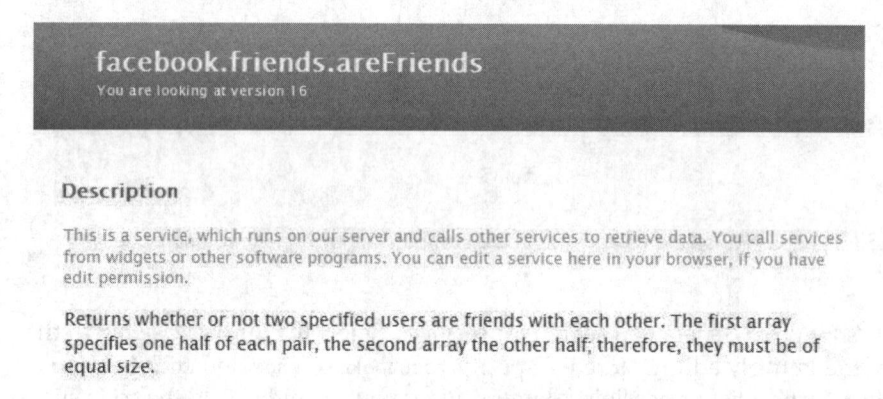

Figure 5.35 zembly adapter documentation page

- Find & Use also lets you call services within your application. For example, Figure 5.36 shows services within the BuddyPics application. Select **Add to editor** to add the code snippet (the correct code is added, depending on whether you are editing a widget or service). Select the service name for more documentation in a pop up window. zembly takes you to the service page if you select the name inside the pop up window.

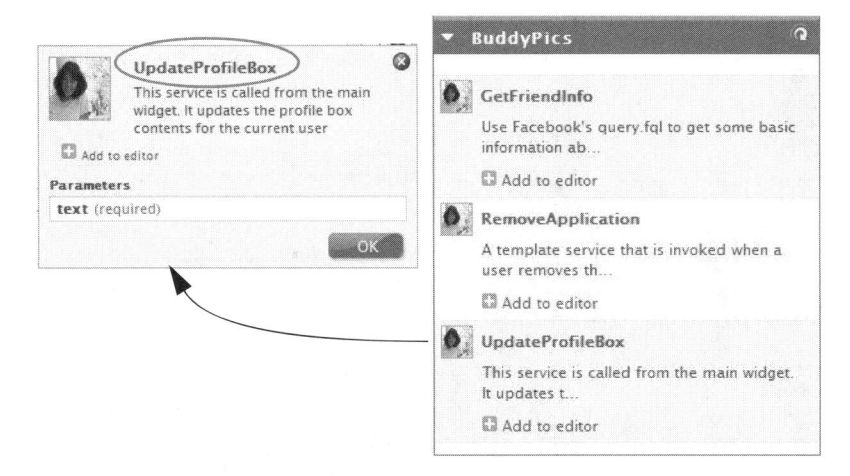

Figure 5.36 Accessing your applications's services with Find & Use

- The Facebook Developers' Wiki, found at http://wiki.developers.facebook.com/index.php/Main_Page describes the Facebook platform as well as the API methods (see Figure 5.37). There is a link to the wiki from your Facebook application page on zembly. From there, you can access the documentation for all of the API calls at http://wiki.developers.facebook.com/index.php/API. Each API has its own page with detailed description, parameters, error codes, and example sections.

Figure 5.37 Navigating to the Facebook Developers' Wiki from zembly

Facebook Code Testing Tools

Facebook provides four extremely helpful testing environments: the API test console, the FBML test console, the Feed Preview console, and the Registered Templates console. All are available from a link on the Developers' Wiki Main Page. You will find these test consoles invaluable for discovering how FBML tags work, how to make calls to the Facebook API, and how to build templatized feeds. (Or you can look at the applications we've built; we've done all the hard work for you!)

Use the API test console to see how an API method works. For example, method `Facebook.friends.areFriends` takes two lists of uids to compare for friendship status. Figure 5.38 shows a sample run with two uids in each argument and the response in XML format.

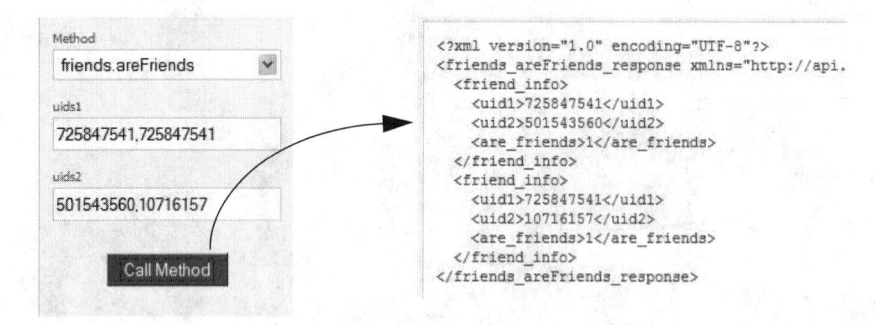

Figure 5.38 Using the Facebook API Test console to explore Facebook API methods

Application Context and Permissions

When a Facebook user invokes your application, Facebook creates the appropriate context and passes it to zembly. zembly captures this information and makes it available to your widgets and services through an Application object. zembly verifies the request (using your API and secret keys) so that you know the request is valid. The Application object contains Facebook-specific information as well as information that zembly maintains, such as `Application.keychain`.

As it turns out, if a user has logged into your Facebook application (`Application.fb_sig_added` is "1"), the Application object includes a valid session key, the Facebook user's id (`Application.fb_sig_user`), a comma-separated list of the user's friends' Facebook ids (`Application.fb_sig_friends`), and other information related to the session. In this case, the Application object also includes the Facebook-specific `Application.fbSessionKey` (the valid session key) and `Application.fbUserID` (the logged-in user id).

If, however, the user has *not* added your application (`Application.fb_sig_added` is then "0"), the Application object still includes the Facebook user id of the user (now in `Application.fb_sig_canvas_user`), and the user's friends' Facebook user ids (`Application.fb_sig_friends`). But, there is no valid session key and `Application.fbSessionKey` and `Application.fbUserID` are not defined. Table 5.2 summarizes the context data Facebook provides to your widgets (and services).

TABLE 5.2 Facebook `fb_sig` Context Data Provided for Widgets/Services

Name	Description	Example Value
[a]`fb_sig_session_key`	Session key (includes user id)	`long_number-1234`
[a]`fb_sig_expires`	Expiration time (in seconds since epoch) of session key or 0 if never expires, int	1221266634
[a]`fb_sig_user`	User ID of logged in user	1234
[b]`fb_sig_canvas_user`	User ID of user (not logged in)	1234
`fb_sig_time`	Time of request, float seconds since epoch	1220047518.2507
`fb_sig_in_new_facebook`	True if user is using new Facebook (should always be true)	1
`fb_sig_profile_update_time`	Last time user's profile was updated, int, seconds since epoch	1219817169
`fb_sig_position_fix`	True if Facebook wrapped canvas page in `position:relative` style (should always be true)	1
`fb_sig_added`	True if user has authorized your application	0/1
`fb_sig_request_method`	Request method	`GET` or `POST`
`fb_sig_friends`	User's friends, comma separated list of uids	1234,5678,10101112
`fb_sig_in_canvas`	True if user is on a canvas page (will be true for your widgets, false when using the application tab)	0/1
`fb_sig_locale`	User's locale	`en_US`
`fb_sig`	Signature of the request for validating that request actually came from Facebook	
`fb_sig_api_key`	Application's API key	

a. Only defined if `fb_sig_added` is 1.
b. Only defined if `fb_sig_added` is 0.

One of the goals of the latest Facebook user interface is letting users interact with applications without having to "add" them to their profiles. To do this, Facebook provides baseline user information to all applications and has opened up more API calls that don't require session keys. We'll address these new access levels as we discuss the example applications in this chapter and the next chapter.

When you call services within your Facebook application (such as UpdateProfileBox) or Facebook adapters (such as `facebook.fql.query`) the application context is automatically preserved and accessible from these services and adapters. This means that **zembly** injects for you (seamlessly behind the scenes) the session key (if you have a valid session) and keychain data.

If, however, you call services that are outside your Facebook application, the application context is not preserved. In this case, you would need to pass the keychain data and session key (if applicable) explicitly by extracting them from the Application object.

> **zembly Tip**
>
> *Since **zembly** takes care of the session authorization work for you, you probably won't need to access most of the fb_sig data values. For example, BuddyPics accesses only fb_sig_friends and MoodPix accesses fb_sig_added, fb_sig_user, and fb_sig_canvas_user.*

Controlling the Allow Access Process

zembly and Facebook give developers several options for letting users login to your applications. Facebook provides the utility `login.php` (www.facebook.com/login.php) to help with this authorization step. You control how and when you want your users to login as follows. Users need only grant access to your application once.

- Lock the widget or service on **zembly** (toggle the lock icon so that its status is "locked"). This is the easiest way and this method will work for many Facebook applications. When a widget or service is locked, **zembly** generates code to redirect users to the Allow Access page (`login.php`). After selecting "Allow," Facebook redirects users to the widget canvas page (for widgets) or calls the service (for services). The BuddyPics Home widget uses this method (see "The BuddyPics Application" on page 139). You can use this method with both HTML and FBML widgets.

- Detect user access state programmatically in widget JavaScript or FBJS code. You can then redirect users to `login.php`. For example, the following snippet redirects to `login.php` if `Application.fbUserID` is null.

```
if (Application.fbUserID == null)
    // redirect to login.php
    top.location.href="http://www.facebook.com/login.php?api_key="
        + Application.fb_sig_key + "&v=1.0&next=Home&canvas=1";
```

`Application.fbUserID` is null if the user has not yet granted access to your application. Utility `login.php` requires the application API key. Parameter `next` specifies the next redirection page. Use `canvas=1` for widgets within your application or canvas=0 (the default) when you want the callback URL prepended to the next parameter instead.

The Capital Punishment Home widget uses canvas=1 to call widget SendInvitation (see Listing 6.8 on page 176). The Capital Punishment iPhoneHome widget calls login.php using the callback URL option instead (see Listing 9.14 on page 345).

- Specify option requireLogin: true when calling a service from FBML. This method pops up an Allow Access dialog when the user has not yet logged into your application. No page redirection occurs. After the user grants access, the call to the service proceeds. Capital Punishment widget SeeScores uses this method (see Listing 6.25 on page 207).

Facebook Tip

Note that your widget must be FBML/FBJS in order to use option requireLogin.

5.5 BuddyPics—Using FBML and FBJS

The Facebook application you just built (Loan Calculator) consists of a standard widget (Home) using HTML for markup, CSS for styles, and JavaScript for program logic. With Facebook applications, however, you have another choice. You can create widgets that use Facebook Markup Language (FBML) for markup, CSS for styles, and Facebook JavaScript (FBJS) for program logic. In this section, you'll build an application—BuddyPics—using FBML for its Home widget. You'll see that FBML is a powerful choice and lets you leverage many Facebook features with its high-level components and tags.

The BuddyPics application shows you how to do the following.

- Build an FBML widget
- Code with FBJS
- Use **zembly** to control access to your Facebook application
- Build and test a service to access the Facebook API
- Add content to a profile box
- Create dynamic FBML content
- Use the Facebook animation library

FBML Overview

FBML is a subset of HTML, but it also has enhancements for leveraging the Facebook platform. For example, with HTML and JavaScript, you must call the Facebook API adapter `facebook.users.getinfo` to get a user's profile picture URL. Then, you can set the `<img>` tag `src` attribute using (for example)

```
document.getElementById("mytag").src = pic_url;
```

where `pic_url` is the user's profile picture URL and element `"mytag"` might be

```
<img id="mytag" />
```

With FBML, however, you use a special tag `<fb:profile-pic>` to display a Facebook user's profile picture, as follows.

```
<fb:profile-pic uid="12345" size="normal" linked="true" />
```

Attribute `size` can be `thumb` (the default), `normal`, `small`, or `square`. Attribute `linked=true` makes the image a link to the user's profile page and `uid` is the Facebook user's ID. So it is quite easy to display a Facebook user's profile picture that links to his or her profile page and displays the user's name when you hover over the profile image. That's quite a bit of functionality with a single FBML tag!

Of course, you must either know the user `uid` statically or make a service call to inject FBML markup into the canvas page dynamically. We'll show you how to do that with BuddyPics (see "Creating Dynamic Content with FBML" on page 142).

Here's a small sampling of some of the high-level Facebook tags available to you as widget building blocks. These tags all manipulate user information.

- `fb:name`—render a user name with options for constructing action sentences involving subject-names, object-names, pronouns, possessives, and reflexive pronouns.

- `fb:user`—hide content if the content belonging to the user identified with attribute `uid` is not visible to the logged in user.

- `fb:pronoun`—generate a pronoun for the user identified with attribute `uid` with options for the type of pronoun (possessive, reflexive, capital letter).

- `fb:profile-pic`—create an `img` tag showing the user identified with attribute `uid` profile picture with options for a link to the profile page and picture sizes.

These tags help you build conditional/logic decisions within FBML.

- `fb:if-is-app-user`—only render the content inside the tag if the user has given access permission to your application.

- `fb:if`—only render the content inside the tag if the value attribute is true.
- `fb:else`—handle the else case inside any `fb:if` tag.

Here is a code snippet that shows you some of these tags.

```
<fb:if-is-app-user>
   <fb:pronoun capital="true"> is a logged in user
   <fb:else>
      <fb:pronoun capital="true"> is not a logged in user
   </fb:else>
</fb:if-is-app-user>
```

The following tags provide complete Facebook components you can embed in your widget.

- `fb:board`—create a discussion board.
- `fb:comments`—create a comment component.
- `fb:rock-the-vote`—create a voter registration component. (This tag appears in the Home widget for the BuddyPics application. This is an example of a single tag that provides an entire component!)
- `fb:friend-selector`—create a friend selection component.

Consult http://wiki.developers.facebook.com/index.php/FBML for a complete reference of the Facebook tags. We'll point out additional FBML and FBJS differences throughout this example. See "Summary of Differences with FBML Widgets" on page 158 for an extended list.

The BuddyPics Application

Before you build BuddyPics, go ahead and run this application on Facebook so you can see how it works. Use the **Search** menu item on zembly to find the application, as shown in Figure 5.39.

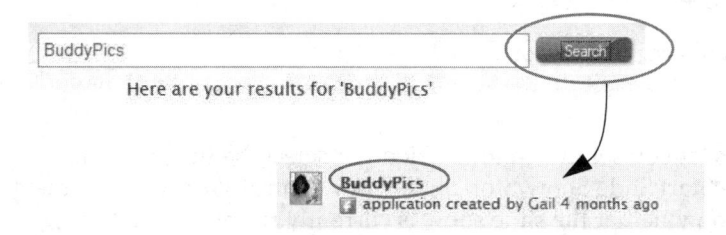

Figure 5.39 Searching for BuddyPics

Follow these steps to run BuddyPics on Facebook.

1. Select **BuddyPics** from the search results displayed on zembly. zembly takes you to the zembly application page for BuddyPics.
2. Select **View about page**. This will take you to the BuddyPics About Page on Facebook.
3. Select **Go to Application**. Facebook displays the Allow Access dialog since BuddyPics requires users to login to the application. (The Home widget is locked.)
4. Select **Allow**. You are now using BuddyPics.

BuddyPics displays a slide show of your friends on Facebook, as shown in Figure 5.40. Depending on what information your friends have set (status, about_me, profile picture, and birthday), BuddyPics displays the available information. You'll see an application header, a link to a Help page, a Register to Vote component, and slide show controls. Figure 5.40 shows BuddyPics when you've paused the slide show.

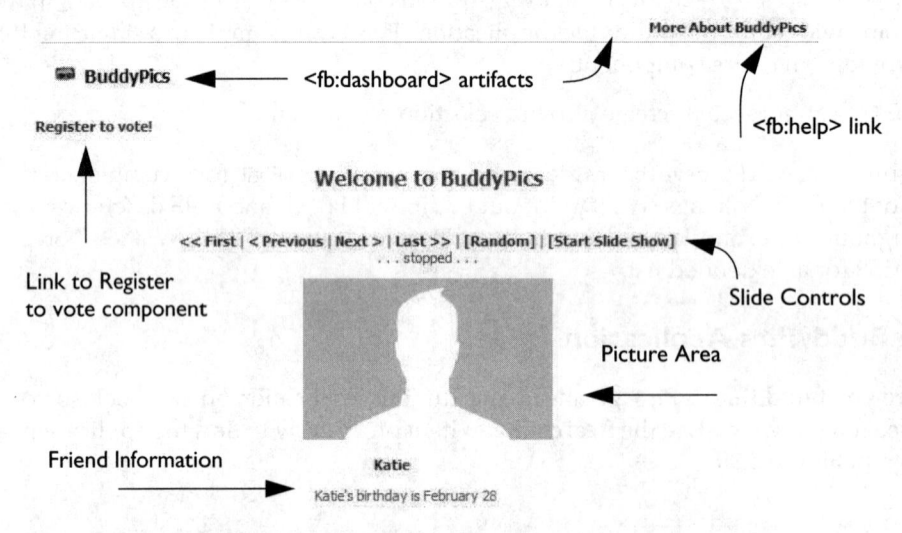

Figure 5.40 BuddyPics running on Facebook

The slide show controls let you select a random friend or select the first, previous, next, or last friend. The Start Slide Show/Stop Slide Show control starts or stops the slide show depending on whether the slide show is currently running or not.

Adding Content to Your Profile

Return to the zembly application page for BuddyPics and run BuddyPics again. You'll notice some differences. First, you won't see the Allow Access dialog this time. You have already given your permission so Facebook sets up a valid session for a logged in user automatically. Second, you'll see an Add to Profile button, as shown in Figure 5.41. Click it and Facebook asks you if it's okay to add the BuddyPics profile box to your profile.

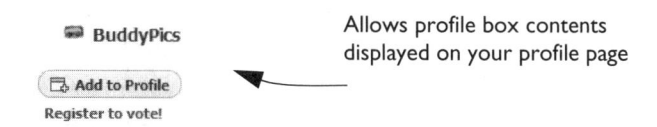

Figure 5.41 Displaying the Add to Profile button for BuddyPics

Facebook then pops up a confirmation dialog, as shown in Figure 5.42. If you click **Add**, Facebook takes you to your profile so that you can confirm the contents.

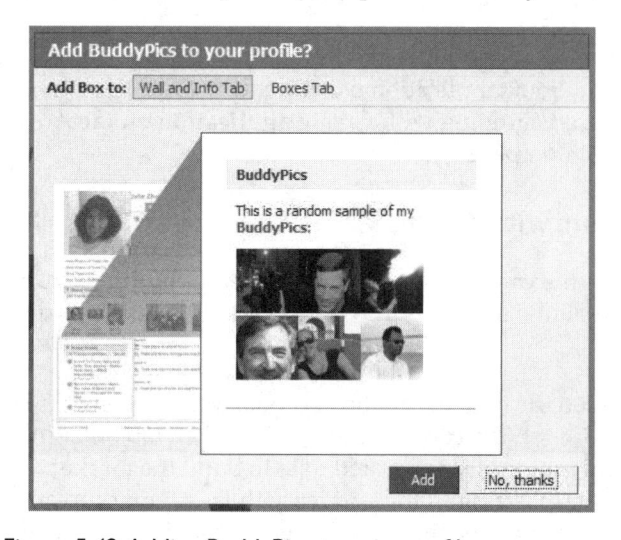

Figure 5.42 Adding BuddyPics to your profile

Building the BuddyPics Facebook Application

You'll now build the BuddyPics application. Although you'll examine each part in detail, you don't need to build it from scratch. Instead, clone the application you've just used. Here's a summary of the steps you'll follow for the rest of this example.

1. Clone the BuddyPics application and rename it
2. Create an application on Facebook.com
3. Examine FBML widget Home
4. Examine and test service GetFriendInfo
5. Examine service UpdateProfileBox
6. Run BuddyPics on Facebook

Return to the BuddyPics application page on zembly. Under Actions, select **Clone this application**. zembly builds you a copy of the BuddyPics application and names it CloneOfBuddyPics. Select **Rename** to rename the application (this is optional), as shown in Figure 5.43.

Figure 5.43 Renaming CloneOfBuddyPics

When you clone an application, you must still create the application on Facebook. Follow the procedure to create a Facebook application using zembly (see "Facebook Application Wizard" on page 115) beginning with **Create application on facebook.com** as shown in Figure 5.14 on page 115.

Creating Dynamic Content with FBML

BuddyPics dynamically updates the canvas page with your friend's profile picture and other markup. Since this dynamic update is a common task with FBML widgets, let's see how this is done.

FBML markup has to be processed into HTML by the Facebook servers before it gets to the browser. The FBML in a widget (the code you see in the FBML tab on zembly) is static; that is, you cannot use dynamically generated data to build the markup. This means you cannot create a JavaScript string in the widget with FBML markup and pass it to the FBJS `setInnerFBML` function. So, how do you get dynamically created FBML processed?

To process dynamically created FBML, you create a service within your application that returns FBML markup in response. This response is processed by the Facebook servers on the way back to the browser and is then usable with `setInnerFBML`. Listing 5.1 shows an example of a service that generates FBML to display a Facebook user's profile picture. (Assume that this service takes a single parameter, uid, the Facebook user ID.)

Listing 5.1 Example FBMLService with FBML response

```
var fbstring = "<fb:profile-pic uid='"
   + Parameters.uid + "' size='normal' linked='true' />";
return fbstring;
```

Listing 5.2 shows how you call this service. In order for Facebook to process the FBML response you must include responseType: Ajax.FBML with the service call. zembly includes this flag in the actual request and the Facebook servers process the response as FBML. (Note that the code name and application name for your application appear in place of mycodename.MyApName.)

The (processed) FBML response string is returned in data (accessible in the onSuccess handler). You then pass it to the FBJS function setInnerFBML using the id of the target element in your FBML code.

Listing 5.2 Example Call of FBMLService

```
    var myuid = "1234";   // facebook user id
    Things.callService("mycodename.MyAppName.FBMLService",
    {
       uid: myuid // facebook uid
    },
    {
       onSuccess: function(data) {
          document.getElementById('results').setInnerFBML(data);
          },
       onFailure: function(error) {
          // process error
          },
       responseType: Ajax.FBML    // required for dynamic FBML
    });
```

BuddyPics uses this technique to display the FBML markup about each friend in the slide show. For each user, the Home widget calls service GetFriendInfo, which returns the generated FBML that is injected into the browser page using setInnerFBML.

Let's now examine the Home (FBML) widget in the BuddyPics application.

BuddyPics Home Widget (FBML)

The BuddyPics Home Widget consists of FBML, CSS, and FBJS for program logic. The widget creates the friend slide show that you've already seen. From the cloned BuddyPics application page on zembly, select widget **Home**. You'll see the Home widget page. Click **Edit** to open the widget for viewing and editing.

> **zembly Tip**
>
> *Note that you cannot preview FBML widgets using the Preview tab on **zembly**.*

Let's look at the FBML first, as shown in Listing 5.3.

The FBML tag `<fb:dashboard>` renders a "dashboard" for your application that includes zero or more `<fb:action>` links (BuddyPics has none) and an optional `<fb:help>` link that appears on the right. Note that the `href` attribute uses the relative URL `"./Help"` which points to the Help widget within the BuddyPics application. The dashboard also renders your application's name and icon below the dashboard menu line.

FBML tags `<fb:if-section-not-added>` and `<fb:add-section-button>` display the Add to Profile button. This button appears only after BuddyPics has generated profile box contents. Users won't see the button when they first run BuddyPics and it won't appear *after* the user adds the profile box.

BuddyPics also includes Facebook's Rock the Vote tag (`fb:rock-the-vote` FBML tag), a component that lets you to register to vote.

Following the welcome message, BuddyPics displays a loading message. This FBML code is interesting for two reasons. First, FBJS can dynamically control whether this markup is rendered using

```
// not visible
document.getElementById("loadingmsg").setStyle({display: 'none'});

// visible
document.getElementById("loadingmsg").setStyle({display: 'block'});
```

Second, the number of friends is dynamically injected into the markup using

```
document.getElementById("numfriends").setValue(number_of_friends);
```

> **FBML/FBJS Tip**
>
> *While it is true that Facebook restricts how you can dynamically generate markup, you can perform markup modifications by calling methods that manipulate tag attributes as illustrated above.*

The HTML a tags invoke FBJS functions `setStart`, `setPrev`, `setNext`, `setEnd`, and `setRandom`. Two separate HTML a tags invoke function `goSlideShow` (which starts the slide show) and `stopSlideShow` (which stops it). These are embedded in `span` tags (`id="stoplink"` and `id="startlink"`) to control their visibility with the style `display` attribute.

The div tag (id="waittest") lets users know when the slide show is stopped and is also controlled with the style display attribute.

The span tag (id="results") is a placeholder for generated FBML that contains the user's friend's profile picture and additional user information. (The widget's FBJS code sets this by calling function setInnerFBML(data) using the dynamic FBML technique already described.)

Listing 5.3 Home (FBML)—BuddyPics

```
<fb:dashboard>
   <fb:help href="./Help">More About BuddyPics</fb:help>
</fb:dashboard>

<!-- Tags to show Add to Profile button -->
<fb:if-section-not-added section="profile">
   <fb:add-section-button section="profile"/>
</fb:if-section-not-added section="profile">

<div id="votediv">
   <fb:rock-the-vote>Register to vote!</fb:rock-the-vote>
</div>


<div id="welcomediv">Welcome to BuddyPics</div>

<!-- Display a loading message that includes how many friends user has -->
<div id="loadingmsg">
   Loading some really cool stuff about your
   <input id="numfriends" type="text" value=" ?? " size='5'
   style='text-align: center;' disabled='true' />
   friends . . .
</div>
<div id="fbwidget">
   <br />

   <!-- Slide show controls that call FBJS functions -->
   <a href="#" onclick="setStart(); return false;"><< First </a> |
   <a href="#" onclick="setPrev(); return false;">< Previous </a> |
   <a href="#" onclick="setNext(); return false;"> Next > </a> |
   <a href="#" onclick="setEnd(); return false;">Last >></a> |
   <a href="#" onclick="setRandom(); return false;">[Random]</a> |

   <!-- Show span startlink or stoplink depending on slide show status -->
   <span id="startlink" style="display:none">
   <a href="#" onclick="goSlideShow(); return false;"> [Start Slide Show] </a>
   </span>
   <span id="stoplink" style="display:none">
   <a href="#" onclick="stopSlideShow(); return false;"> [Stop Slide Show] </a>
   </span>
   <br />
```

```
<!-- Show div when user stops the slide show -->
<div id="waittext" style="display:none"> . . . stopped . . . </div>

    <!-- Placeholder tags that get injected with FBML during execution -->
    <div id="fbresults">
       <span id="results"></span>
    </div>
</div>
```

Listing 5.4 shows the CSS styles for the BuddyPics Home widget. In general, the styles are centered. The font-size attribute for #welcomediv makes the title stand out. Style #votediv defines margins and font styles for the link to the Facebook Rock the Vote component. Finally, the styles for the links specify different background and color settings that reflect hover events.

Listing 5.4 Home (CSS)—BuddyPics

```
#fbwidget {
    font-family: Calibri,Tahoma, Arial, sans-serif;
    text-align: center;
    color: #666666;
    padding: 5px;
    display: none;
}

#welcomediv {
    font-weight: bold;
    padding: 15px;
    font-size: 150%;
    font-family: Calibri,Tahoma, Arial, sans-serif;
    text-align: center;
    color: #666666;
}

#loadingmsg {
    text-align: center;
    font-family: Calibri,Tahoma, Arial, sans-serif;
    font-style: italic;
    text-align: center;
    color: #666666;
    padding: 10px;
}

#votediv {
    padding: 5px;
    font-family:Calibri,Tahoma, Arial, sans-serif;
    margin-bottom: 5px;
}
```

```
a { color: #305090; font-weight: bold; text-decoration:none; }
a:visited { color: #305090; }
a:hover { background-color: #305090; color: #fff; }

#fbresults {
   padding: 10px;
}
```

Listing 5.5 through Listing 5.9 show the Facebook JavaScript (FBJS) code for the BuddyPics Home widget. The FBJS for this widget is divided into five parts for display convenience only. You'll see that much of the code looks exactly like regular JavaScript, while other code contains the more verbose FBJS using explicit setters and getters.

The BuddyPics Home widget displays information about a user's friends. The user's list of friends, `Application.fb_sig_friends`, is a comma-separated string of user ids (see Table 5.2 on page 135 for the Application object fields). The FBJS code uses JavaScript regular expressions to parse the string, count the number of friends, find the next friend in the string, and find the previous friend. While it would arguably be easier to create an array of user ids from this string (using the JavaScript `split` function), we want to make sure the widget works for any number of friends (some Facebook users have more than 1,000 friends). Therefore, the Home widget works solely with string `fb_sig_friends`.

Listing 5.5 includes variables that keep track of the indices into the `fb_sig_friends` string and the slide show controls, as well as functions `goSlideShow`, which starts the slide show, and `stopSlideShow`, which stops it. These functions toggle the visibility of document elements `startlink`, `stoplink`, and `waittext` using `setStyle` instead of a direct assignment to attribute `style` (a restriction with FBJS).

Functions `goSlideShow` and `stopSlideShow` use `setTimeout` and `clearTimeout` to control the slide show. Function `setInterval` is not used because, in between each friend display, the widget makes a service call to get the friend information, format the FBML, and render the markup. Since the round trip elapsed time is indeterminate, it's not possible to pick an interval that will display each new friend smoothly. Instead, with `setTimeout`, a new timer is initiated after the round trip service call for the current friend display is complete.

Those familiar with `setTimeout` and `clearTimeout` will notice that in FBJS these functions are not invoked using object `window` and arguments require explicit JavaScript. Moreover, you cannot provide a function name within a string. This is because Facebook prepends all function and variable names with your Facebook application ID. (See "Summary of Differences with FBML Widgets" on page 158 for more examples of FBJS coding differences.)

Listing 5.5 Home (FBJS)—BuddyPics Part 1

```
// variables to keep track of indices into fb_sig_friends string
var NextIndex = 0;
var CurrentIndex = 0;
var LastUidIndex = 0;
var NumFriends = 0;

// variables for the slide show timer
var ShowTimer = 3500;
var AnimationTime = 1000;
var PauseTime = 500;
var run;
var start_new = true;
var AutoRun = false;

// start the slide show
function goSlideShow() {
   if (!AutoRun) {
      AutoRun = true;
      document.getElementById("startlink").setStyle({display: 'none'});
      document.getElementById("stoplink").setStyle({display: ''});
      document.getElementById("waittext").setStyle({display: 'none'});
      displayFriendInfo(getNextUid(NextIndex));
   } else
      run = setTimeout(
         function() { displayFriendInfo(getNextUid(NextIndex)); }, ShowTimer);
}

// stop the slide show
function stopSlideShow() {
   if (!AutoRun) return;
   AutoRun = false;
   clearTimeout(run);
   document.getElementById("stoplink").setStyle({display: 'none'});
   document.getElementById("startlink").setStyle({display: ''});
   document.getElementById("waittext").setStyle({display: 'block'});
}
```

Listing 5.6 contains the onclick event handlers specified in the FBML code in Listing 5.3 on page 145. These functions first stop the slide show, then display the friend information (start, previous, next, last, or random) after a slight delay. (The delay allows the current friend information display to complete.)

Listing 5.6 Home (FBJS)—BuddyPics Part 2

```
function setStart() {
   stopSlideShow();
   setTimeout(function() { displayFriendInfo(getNextUid(0)); }, PauseTime);
}
```

```
function setPrev() {
   stopSlideShow();
   setTimeout(function() { displayFriendInfo(getPrevUid()); }, PauseTime);
}

function setNext() {
   stopSlideShow();
   setTimeout(function() { displayFriendInfo(getNextUid(NextIndex)); },
      PauseTime);
}

function setEnd() {
   stopSlideShow();
   setTimeout(function() { displayFriendInfo(getNextUid(LastUidIndex)); },
      PauseTime);
}

function setRandom() {
   stopSlideShow();
   setTimeout(function() { displayFriendInfo(getRandomStart()); }, PauseTime);
}
```

Listing 5.7 shows the code to initialize the widget (function init). You cannot use window.onload to invoke a function at start up. Instead, you call a function within global scope to provide code initialization. First, function init counts and displays the number of friends by updating the value attribute of element numfriends. When the last index (in the fb_sig_friends string) is set and the user's profile contents is updated, the slide show starts.

Functions getHowManyFriends and findLastIndex both use JavaScript regular expressions to parse the fb_sig_friends string.

Listing 5.7 Home (FBJS)—BuddyPics Part 3

```
init(); // get everything going

// initialize the widget
function init() {
   // count how many friends & display
   NumFriends = getHowManyFriends();
   document.getElementById("numfriends").setValue(NumFriends);
   findLastIndex();

   // generate content for the profile box
   updateprofile();
   // start the timer for the slide show
   setTimeout(function() { goSlideShow(); }, ShowTimer + AnimationTime)
}
```

```
function getHowManyFriends() {
   // use regular expressions to count commas
   var result;
   var pattern = /,/g;
   var fr = 0;
   while ((result = pattern.test(Application.fb_sig_friends)) != null) {
      fr++;
      if (pattern.lastIndex == 0) break;
   }
   return fr;
}

function findLastIndex() {
   // use regular expressions to find the last friend
   var pattern = /\d+$/;
   var result = pattern.exec(Application.fb_sig_friends);
   LastUidIndex = result.index;
}

function getPrevUid() {
   var index = CurrentIndex - 2;
   if (index < 0) return getNextUid(LastUidIndex);

   while (Application.fb_sig_friends[index] != ',') {
      index--;
      if (index == 0) return getNextUid(0);
   }
   return getNextUid(index);
}

function getRandomStart() {
   return getNextUid(Math.floor(
      Application.fb_sig_friends.length * Math.random()));
}
```

Listing 5.8 includes function getNextUid, the main function for parsing and returning the next friend user id from fb_sig_friends. The JavaScript regular expression pattern /\b\d+\b/g looks for one or more digits (\d+) within a word boundary (\b) (comma is a word delimiter). The global flag g allows the expression engine to update the indices for keeping track of the fb_sig_friends string.

Function displayFriendInfo invokes GetFriendInfo within the BuddyPics application. Service GetFriendInfo makes a call to the Facebook API to retrieve information about its user id parameter. It then formats it into FBML, returning an FBML string. Note that the call specifies option responseType: Ajax.FBML. Facebook processes the return FBML which is then valid to pass to setInnerFBML in the onSuccess handler, as described in "Creating Dynamic Content with FBML" on page 142.

As noted earlier, since GetFriendInfo is defined inside application BuddyPics, the application context is retained and **zembly** provides the session key and key chain data for you.

zembly Tip

When you add code to call a service, use the Find & Use feature to search for services within your application. (This is described in Figure 5.36 on page 133.) Using Find & Use ensures you get the code snippet correct and it includes any parameter descriptions you (of course!) write.

Function `displayFriendInfo` calls the Facebook Animation library to animate element `results`. Briefly, the Animation library lets you chain together CSS styles for animation. First, you call `Animation()` with the element id you want to animate as the first parameter. Then you chain the CSS styles you'd like to animate. In this example, we animate the height (from 0 to auto) and opacity (from 0 to .5) for div `results`. Method `checkpoint` lets you string together separate animations. Here we animate the height and opacity together, then in a separate animation sequence, we bring the opacity up to 1 (full saturation). Call `go` to let Animation know that you are done chaining. Method `blind` keeps text from wrapping during the div-level animation and `show` indicates that the div ends up visible. Method `duration` lets you specify a different animation time from the default 1000 milliseconds.

You'll find more about the Animation library on Facebook at

http://wiki.developers.facebook.com/index.php/FBJS/Animation

Listing 5.8 Home (FBJS)—BuddyPics Part 4

```
function getNextUid(start) {
   // RegExp pattern is one or more digits (\d+) on a word boundary (\b)
   var mypat = /\b\d+\b/g;
   var result;
   mypat.lastIndex = start;
   result = mypat.exec(Application.fb_sig_friends);
   if (result == null) {
      mypat.lastIndex = 0;
      result = mypat.exec(Application.fb_sig_friends);
   }
   // update all the index variables & return the uid
   CurrentIndex = result.index;
   NextIndex = mypat.lastIndex;
   return result[0];
}

function displayFriendInfo(uid) {
   Things.callService("ganderson.BuddyPics.GetFriendInfo",
   {
```

```
      target_uid: uid // facebook friend's uid
   },
   {
      onSuccess: function(data) {
         Log.write(data);
         if (start_new) {
            start_new = false;
            document.getElementById("fbwidget").setStyle({display: 'block'});
            document.getElementById("loadingmsg").setStyle({display: 'none'});
         }
         document.getElementById('results').setStyle({display: 'none'});
         document.getElementById('results').setInnerFBML(data);
         Animation(document.getElementById('results')).to(
            'height', 'auto').from('0px').to(
            'opacity', .5).from(0).blind().show().checkpoint().to(
            'opacity', 1).duration(AnimationTime).go();
         if (AutoRun) goSlideShow();
      },
      onFailure: function(error) {
         Log.write("Error: " + error.code + " : " + error.message);
      },
      responseType: Ajax.FBML    // required for dynamic FBML
   });
}
```

Listing 5.9 contains the code to generate the BuddyPics profile box. It generates a random sampling of six friends and displays their square-format profile pictures. Function `updateprofile` shows how to declare and manipulate a JavaScript array using FBJS. It calls service UpdateProfileBox to update the profile box.

In function `updateprofile`, change variable text to use your Facebook application id. This builds the correct link to your application's About Page.

Function `updateprofile` is called during initialization (from `init`), setting `NextIndex` to a random index value. This makes the slide show start with a random friend, instead of always starting at the beginning of the friend list.

Listing 5.9 Home (FBJS)—BuddyPics Part 5

```
function getRandom(cursize, rArray) {
   // get random friend uids from Application.fb_sig_friends
   while (1) {
      var uid = getRandomStart();
      var duplicate = false;
      for (var i = 0; i < cursize; i++) {
         if (rArray[i] == uid) {
            duplicate = true;
            break;
         }
```

```
        }
        if (duplicate) continue;
        return uid;
    }
}

function updateprofile() {
    // grab a few random pics and put them in the profile box
    var text = "This is a random sample of my "
        + "<a href=\"http://www.facebook.com/apps/applica-
tion.php?id=15375481317\">"
        + "BuddyPics</a>:<p/>";

    var samplesize = 6;
    if (samplesize > NumFriends)
        samplesize = NumFriends;
    var uidArray = [];
    for (var i = 0; i < samplesize; i++) {
        uidArray[i] = getRandom(i, uidArray);
    }
    for (var i = 0; i < samplesize; i++) {
        var fruid = uidArray[i];
        text += "<fb:profile-pic uid=\""
            + fruid
            + "\" size=\"square\" linked=\"true\" />";
    }
    text += "<br/>";

    Things.callService("ganderson.BuddyPics.UpdateProfileBox",
    {
        "text": text
    },
    {
        onSuccess: function(data) {
        }
        ,onFailure: function(error) {
        }
    });
}
```

Let's now examine the services GetFriendInfo and UpdateProfileBox in the BuddyPics application.

Service GetFriendInfo

From the BuddyPics application page on **zembly**, select service GetFriendInfo. You'll see the GetFriendInfo service page. Click **Edit** to open the service for editing. Listing 5.10 shows the JavaScript source.

Service GetFriendInfo takes a single Facebook user ID as its parameter (`target_uid`) and returns FBML markup to the caller that shows the information you see when you run BuddyPics. That is, the service returns the user id, profile picture, about_me text, birthday, status, first_name, and whether or not the friend uses BuddyPics. All of the information is optional except the user id and first_name. (Facebook displays an anonymous profile picture for friends who haven't set a profile picture.)

Service GetFriendInfo first calls Facebook adapter `facebook.fql.query` to obtain the data from Facebook's user-wide database. (The data returned is subject to access permissions that the friend has given to the logged in user.) Remember that **zembly** supplies the necessary `session_key` and key chain values from the application context for you.

Facebook Tip

Alternatively, you could also call Facebook API `users.getInfo`. In general `fql.query` is more flexible, but in this case there is no advantage in using one over the other. If you restrict the fields to uid, first_name, last_name, name, locale affiliations (regional type only), pic, or profile_url, then you don't need a session key to make a call.

Next, service GetFriendInfo formats the `fql.query` results and returns FBML markup.

Listing 5.10 Service GetFriendInfo (JavaScript)—BuddyPics

```
var info = Things.facebook.fql.query({
    // The query to perform, as described in the FQL documentation.
    query: "select uid,about_me,birthday,status,first_name,is_app_user " +
        "from user where uid in (" + Parameters.target_uid + ")"
});

// info is a JSON array object
var fr = info[0];

// Build FBML and return string
var fbstring = "<fb:profile-pic uid=\""
    + fr.uid
    + "\" size=\"normal\" linked=\"true\" />"
    + "<p /><fb:name uid=\""
    + fr.uid + "\" /><p />";

var morestr = "";
if (fr.about_me != null && fr.about_me != ""){
    morestr += "<p/>" + fr.about_me;
}
if (fr.is_app_user){
    morestr += "<p/>" + fr.first_name
        + " uses BuddyPics.";
}
```

```
if (fr.status != null && fr.status.message != ""){
   morestr += "<p/>" + fr.first_name
       + " " + fr.status.message;
}
if (fr.birthday != null && fr.birthday != ""){
   morestr += "<p/>" + fr.first_name + "'s birthday is " + fr.birthday + ".";
}

fbstring += morestr;

return fbstring;
```

Testing a Facebook Service

When you write a service that makes a Facebook API call, you can test your service from the service page on zembly. Let's step through the process of testing a service that makes a Facebook API call using service GetFriendInfo. In the JavaScript editor for service GetFriendInfo, add the code

```
return info;
```

after the call to `fql.query`. In the Call box, acquire a Facebook session, as shown in Figure 5.44. This enables you to test drive your service in session context.

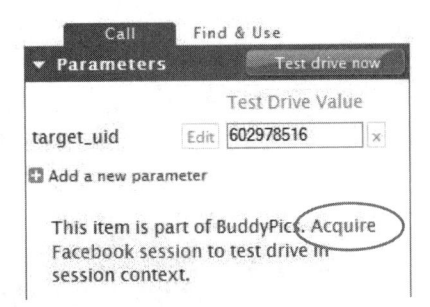

Figure 5.44 Acquiring a Facebook session for testing

Now enter a value into the `target_uid` parameter (go to a friend's profile on Facebook and copy his or her user ID from the URL). Click **Test drive now** as shown in Figure 5.45.

156   Chapter 5   Facebook Basics

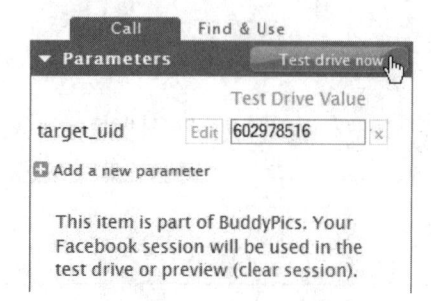

```
   Call        Find & Use
▼ Parameters        Test drive now
                 Test Drive Value
target_uid    Edit  602978516    x
➕ Add a new parameter

This item is part of BuddyPics. Your
Facebook session will be used in the
test drive or preview (clear session).
```

Figure 5.45 Testing a service in context

The fql query returns the data in JSON format, with each data field requested accessible as a JSON property. Figure 5.46 shows sample data as displayed in the Result window.

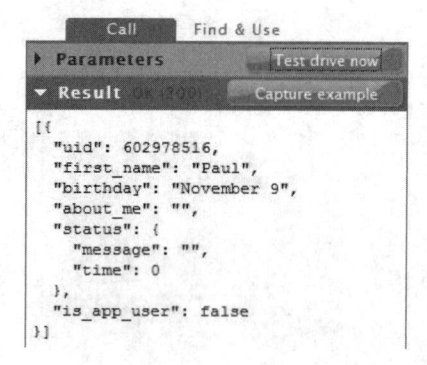

```
   Call        Find & Use
▶ Parameters        Test drive now
▼ Result  Ok (200):  Capture example
[{
   "uid": 602978516,
   "first_name": "Paul",
   "birthday": "November 9",
   "about_me": "",
   "status": {
      "message": "",
      "time": 0
   },
   "is_app_user": false
}]
```

Figure 5.46 Viewing the results

Service GetFriendInfo then generates FBML tags inserting the returned data values. Remove (or comment out) the `return info` code you added and re-test the service. Figure 5.47 displays the generated FBML in the Result window that service GetFriendInfo returns.

BuddyPics—Using FBML and FBJS   157

```
<fb:profile-pic uid="602978516"
size="normal" linked="true" /><p
/><fb:name uid="602978516" /><p
/><p/>Paul's birthday is November 9.
```

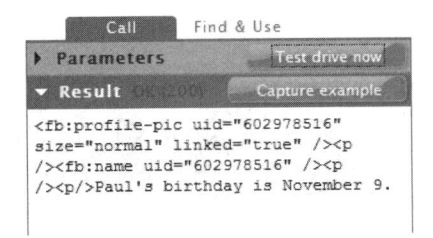

Figure 5.47 Viewing the results (FBML)

Service UpdateProfileBox

Service UpdateProfileBox updates the user's profile using FBML markup. Listing 5.11 shows service UpdateProfileBox for BuddyPics. Note that this service takes one parameter (`text`), type String, required, and Escape value is *unchecked*. Examine this parameter (click **Edit** in the Call window). **zembly** displays the Parameter Editor, as shown in Figure 5.48.

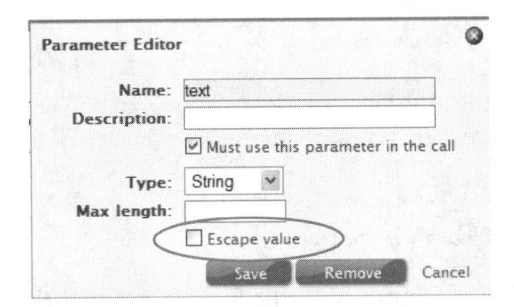

Figure 5.48 zembly's Parameter Editor

Why is it necessary to uncheck the Escape value? By default all String parameters are escaped on input. If Escape value is checked, **zembly** converts all the HTML-specific characters to HTML entities (for example, < is converted to <). However, service UpdateProfileBox requires untouched FBML markup (otherwise your profile box will contain escaped character sequences instead of correctly rendered markup).

Facebook adapter `facebook.profile.setFBML` updates the logged in user's profile box contents. Service UpdateProfileBox passes parameter `text` for both `profile_main` and `profile`. Parameter `profile` is the FBML intended for the application profile box that appears on the Boxes tab on the user's profile. Parameter `profile_main` is the FBML intended for the narrow profile box on user's main profile area (the left-hand column).

Listing 5.11 Service UpdateProfileBox (JavaScript)—BuddyPics

```
Things.facebook.profile.setFBML({
   // uid: 0
   profile_main: Parameters.text, // FBML intended for the Wall
   // mobile_profile: "" // FBML intended for mobile devices.
   profile: Parameters.text // FBML intended for the application profile box
});
```

Figure 5.49 shows the BuddyPics profile box in the left-hand column (FBML passed in `profile_main`).

Figure 5.49 BuddyPics on main profile (left-hand column)

As you test this application, you'll see that BuddyPics is a nice, relaxing way to sit back and peruse your friends' profile information without having to visit each of their profile pages.

Summary of Differences with FBML Widgets

FBML and FBJS use alternative coding styles. For example, the Prototype JavaScript library is not available for FBML widgets, so you cannot use the shorthand notation `$("elemId")` when referencing elements by id. `Event.observe` is also unavailable.

Here is a summary of some of the important differences. The list is not complete, but it should help you identify potential problem areas and give you the code that works with FBJS and FBML.

- Images

  For privacy reasons, Facebook does not display images when the `src` attribute is from `Facebook.com` with FBML. Facebook displays a blank image if the URL is from the Facebook domain. Instead, use tag `<fb:profile-pic>`.

- Arrays

  ```
  // Doesn't work
  ```

```
var myarray = new Array();

// Use
var myarray = [];
```

- 'click' Event Handlers

  ```
  // Doesn't work
  Event.observe($("elemId"), 'click', function() {
     // function body
  });

  // Use
  document.getElementById("elemId").addEventListener('click', function() {
     // function body
  });

  // Alternatively, from FBML use
  <a href="#" onclick="myfunc(); return false;"> Call My Func </a>
  ```

- Buttons

  ```
  // Unsupported
  <button id="makeslow">Slow Down</button>

  //Use
  <input type="button" id="makeslow" class="Inbutton" value="Slow Down" />
  ```

- Dynamic Modifications to Element Attributes

  ```
  // Doesn't work
  document.getElementById("elemId").style.display = "block";

  // Use
  document.getElementById("elemId").setStyle({display: 'block'});
  ```

- Setters and Getters for Attributes

  ```
  // Doesn't work
  var answer = document.getElementById("elemId").value;
  document.getElementById("elemId").value = answer;

  // Use
  var answer = document.getElementById("elemId").getValue();
  document.getElementById("elemId").setValue(answer);
  ```

- Popup Alerts

  ```
  // Doesn't work
  alert("Your profile has been updated.");

  // Use
  new Dialog().showMessage("Successful Update",
  ```

"Your profile has been successfully updated.", "Okay");

- Window Events and Timers

```
// Doesn't work
var run = setInterval("getNextFriend(1)", 2000);
window.clearInterval(run);

// Use
var run = setInterval(function() { getNextFriend(1); }, 2000);
clearInterval(run);

// Doesn't work
Event.observe(window, 'load', function() {
// function body
});

// Use
function init() {
// function body
}
init();  // call in global scope
```

The HTML Alternative

Application BuddyMugs is a similar application to BuddyPics—it displays a slide show of your Facebook friends. BuddyMugs is an HTML version of BuddyPics. For those who are more comfortable with HTML, or those who just want to see some of the differences in coding styles between JavaScript and FBJS, check out BuddyMugs. Use **zembly**'s Search mechanism to locate this application.

What's Next

This chapter covers basic Facebook application development with **zembly**. In the next chapter, you'll see how to build applications that leverage Facebook integration points, including issuing challenges to friends, using the Facebook DataStore API, and using the new templatized feed story bundles. You'll also see how to use the new Publisher, create an application tab, interface with the new profile Info tab, and use the new feed forms. All of these features are used in the chapter's two example applications: Capital Punishment and Mood Pix.

6 Facebook Integration

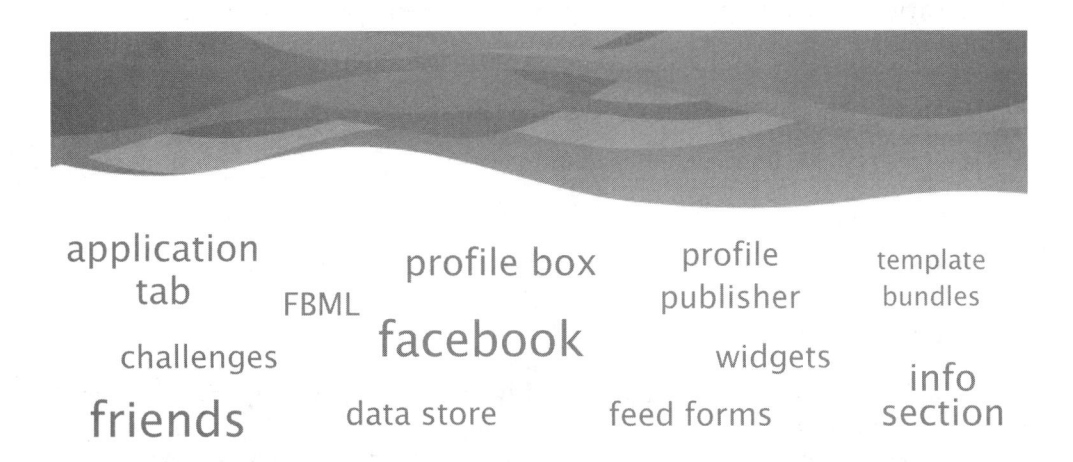

application tab profile box profile publisher template bundles
FBML
challenges **facebook** widgets
friends data store feed forms info section

The previous chapter gives you an overview of the Facebook integration points (see Table 5.1, "Summary of Facebook Features and Integration Points" on page 104). Application BuddyPics shows you FBML, FBJS, and generating markup for the new profile box features. In this chapter, we'll continue with more Facebook integration points.

Capital Punishment, our flagship Facebook application on zembly, shows you how to challenge friends with invitations and create registered template bundles. With templates, you can publish stories about an application. You'll learn how to detect whether users have granted access to your application. Capital Punishment also shows you how to store application data using the Facebook data store API.

The second example, Facebook application Mood Pix, shows how to leverage every integration avenue that Facebook offers. These include application tabs, the profile publisher, application info sections, feed forms, and using `fb:friend-selector` and FBML to send friend notifications. Like Capital Punishment, Mood Pix uses the Facebook data store API, registered template bundles, and the add-to-profile button with the new profile box layout.

What You Will Learn

- Using HTML with Facebook integration
- Selecting a single friend for notifications
- Selecting multiple friends for notifications or requests
- Displaying the add-to-profile button with both FBML and HTML widgets
- Detecting whether a user is logged in to your application
- Registering template bundles and creating news feed stories
- Using the profile publisher and feed forms
- Using the Application Tab and Application Info Sections
- Using the Facebook Data Store API and Facebook Query Language (FQL)

Examples in This Chapter

All examples in this chapter are tagged **zembly-book-facebookintegration**. To search for these examples on **zembly**, select **Search** at the top of any **zembly** page. Supply the search term **zembly-book-facebookintegration** and click **Search** as shown in Figure 6.1.

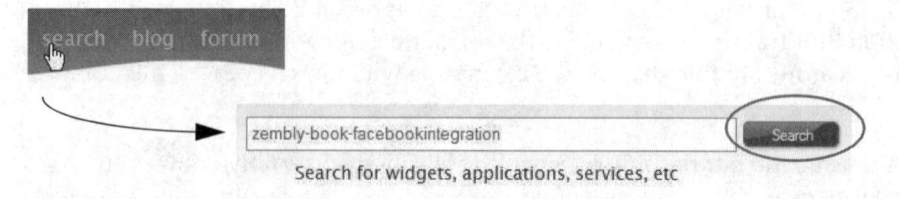

Figure 6.1 Searching for the examples in this chapter

6.1 Capital Punishment—A Challenging Facebook Application

The trick to writing an engaging Facebook application is to involve users and their friends. With Facebook, you can publish "stories" about user achievements or user challenges. These extra features help introduce your application to more people. After all, the goal is to create "viral" applications that are quickly added by more and more friends (and their friends as well).

Capital Punishment—A Challenging Facebook Application

Capital Punishment is a good example of an engaging Facebook application. With a multiple choice format, a 20-question quiz prompts users to identify the capitals of various countries in the world and provides feedback. Google maps helps make the quiz educational—you learn about new cities and countries and see exactly where these little-known places are located. Capital Punishment uses Google maps zoom level three, which is just about the right zoom level to study a country and its neighbors. Of course, you can always zoom out to see more of the area or zoom in for a closer look using the provided map controls.

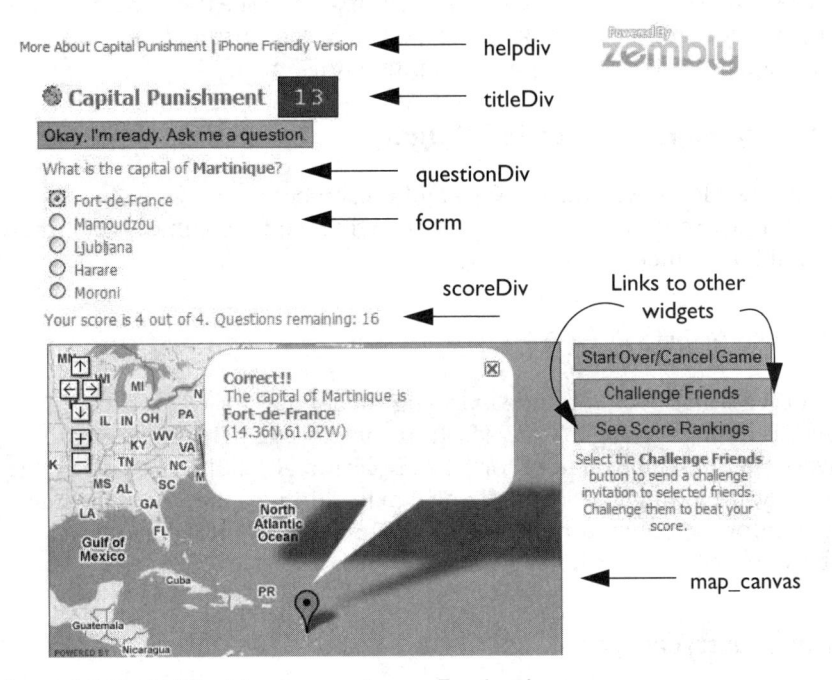

Figure 6.2 shows Capital Punishment running on Facebook. The top half of the screen contains the question and multiple-choice selections for the capital of the named country. After you select your answer (within the allotted time frame), the Google map displays the correct response. The application updates your score and displays how many questions remain in the current quiz. When you're ready, click **Okay, I'm ready** and you're given the next question. You can challenge friends or start over at any time. You can also see your previous scores and your friends' rankings. (The Start Over, Challenge Friends, and See Score Rankings options appear to the right of the map.) Several div tags are labeled in Figure 6.2.

Figure 6.2 Capital Punishment running on Facebook

After at least one quiz is complete, the application generates markup in the application's profile box showing the countries' capitals you correctly named, your diplomatic rank (from "Lackey" to "Top Diplomat"), and a color-coded map showing the capitals you identified. The Challenge Friends and See Score Rankings buttons take you to separate widgets, both implemented with FBML and FBJS.

The Capital Punishment widget also includes a link to a Help page that displays additional information about the application and the iPhone-friendly version of the quiz. (See "Facebook Integration—iPhoneHome Widget" on page 337 for a discussion of the iPhone-friendly version.)

Cloning the Facebook Application

A straightforward way to learn about this application is to clone it. This approach lets you own your own copy so you can modify it as much as you'd like. When you clone the application, zembly uses the default name CloneofCapitalPunishment (which you can change). Once the application is cloned, follow the instructions presented earlier to create an application on Facebook (see "Facebook Application Wizard" on page 115). When you're finished with this basic setup, you'll see the widgets and services zembly provides for a Facebook application as well as the modified and added services and widgets created to implement Capital Punishment.

The Capital Punishment Home Widget

Let's begin with the Home widget. The Capital Punishment Home widget uses HTML, CSS, and JavaScript code. Click the Home widget on the zembly application page for Capital Punishment.

Using Google Maps

Previously, you've seen how to provide mapping capabilities for widgets using Google Maps (see "Building a Google Maps Mashup" on page 92). This Zillow-based mashup covers most of what you need for map applications: loading the Google Maps JavaScript library, providing a key, initializing a map, adding a marker to the map, and adding an information window. Capital Punishment uses markers to provide visual feedback for the correct capital cities.

JavaScript countrydata.js

Information about each country (name, capital, country "code", and map coordinates) is kept in a JavaScript file that you upload to the widget. (When you clone the application, this resource is included for you.) Listing 6.1 shows the format of file `countrydata.js`.

Listing 6.1 countrydata.js (JavaScript)—Capital Punishment

```
function init_country_data() {
   var countries = new Array();
   countries = [

{name: "Afghanistan", code: "AF", capital: "Kabul", latitude: "34.28N",
   longitude: "69.11E" },
{name: "Albania", code: "AL", capital: "Tirane", latitude: "41.18N",
   longitude: "19.49E" },

. . . [many countries omitted] . . .

{name: "Zambia", code: "ZM", capital: "Lusaka", latitude: "15.28S",
   longitude: "28.16E" },
{name: "Zimbabwe", code: "ZW", capital: "Harare", latitude: "17.43S",
   longitude: "31.02E" }
   ];
   return countries;
}
```

Function `init_country_data` builds an array of objects that includes name (such as "Afghanistan"), code (the code corresponds to country codes used by web site http://www.world66.com/myworld66/visitedCountries to generate a visited countries world map), capital, and latitude and longitude data. The Capital Punishment Home widget uses this data to map capital cities, look up correct answers, and generate choices for the multiple choice questions.

Including Library Prototype JS

The Capital Punishment widget requires the Prototype JavaScript library. From the Resources tab, select **Libraries** (at the bottom) and choose **Prototype** from the list of libraries, as shown in Figure 5.24 on page 124. (This step is already done for you when you clone the application.) Recall that Prototype lets you use the syntactic shortcut `$("element_id")` instead of `document.getElementById("element_id")`. It also supports

```
Event.observe(DOM object, Event, func_name);
```

which is a safe and portable way to register event handlers with events in JavaScript.

Capital Punishment Home Widget Code

Now let's examine the code for the Capital Punishment Home widget. Listing 6.2 (Part 1) and Listing 6.3 (Part 2) show the HTML. Refer to Figure 6.2 on page 163 for placement of many tag elements listed in the code.

Script tags and link tags import JavaScript and CSS code. The Capital Punishment Home widget supports the dynamic display of the Facebook add-to-profile button. While this is straightforward with FBML, it requires more effort with HTML. The HTML includes the necessary Facebook support (JavaScript and CSS) to display the add-to-profile button.

JavaScript file `countrydata.js` contains the previously discussed data for the capital cities quiz. The next script tag imports the Google Maps JavaScript library, which requires a key value (you provide your own key).

The `"poweredBy"` div tag provides placement for the **zembly** logo. The `"tabdiv"` div tag holds links for the Capital Punishment Help widget and the iPhone-friendly version of this widget (see "iCapitalPunishment Widget" on page 331). The Help widget explains in more detail how the Home widget behaves.

Listing 6.2 Home (HTML)—Capital Punishment Part I

```
<!-- CSS & Javascript code to support Facebook add-to-profile button -->
<link rel="stylesheet" href="http://static.ak.facebook.com/css/fb_connect.css"
   type="text/css" />
<script src=
   "http://static.ak.facebook.com/js/api_lib/v0.4/FeatureLoader.js.php"
   type="text/javascript"></script>

<!-- Data to look up capitals, map coordinates, codes, country names -->
<script src="${res('countrydata.js')}" type="text/javascript"></script>

<!-- Google Javascript support library -->
<script src="http://maps.google.com/maps?file=api&amp;v=2&amp;key=Google Key"
   type="text/javascript"></script>
<body onunload="GUnload()">
<div id="poweredBy"></div>
<div id="tabdiv">
   <a href="http://apps.facebook.com/capitalpunish/Help" target="_new">
   More About Capital Punishment</a> |
   <a href="http://a3b0707f76ea498391d9da8621def5dd.zembly.com/things/
   9169cabb2b9c4fedb9ba12b19858676e;iframe" target="_top">
   iPhone Friendly Version</a>
</div>
```

The `"widgetDiv"` div tag holds the rest of the Home widget markup shown in Listing 6.3.

The `"titleDiv"` div tag contains the application's icon, the widget's title, and a placeholder for the timer mechanism. The `"addtoProfileButton"` span tag is a place holder for the Facebook-styled button that lets users interactively add a profile box to their profiles.

The "nextQ" input tag (button) lets users control the pace of the quiz. It gets the next question and starts the timer.

The "questionDiv" div tag is a placeholder for the generated question. Next, a form element holds the input elements that let you respond to the quiz. A set of radio buttons displays five choices. Radio buttons that share the same name attribute (here, "capital") provide standard radio button behavior, allowing only one selection at a time. Each radio button invokes function getGeo after a "change" event to process your response.

The "scoreDiv" div tag holds the generated score as you work through the quiz and the "map_canvas" div defines the view port for the Google map. The "buttonDiv" tag contains the buttons that let you start over (id="startover"), challenge friends (id="challengeButton"), or see scores (id="seeScores"). The following div (class="small_note") provides instructions for challenging friends.

Finally, the "profilebox" div tag is a placeholder for the color-coded world map showing the countries whose capital cities you correctly name. Its style attribute is initially "display:none", making the content hidden until its style attribute is changed to "display:block" (in the JavaScript code). This allows the widget's JavaScript code to display or hide portions of the widget markup.

Listing 6.3 Home (HTML)—Capital Punishment Part 2

```
<div id="widgetDiv">
   <div id="titleDiv">
      <img id="globe" src="${res('globeicon.png')}"> Capital Punishment
      <span id="timer"></span>
      <span id="addToProfileButton" style="display:inline"></span>
   </div>
   <input type="button" class="buttonQ"
      value="Okay, I'm ready. Ask me a question." id="nextQ" />
   <div id="questionDiv"></div>
   <form name="myform" onsubmit="getGeo(); return false;">
   <div class="adiv">
      <input name="capital" type="radio" class="radio" id="r0" />
      <span id="radio0"></span><br />
      <input name="capital" type="radio" class="radio" id="r1" />
      <span id="radio1"></span><br />
      <input name="capital" type="radio" class="radio" id="r2" />
      <span id="radio2"></span><br />
      <input name="capital" type="radio" class="radio" id="r3" />
      <span id="radio3"></span><br />
      <input name="capital" type="radio" class="radio" id="r4" />
      <span id="radio4"></span><span id="errstr"></span>
   </div>
   </form>
   <div id="scoreDiv"></div>
```

```
<p/>
<div class="adiv" id="buttondiv">
   <input type="button" class="button" value="Start Over/Cancel Game"
      id="startOver" /><br />
   <input type="button" class="button" value="Challenge Friends"
      id="challengeButton" /><br />
   <input type="button" class="button" value="See Score Rankings"
      id="seeScores" /><br />
   <div class="small_note">
   Select the <b>Challenge Friends</b> button to send a challenge
   invitation to selected friends. Challenge them to beat your score.
   </div>
</div>
<div id="map_canvas"></div>
<div id="profilebox" style="display:none"></div>
</div>
```

Listing 6.4 shows the CSS styles for the Capital Punishment widget. The buttons are styled with blue background and black text. Links (tag a) have a gray color (#666666), no text decoration, and a dark background and white text for hover events.

Listing 6.4 Home (CSS)—Capital Punishment

```
.fb_addSection {
   height:22px;
   width:116px;
   margin-left: 20px;
}
#widgetDiv {
   color: #647A88;
   padding: 5px;
   font-family: Calibri,Tahoma, Arial, sans-serif;
   margin: 5px 5px 0px 5px;
   font-size: 75%
}
#tabdiv {
   font-family: Calibri,Tahoma, Arial, sans-serif;
   font-size: 70%
}
#globe { width: 16px; height: 16px }
#poweredBy{
   background : url(../resources/poweredByZembly.png);
   width : 116px;
   height : 43px;
   position : absolute;
   top : 0px;
   right : 40px;
   cursor : pointer;
   z-index : 10;
}
```

```css
#buttondiv {
   position : absolute;
   top : 238px;
   left : 440px;
   width : 160px;
}
#timer {
   border:1px solid #000000;
   font-family:courier ;
   font-size:16pt;
   font-weight:bold;
   background-color: #ff0000 ;
   color: #FFFF00;
   padding: 5px 10px 5px 10px;
   margin: 5px;
}
.small_note { font-size:0.9em; color:#666; margin:3px; text-align: center; }
.small_note_left { font-size:0.9em; color:#666; margin:3px; }
.adiv { margin: 7px; }

h4 {margin:6px 0px}

a { text-decoration: none; }
a:link { color: #666666; }
a:visited { color: #666666; }
a:hover { background-color: #222; color: #fff; }

.button,.buttonQ {background-color:#99B3CC; color:#000;
   border:1px solid #647A88; text-align:center;
   cursor:pointer; padding: 1px; margin: 3px; }
.button:hover, .linkbutton:hover, .buttonQ:hover { background-color:#557FFF;
   color:#fff}
.button {width: 160px; }
.buttonQ:disabled {background-color: #aaa }

#scoreDiv, #questionDiv {
   margin: 5px 5px 5px 7px;
}

#titleDiv {
   margin: 5px 5px 3px 7px; font-weight: bold; font-size: 1.3em;
}
#profilebox {
   width: 400px;
   padding: 5px;
   border: 1px solid #647A88;
   margin: 10px;
}

#map_canvas {
   height: 260px;
   width: 400px;
```

```
    padding: 5px;
    border: 1px solid #647A88;
    margin: 2px 5px 0px 10px;
}
```

Listing 6.5 through Listing 6.9 show the JavaScript code for the Capital Punishment Home widget. The Home widget has five distinct areas of logic, and we show you the JavaScript code for each part separately. Part 1 contains the global data for the quiz and the code to implement the timer. Part 2 includes the interface with Google maps and the code to initialize the widget. Part 3 processes user input and controls progress through the quiz, including building the question and selection choices. Part 4 processes the Challenge Friends, Start Over, and See Score Rankings buttons. Part 5 provides the quiz completion code. This part saves the user's score, publishes the news feed story, and builds the application's profile box.

Widget Home has optional parameter `ids` of type JSON. Parameter `ids` contains the Facebook user IDs who have been challenged. Widget Home publishes a story when users issue challenges to their friends.

Listing 6.5 contains the global variables and includes the timer code that starts at the beginning of each question. A display counts down and is updated every second. Users have 15 seconds to answer each question to record a correct response. The timer is stopped when the user answers the question or selects a button that navigates away from the main quiz.

Listing 6.5 Home (JavaScript)—Capital Punishment Part 1

```
var map;
var countries;
var myscore = { };
var countrydata = { };
var mycountries = { };
var usedcountries;
var choicesArray;
var QuizTotal = 20;
var rank = "Lackey";
// Coordinates for Senegal, nice for centering map
var InitLat = "14.34N";
var InitLng = "17.29W";

//Code to implement the timer
var secs;
var TIME_LIMIT = 16;
var timerHandle;

function stopTimer() {
    clearTimeout(timerHandle);
}
```

```
function startTimer() {
   secs = 0 + TIME_LIMIT;
   redo();
}

// format the display
function disp(secs) {
   var dis;
   if (secs <= 9) dis = "0" + secs;
   else dis = secs + "";
   return dis;
}

// count down and update every second
function redo() {
   secs--;
   $("timer").innerHTML = disp(secs);
   if(secs <= 0) {
      alert("Sorry. Time is up. Press OK to continue.");
      getGeo();
   } else {
      timerHandle = setTimeout("redo()",1000);
   }
}
```

Listing 6.6 contains the initialization code and the Google maps support functions. First, function init_app initializes the countries array (containing country names, capitals, code, and coordinates) and Google maps. Function parsecoord converts coordinate values from degrees and minutes to a decimal-format degree value. Southern latitudes and western longitudes are converted to negative values. The conversion to geocodes is necessary to add markers for the capital city location using the Google maps interface. For more details on these Google maps functions, see the Zillow mashup widget shown in Listing 4.12 on page 97.

Listing 6.6 Home (JavaScript)—Capital Punishment Part 2

```
Event.observe(window, 'load', function() {
   init_app();
   });

function init_app() {
   countries = init_country_data();
   init_map(parsecoord(InitLat), parsecoord(InitLng),2);
   $("profilebox").style.display = "none";
   $('poweredBy').onclick = function(){ window.open('http://www.zembly.com');
}
   checkChallenges();
   reset_score();
```

```
}
function init_map(lat, lng, zoomlevel) {
   if (GBrowserIsCompatible()) {
      map = new GMap2(document.getElementById("map_canvas"));
      map.addControl(new GSmallMapControl());
      map.setCenter(new GLatLng(lat, lng), zoomlevel);
   }
}

function add_marker(lat, lng, htmlstr) {
   var point = new GLatLng(lat, lng);
   var marker = new GMarker(point);
   GEvent.addListener(marker, "click", function() {
      marker.openInfoWindowHtml(htmlstr);
   });

   map.addOverlay(marker);
   // open window by default
   marker.openInfoWindowHtml(htmlstr);
}

function parsecoord(geo) {
   // convert coordinates which are deg.min to deg (decimal)
   var n = new String(geo.substring(0,geo.length-1));
   n = Number(n);
   var c = geo.charAt(geo.length-1);
   var m = (n-Math.floor(n)) * 100;
   n = Math.floor(n) + (m * (1/60));
   if (c == 'S' || c == 'W') {
      var nn = n * (-1);
      n = nn + "";
   }
   return n;
}
```

Listing 6.7 includes the code that sets up the radio button event handler, getGeo. Function getGeo contains the main code for processing user input for the quiz. First, it stops the timer. Users who have not added the application are allowed three questions before they are asked to login to Capital Punishment.

zembly Tip

See "Application Context and Permissions" on page 134 for details about the Application object and "Controlling the Allow Access Process" on page 136 for information on Facebook's application login process.

Function `processAnswer` returns true if the answer is correct or false if incorrect. Function `init_map` centers the map on the capital city in question and `add_marker` adds a marker to the map with the country's name, its capital, and the latitude and longitude of the capital city. After each question, `getGeo` displays the current score and quiz progress number. After `QuizTotal` (20) questions, the quiz is complete and `getGeo` calls function `quizend` (shown in Listing 6.9 on page 179).

When users are ready for the next question, they click button "Okay, I'm ready." Function `getNextQuestion` builds each question by choosing a target country randomly (avoiding duplicates) and filling the `choicesArray` with the correct answer and four incorrect answers. It updates the HTML markup with the newly generated choices, resets the radio buttons, and restarts the timer.

Listing 6.7 Home (JavaScript)—Capital Punishment Part 3

```
// set up the event handlers for the radio buttons
Event.observe($("r0"), "change", getGeo);
Event.observe($("r1"), "change", getGeo);
Event.observe($("r2"), "change", getGeo);
Event.observe($("r3"), "change", getGeo);
Event.observe($("r4"), "change", getGeo);
Event.observe($("nextQ"), 'click', getNextQuestion);

function getGeo() {
   stopTimer();
   // user can go through 3 questions before being asked to
   // log in to the application
   if (Application.fbUserID == null && myscore.total >= 3) {
      if (confirm("Trial quiz complete. " +
         " \n\nClick 'OK' to log in to the application.")) {
         top.location.href="http://www.facebook.com/login.php?api_key="
            + Application.fb_sig_api_key +
            "&v=1.0&next=Home&canvas=1";
      }
      else {
         startover();
         return;
      }
   }

   // update question counter, see if response is correct & update score
   myscore.total++;
   var feedback = "";
   if (processAnswer()) {
      feedback = "<b>Correct!!</b>";
      myscore.score++;
   } else {
      feedback = "<b>Sorry . . .</b> ";
   }
```

```javascript
    // map it on the Google maps and put a marker at the capital city
    init_map(parsecoord(countrydata.latitude),
        parsecoord(countrydata.longitude),3);
    add_marker(parsecoord(countrydata.latitude),
        parsecoord(countrydata.longitude),
        feedback + "<br/>The capital of " + countrydata.name + " is<br/><b> " +
        countrydata.capital + "</b><br/>(" +
        countrydata.latitude + "," +
        countrydata.longitude + ")");

    // display the running score
    displayScore();
    if (myscore.total >= QuizTotal) quizend();
    $("nextQ").disabled = false;// Enable get next question button
}

function processAnswer() {
    var s = countrydata.capital;
    var answer = -1;
    // find which radio button was checked
    for (var i = 0; i < document.myform.capital.length; i++) {
        if (document.myform.capital[i].checked) {
            answer = i;
            break;
        }
    }
    if (answer >= 0) {
        // save country codes & names for correct answer and return true
        if (countries[choicesArray[answer]].capital == s) {
            //get code and save countryname
            mycountries.codestring += countrydata.code;
            if (mycountries.namestring.length > 0)
                mycountries.namestring += ", ";
            mycountries.namestring += countrydata.name;
            return true;
        }
    }
    return false;
}

function displayScore() {
    $("scoreDiv").innerHTML = "Your score is "
        + myscore.score + " out of "
        + myscore.total + ". Questions remaining: "
        + (QuizTotal - myscore.total) + "";
}

// user is ready for a new question
function getNextQuestion() {
    $("nextQ").disabled = true;// Don't allow a new question now
    choicesArray = new Array();
    var i;
```

```javascript
      // randomly choose a new country, but make sure we haven't already
      // asked the same question in this quiz
      while(1) {
         i = Math.floor((Math.random() * countries.length));
         var duplicate = false;
         for (var n = 0; n < usedcountries.length; n++) {
            if (usedcountries[n] == i) {
               duplicate = true;
               break;
            }
         }
         if (duplicate) continue;
         break;
      }
      // put the current country question into the used countries
      // and as one of the choices
      usedcountries.push(i);
      choicesArray.push(i);
      // remember the correct answer
      countrydata = countries[i];
      // find 4 more selections for wrong answers
      for (i = 0; i < 4; i++)
         fillchoices();
      // sort the choices by the index number of the country
      choicesArray.sort();
      $("questionDiv").innerHTML = "What is the capital of <b>"
         + countrydata.name + "</b>?";
      // uncheck all of the radio buttons and fill in the labels with the choices
      for (i = 0; i < document.myform.capital.length; i++) {
         document.myform.capital[i].checked = false;
         $("radio"+i).innerHTML = countries[choicesArray[i]].capital;
      }
      startTimer();
   }

   function fillchoices() {
      var i;
      while(1) {
         // randomly select wrong answers
         // make sure there's no duplicates
         i = Math.floor((Math.random() * countries.length));
         var duplicate = false;
         for (var n = 0; n < choicesArray.length; n++) {
            if (choicesArray[n] == i) {
               duplicate = true;
               break;
            }
         }
         if (duplicate) continue;
         // make sure that none of the wrong answers were already correct
         // answers earlier
         for (var nn = 0; nn < usedcountries.length; nn++) {
```

```
            if (usedcountries[nn] == i) {
                duplicate = true;
                break;
            }
        }
        if (duplicate) continue;
        break;
    }
    choicesArray.push(i);
}
```

Listing 6.8 sets up event handlers for the buttons. The `doChallenge` function lets you send challenge invitations to friends. It invokes SendInvitation, a separate widget that is part of the Capital Punishment application (see "Sending Challenge Invitations" on page 186.) During widget initialization, function `checkChallenges` checks the query parameters (`Parameters.ids`), and if set, generates a news feed story for each user who was challenged.

Facebook Tip

Facebook API method `publishUserAction` returns false if users haven't granted permission to publish stories to their Walls. Here, we let users know so they can grant permission through the Applications Edit settings on Facebook.

Function doRankings invokes SeeScores, also a separate widget. Widget SeeScores uses the Facebook Data Store API, which is discussed in Section 6.2 (see "Using the Facebook Data Store and FQL" on page 191).

Function `startclean` calls `startover`, which resets the score-keeping variables and starts a new quiz. The Start Over button (`id="startOver"`) invokes function `startclean`.

Function `addAddToProfileButton` injects an Add to Profile button in the markup using the Facebook JavaScript client library and integrates Facebook's dialogs that let the user approve adding the profile box.

Listing 6.8 Home (JavaScript)—Capital Punishment Part 4

```
// set up the button event handlers
Event.observe($("seeScores"), 'click', doRankings);
Event.observe($("challengeButton"), 'click', doChallenge);
Event.observe($("startOver"), 'click', startclean);

// go to widget SendInvitation to issue challenges
function doChallenge() {
    stopTimer();
```

Capital Punishment—A Challenging Facebook Application 177

```
   // Do our own checking of valid login so we can control next
   // URL with next query parameter
   if (Application.fbUserID == null) {
      top.location.href = "http://www.facebook.com/login.php?api_key="
         + Application.fb_sig_api_key + "&v=1.0&next=SendInvitation&canvas=1";
   }
   else {
      top.location.href =
         "http://apps.facebook.com/capitalpunish/SendInvitation";
   }
}

// Widget SendInvitation sends parameter ids via widget GetIds
// (user ids of those challenged)
// Publish a news story for challenges sent
function checkChallenges() {
   if (Parameters.ids == null) return;

   Things.callService("ganderson.CapitalPunishment.PublishChallenge",
      {
         friends: Parameters.ids
      },
      {
         onSuccess: function(data) {
            // Facebook returns false if user has not granted
            // permission to publish
            if (!data[0])
               alert("We attempted to publish your challenge,"
               + " but Facebook requires your permission. "
               + "From the Applications menu on Facebook, "
               + "click Edit and enable Wall permissions for publishing."
               + " This will allow future challenges to be published.");
         },
         onFailure: function(error) {
         }
      });
}

// go to widget SeeScores to look at user and friends' scores
function doRankings() {
   stopTimer();
   top.location.href="http://apps.facebook.com/capitalpunish/SeeScores";
}

function startclean() {
   stopTimer();
   if (confirm(
      "Click OK to Start a new quiz. Cancel will Stop/Reset current quiz.")) {
      startover();
   }
   else {
   // wipe out score and don't restart timer
```

```
      myscore.score = 0;
      myscore.total = 0;
      mycountries.codestring = "";
      mycountries.namestring = "";
      usedcountries = new Array();
      displayScore();
      return;
   }
}

function startover() {
   init_map(parsecoord(InitLat),
   parsecoord(InitLng),2);
   reset_score();
}

function reset_score() {
   myscore.score = 0;
   myscore.total = 0;
   mycountries.codestring = "";
   mycountries.namestring = "";
   usedcountries = new Array();
   displayScore();
   // display the time, but don't start it yet
   $("timer").innerHTML = disp(TIME_LIMIT - 1);
   // show add-to-profile button if user hasn't added profile box yet
   if (Application.fbUserID != null) addAddToProfileButton();
   $("nextQ").disabled = false;      // Let user start the quiz when ready
}

////////////////
// add to profile button
////////////////
function addAddToProfileButton(){
   FB_RequireFeatures(["Integration"], function(){
      FB.Facebook.init(Application.fb_sig_api_key,
         "./Home/resources/xd_receiver.html", null);
      FB.Integration.showAddSectionButton("profile", $("addToProfileButton"));
   });
}
```

Listing 6.9 consists of functions quizend, saveScore, doprofile, and publishScore. Function doprofile updates the application's profile box and creates a color-coded world map showing the countries whose capitals you correctly named. It generates different markup for the main profile box and the larger box that appears under the Boxes tab (Figure 6.3 shows both profile boxes for Capital Punishment). It also generates the map on the widget's canvas page and calls service UpdateProfileBox to update the profile. Function publishScore publishes your quiz results by invoking service PublishScore. (The user is alerted if permission has not been granted to publish the score.) We discuss these services in the next sections.

Lastly, function `quizend` provides the housekeeping details required when you complete a quiz, including saving your score, updating your profile, and publishing a story. Function `saveScore` calls service SaveScore to store your score (the data store mechanism is discussed in "Using the Facebook Data Store and FQL" on page 191).

"Main" profile box   "Boxes Tab" profile box

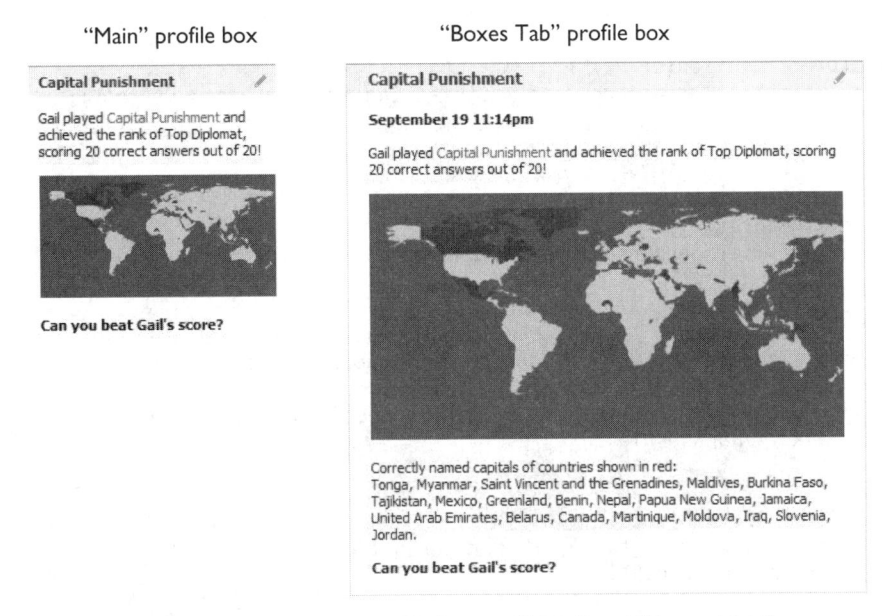

Figure 6.3 Capital Punishment profile boxes: "Main" and "Boxes Tab"

Listing 6.9 Home (JavaScript)—Capital Punishment Part 5

```
function quizend() {
   if (myscore.score >= 20) rank = "Top Diplomat";
   else if (myscore.score >= 15) rank = "Senior Diplomat";
   else if (myscore.score >= 10) rank = "Career Diplomat";
   else if (myscore.score >= 5) rank = "Junior Diplomat";
   else rank = "Lackey";
   // save score to application data store
   saveScore();
   alert("Congratulations! \n\nYou have completed the Quiz\n"
      + "and your score has been saved. "
      + "\n\nYour score is " + myscore.score + " out of " + myscore.total
      + ".\n\nYou have achieved the rank of " + rank + ".");
   // generate a news feed story
   publishScore();
}

function saveScore() {
   // save user's score to data store
```

```
    Things.callService("ganderson.CapitalPunishment.SaveScore",
    {
       score: myscore.score // user's capital punishment score
    },
    {
       onSuccess: function(data) {
       },
       onFailure: function(error) {
          Log.write("An error occurred while saving score to data store.");
       }
    });
}

function publishScore() {
    Things.callService("ganderson.CapitalPunishment.PublishScore",
    {
       score: myscore.score, // the score earned by the user
       total: myscore.total, // possible total number correct
       // A comma-separated list of correct answer country names.
       countries: mycountries.namestring,
       codes: mycountries.codestring, // Country codes to produce map
       rank: rank // Rank achieved by user
    },
    {
       onSuccess: function(data) {
          // Facebook returns false if user has not granted
          // permission to publish
          if (!data[0])
             alert("We attempted to publish your score ("
             + myscore.score + "), but Facebook requires your permission. "
             + "From the Applications menu on Facebook, "
             + "click Edit and enable Wall permissions for publishing."
             + " This will allow future quiz scores to be published.");
          // generate profile box
          doprofile();
       },
       onFailure: function(error) {
          Log.write("Error: " + error.code + " : " + error.message);
       }
    });
}

function doprofile() {
    // FBML to appear on profile
    var nameinfo = "<fb:name uid='" + Application.fbUserID
       + "' firstnameonly='true' useyou='false' />";
    var fbtext = " played <a
       href='http://www.facebook.com/apps/application.php?id=12659122390'>"
       + "Capital Punishment</a> and achieved the rank of "
       + rank + ", scoring "
       + myscore.score + " correct answers out of "
       + myscore.total + "! <br/><br/>";
```

```
var maptextb =
   "<a href=\"http://www.world66.com/myworld66/visitedCountries\">" +
"<img width=\"385px\" "
src=\"http://www.world66.com/myworld66/visitedCountries/worldmap?visited="
+ mycountries.codestring +
"\"></a><br/><br/>Correctly named capitals of countries shown in red:<br/>"
+ mycountries.namestring + ".<br/><br/>";
var maptext_main =
"<a href=\"http://www.world66.com/myworld66/visitedCountries\">" +
"<img width='190px' " +
"src='http://www.world66.com/myworld66/visitedCountries/worldmap?visited="
+ mycountries.codestring + "'></a><br/><br/>";

var name2info = "<b>Can you beat "
   + "<fb:name uid='" + Application.fbUserID +
   "' firstnameonly='true' useyou='false' possessive='true' /> score?</b>";

// display on canvas page too
$("profilebox").innerHTML = "I" + fbtext + maptextb;
$("profilebox").style.display = "block";

Things.callService("ganderson.CapitalPunishment.UpdateProfileBox",
{
   text: nameinfo + fbtext + maptextb + name2info,
   text_main: nameinfo + fbtext + maptext_main + name2info
},
{
   onSuccess: function(data) {
      Log.write("Your profile has been updated.");
      startover();
   },
   onFailure: function(error) {
      Log.write("Error: " + error.code + " : " + error.message);
   }
});
}
```

Service UpdateProfileBox

By default, zembly creates a service called UpdateProfileBox within your application. For Capital Punishment, the Home widget provides markup for both parameters profile and profile_main. Make sure both parameters have the Escape value *unchecked*. The FBML must arrive at the service untouched (it cannot contain HTML escape characters). Parameter session_key is optional and service UpdateProfileBox uses the application context to determine the value when it is not provided by the caller. (Only widget iPhoneHome provides parameter session_key since iPhoneHome runs outside the normal application context. See "iCapitalPunishment Widget" on page 331 for details.) Listing 6.10 shows the source for service UpdateProfileBox.

Listing 6.10 Service UpdateProfileBox (JavaScript)—Capital Punishment

```
var fbSessionKey = Parameters.session_key;
if (fbSessionKey == null) fbSessionKey = Application.fbSessionKey;
var d = new Date().getTime();
var now = new Number(d/1000).toFixed();
var heading = "<b><fb:time t='" + now
    + "'/></b><br/><br/>";
var text_main = Parameters.text_main;
if (text_main == null) text_main = "";

return Things.facebook.profile.setFBML({
    // uid: 0
    // markup: heading + Parameters.text, // Deprecated parameter
    // profile_action: "" // The FBML intended for the user's profile actions.
    session_key: fbSessionKey,
    profile_main: text_main, // The FBML intended for the left-hand profile col-
umn
    // mobile_profile: "" // The FBML intended for mobile devices.
    profile: heading + Parameters.text // The FBML intended for Boxes tab
});
```

Function `doprofile` (Listing 6.9 on page 179) generates the FBML markup and calls this service.

Publishing Feed Stories

One of the most effective ways to introduce new users to your application is to publish stories about how people use it. Capital Punishment publishes two stories: one when a user earns a new score (completes a quiz) and the other when a user challenges one or more friends. Before you can publish a story, however, you must register a *template bundle* for your application with Facebook. The template bundle consists of three story types: one line, short, and full. In addition, the one line and short story types can specify multiple versions, where the first version has the most data and any subsequent versions are more general. Facebook encourages this multi-level story template so that Facebook can aggregate stories over multiple users when possible.

Template Bundles

Facebook provides two interfaces to register template bundles. One is to submit a template bundle for registration through the API. This gives you the most flexibility and lets you edit a template bundle by editing service source code. The service returns your template bundle ID, which you use when publishing to the template. You can also use the Registered Template Bundles Console, although you can only specify one level for each story type and you cannot edit previously submitted template bundles.

All templates include token {*actor*}, which Facebook replaces with the user id of the person using your application. Templates may also include {*target*}, which is replaced by the Facebook user id(s) of the target of the story (such as, the receiver of gifts, challenges, or invitations).

Listing 6.11 contains the template bundle for the story in which the user completes the quiz and earns a new score. The one line story is a JSON-encoded array of template strings. The first template contains the most data (tokens {*actor*}, {*countries*}, {*score*}, {*total*}, and {*rank*}) and the second one is more general (only tokens {*actor*}, {*score*}, and {*total*} are defined).

The short story is a JSON-encoded array of template objects consisting of a template title (property `template_title`) and template body (property `template_body`). Like the one line story, the first template has more detail and the second one is more general.

Finally, the full story template is not an array, but a JSON object with both a template title and body. In the Capital Punishment example, the full story displays a small version of the color-coded map that appears in the profile box, as shown in Figure 6.4.

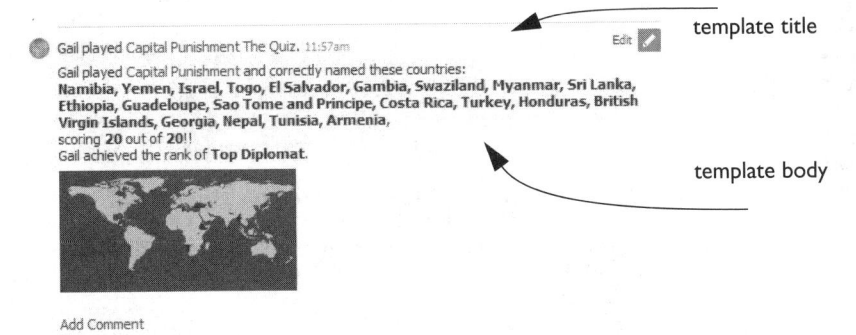

Figure 6.4 Capital Punishment's full story appearing on the user's profile

Users choose which story size they want displayed on their profile and Facebook chooses the story size and specificity level for the News Feed (depending on aggregation possibilities). After you register a template bundle, you can publish stories against it. You can also register a new template bundle if you need to make changes (you'll get a new template bundle ID). You can always retrieve your registered template bundle ID from the Registered Template Bundles Console.

Facebook Tip

The only HTML and FBML tags Facebook supports for one line story templates are `<br />`, `<a>`, `<small>`, `<fb:name>`, `<fb:pronoun>`, *and* `<fb:if-multiple-actors>`. *Facebook eliminates any other tags (and enclosed data) from the markup.*

Listing 6.11 Service RegisterTemplates (JavaScript)—Capital Punishment

```javascript
// Bundle 1: User earns a new score
var onelinestory = [
   "{*actor*} played <a href='http://apps.facebook.com/capitalpunish/Home'>
   Capital Punishment</a> and correctly named these countries:
   {*countries*}, scoring {*score*} out of {*total*}!!
   {*actor*} achieved the rank of {*rank*}.",

   "{*actor*} played <a href='http://apps.facebook.com/capitalpunish/Home'>
   Capital Punishment</a> and scored {*score*} out of {*total*}!!"
];

var shortstory = [
   // version 1, most detail
   {"template_title":
   "{*actor*} played <a href='http://apps.facebook.com/capitalpunish/Home'>
   Capital Punishment The Quiz</a>.",

   "template_body":
   "{*actor*} played <a href='http://apps.facebook.com/capitalpunish/Home'>
   Capital Punishment</a> and correctly named these countries:
   <b>{*countries*}</b>, scoring <b>{*score*}</b> out of <b>{*total*}</b>!!"
   + " <br/>{*actor*} achieved the rank of <b>{*rank*}</b>."},

   // version 2, more general
   {"template_title":
   "{*actor*} played <a href='http://apps.facebook.com/capitalpunish/Home'>
   Capital Punishment The Quiz</a>.",

   "template_body":
   "{*actor*} played <a href='http://apps.facebook.com/capitalpunish/Home'>
   Capital Punishment</a> and scored <b>{*score*}</b> out of
   <b>{*total*}</b>!!"
   + " <br/>{*actor*} achieved the rank of <b>{*rank*}</b>."},

   // version 3, most general
   {"template_title":
   "{*actor*} played <a href='http://apps.facebook.com/capitalpunish/Home'>
   Capital Punishment The Quiz</a>.",
   "template_body":
   "{*actor*} played <a href='http://apps.facebook.com/capitalpunish/Home'>
   Capital Punishment</a> and achieved the rank of <b>{*rank*}</b>!!"}
];
```

```
var fullstory =
  {"template_title":
  "{*actor*} played <a href='http://apps.facebook.com/capitalpunish/Home'>
  Capital Punishment The Quiz</a>.",

  "template_body":
  "{*actor*} played <a href='http://apps.facebook.com/capitalpunish/Home'>
  Capital Punishment</a> "
  + "and correctly named these countries:<br/> <b>{*countries*}</b>,
  <br/> scoring <b>{*score*}</b> out of <b>{*total*}</b>!!"
  + "<br/>{*actor*} achieved the rank of <b>{*rank*}</b>."
  + "<p/><a href='http://www.world66.com/myworld66/visitedCountries'>" +
  "<img width='190px' src='http://www.world66.com/myworld66/visitedCountries/
  worldmap?visited={*codes*}'>
  </a>"
};

// save template_id to use with publishUserAction API call
var template_id = Things.facebook.feed.registerTemplateBundle({
  short_story_templates: shortstory.toJSON(), // A JSON-encoded array
  one_line_story_templates: onelinestory.toJSON(), // A JSON-encoded array
  full_story_template: fullstory // // A JSON-encoded string
});
// template bundle id returned: 30393407390
return template_id;
```

Facebook displays registered template bundles for your application with the Registered Templates Console. You can find the Registered Templates Console with the other code testing tools at http://developers.facebook.com/tools.php. Figure 6.5 shows the Capital Punishment template bundle using the Facebook Registered Templates Console for a user earning a new score. The template bundle ID is circled below.

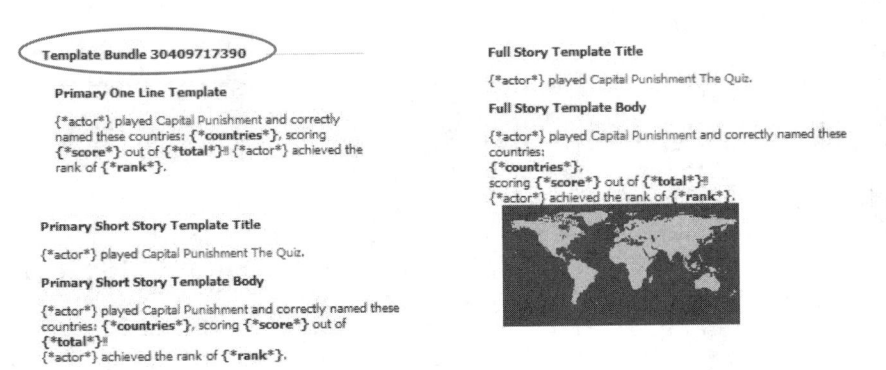

Figure 6.5 Using the Registered Templates Console for Capital Punishment

Using the New Publisher

Service PublishScore calls Facebook API method `feed.publishUserAction` to publish a user's new score.

Listing 6.12 shows the JavaScript for service PublishScore. Parameter `session_key` is optional (only iPhoneHome supplies it; normally the session key is available from the application context, `Application.fbSessionKey`). API method `feed.publishUserAction` requires `template_data` (a JSON object consisting of the template bundle's tokens as property names and the corresponding data as property values) and the template bundle ID. Parameter `target_ids` is required when the template bundle includes token `{*target*}` (not used with this template bundle).

This service is called from function `publishScore` (see Listing 6.9 on page 179).

Listing 6.12 Service PublishScore (JavaScript)—Capital Punishment

```
var fbSessionKey = Parameters.session_key;
if (fbSessionKey == null) fbSessionKey = Application.fbSessionKey;

var token_data = [{"countries": Parameters.countries,
   "codes": Parameters.codes,
   "score": Parameters.score,
   "total": Parameters.total,
   "rank": Parameters.rank
}];
return Things.facebook.feed.publishUserAction({
   template_data: token_data, // A JSON-encoded associative array of the values

   template_bundle_id: 33614232390,// ID of a registered template bundle.
   // body_general: "" // Additional markup extending body of short story.
   // target_ids: "" // A comma-delimited list of IDs of friends of the actor
   session_key: fbSessionKey
});
```

Sending Challenge Invitations

One big advantage of FBML widgets (over HTML) is that you have access to Facebook high-level `<fb>` tags. To build a widget that lets you send invitations to selected friends is ridiculously easy with FBML. Let's look at how to do this with widget Send-Invitation.

Widget SendInvitation

In the Capital Punishment application page on zembly, select widget SendInvitation. Listing 6.13 shows the widget's FBML source and Figure 6.6 shows how it is rendered on the page. (Note that there's no CSS or FBJS defined for this widget—just FBML!)

Tag `fb:dashboard` lets you specify links to other widgets in your application. Here, you see three links. The `fb:help` link renders on the right side of the dashboard and takes you to a help widget. Link `fb:action` takes you back to the Capital Punishment Home widget. A second `fb:action` link invokes the SeeScores widget (see "Widget See-Scores" on page 205).

Tag `fb:request-form` lets users select friends and send them a request. Attribute `action` is the URL loaded after users submit the request form. Here, the attribute `action` specifies Home. Widget Home checks for parameter `ids`, Facebook user ids of those who were challenged (see function `checkChallenges` in Listing 6.8 on page 176 for the code that actually publishes the challenge story). If the user does not select any friends to challenge, control is still passed to widget Home. Attribute `content` holds the request's text. When attribute `invite` is set to `true`, the request is an invitation. Attribute `type` specifies a name for your invitation so that friends can identify it. Note that Facebook always includes a Skip button to avoid forced (spam) invitations to friends.

Tag `req-choice` includes a `label` attribute (its text shows up on the button that the invited friend will click to accept the invitation). Tag `fb:multi-friend-selector` builds a full-page friend selector widget. The `actiontext` attribute tells the user what sort of invitation it will send.

The `fb:request-form` tag lets you add a personalized message and lets you preview exactly what your invited friends will see.

Listing 6.13 Widget SendInvitation (FBML)—Capital Punishment

```
<fb:dashboard>
    <fb:help href="http://apps.facebook.com/capitalpunish/Help">Help</fb:help>
    <fb:action href="http://apps.facebook.com/capitalpunish/Home">
        Back to Capital Punishment Page</fb:action>
    <fb:action href="http://apps.facebook.com/capitalpunish/SeeScores">
        Score Rankings</fb:action>
</fb:dashboard>

<fb:request-form action="./Home" method="POST" invite="true"
    type="Capital Punishment"
    content="How well do you know the World's Capitals?
    Take the Capital Punishment Quiz and see (it's fun)."
    <fb:req-choice
        url='http://apps.facebook.com/capitalpunish/Home'
```

```
        label='Take the Capital Punishment Quiz' />"
    <fb:multi-friend-selector showborder="true"
    actiontext="Challenge (invite) your friends to play Capital Punishment." />
</fb:request-form>
```

Figure 6.6 shows the widget rendered on a page. If you have many friends, Facebook provides paging. Furthermore, the multi-friend-selector widget provides a friend finder. That is, you start typing your friend's name and all matching friends immediately become selectable. If you select the Skip button, Facebook takes you to the URL specified in the request-form `action` attribute.

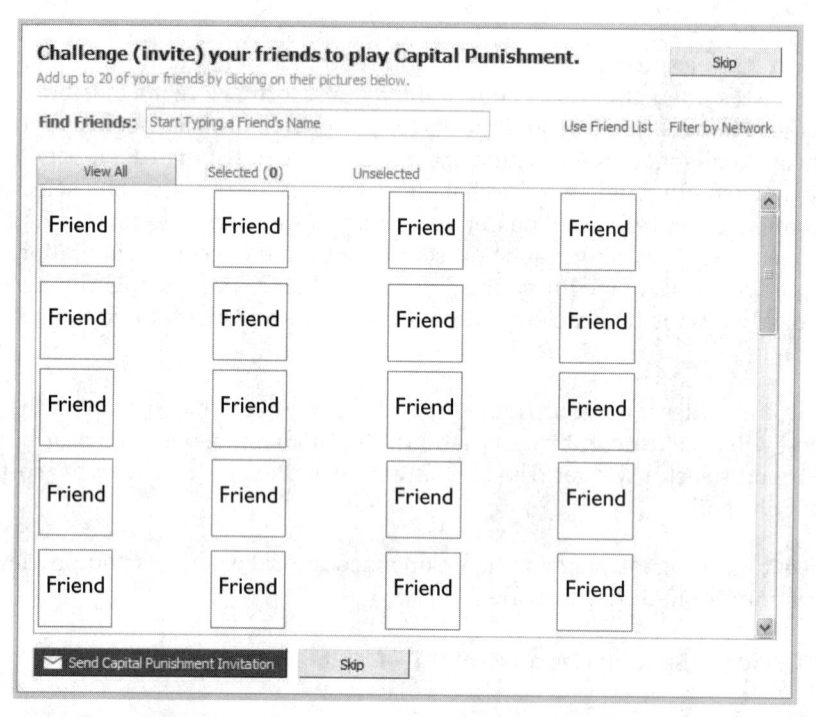

Figure 6.6 Facebook's request form and multi-friend selector (friend names omitted and images blocked)

Once you select one or more friends and click Send Capital Punishment Invitation, the request widget pops up a personalization and confirmation dialog as shown in Figure 6.7.

You can personalize any invitation. As you type text for your invitation, Facebook displays it in the invitation preview area so that you see what your friends will see when they receive the invitation. Each invitation includes your profile picture, the content specified in the request-form tag, and any personalized text.

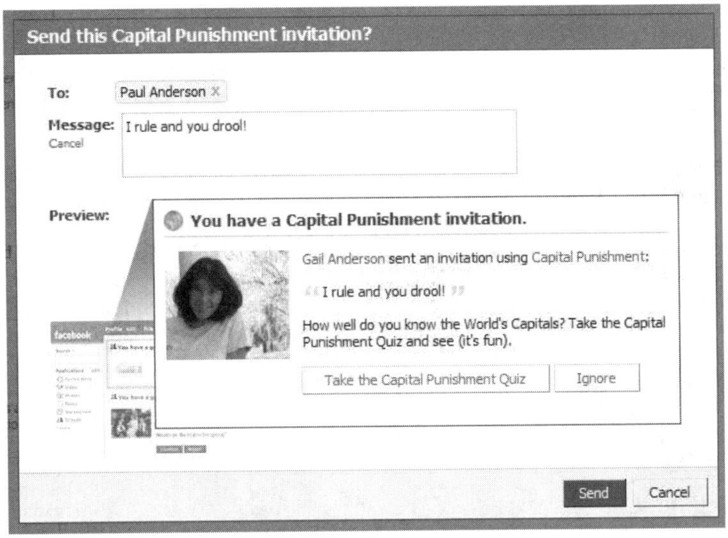

Figure 6.7 Request form and request choice pop up confirmation window

Registered Template Bundle for PublishChallenge

The template bundle for publishing a story on a Capital Punishment challenge takes tokens {*actor*} (the challenger) and {*target*} (one or more invitees). Since no other data is specified, no other tokens are required and no template data is necessary for this template bundle. Listing 6.14 shows the JavaScript code for registering this template bundle.

Listing 6.14 Service RegisterTemplates (JavaScript)—Capital Punishment

```
// Bundle 2: User issues a challenge
var onelinestory = [
    "{*actor*} challenged {*target*} to play <a href='http://www.facebook.com/
    apps/application.php?id=12659122390'>Capital Punishment</a>." ];

var shortstory = [
   {"template_title":
    "{*actor*} issued a <a href='http://apps.facebook.com/capitalpunish/Home'>
    Capital Punishment</a> challenge.",

    "template_body":
    "{*actor*} challenged {*target*} to play <a href='http://www.facebook.com/
    apps/application.php?id=12659122390'>Capital Punishment</a>."}
];
```

```
var fullstory =
  {"template_title":
  "{*actor*} issued a <a href='http://apps.facebook.com/capitalpunish/Home'>
  Capital Punishment</a> challenge.",

  "template_body":
  "{*actor*} challenged {*target*} to play <a href='http://www.facebook.com/
  apps/application.php?id=12659122390'>Capital Punishment</a>."};

var template_id = Things.facebook.feed.registerTemplateBundle({
  short_story_templates: shortstory.toJSON(), // A JSON-encoded array
  one_line_story_templates: onelinestory.toJSON(), // A JSON-encoded array
  full_story_template: fullstory // A string of a JSON-encoded dictionary
});
// template bundle id returned: 30421277390
return template_id;
```

Service PublishChallenge

When a challenge invitation goes out, the Home widget is invoked with the user ids of the friends who have been challenged. Function `checkChallenges` (see Listing 6.9 on page 179) then calls service PublishChallenge to issue a story. Listing 6.15 shows the JavaScript source for service PublishChallenge.

Service PublishChallenge has one parameter (`friends`) of type JSON.

Facebook API method `feed.publishUserAction` requires a template bundle ID of a previously registered template bundle (see Listing 6.14) and `target_ids`, a comma-delimited list of Facebook user ids of friends who were challenged. The call does not require `template_data` since the only tokens used by the template bundle are {*actor*} and {*target*}. With token {*target*}, you must include parameter `target_ids`.

Listing 6.15 Service PublishChallenge (JavaScript)—Capital Punishment

```
if (Parameters.friends != null) {
  return Things.facebook.feed.publishUserAction({
    // template_data: "", // A JSON-encoded associative array
    template_bundle_id: 30421277390, // The template bundle ID
    // body_general: "" // markup to extends the body of a short story.
    target_ids: Parameters.friends.toString() // Comma-delimited list of IDs
  });
}
```

Application FriendChooser

What if you don't want to use Facebook FBML to provide an invitation feature for your application? You can always build your own invitation with standard HTML, CSS, and JavaScript. You can bundle this feature in the Home widget with other code that supports the actions of the application. Alternatively, you can build a separate widget as we have shown with widget SendInvitation. Building separate widgets helps modularize your application, keeping friend challenge code apart from your application's other functions.

To show how to build a widget to challenge friends using HTML and JavaScript, we have created a separate application that consists only of this widget, application FriendChooser. You can view its source on **zembly** (use **zembly**'s Search mechanism).

6.2 Using the Facebook Data Store and FQL

Part of making a Facebook application "social" is providing links between you and your friends. You can do this by publishing news stories, updating profiles, and sending invitations and notifications to your friends. But, perhaps the best way to keep an active connection with friends is to see their activities with a particular application. For example, suppose you'd like to compare your Capital Punishment scores with your friends' scores. In order to provide this highlight, you must store Capital Punishment scores. Fortunately, Facebook provides a Data Store API and an FQL (Facebook query language) API call to query your application's data. Figure 6.8 shows the Capital Punishment widget SeeScores running on Facebook.

As the screen shot shows, the application stores users' scores, the time the score was saved, and the Facebook uid (which allows you to access Facebook user data such as the profile picture and user name).

Before we show you the code to implement widget SeeScores, let's look at the Facebook Data Store API. You'll see how to define the data store for the Capital Punishment application and how data is saved. You'll also see the low-level services this widget uses to query the data and return FBML to the calling widget. Finally, you'll see the FBML, CSS, and FBJS code from the SeeScores widget.

Let's begin with an overview of the Facebook Data Store facility.

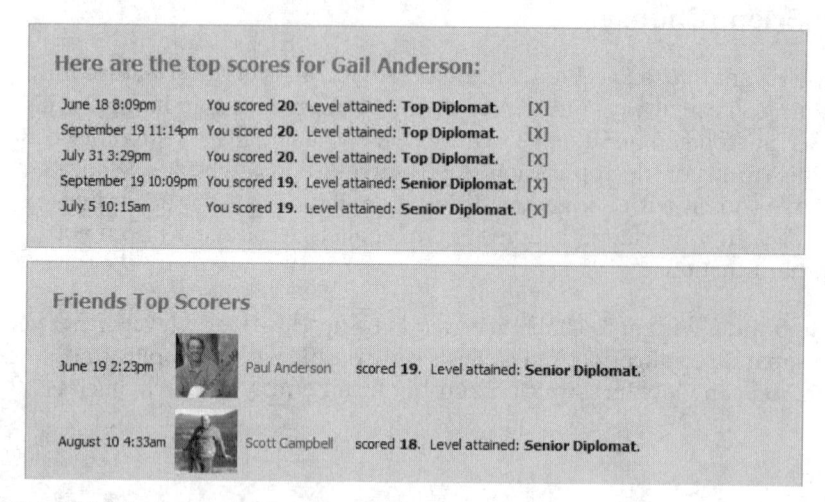

Figure 6.8 SeeScores widget running on Facebook

Facebook Data Store Model

The Facebook Data Store API uses an object model for its database. This is different than the traditional table-based model used by most databases, but it is straightforward to correlate the object model to the relational database model.

Each application is given its own Data Store "space." This means you can't access data across applications. You can, of course, access the Facebook-wide user database and build queries with criteria for both your application data store and the global Facebook user database.

The Facebook Data Store API supports Object Types and Properties, Objects, and Associations. Object Types represent tables, Object Type Properties represent table columns, Objects represent rows in tables, and Associations represent foreign keys. The Data Store API returns a unique object id (object property _id) when you create an object; this represents the object's primary key. However, Associations are the only way to retrieve your data with a query.

Facebook Tip

You can, of course, query the data store with the object property _id directly, but typically the only way you know this value is to store it in an association. That is precisely why you need associations.

The combination of Object Types (and their properties) and Associations defines your database schemata. You can define Object Types, Properties, Objects, and Associations programmatically using the Data Store API or manually using the Data Store Admin tool. Both have advantages, but the best approach is to use a combination of the two.

Data Model for Capital Punishment

Capital Punishment stores the score, time, and user id (uid) in an object. First, you define a ranking object type. Next, you give the object type three properties: score, time, and uid. Once you have an object type, you can create objects of that type. Each object has a unique object id (property _id). You can always access an object using its object id. However, unless you store these object ids somewhere, this isn't practical. What you need is a way to search objects with a query (such as looking for objects with a particular uid value). For this, you need an association. Associations create links between properties (such as user ids) and objects; they are required to search your data.

Figure 6.9 shows the object type (ranking), object type properties (uid, time, score), and association (user_to_score) defined for Capital Punishment.

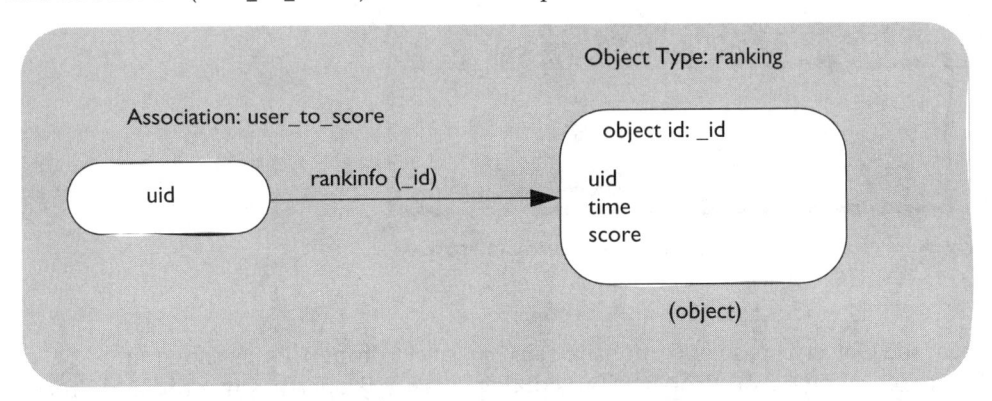

Figure 6.9 Association user_to_score links user ids to ranking object types

Let's examine the Data Store Admin tool first.

Facebook Data Store Admin Tool

Within the Developer application, Facebook provides a Data Store Admin tool. This tool lets you define your database schemata and submit queries against it (once you have data stored). From the Developer application on Facebook, select your application (Capital Punishment) and then select **DataStoreAdmin** as shown in Figure 6.10.

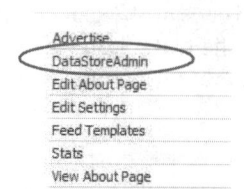

Figure 6.10 Accessing the DataStoreAdmin tool for you application

From the Object Types page, select **Create Object Type** and specify name **ranking** in the Add Object Type dialog, as shown in Figure 6.11. You can now specify Object Type Properties.

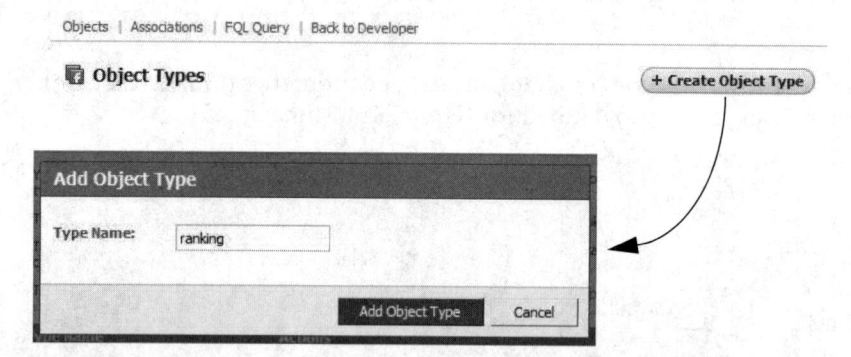

Figure 6.11 Adding an object type to your data store

From the Object Types page opposite ranking, select **Properties**, as shown in Figure 6.12. In the Add Property Type dialog, specify Property Name **uid** and Property Type **String**. Click the Add Object Type button.

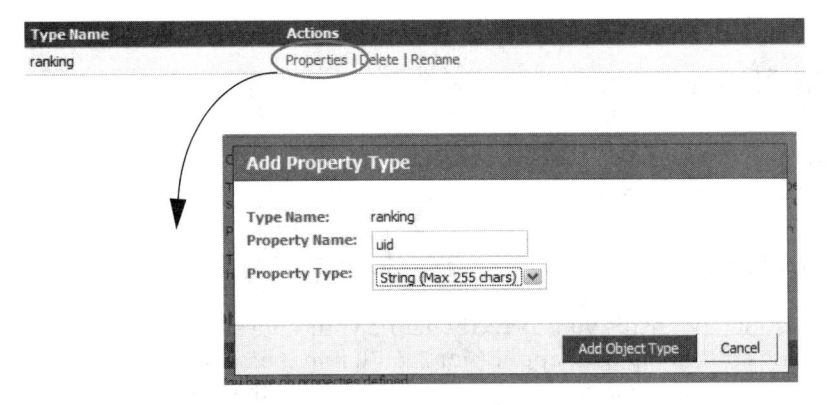

Figure 6.12 Adding property types to your data store object

Repeat this step and add property types score (integer) and time (string). Figure 6.13 shows object type ranking with its three property types added.

Figure 6.13 Object type ranking has three properties: uid, score, and time

After defining an Object Type and its Object Type Properties, you can now define an Association. The Data Store API provides three associations types: one way, two-way symmetrical, and two-way asymmetrical. One-way associations are applicable when a reverse lookup is not necessary (such as this Capital Punishment association where we find ranking objects from user ids). Two-way symmetrical associations (such as Facebook friends) allow lookups in either direction and the association has the same meaning in both directions (friendship). Finally, two-way asymmetrical associations provide two-way lookup, but the meaning is different depending on the direction. A parent-child association illustrates a two-way asymmetrical association, where the association name is "parent" in one direction and "child" in the reverse direction.

You specify an alias for each end of an association. In one-way associations, provide Object 2 Info (the Object Type that the forward lookup returns). In two-way associations, provide both Object 1 Info (the Object Type that the reverse lookup returns) and Object 2 Info. Figure 6.14 shows the user_to_score association with aliases "uid" and "rankinfo" and Object 2 Info set to "ranking." Association alias `rankinfo` is the object id of object type `ranking`.

Name	Association	Object 1 Info	Object 2 Info	Actions
user_to_score	uid ---> rankinfo		ranking	Delete | Rename

Figure 6.14 Defining an association for uid and ranking

Service CreateDataStore

The Data Store Admin Tool helps you correctly define your data store schema. However, when building and testing your application, you'll find it useful to re-create your data store programmatically. You do this by building a service that creates object types, object type properties, and associations. You can then run the service (using the **Test drive now** button in the zembly call window for that service).

> **zembly Tip**
>
> *Note that if you call this service after you've already created your data store, you'll need to write calls that remove these object types, associations, and properties (as shown below). These "undo" methods will fail if you haven't defined the data store schemata yet.*

Listing 6.16 shows the JavaScript code for service CreateDataStore. First, it calls the Facebook data store adapters `dropObjectType` and `undefineAssociation` (which also removes all data associated with these types) so that the create services will succeed.

Adapter `createObjectType` creates object type `ranking`. Next, `defineObjectProperty` is called three times to define properties `uid`, `score`, and `time`. Service `defineAssociation` sets up a one way association (`user_to_score`) between a user id (`uid`) and a ranking object (alias `rankinfo`).

Finally, two adapter calls (`getObjectTypes` and `getAssociationDefinitions`) return the data store definitions you set up. These are diagnostic calls you can use to check the structure of your data store.

Listing 6.16 Service CreateDataStore (JavaScript)—Capital Punishment

```
/////////////////////////////////
// Note: Comment out all dropObjectType() and undefineAssociation() calls
// if you haven't defined any objects or associations yet.
/////////////////////////////////

Things.facebook.data.dropObjectType({
    session_key: Application.fbSessionKey,
```

```javascript
    obj_type: "ranking", // Name of the object type to delete.
    keys: Application.keychain
});

Things.facebook.data.undefineAssociation({
    name: "user_to_score", // Name of the association to remove.
    session_key: Application.fbSessionKey,
    keys: Application.keychain
});

Things.facebook.data.createObjectType({
    name: "ranking", //Name of this new object type.
    session_key: Application.fbSessionKey,
    keys: Application.keychain
});

Things.facebook.data.defineObjectProperty({
    prop_type: 2, // Type of the new property:
    // * 1 for integer
    // * 2 for string (max. 255 characters)
    // * 3 for text blob (max. 64kb)
    prop_name: "uid", //Name of the new property to add.
    session_key: Application.fbSessionKey,
    obj_type: "ranking", // Object type to add a new property to.
    keys: Application.keychain
});

Things.facebook.data.defineObjectProperty({
    prop_type: 2, // Type of the new property:
    // * 1 for integer
    // * 2 for string (max. 255 characters)
    // * 3 for text blob (max. 64kb)
    prop_name: "time", //Name of the new property to add.
    session_key: Application.fbSessionKey,
    obj_type: "ranking", // Object type to add a new property to.
    keys: Application.keychain
});

Things.facebook.data.defineObjectProperty({
    prop_type: 1, // Type of the new property:
    // * 1 for integer
    // * 2 for string (max. 255 characters)
    // * 3 for text blob (max. 64kb)
    prop_name: "score", //Name of the new property to add.
    session_key: Application.fbSessionKey,
    obj_type: "ranking", // Object type to add a new property to.
    keys: Application.keychain
});

Things.facebook.data.defineAssociation({
    //inverse: "", // Name of backward association, if two-way asymmetrical.
    name: "user_to_score", //Name of forward association to create.
```

```
      assoc_info2: { "alias": "rankinfo",
         "object_type": "ranking", unique: false},
      assoc_info1: { "alias": "uid", "object_type": "", },
      assoc_type: 1,
      session_key: Application.fbSessionKey,
      keys: Application.keychain
});

// testing adapter calls to get back the ObjectTypes or AssociationDefinitions
// (call one or the other)

return Things.facebook.data.getObjectTypes({
   session_key: Application.fbSessionKey,
   keys: Application.keychain
});

/*
return Things.facebook.data.getAssociationDefinitions({
   session_key: Application.fbSessionKey,
   keys: Application.keychain
});
*/
```

Service SaveScore

Once you've defined your data store, storing actual data is straightforward. First, create an object with the property values (the data you want to store) and then set an association. Use the return value from the createObject call as the obj_id2 parameter in the setAssociation call. (Two-way associations have another return value from a second createObject call that you pass as the obj_id1 parameter in the setAssociation call.)

Listing 6.17 shows the source code for service SaveScore. The userid comes from the application context (the logged-in user), the score comes from the caller as Parameters.score, and the time is generated from a call to new Date().getTime(). These values are stored in the properties argument as a JSON object property value pairs, as shown below. Argument obj_type is "ranking".

Adapter setAssociation requires a name ("user_to_score"), obj_id2 (the createObject return value), and obj_id1 (the user id in question). The Home widget calls service SaveScore when the user completes a quiz (see function saveScore in Listing 6.9 on page 179).

Listing 6.17 Service SaveScore (JavaScript)—Capital Punishment

```javascript
// set up variables
// only iPhoneHome provides Parameters.fb_userid and Parameters.session_key
var userid = Parameters.fb_userid;
if (userid == null) userid = Application.fbUserID;
var fbSessionKey = Parameters.session_key;
if (fbSessionKey == null) fbSessionKey = Application.fbSessionKey;
var score = Parameters.score;
var d = new Date().getTime();
var now = new Number(d/1000).toFixed();

// create the object
var id = Things.facebook.data.createObject({
   properties: {"uid": userid, "score": score, "time" : now},
   session_key: fbSessionKey, // Use Application.fbSessionKey
   obj_type: "ranking" // Specifies which type of new object to create.
});

// set the association, use the object id returned from createObject
Things.facebook.data.setAssociation({
   //assoc_time: 0, // Default to association creation time.
   name: "user_to_score", // Name of the association to set.
   // data: "", // An arbitrary data (max. 255 characters)
   obj_id2: id, // Object identifier 2.
   session_key: fbSessionKey,
   obj_id1: userid // Object identifier 1.
});
return id;
```

Using FQL with DataStoreAdmin

Once you start collecting data, the Facebook Query Language (FQL) can retrieve data for you. FQL is similar to SQL, but it has some restrictions. For example, you cannot construct a query without a WHERE clause. The following query returns a parser error (WHERE clause is required).

```
// Error
SELECT uid, time, score FROM app.ranking
```

The Data Store Admin tool will help you experiment with valid queries. In Capital Punishment, the association user_to_score is defined so that you can access the application's ranking objects through a user id (uid). For example, in the first use case, you want to see all of the logged-in user's scores (or perhaps just the top five scores). Here is the query.

```
select _id, time, score  from app.ranking where _id in (select rankinfo from
   app.user_to_score where uid = 1234) order by score desc limit 5
```

This query effectively says, grab all objects from object type `ranking` that the association `user_to_score` points to where the uid is 1234. From this object provide properties (fields) `_id`, `time`, and `score`. Sort the results by score (descending) and return at most five objects. (Property `_id`, which is the stored object id, is included in the results so that we can easily delete this object from the data store.)

zembly Tip

Supply your own user id for testing. In the live application context, the user id of the logged-in user is accessible through Application.fbUserID.

If you type the query into the query window on the Data Store Admin tool FQL page, you'll see the results displayed. Figure 6.15 shows an example.

no.	_id	time	score
1	5002249968540	1213844971	20
2	5002260104143	1221891282	20
3	5002256878634	1217543343	20
4	5002259963225	1221887349	19
5	5002254082886	1215278141	19

Figure 6.15 Results from running FQL query

The second use case for the SeeScores widget is retrieving the top scores of the logged-in user's friends. This query is a bit more complicated, but we'll break it up into clauses. The first step is to get the logged-in user's friends. Use the Data Store Admin tool FQL page to build the correct query. Here's the query to get a user's friends sorted by name:

```
SELECT uid, name FROM user WHERE  uid IN
(SELECT uid2 FROM friend WHERE uid1 = 1234) order by name
```

This query returns all user ids from the Facebook `user` data store in which the logged-in user (`uid1`) is friends with (`uid2`). Note that this example requires the Facebook `user` table since `name` is not a member of the `friend` table. If all you need are friend uids, however, you can simplify the query as follows.

```
SELECT uid2 FROM friend WHERE uid1 = 1234
```

Once you have the list of friend uids, you can build a query similar to the first use case. The only difference is the target uids come from the friends list instead of the single logged-in user. Here is the complete query.

```
SELECT time, score, uid FROM app.ranking WHERE _id IN
(SELECT rankinfo FROM app.user_to_score WHERE uid IN
```

```
    (SELECT uid2 FROM friend WHERE uid1 = 1234)) ORDER BY score DESC LIMIT 25
```

Let's examine the services that implement these two use cases, as well as the service that deletes a user's score.

Services FBMLGetMyScores and FBMLGetFriendScores

Service FBMLGetMyScores queries the data store for the user's top five scores and generates FBML. The returned FBML is processed by the Facebook servers so that the caller (widget SeeScores) can inject it into the FBML markup dynamically.

Service FBMLGetMyScores gets the _id, time and score properties of the top five ranking objects for the logged-in user. The logged-in user is Application.fbUserID and the service calls the Facebook adapter fql.query.

Array myScores holds the data returned from the fql.query call. The service generates FBML to format the score, time, and rank attained. The FBML includes markup that lets users delete any of their own scores. Listing 6.18 shows the JavaScript for service FBMLGetMyScores.

Listing 6.18 Service FBMLGetMyScores (JavaScript)—Capital Punishment

```
function getRank(score) {
   var rank = "Lackey";
   if (score >= 20) rank = "Top Diplomat";
   else if (score >= 15) rank = "Senior Diplomat";
   else if (score >= 10) rank = "Career Diplomat";
   else if (score >= 5) rank = "Junior Diplomat";
   return rank;
}

var fbmlstring = "";

// variables to call fql.query
var userid = Application.fbUserID;
var query = "SELECT _id, time, score FROM app.ranking "
   + "WHERE _id IN (SELECT rankinfo FROM app.user_to_score WHERE uid = "
   + userid + ") ORDER BY score DESC LIMIT 5";

// Get the data
var myScores = Things.facebook.fql.query({
   query: query // The query to perform, as described in the FQL documentation.
});

// Generate FBML
// include markup to call a function to delete an object

// Any scores yet?
if (myScores.length == null) {
```

```
        fbmlstring = "You don't have any scores stored yet.<br/>" +
            "Once you complete a Capital Punishment Quiz, " +
            "<br/>your score will be stored automatically.";
        return (fbmlstring);
    }

    // use some of the facebook CSS classes and build a <table>
    // function deleteScore is in widget SeeScores
    fbmlstring = "<div class='mytitle'>Here are the top scores for "
        + "<fb:name uid='" + userid
        + "' useyou='false' linked='false' />:</div>"
        + "<table class='editorkit' border='0' cellspacing='5px'>";

    for (var i = 0; i < myScores.length; i++) {
        fbmlstring += "<tr><td class='editorkit_row'>"
        + "<fb:time t='" + myScores[i].time + "'/></td>"
        + "<td class='editorkit_row'>You scored <b>"
        + myScores[i].score
        + "</b>.</td><td class='editorkit_row'>Level attained: <b>"
        + getRank(myScores[i].score) + "</b>.</td>"
        + "<td class='editorkit_row'>"
        + "<a href='#' onclick='deleteScore("
        + myScores[i]._id
        + "); return false;'><b>[X]</b></a></td></tr>";
    }
    fbmlstring += "</table>";
    return fbmlstring;
```

Note that the return from the `fql.query` API call is an array of JSON objects consisting of property value pairs. Listing 6.19 shows sample output.

Listing 6.19 Sample Output from fql.query (JSON)

```
[
    {
      "time": "1217102290",
      "_id": 5002256011072,
      "score": 20
    },
    {
      "time": "1217196433",
      "_id": 5002256320737,
      "score": 20
    }
]
```

Service FBMLGetFriendScores also uses the logged-in user's id to build the query and call the Facebook adapter `fql.query` to obtain friend scores. It then generates FBML to return to the caller. Here, we've added processing to remove multiple scores for the same user (leaving the top score only). This service generates the user's picture, name, score, time (or date) and rank of each friend.

Listing 6.20 shows the JavaScript for service FBMLGetFriendScores.

Listing 6.20 Service FBMLGetFriendScores (JavaScript)—Capital Punishment

```javascript
function getRank(score) {
   var rank = "Lackey";
   if (score >= 20) rank = "Top Diplomat";
   else if (score >= 15) rank = "Senior Diplomat";
   else if (score >= 10) rank = "Career Diplomat";
   else if (score >= 5) rank = "Junior Diplomat";
   return rank;
}

function isduplicate(uid) {
   for (var i = 0; i < uidsArray.length; i++) {
      if (uid == uidsArray[i]) return true;
   }
   return false;
}

// variables to build the fbml string
var uidsArray;
var fbmlstring = "";

// set up query
var userid = Application.fbUserID;
var query = "SELECT time, score, uid FROM app.ranking WHERE _id IN " +
   "(SELECT rankinfo FROM app.user_to_score WHERE uid IN " +
   "(SELECT uid2 FROM friend WHERE uid1 = " +
   userid + ")) ORDER BY score DESC LIMIT 50";

var scores = Things.facebook.fql.query({
   query: query // The query to perform, as described in the FQL documentation.
});

// build the fbml string
if (scores.length == null) {
   fbmlstring = "No friends have saved any scores yet.<br/>" +
   "<a href='http://apps.facebook.com/capitalpunish/SendInvitation' " +
   "target='_top'>" +
   "Challenge them to play Capital Punishment</a> and complete a quiz.";
   return (fbmlstring);
}

// build a table and use Facebook CSS class editorkit and editorkit_row
uidsArray = new Array();
fbmlstring = "<div class='mytitle'>Friends Top Scorers</div>" +
   "<table class='editorkit' border='0' cellspacing='5px' >";
```

```
for (var i = 0; i < scores.length; i++) {

    // only display one score per friend
    if (isduplicate(scores[i].uid)) continue;
    else uidsArray.push(scores[i].uid);

    fbmlstring += "<tr><td class='editorkit_row'>"
      + "<fb:time t='" + scores[i].time
      + "' /></td>"
      + "<td class='editorkit_row'>"
      + "<fb:profile-pic uid='" + scores[i].uid
      + "' size='square' linked='true' /></td>"
      + "<td class='editorkit_row'><fb:name uid='"
      + scores[i].uid
      + "' capitalize='true' /></td>"
      + "<td class='editorkit_row'> scored <b>"
      + scores[i].score
      + "</b>.</td><td class='editorkit_row'> Level attained: <b>"
      + getRank(scores[i].score) + "</b>.</td></tr>";
}
fbmlstring += "</table>";
return fbmlstring;
```

Listing 6.21 shows sample output from the fql.query adapter call in service FBML-GetFriendScores.

Listing 6.21 Sample Output from fql.query (JSON)

```
[
  {
    "uid": "12345",
    "time": "1213910590",
    "score": 19
  },
  {
    "uid": "54321",
    "time": "1213917805",
    "score": 15
  }
]
```

Service DeleteScore

Finally, Listing 6.22 shows the code to delete an object from the Capital Punishment data store. This service requires the unique object id of the target object, parameter obj_id. First, the association between the target object and the user id must be removed. Only then can you delete the actual object.

Listing 6.22 Service DeleteScore (JavaScript)—Capital Punishment

```
var userid = Application.fbUserID;
Things.facebook.data.removeAssociation({
   name: "user_to_score", // Name of the association.
   obj_id2: Parameters.obj_id, // Object identifier 2.
   obj_id1: userid // Object identifier 1.
});
return Things.facebook.data.deleteObject({
   obj_id: Parameters.obj_id // Numeric identifier (fbid) of the object to
delete.
});
```

Widget SeeScores

This FBML widget provides scores for logged-in users and their friends. Setting up the data store and writing the services to store, retrieve, delete, and format the data are the challenging parts. With all the hard work already finished, Widget SeeScores is relatively straightforward.

Recall that you cannot display dynamic FBML directly from your widget. You must get the generated FBML from a service call so that the Facebook servers can process it (see "Creating Dynamic Content with FBML" on page 142 for an explanation of this technique). Therefore, the services that read the data return FBML instead of JSON data to the caller.

Listing 6.23 shows the FBML source for widget SeeScores. It defines a dashboard so the user can either return to the main Capital Punishment widget, challenge friends (especially after seeing what the competition is up to), or go to the Help page.

The remaining FBML consist of placeholders to display the generated markup.

Listing 6.23 Widget SeeScores (FBML)—Capital Punishment

```
<fb:dashboard>
   <fb:help href="./Help">Help</fb:help>
   <fb:action href="./Home">Back to Capital Punishment Page</fb:action>
   <fb:action href="./SendInvitation">Challenge Friends</fb:action>
</fb:dashboard>

<div class="fbresults">
   <span id="results"></span>
</div>
<div class="fbresults">
   <span id="friends"></span>
</div>
```

Listing 6.24 includes the CSS for widget SeeScores. CSS class `fbresults` formats the `<div>` tags that hold the results from the queries.

Listing 6.24 Widget SeeScores (CSS)—Capital Punishment

```
.inputElements {
   border: 1px solid #BDC7D8;
   font-family: "lucida grande,tahoma,verdana,arial,sans-serif";
   font-size: 11px;
   padding: 3px;
}
.fbresults {
   padding: 20px;
   margin: 10px;
   background-color: #D2D9E6;
   border: 1px solid #ababab;
}
.mytitle {
   font-size: 150%; font-weight: bold; color: #787878;
   padding-bottom: 10px;
}
```

Listing 6.25 contains the FBJS code that displays the logged-in user's scores (function `displayMyScores`) and the user's friends' scores (function `displayFriendScores`). Note that both functions call services that generate FBML and include the Facebook option `responseType: Ajax.FBML` with the call. Results are displayed using FBML method `setInnerFBML`. Furthermore, the service calls also include `requireLogin: true`. This option tells Facebook to display pop up dialog Allow Access if the user has not yet logged into the application. (From the Capital Punishment Home widget, you can immediately select the See Scores button without ever completing a quiz and logging in to the application.) This is a light-weight method for ensuring a user has logged in.

> **Facebook Tip**
>
> *The Home widget uses Facebook utility* `login.php` *to redirect users to a separate page for the login process. Here, you can use option* `requireLogin: true` *within FBML widgets making service calls that need login permission. This method provides a simple pop up dialog without redirecting users to a separate page. See "Controlling the Allow Access Process" on page 136 for options on letting users login to your applications.*

Function `deleteScore` calls service DeleteScore to remove an object from the data store. Recall that service FBMLGetMyScores generates a link with the `onclick` event handler to invoke function `deleteScore` with the selected object id.

Listing 6.25 Widget SeeScores (FBJS)—Capital Punishment

```
function displayMyScores() {
   Things.callService("ganderson.CapitalPunishment.FBMLGetMyScores",
   {
   },
   {
      onSuccess: function(data) {
         document.getElementById('results').setInnerFBML(data);
      },
      onFailure: function(error) {
         Log.write("Error: " + error.code + " : " + error.message);
      },
      responseType: Ajax.FBML,
      // pop up Allow Access dialog if user not yet logged into application
      requireLogin: true
   });
}

function displayFriendScores() {
   Things.callService("ganderson.CapitalPunishment.FBMLGetFriendScores",
   {
   },
   {
      onSuccess: function(data) {
         document.getElementById('friends').setInnerFBML(data);
      },
      onFailure: function(error) {
         Log.write("Error: " + error.code + " : " + error.message);
      },
      responseType: Ajax.FBML,
      // pop up Allow Access dialog if user not yet logged into application
      requireLogin: true
   });
}

function deleteScore(obj_id) {
   var dialog = new Dialog().showChoice(
      'Are you sure you want to delete this score?',
      'This cannot be undone.', 'Delete', 'Cancel');
   dialog.onconfirm = function() {
      Things.callService("ganderson.CapitalPunishment.DeleteScore",
      {
         obj_id: obj_id // Numeric identifier (fbid) of the object to delete.
      },
      {
         onSuccess: function(data) {
            Log.write(data);
            // refresh display after the delete is finished
            displayMyScores();
         },
         onFailure: function(error) {
```

```
            Log.write("Error: " + error.code + " : " + error.message);
        },
        requireLogin: true
    });

    };
}

displayMyScores();
displayFriendScores();
```

6.3 Mood Pix—Leveraging Facebook Integration

The Facebook Mood Pix application is conceptually a simple application that lets you choose a mood image and display it in your profile box. It also lets you send a mood "pix" to a friend with a personal "thinking of you" message. But Mood Pix is much more than this. You'll see that Mood Pix actually leverages the latest Facebook integration points—all of them. Here's a summary of the Facebook features you'll see with Mood Pix.

- Publishing with feed forms
- Providing Add to Profile and Add to Info buttons
- Reading users' profile and info section data
- Adding data to users' Info section from the application
- Providing direct editing of users' Info section
- Providing an Application Tab
- Providing a profile publisher
- Using FBML tag `fb:friend-selector` to select a friend
- Publishing with `publisherUserAction` API method

Before we launch into how Mood Pix hooks into these Facebook features, we give you a high-level overview of the application.

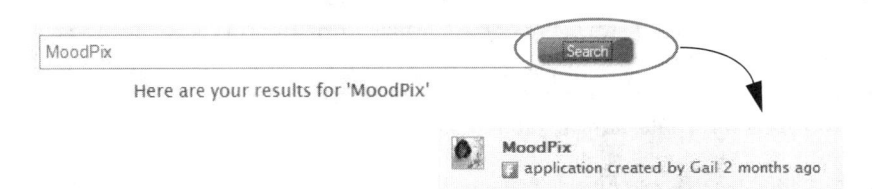

Figure 6.16 Finding the Mood Pix application on zembly

Go To Application

First, run the Mood Pix application on Facebook. Begin by searching for Mood Pix on zembly and bring up the application page as shown in Figure 6.16.

Click **View about page** on zembly, which takes you to the Mood Pix About page on Facebook. Click **Go to Application** to run Mood Pix, as shown in Figure 6.17.

Figure 6.17 Running the Mood Pix application on Facebook

About Mood Pix

Figure 6.18 shows the Mood Pix Home widget running on Facebook. You select moods by either selecting a photo or the associated mood name. You can also provide an optional description (why are you feeling this?). The selection process ends when you click button **Update Mood Pix Profile**.

Facebook Tip

Note that you are not required to "login" to Mood Pix before using the application. However, as soon as you click the Update Mood Pix Profile button, a pop up dialog asks you to Allow Access. This provides a light-weight method for logging into applications, as described in "Controlling the Allow Access Process" on page 136.

Mood Pix also lets you designate any mood as your current "favorite," which posts this information under the Info tab on your profile.

When you select a mood and update your profile or make a selected mood your favorite, Mood Pix publishes a feed story. Whereas Capital Punishment uses Facebook API method `publisherUserAction`, the Mood Pix Home widget publishes its stories with feed forms. Feed forms let users approve a story for publication interactively. You still need to register feed template bundles to use feed forms.

Mood Pix has a dashboard (see Figure 6.18) with widgets to send a Mood Pix message to a friend and examine a Mood Pix message box (showing both messages sent and received). Mood Pix uses the Facebook Data Store API to record and retrieve these messages.

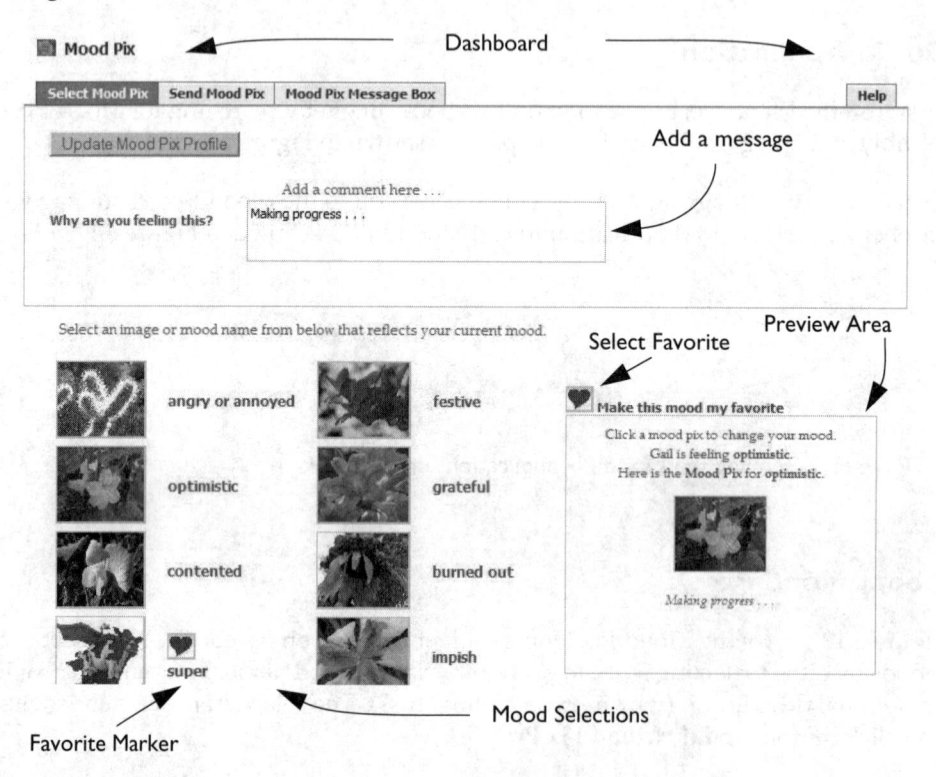

Figure 6.18 Mood Pix Home widget running on Facebook

Go ahead and select a mood pix, optionally provide text, and click **Update Mood Pix Profile**. Mood Pix pops up a preview that lets you see the profile box content (see Figure 6.19). Select either **Update Profile** (create content for your profile box) or **Edit** (make changes).

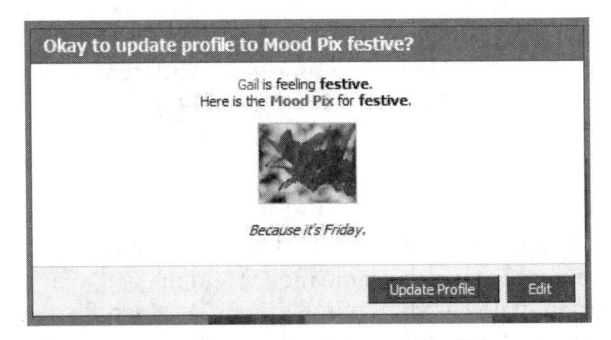

Figure 6.19 Mood Pix pop up confirmation dialog

Feed Forms

If you elect to update your profile, Mood Pix displays button **Publish Mood Story**. A pop up dialog (feed form) then prompts you before publishing a story (see Figure 6.20). The feed form shows you the story contents and lets you select among one line, short, or full versions. (If you check **Save my answer for Mood Pix**, you will no longer be asked to confirm story publications.) Note that the feed form also lets you add a comment to the story.

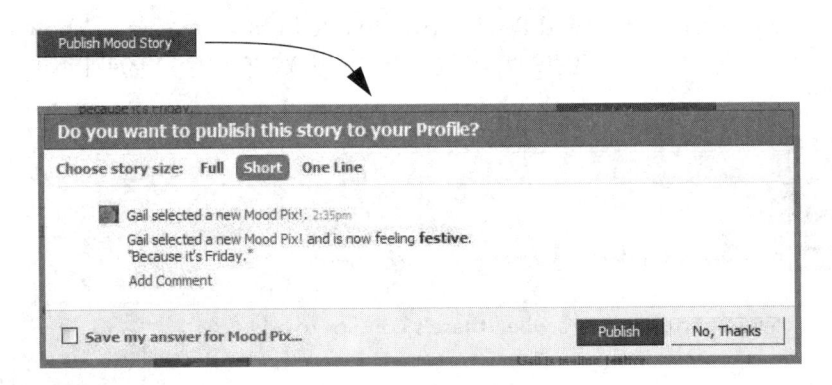

Figure 6.20 Facebook feed form for Mood Pix

Click **Publish**; then navigate to your Facebook profile page and the newly published story will appear.

Now return to Mood Pix. You'll see the Add to Profile button that Facebook generates when the application created profile box content. Follow the steps described for application BuddyPics to add the Mood Pix content to your profile (see "Adding Content to Your Profile" on page 141 and Figure 5.40 and Figure 5.42 on page 141).

Application Info Section

When you select a favorite mood, Mood Pix displays content in your profile Info section. Return to Mood Pix, select a mood (or use the same mood) and make it a favorite. Mood Pix pops up a confirmation dialog as shown in Figure 6.21. Mood Pix uses feed forms again to publish a story about specifying a favorite mood.

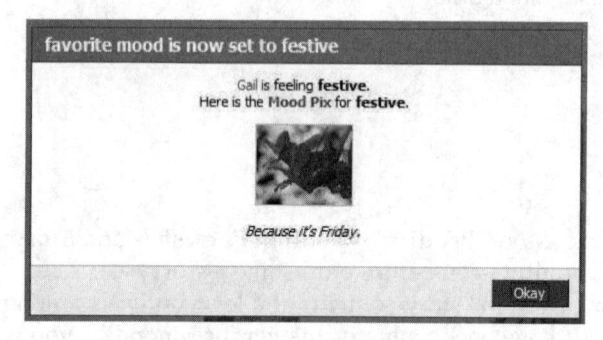

Figure 6.21 Selecting a favorite mood

Now the next time you return to Mood Pix, the Add to Info button appears, as shown in Figure 6.22. This lets you know there is content to add to your Mood Pix application Info section.

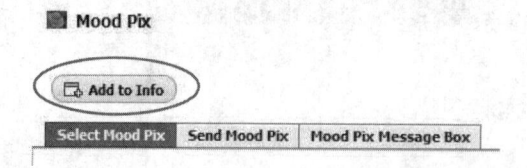

Figure 6.22 Add to Info button appears when there's content to add

If you select **Add to Info**, Mood Pix pops up a confirmation dialog with the Info section content (see Figure 6.23).

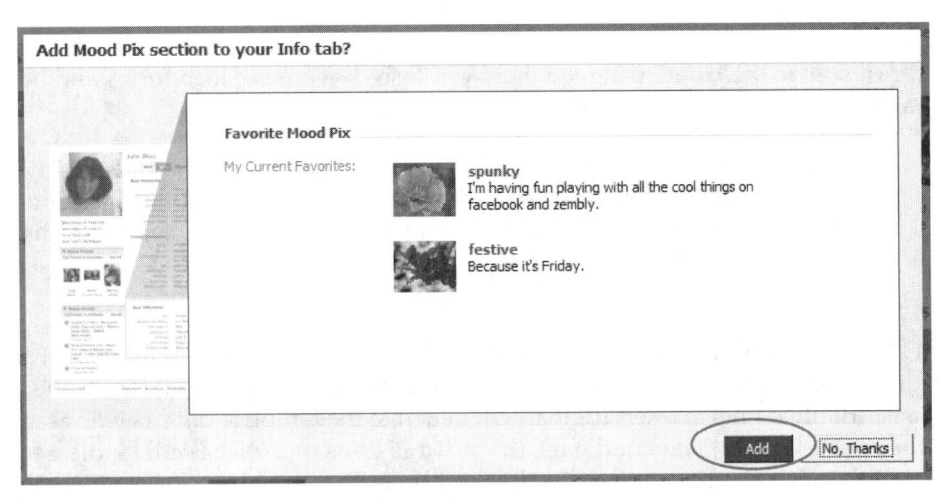

Figure 6.23 Facebook lets you confirm Info section content

After selecting **Add**, return to your profile, select tab **Info**, and you'll see the content added under application Mood Pix.

Mood Pix also lets you add content directly to the Info section. Figure 6.24 shows sample content that you can add to the Mood Pix Info section.

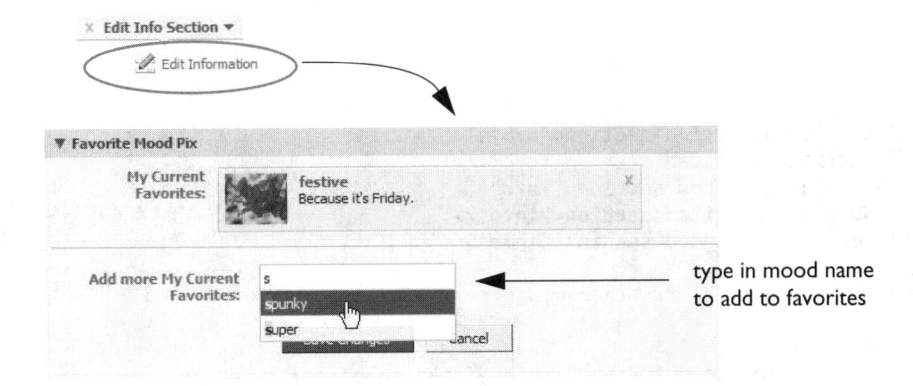

Figure 6.24 Select Edit Information to add content to Favorite Mood Pix section

Widget Home

Let's turn now to the Home widget, where you'll see how to use feed forms and how to manipulate the application-specific Info section on your profile.

Listing 6.26 shows the FBML code for the Mood Pix Home widget. (Some repetitive code is omitted.) First, the Home widget includes FBML tags to conditionally render the Add to Profile and Add to Info buttons. You've already seen how Facebook displays these buttons after the application generates content for the profile or info section.

Next, look at the FBML code that supports feed forms (labeled with comments). Facebook feed forms require a form tag with special attribute `fbtype="feedstory"`. The `action` attribute points to a service that will generate the template data as well as supply the registered template bundle ID. (In Mood Pix this is service FeedHandlerService, but the `action` attribute specifies the corresponding zembly callback URL.) The form element provides data to the feed handler using hidden elements. We discuss service FeedHandlerService in Listing 6.28 on page 219. Note that the enclosing div (`feedDiv`) does not become visible until after the user selects a mood.

The profile box preview div will change as the user selects new moods. This content comes from service calls that generate FBML.

Listing 6.26 Home (FBML)—Mood Pix

```
<fb:dashboard />

<!-- Add to Profile and Add to Info buttons-->

<fb:if-section-not-added section="profile">
    <fb:add-section-button section="profile"/>
</fb:if-section-not-added section="profile">
<fb:if-section-not-added section="info">
    <fb:add-section-button section="info"/>
</fb:if-section-not-added section="info">

<!-- Mood Pix tab/links to other widgets -->

<fb:tabs>
<fb:tab-item title="Select Mood Pix" href="#" selected="true" />
<fb:tab-item title="Send Mood Pix" href="./SendMoodPix" selected="false" />
<fb:tab-item title="Mood Pix Message Box" href="./SeeMessages" selected="false" />
<fb:tab-item title="Help" href="./Help" selected="false" align="right" />
</fb:tabs>

<!-- Update Profile and Add comment box -->
```

```html
<div class="requestDiv">
   <form id="myForm" onsubmit="return doUpdate(this);">
   <input class="button" value="Update Mood Pix Profile" type="submit"/>
   </form>

   <table class="editorkit" border="0" cellspacing="0" style="width:720px">
   <tr class="width_setter"><th style="width:170px"></th>
   <td></td>
   <td></td></tr>
   <tr><th class="detached_label"><label>Why are you feeling this?</label></th>
   <td class="editorkit_row">
   <span class="notes">
   Add a comment here . . .
   </span>
   <br/>
   <textarea id="messagenote" style="width:300px"
   onchange="saveMessage(); return false;"></textarea></td>
   <td>

<!-- FBML to support feed forms -->

   <div id="feedDiv" style="display: none">
   <form fbtype="feedStory"
   action="http://zembly.com/things/d43d457812324ad094d794f369187e48;exec?">
   <input class="button" value="Publish" label="Publish Mood Story"
      type="submit"/>
   <input type="hidden" id="moodname" name="moodname" value="" />
   <input type="hidden" id="picurl" name="picurl" value="" />
   <input type="hidden" id="storytype" name="storytype" value="" />
   <input type="hidden" id="moodmessage" name="moodmessage" value="" />
   </form>
   </div>

   </td>
   </tr>
   </table>
</div>

<div id="main_body">
   <div class="notes">
   Select an image or mood name from below that reflects your current mood.
   </div>
   <table><tr><td>

<!-- mood is angry or annoyed -->

   <div class="moodbox">
         . . .
   </div>
   </td><td>

<!-- mood is festive -->
```

```
    <div class="moodbox">
        . . .
    </div>
    </td>

<!-- put the profile box preview in the 3rd column -->

    <td rowspan="4">
    <span id="ajaxmoodmsg">
    <a href="#" onclick="setFavorite(); return false;">
    <img src="${res('heart.jpg')}" style="width: 21px; height: 19px;"/>
    </a></span>
    <label><a href="#" onclick="setFavorite(); return false;">
    Make this mood my favorite</a>
    </label>
    <div id="displaymood">
    Click a mood pix to change your mood.
    <div id="ajaxmoodbox">
    </div>
    </div>
    </td>

    </tr><tr><td>

<!-- other moods omitted -->

    </td></tr></table>
</div>
```

Listing 6.27 shows a partial listing of the FBJS functions found in the Home widget.

Function init checks to see if the user has logged into the application (Application.fb_sig_added is "1") so that it can set the user id (fbUserID) correctly. Service GetProfileInfo gets both the user's profile and info data for Mood Pix and initializes the canvas with this information (if there is data).

Function doUpdate is the event handler for the **Update Mood Pix Profile** button. This handler reads the text area element and sets the hidden elements in the Facebook feed story form tag. Service AjaxFBML returns its text argument so Facebook servers can process the FBML prior to rendering. If the user confirms updating the profile with the generated FBML, the confirm function calls function updateProfile.

Function updateProfile displays the **Publish Mood Story** button so the user can publish a story (see Figure 6.20 on page 211). It also calls service UpdateProfileBox to write new content to the profile box. Note that service call option requireLogin: true verifies that the user is logged in before it actually updates the user's profile.

Listing 6.27 Home (FBJS)—Mood Pix Partial Listing

```
function init() {
   // get the Facebook user id
   // (user does not have to be logged in)
   if (Application.fb_sig_added == "1")
      fbUserID = Application.fb_sig_user;
   else
      fbUserID = Application.fb_sig_canvas_user;

   // Check to see if user has saved a profile mood/info data
   Things.callService("ganderson.MoodPix.GetProfileInfo",
   {
      userid: fbUserID // optional userid
   },
   {
   onSuccess: function(data) {
      Log.write(data);
      // display profile and info information
      displayProfileBox(data.profile);
      displayInfoData(data.info);
      },
   onFailure: function(error) {
      Log.write("Error: " + error.code + " : " + error.message);
      },
   responseType: Ajax.JSON
   });
}

function doUpdate(form) {
   message = document.getElementById("messagenote").getValue();

   // set values for the feed form hidden elements
   document.getElementById("moodmessage").setValue(message);
   document.getElementById("moodname").setValue(moods[moodindex]);
   document.getElementById("picurl").setValue(image_head + imgs[moodindex]);
   document.getElementById("storytype").setValue("1");
   var text = setFBMLText();

   // Let Facebook process the FBML so we can inject it into page dynamically
   Things.callService("ganderson.MoodPix.AjaxFBML",
   {
      text: text
   },
   {
      onSuccess: function(data) {
         Log.write(data);
         document.getElementById('ajaxmoodbox').setInnerFBML(data);
         var dialog = new Dialog().showChoice(
            "Okay to update profile to Mood Pix "
            + moods[moodindex] + "?",
            data,
```

```
                button_confirm="Update Profile", button_cancel="Edit");
            dialog.onconfirm = function()
            {
                updateProfile(text);
            }
            dialog.oncancel = function() {}
        },
        onFailure: function(error) {
            Log.write("Error: " + error.code + " : " + error.message);
        },
        responseType: Ajax.FBML
    });
    return false;
}

// Update the profile box
function updateProfile(text) {
    // make feed form publish button visible
    showPublishButton(PROFILESTORY);
    Things.callService("ganderson.MoodPix.UpdateProfileBox",
    {
        userid: fbUserID,
        text: text
    },
    {
        onSuccess: function(data) {
            Log.write(data);
        },
        onFailure: function(error) {
            Log.write("Error: " + error.code + " : " + error.message);
        },

        // User must authorize Mood Pix
        requireLogin: true
    });
}

// show the Publish Story feed form
function showPublishButton(storytype) {
    document.getElementById('feedDiv').setStyle({display: 'block'});
    document.getElementById('storytype').setValue(storytype);
}
```

Service FeedHandlerService

The Facebook feed form pops up a confirmation dialog, as shown in Figure 6.20 on page 211. If a user clicks **Publish**, the callback URL specified in the form's action attribute is invoked. This calls service FeedHandlerService shown in Listing 6.28. This service builds a response object (response.content) consisting of template data (feed.template_data) and template bundle ID (feed.template_id). The template ID refers to a previously registered template bundle ID. (We discuss registered template bundles in "Publishing Feed Stories" on page 182.) The response object method (response.method) is set to "feedStory".

FeedHandlerService's parameters (moodname, moodmessage, picurl, and storytype) come from the FBML form's hidden elements. The template data replaces the tokens in the registered template. The response returned to Facebook is a JSON-encoded object.

Listing 6.28 Service FeedHandlerService (JavaScript)—Mood Pix

```
var response = {};
response.content = {};
response.content.feed = {};

// assume that user has selected a new profile mood
response.content.feed.template_id = 22716163702;

if (Parameters.storytype && Parameters.storytype == "2")
   // user has selected a new favorite mood
   response.content.feed.template_id = 22738998702;

// build the template data
response.content.feed.template_data =
   {"mood": Parameters.moodname,
    "message": Parameters.moodmessage,
    "moodpic": Parameters.picurl,
    "images": [{"href": Parameters.picurl},
    {"href": "http:\/\/apps.facebook.com\/moodpix\/Home"}]
};
response.method = "feedStory";
// return to Facebook
return response.toJSON();
```

Application Info Section

You've seen how Mood Pix updates your application Info section when you select a favorite mood (shown in Figure 6.25). Listing 6.29 shows the FBJS code that generates the Info section for Mood Pix.

Figure 6.25 Making a mood a favorite adds content to your Info section

Selecting a favorite mood invokes function `setFavorite`, which resets the heart symbol image (if it was marking a previous mood as favorite). Service AjaxFBML lets Mood Pix display dynamic FBML (Facebook processes the FBML prior to rendering). After displaying a popup dialog, the `onSuccess` handler invokes function `configureInfo`.

Function `configureInfo` sets the Facebook feed story form's hidden elements with the appropriate data, enables the **Publish Mood Story** button, and calls service SetInfo. Service SetInfo (shown in Listing 6.30) writes the data to the user's Info section.

Listing 6.29 Home (FBJS)—Mood Pix Partial Listing

```
function setFavorite() {
  // if the favorite was previously set, hide the former setting
  if (favorite_mood != -1) document.getElementById("mood" +
        favorite_mood).setStyle({display: 'none'});
  favorite_mood = moodindex;
  message = document.getElementById("messagenote").getValue();
  favorite_message = message;
  var text = setFBMLText();

  //launder the FBML through Facebook servers
  Things.callService("ganderson.MoodPix.AjaxFBML",
  {
    text: text
  },
  {
    onSuccess: function(data) {
      Log.write(data);
      document.getElementById('ajaxmoodbox').setInnerFBML(data);
      new Dialog().showMessage("favorite mood is now set to "
          + moods[favorite_mood], data, "Okay");

      // display the new favorite "heart"
      document.getElementById(
          "mood" + favorite_mood).setStyle({display: 'block'});
      configureInfo();
    },
    onFailure: function(error) {
      Log.write("Error: " + error.code + " : " + error.message);
    },
    responseType: Ajax.FBML
  });
}

function configureInfo() {
  // set values for the feed form hidden elements
  document.getElementById("moodname").setValue(moods[favorite_mood]);
  document.getElementById("moodmessage").setValue(favorite_message);
  document.getElementById("picurl").setValue(image_head
        + imgs[favorite_mood]);
  showPublishButton(FAVORITESTORY);
```

```
   // Configure an application info section with the user's favorite mood
   Things.callService("ganderson.MoodPix.SetInfo",
   {
      label: moods[favorite_mood], // label for the item
      link: "http://apps.facebook.com/moodpix/Home", // a hyperlink
      description: favorite_message, // a description of the item
      image: image_head + imgs[favorite_mood], // absolute URL of mood image
      userid: fbUserID // facebook userid who owns the Info section
   },
   {
      onSuccess: function(data) {
         Log.write(data);
      },
      onFailure: function(error) {
         Log.write("Error: " + error.code + " : " + error.message);
      },
      requireLogin: true
   });
}
```

Listing 6.30 is the JavaScript code for service SetInfo. This service builds the `opt_info` object from the parameters' data. It then gets the current information from the user's Info section (with Facebook API method `profile.getInfo`) and adds the new information to the end of the `items` array. Invoking Facebook API method `profile.setInfo` updates the Info section.

Listing 6.30 Service SetInfo (JavaScript)—Mood Pix

```
var opt_info = {};
var field = "Favorite Mood Pix";

opt_info["label"] = Parameters.label;
opt_info["link"] = Parameters.link;
opt_info["description"] = Parameters.description;
opt_info["image"] = Parameters.image;

// get what is already there so we can add to it
var oldinfo = Things.facebook.profile.getInfo({
   uid: Parameters.userid // User ID of the user who added the application info
});

var newItems = oldinfo.info_fields[0];
newItems.items[newItems.items.length] = opt_info;

var info_fields = [{"field": "My Current Favorites", "items": newItems.items
}];

return Things.facebook.profile.setInfo({
   uid: Parameters.userid, // The user ID of user adding the application info
```

```
    title: field, // The title or header of the application info section.
    info_fields: info_fields.toJSON(), // A JSON-encoded array of elements.
    type: 5 // 5 for a thumbnail configuration.
});
```

To directly edit your Info section, the developer must provide options to add to the application-specific Info section. Listing 6.31 shows the JavaScript code for service SetInfoOptions. Service SetInfoOptions builds the list of options users select when adding favorite moods directly to their Mood Pix Info section. Note that this service is called only once.

zembly Tip

You can invoke service SetInfoOptions manually from **zembly**. *Acquire a Facebook session and click button* **Test drive now** *in the service Call box.*

The `opt_info` object includes a label, a link (which always points to the Mood Pix Home widget), a description, and an image. There are ten `opt_info` objects from which users can add to their profile Info section.

Listing 6.31 Service SetInfoOptions (JavaScript)—Mood Pix

```
var moods = [ ];
var imgs = [ ];
var descr = [ ];
var image_head = "http://f33f7b88bb1440b99edfbbfd1d654f90.zembly.com/things/
ganderson/MoodPix/dev/Home/resources/";

var optArray = new Array();

moods[0] = "angry and annoyed";
          . . . [moods omitted] . . .
moods[9] = "grateful";

imgs[0] = "annoyed_angry_sm.jpg";
          . . . [images omitted] . . .
imgs[9] = "grateful_sm.jpg";

descr[0] =
"The silver cholla is brash, prickly and connotes anger or annoyance.";
          . . . [descriptions omitted] . . .
descr[9] =
"Wild pink lilies evoke beauty; of which there is a lot to be thankful for.";

function buildOptions() {
   for (var i = 0; i < moods.length; i++) {
      var opt_info = {};
      opt_info["label"] = moods[i];
```

```
        opt_info["link"] = "http://apps.facebook.com/moodpix/Home";
        opt_info["description"] = descr[i];
        opt_info["image"] = image_head + imgs[i];
        optArray.push(opt_info);
    }
}

buildOptions();

Things.facebook.profile.setInfoOptions({
    field: "My Current Favorites", // The title of the field.
    options: optArray.toJSON() // A JSON-encoded array of items for a thumbnail
});
return Things.facebook.profile.getInfoOptions({
    field: "My Current Favorites" // The title of the field.
});
```

Mood Pix Application Tab

Facebook lets users add application-specific tabs to their profile. To do this, developers must provide an appropriate widget and configure their applications with the Facebook Developer. Mood Pix includes widget TabHome, which is the application-specific tab widget for this application. Figure 5.9 on page 111 shows how to add a new application tab with Mood Pix. Once you add Mood Pix to your profile tab, friends who visit your profile will see the Mood Pix tab and can execute the Mood Pix tab widget (TabHome).

Application tab widgets have restrictions. The widget is "passive," that is, it can only execute FBJS code after the visitor has interacted with the widget by clicking a button, for example. The widget must be FBML/FBJS, is read-only, and excludes advertising. The application tab widget does not know who the viewer is, but the profile owner is known (`Application.fb_sig_profile_user`). Figure 6.26 shows widget TabHome when you first select the Mood Pix tab.

224   Chapter 6   Facebook Integration

Figure 6.26 Mood Pix tab (widget TabHome) running on Facebook

After clicking **Peak at Profile Owner's Moods**, widget TabHome displays the owner's profile and info section moods.

Widget TabHome is included with the Mood Pix application services and widgets on **zembly**. Its code is a subset of the code in widget Home. Note that you don't select new moods, but only view those previously selected by the profile owner.

In order to supply an application tab, you must configure your application on Facebook. From the Developer application on Facebook, select your application and choose option **Edit Settings**. Figure 6.27 shows a portion of the configuration page for Mood Pix. Supply a widget name that will execute when users select the Mood Pix tab (TabHome) and supply a name that will appear on the tab (Mood Pix).

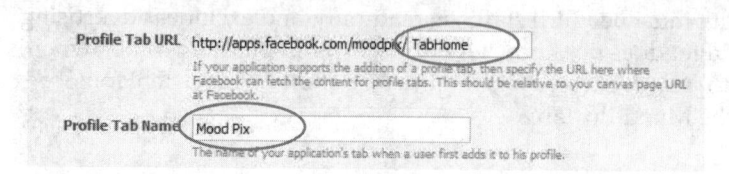

Figure 6.27 Configuring the Mood Pix application tab

Profile Publisher

Another important Facebook integration point with Mood Pix is the profile publisher. Facebook applications can provide an interface that lets users instantly publish content to their wall. For example, Update Status lets you update your Facebook status and Share Link lets you share an internet page with friends. Add Photos lets you post photos to your wall and Write lets you write on your own wall (or another's wall if you're viewing a friend's profile).

Figure 6.28 shows these profile publishers and a new one called New Mood Pix. New Mood Pix lets you update your profile Mood Pix directly (this is the self publisher). If you visit a friend's profile, you'll see Send Mood Pix instead (this is the friend publisher) and you'll be able to send a Mood Pix to your friend's wall.

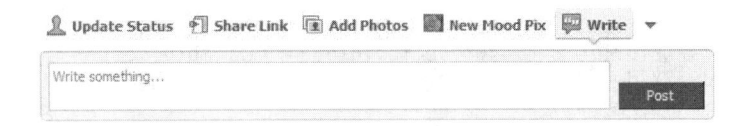

Figure 6.28 Several Facebook profile publishers

Figure 5.12 on page 113 shows how to add the profile publisher for Mood Pix to your profile. Figure 6.29 shows the New Mood Pix publisher interface. Here, you select a new mood from the drop down menu, add an optional comment, and click **Post**. Before users can invoke a profile publisher for an application, you must provide services and configure your application on Facebook.

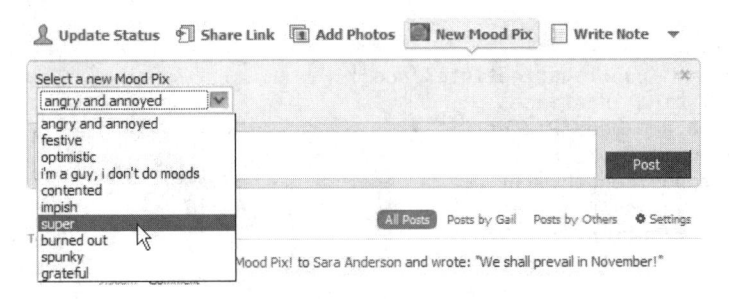

Figure 6.29 Using the New Mood Pix profile publisher

Listing 6.32 is the JavaScript for service PublisherSelf. This service is invoked by Facebook when you select New Mood Pix on your wall.

Service PublisherSelf includes two parameters. Parameter method is type String and indicates if the caller is getting the interface ("publisher_getInterface") or the feed story ("publisher_getFeedStory"). The second parameter, app_params, is a JSON object that includes integer moodnum (defined in the publisher interface) and string comment_text (available when the publisher interface enables comments).

The service first determines if it needs to provide FBML for the publishing interface or provide data for the feed story. The publishing interface lets you select a mood, provide an optional comment, and post the content. When you select Post, Facebook invokes service PublisherSelf a second time, requesting the information it needs (including the template feed bundle ID) to publish the content.

Listing 6.32 Service PublisherSelf (JavaScript)—Mood Pix

```
var moods = [ ];
var imgs = [ ];
var image_head = "http:\/\/f33f7b88bb1440b99edfbbfd1d654f90.zembly.com\/
things\/ganderson\/MoodPix\/dev\/Home\/resources\/";

// mood variables
var moodindex = 1;
var message = "";

moods[0] = "angry and annoyed";
   . . .
moods[9] = "grateful";

imgs[0] = "annoyed_angry_sm.jpg";
   . . .
imgs[9] = "grateful_sm.jpg";

var response = {};
response.content = {};
if (Parameters.method == "publisher_getInterface") {
   // Supply the publishing interface
   var fbml = "Select a new Mood Pix<br />" +
   "<form><select name='moodnum' >" ;
   for (var i=0; i < moods.length; i++) {
      fbml += "<option value='" + i + "'>"
         + moods[i] + "</option>";
   }
   fbml += "</select></form>";
   response.content.fbml = fbml;
   response.content.publishedEnabled = true;
   response.content.commentEnabled = true;
   response.method = "publisher_getInterface";
}
   else // method is "publisher_getFeedStory"
{
   var moodindex = 2;
   var message = "This feature is currently in test mode.";
   if (Parameters.app_data != null) {
      moodindex = Parameters.app_data['moodnum'];
      message = Parameters.app_data['comment_text'];
   }

   response.content.feed = {};
   response.content.feed.template_id = 22716163702;
   response.content.feed.template_data = {"mood": moods[moodindex],
      "message": message,
      "moodpic": image_head + imgs[moodindex],
```

```
        "images": [{"href": image_head + imgs[moodindex]},
        {"href": "http:\/\/apps.facebook.com\/moodpix\/Home"}]};
    response.method = "publisher_getFeedStory";
}
return response.toJSON();
```

Service PublisherFriend performs the same function as service PublisherSelf, except it publishes to a friend's wall instead of the user's wall. (We don't include the listing here since the code is similar to Listing 6.32.)

Finally, to enable the profile publishers for Mood Pix, you must configure the application on Facebook. From the Developer application on Facebook, select your application and choose option **Edit Settings**. Figure 6.30 shows a portion of the configuration page for Mood Pix. Supply a name for the publisher tab (here you see **Send Mood Pix** for publishing content to friends and **New Mood Pix** for publishing content to your own wall). Use the URLs from zembly's service page for the callback URLs. For example, the callback URL for publishing content to self is

```
http://zembly.com/things/3ffb71a6944e4927b9510cef0ce61f52;exec
```

which invokes service PublisherSelf.

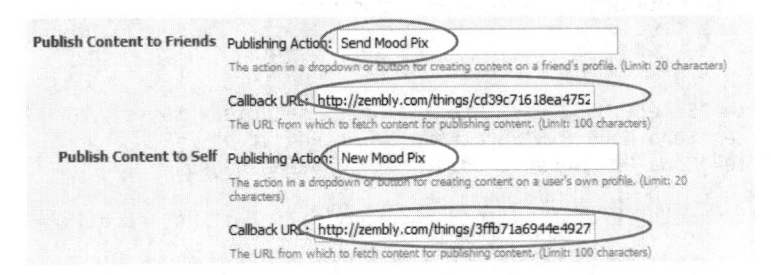

Figure 6.30 Configuring the Mood Pix profile publishers

Widget SendMoodPix

Widget SendMoodPix is an FBML/FBJS widget that lets you send a mood pix to a friend. Service SendMoodPixService sends a notification to your friend and publishes the story with Facebook API method `publishUserAction`. Service StoreMessage uses the Facebook data store API to store the sender, receiver, the mood, and any message text.

Widget SendMoodPix is similar in principle to Capital Punishment's SendInvitation; the biggest difference is that with widget SendMoodPix you select a single friend. We once again take advantage of Facebook's high level tags—this time we use tag `fb:friend-selector`. Figure 6.31 shows the friend selector component in action. As

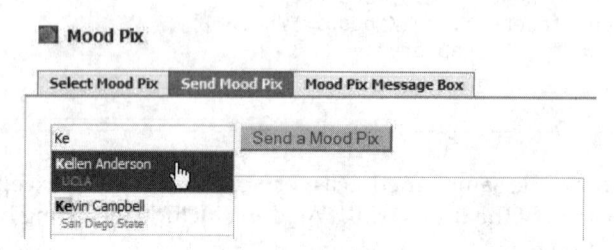

Figure 6.31 Using the Facebook friend selector component

you start typing a friend's name, a matching list of friends appears from which you can select one name.

Listing 6.33 shows the FBML for widget SendMoodPix (we've eliminated repetitive code). After the dashboard (fb:dashboard) and tab menu (fb:tabs), you see a form tag coupled with fb:friend-selector and an input tag (type="submit"). These three tags (form, fb:friend-selector, and input) provide the friend selection mechanism. Function checkForm is the event handler called after the user clicks **Send a Mood Pix**.

Listing 6.33 Widget SendMoodPix (FBML)—Mood Pix

```
<fb:dashboard />
<fb:tabs>
   <fb:tab-item title="Select Mood Pix" href="./Home" selected="false" />
   <fb:tab-item title="Send Mood Pix" href="#" selected="true" />
   <fb:tab-item title="Mood Pix Message Box" href="./SeeMessages"
      selected="false"/>
   <fb:tab-item title="Help" href="./Help" selected="false" align="right" />
</fb:tabs>
<div class="requestDiv">
   <form id="myForm" onsubmit="return checkForm(this);">
      <fb:friend-selector />
      <input class="button" value="Send a Mood Pix" type="submit"/>
      <table class="editorkit" border="0" cellspacing="0" style="width:720px">
      <tr class="width_setter"><th style="width:120px"></th>
      <td></td>
      <td></td></tr>
      <tr><th class="detached_label"><label>Add a personal note:</label></th>
      <td class="editorkit_row">
         <textarea id="messagenote" style="width:300px">
         </textarea></td>
      <td class="editorkit_row" style="padding-left:5px">
      <div id="displaymsg" style="display:none">
      <br />
      Here is your message:
      <div id="ajaxmoodmsg">
      </div>
```

```
        </div></td></tr>
      </table>
    </form>
</div>

<div id="main_body">
    <table><tr><td>

        <!-- mood is angry or annoyed -->
        <!-- code for rest of the moods is omitted -->

    </td></tr></table>
</div>
```

Listing 6.34 shows the FBJS for function checkForm. This function calls FBJS function serialize, which returns an associative array of elements in the form. The associative array contains key-value pairs, where key is the name of the form element and value is the input. With the fb:friend-selector tag, the default name for the friend id is friend_selector_id and the default name for the friend name is friend_selector_name.

As seen previously, service AjaxFBML returns processed FBML so the onSuccess handler can inject it into the page. The user is asked to confirm before calling function sendNotification, which actually sends the notification and publishes the story.

Listing 6.34 Function checkForm (FBJS)—Widget SendMoodPix

```
function checkForm(form) {
   // get the elements in the form
   var params=form.serialize();
   if (params.friend_selector_id==null || params.friend_selector_name=='') {
      new Dialog().showMessage("Please select a friend",
         "Select a friend first, then send the mood pix message.", "Okay");
   } else {
      friendname = params.friend_selector_name;
      friendid = params.friend_selector_id;
      message = document.getElementById("messagenote").getValue();
      var text = setFBMLText();
      Things.callService("ganderson.MoodPix.AjaxFBML",
      {
         text: text
      },
      {
         onSuccess: function(data) {
            Log.write(data);
            document.getElementById('ajaxmoodbox').setInnerFBML(data);
            var dialog = new Dialog().showChoice("Okay to send Mood Pix " +
               moods[moodindex] + " to " + friendname + "?",
               data, button_confirm="Send It", button_cancel="Edit");
```

```
            dialog.onconfirm = function()
            {
               document.getElementById("messagenote").setValue("");
               sendNotification();
            }
         },
         onFailure: function(error) {
            Log.write("Error: " + error.code + " : " + error.message);
         },
         responseType: Ajax.FBML
      });
   }
   return false;
}
```

Listing 6.35 is the FBJS code for function sendNotification. This function calls service SendMoodPixService with the notification text, the Facebook user id of the recipient, and the data necessary to publish the Mood Pix story. Note that the onSuccess handler checks to see if the story was actually published and displays a message if the user does not have automatic publishing enabled.

Listing 6.35 Function sendNotification (FBJS)—Widget SendMoodPix

```
function sendNotification() {
   var sendtext = "sent you the <b>" + moods[moodindex] + "</b>" +
   "<a href='http://apps.facebook.com/moodpix/SeeMessages'>Mood Pix!</a><i>"
   + message + "</i> ";

   Things.callService("ganderson.MoodPix.SendMoodPixService",
   {
      //testmode: false, // if true, send the message to yourself for testing
      fbml_message: sendtext, // FBML for the message content
      recipient: friendid, // facebook id of the intended receiver
      message_text: message, // personal note of message
      mood_id: moodindex, // mood index of mood pix
      mood_image: image_head + imgs[moodindex], // Absolute URL of image
      mood_name: moods[moodindex] // the actual mood
   },
   {
      onSuccess: function(data) {
      Log.write(data);
      if (!data[0]) new Dialog().showMessage(
         "Your Permission is Needed to Publish",
         "We attempted to publish your challenge,"
         + " but Facebook requires your permission. "
         + "From the Applications menu on Facebook, click Edit and select "
         + "'Allow Mood Pix to publish specific story sizes automatically.'",
         "Okay");
      },
      onFailure: function(error) {
```

```
        Log.write("Error: " + error.code + " : " + error.message);
    },

    requireLogin: true
  });
}
```

Mood Pix Widgets and Services—The Rest of the Story

There's more widgets and services in application Mood Pix. For example, another tab on the Home widget dashboard links to widget SeeMessages (which lets you look at your mood pix message box).

Widget SeeMessages shows you the mood pix messages you've received and sent. This widget is structured very similarly to widget SeeScores in Capital Punishment. Service MessagesSent queries the data store and returns JSON data to the caller. Widget SeeMessages formats the data into FBML and calls service AjaxFBML to update the canvas page dynamically. Similarly, service MessagesReceived queries the data store and returns JSON to the caller. Service DeleteMessage removes the selected mood pix message from the application data store. You can view these services and widgets from the **zembly** Mood Pix application page.

6.4 Facebook Connect—Looking Forward

The Facebook Connect facility is yet another way Facebook lets developers hook into Facebook social networking. Facebook Connect is aimed at developers who have an external web site that supports users' actions (such as logging in or storing data). With Facebook Connect, you (the developer) can connect your web site users to their Facebook accounts, providing several advantages. One, you simplify your users' login or registration by reusing their Facebook credentials. Two, with a user's Facebook identity, you can pull Facebook information about your users, including their basic profile information, profile picture, name, friends, photos, events, groups, and other data. And three, you can push information about what users do on your web site back onto Facebook via publishing stories. All this hopefully results in engaging users' friends and subsequently growing your user base.

> **zembly Tip**
>
> *The material presented here relies on Facebook features that are still in Beta. Furthermore, the* **zembly** *support is new and the specifics for creating Facebook Connect applications and launching them will undoubtedly change and become more automated. The demonstration pro-*

grams presented here will also change as the Facebook and **zembly** *features stabilize. Nevertheless, we thought you'd like a preview.*

Since the Facebook Connect facility is currently in Beta, you can't realize its full functionality yet. But, you can create a Facebook Connect application that lets you access Facebook features without running within the Facebook skin, and more importantly, running on an external web site. What you get is a hybrid environment: Facebook authorization coupled with a subset of FBML (called XFBML). You use JavaScript and HTML as well as some FBML tags.

zembly engineers have created a demo application that lets you try out Facebook Connect. Here's a summary of the steps you'll follow to test your own copy of this demonstration application.

1. Find the demonstration application (use the Search mechanism to search for **zemblyConnectDemo**).
2. Clone the demo application and rename it (renaming is optional).
3. Follow the instructions presented earlier to create an application on Facebook (see "Facebook Application Wizard" on page 115) for your newly cloned application.
4. Replace values assigned to `api_key` in widgets fbConnectDemo1, fbConnectDemo2, and fbConnectDemo3 with your application's API key. Copy and paste the API key from your application's page in the Developer on Facebook. (It's likely **zembly** will do this step for you in the future.)
5. Try out the application with URL

    `{_your_callback_url_}/fbConnectDemoIndex;iframe`

---

zembly Tip

As of this writing, Facebook Connect is still in "sandbox" mode and you must be listed as a Developer of your application to access Facebook Connect. This is why you can't use the demonstration application directly; you must clone it first.

Running the zemblyConnectDemo Widget

When you copy and paste the above URL into your browser's address bar, a widget lets you run three demo programs. The first demo (fbConnectDemo1) connects you to Facebook with a login button and, after connecting, returns a list of your friends' user IDs. Widget fbConnectDemo1 illustrates the structure of a widget that uses Facebook Connect. The other two widgets have similar JavaScript code for connecting with Facebook.

Listing 6.36 shows the XFBML code for this widget. XFBML lets you incorporate a subset of FBML tags in your HTML widgets or on your Facebook Connect site. To use XFBML, you provide some basic handshaking with Facebook. The fbConnectDemo1 widget does this by

- providing a link to Facebook CSS styles
- providing a link to the Facebook FeatureLoader JavaScript support file
- initializing a Facebook Connection in the JavaScript code (see Listing 6.37)

zembly Tip

*When **zembly** supplies the Facebook Client Library for you, this handshaking code will happen automatically. Then, HTML code in widgets can include XFBML implicitly.*

Note that FBML tag `fb:login-button` provides login access for the user.

Listing 6.36 fbConnectDemo1 (XFBML)—zemblyConnectDemo

```
<head>
<title>Facebook Connect Demo 1</title>
<link rel="stylesheet"
href="http://static.ak.connect.facebook.com/css/fb_connect.css" type="text/
css" />
</head>
<body>
<h1>Facebook Connect Demo 1</h1>
<p>Login flow example, with simple API call example</p>
<p>Login Button:</p>
<fb:login-button>
</fb:login-button>

<a href="./fbConnectDemoIndex;iframe">back to index</a>

<script
src="http://static.ak.connect.facebook.com/js/api_lib/v0.4/Feature-
Loader.js.php"
type="text/javascript"></script>

<pre id="friends"></pre>

</body>
</html>
```

Listing 6.37 contains the JavaScript code for widget fbConnectDemo1. Function `FB_RequireFeatures` provides the handshaking with Facebook Connect. After the connection is initialized and the session is established, the code calls Facebook API method `friends_get` to obtain the user's list of friends (IDs). The return data is stored in `result` and displayed on the page using Prototype function `update` with element id `"friends"`.

> **Facebook Tip**
>
> Call `FB_RequireFeatures` and `FB.Facebook.init` to use XFBML with your HTML page. Invoking `get_sessionState` lets you access the Facebook API with the JavaScript client.

Listing 6.37 fbConnectDemo1 (JavaScript)—zemblyConnectDemo

```
var api_key = "Your API Key Here";
var xdPath = "./?xd-receiver";

FB_RequireFeatures(["XFBML"], function() {

  FB.Facebook.init(api_key, xdPath);
  FB.Facebook.get_sessionState().waitUntilReady(function() {

    window.alert("Session is ready, making API call");

    //If you want to make Facebook API calls from JavaScript (example)
    FB.Facebook.apiClient.friends_get(null, function(result, ex) {
      //Do something with result
      $("friends").update(result);
    });

  });
});
```

fbConnectDemo2 and fbConnectDemo3 Widgets

Return to the main widget (fbConnectIndex) and try out the other two demonstration widgets.

Widget fbConnectDemo2 shows several XFBML tags, including profile picture, name, network, group, and event.

Widget fbConnectDemo3 illustrates "Server" FBML tags—Facebook tags that must be hosted on Facebook. Server tags include `fb:request-form`, which is illustrated in Listing 6.38. Note that the request form FBML is embedded within an `fb:fbml` tag as a script for the `fb:serverfbml` tag.

Listing 6.38 fbConnectDemo3 (XFBML)—zemblyConnectDemo

```
<!DOCTYPE html PUBLIC "-//W3C//DTD XHTML 1.0 Strict//EN"
```

Facebook Connect—Looking Forward 235

```html
"http://www.w3.org/TR/xhtml1/DTD/xhtml1-strict.dtd">
<html xmlns="http://www.w3.org/1999/xhtml"
xmlns:fb="http://www.facebook.com/2008/fbml">
<head>
   <title>Facebook Connect Demo 3</title>
   <link
rel="stylesheet" href="http://static.ak.connect.facebook.com/css/
fb_connect.css"
      type="text/css" />
</head>
<body>
   <h1>Facebook Connect Demo 3</h1>
   <p>
   Login flow and serverside XFBML (Request form)
   </p>
   <p>Login Button:</p>
   <fb:login-button>
   </fb:login-button>
   <h2>XFBML rendered as an iframe from facebook.com</h2>

<!-- Server FBML tags are necessary for Facebook elements which must be hosted
on Facebook. The request form is one of these, as demonstrated below. -->

   <fb:serverfbml style="width: 755px;">
   <script type="text/fbml">
      <fb:fbml>
         <fb:request-form
         action="<url for post invite action>"
         method="POST"
         invite="true"
         type="XFBML"
         content="This is a test invitation from XFBML test app
         <fb:req-choice url='req-choice-url'
         label='Ignore the Connect test app!' />">
         <fb:multi-friend-selector
         showborder="false"
         actiontext="Invite your friends to use Connect.">
         </fb:request-form>
      </fb:fbml>
   </script>
</fb:serverfbml>
<a href="./fbConnectDemoIndex;iframe">back to index</a>

<script
src="http://static.ak.connect.facebook.com/js/api_lib/v0.4/Feature-
Loader.js.php"
type="text/javascript"></script>
</body>
</html>
```

7 Working with Dapper

groups   content extractor   dapps   Input Variables

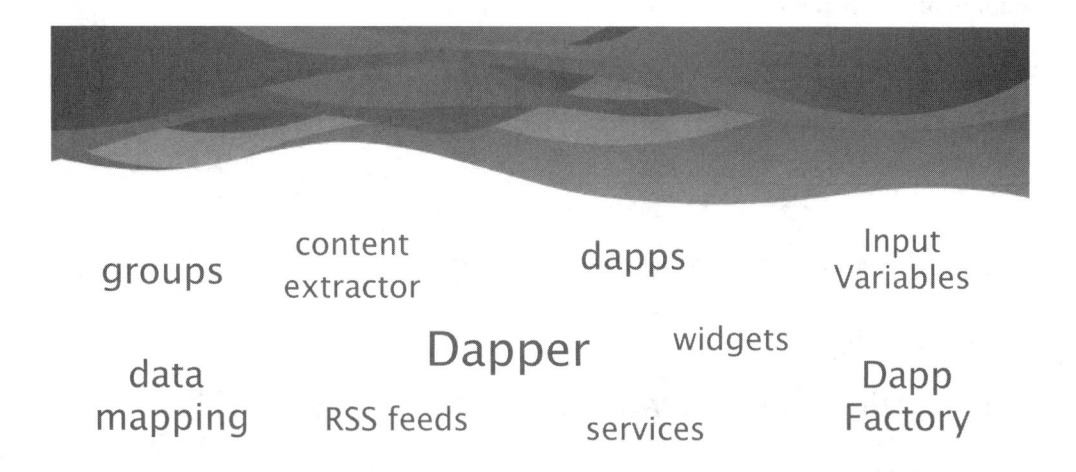

data mapping   **Dapper**   widgets   Dapp Factory

RSS feeds   services

Dapper is a content extractor for feeds and HTML streams. Content extractors let you consume data that is not accessible from existing interfaces. Dapper creates feeds from web site content modified by the input you provide. This feed is called a *Dapp*. With zembly, you can access Dapps you build as services and then build widgets to create your applications. Dapper is particularly useful from zembly, because you can provide an API interface (a Dapp) for content providers that do not have adapters on zembly. In this chapter, you will see how to create several Dapps and use them with zembly to build services and widgets.

What You Will Learn

- Creating a Dapp that has input variables
- Creating a service that calls a Dapp
- Providing Dapp input using service parameters
- Creating a Dapper-based widget
- Creating a Dapper-based feed for content that has no feed

- Creating a Feed Reader widget for a Dapper-based feed

Examples in This Chapter

All examples in this chapter are tagged **zembly-book-dapper**. To search for them, select **Search** at the top of any zembly page. Supply the search term **zembly-book-dapper** and click the search icon as shown in Figure 7.1.

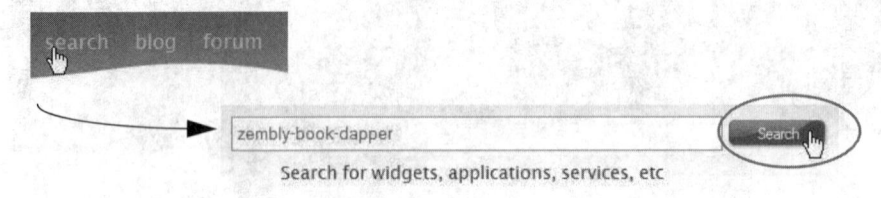

Figure 7.1 Searching for the examples in this chapter

7.1 Getting Content with Dapper

What is Dapper and why is it important to zembly? Dapper (www.dapper.net) is a web-based service that allows users to extract content from feeds or HTML streams. Dapper runs your extractors (or *Dapps*) on its own servers. By default, Dapps are publicly accessible, so you can access any number of Dapps from your applications (even Dapps created by other users).

To build a Dapp, you must first create a Dapper account. For most uses Dapper is free, although there is a multi-level Service Level Agreement. The main limitation is that free account Dapps can only be called once a second. After you create and save it, your Dapp becomes accessible from zembly `things/dapper/dappName`. You can search for Dapps with zembly's Find & Use search mechanism when building services and widgets, and from zembly's general search mechanism.

Dapper is useful with zembly because you are not limited by available adapters. Because Dapper lets you manipulate data from arbitrary sources, you can build a wide range of interesting widgets from zembly.

zembly Axiom

If you can build a Dapp, you can create a widget for that Dapp with **zembly**.

zembly provides a Dapper interface that returns data in JSON format. Thus, Dapper makes it easy to extract data from web sites and **zembly** makes it easy to access that data from services and widgets.

In this chapter we'll show you several examples of Dapps and widgets that use data from these Dapps. The first example uses content from Flickr, a photo sharing web site. Although it's possible to access Flickr directly with **zembly**'s adapters, an example with familiar content will make your introduction to Dapper easier. The second example uses the www.tubeplanner.com site to provide users with routing information when using the London Underground (tube). This example is only possible because **zembly** is "Dapper-aware."

The third example is a Dapper-based widget that reports the day's Major League Baseball scores. Lastly, we show you a feed reader, a widget that formats and displays a Dapper-based RSS feed.

7.2 Photo Search Widget

Dapper requires a bit of practice. Once you get the hang of Dapper, you'll learn to recognize sites that work well with it. You'll also get comfortable identifying variable input to control content and grouping data into logical categories, creating easy to manage JSON objects.

For our first example, let's use Flickr as the content provider. You've already seen how to manipulate Flickr data. While you could build a widget using the adapters provided on **zembly** for Flickr's many APIs, building a Dapp is also a quick way to access content.

zembly Tip

*In general, using content providers through **zembly**'s adapters gives you the most flexibility. Dapper, on the other hand lets you create a service very quickly.*

Figure 7.2 shows the widget you'll build using Flickr and Dapper. The widget provides a text field for a search term and builds a slide show from the returned data. Each photo includes its title, owner, and link to the owner's page on Flickr.

Figure 7.2 FlickrPhotoSearchWidget running in a browser

Creating the flickrPhotoSearch Dapp

Here's a summary of the steps you'll follow to create a Dapp on `dapper.net`.

1. Sign up to create an account on Dapper.
2. Initiate the Dapp Factory to create a Dapp.
3. Specify your content's source URL.
4. Collect sample pages with variable input.
5. Select content from the sample pages.
6. Group the data into a logical structure.
7. Save (publish) your Dapp.

Dapper's Dapp Factory helps you create a Dapp. You must have an account on Dapper; it's free for most applications. Creating a Dapp is a five-step process that starts with specifying your content's source URL. To create a Dapp based on Flickr content, you begin with Flickr's web site on Dapper's Create a Dapp page.

The second step is to collect sample pages, being careful to identify input variables that affect the content. For example, for the flickrPhotoSearch Dapp, you specify the search term Flickr uses to find photos. Each time you generate a new sample page, the search term becomes an input variable for Dapper. (Be sure to specify the input variable exactly the same each time.)

The third step is to select the content you're interested in. In the Flickr example, the example widget displays the photo thumbnail, title, and owner. The owner also contains a link to the owner's Flickr home page. Figure 7.3 shows a sample Flickr page with the selected data (the dark areas) that constitute the Dapp.

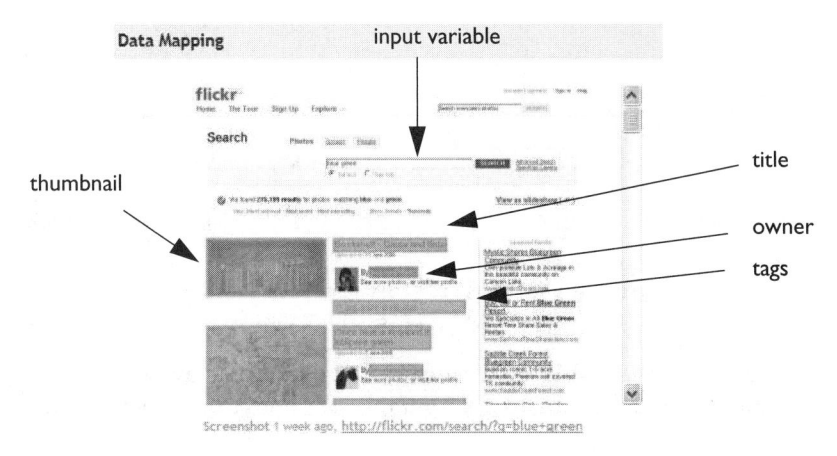

Figure 7.3 Viewing the selected data for the flickrPhotoSearch Dapp

After selecting content, you group the data into a logical structure. You tell Dapper how to view the data; that is, which items are grouped together to form related components. For the Flickr Dapp, the content describes attributes of a photo. It makes sense, then, to group all of the information together into a "photo" object. Listing 7.1 shows a sample of the JSON data that Dapper generates using the structure you define.

Listing 7.1 Sample of JSON Data from the flickrPhotoSearch Dapp

```
{"groups": {"photo": [
  {
    "tags": [{
      "value": "blue, colour, green, book ...",
      "originalElement": "p"
    }],
    "title": [{
      "value": "Bookshelf - Green and Blue",
      "originalElement": "span"
    }],
    "thumbnail": [{
      "value": "",
      "originalElement": "img",
      "src": "http://farm1.static.flickr.com/51/166358847_95892d1d37_m.jpg",
      "href": "http://flickr.com/photos/popsie/166358847/"
```

```
    }],
    "owner": [{
      "value": "popsie@flickr",
      "originalElement": "a",
      "href": "http://flickr.com/photos/popsie/"
    }]
  },
  {
    . . . omitted . . .
  }
}}
```

Suppose you want to access the titles of the first and second photos. Here's the code.

```
var data = data_returned_from_service;
var first_title = data.groups.photo[0].title[0].value;
var second_title = data.groups.photo[1].title[0].value;
```

Referring to the sample in Listing 7.1, node `photo` is a zero-based array, so the first photo is `photo[0]`. Node `title` (also an array) contains the photo title in element `value`.

Dapper Tip

Dapper creates arrays of each data field, even if there's only a single element. This provides more flexibility when the generated content varies and some fields have less content or nonexistent elements.

The final step is to save your Dapp. Figure 7.4 shows a portion of the page that lets you run the Dapp interactively and preview the feed. Once you save your Dapp, it becomes accessible from a service on **zembly**.

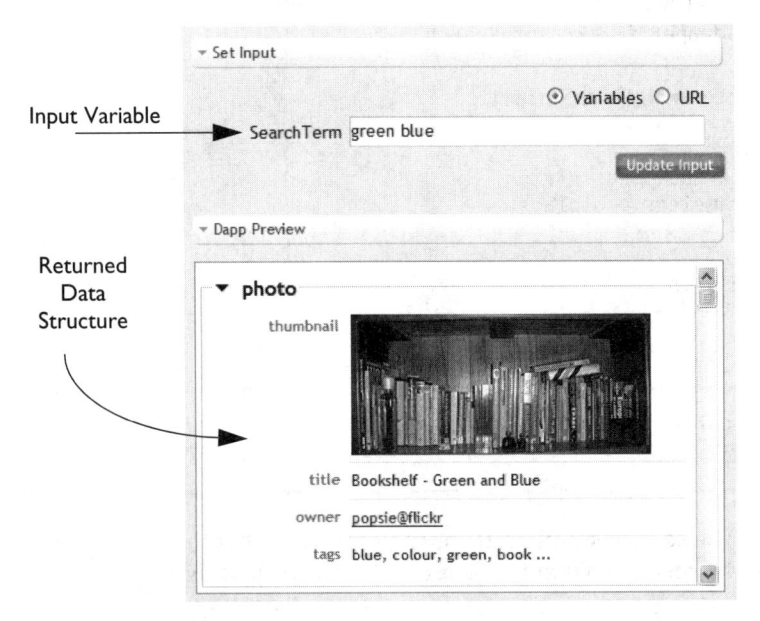

Figure 7.4 Previewing the flickrPhotoSearch Dapp

Creating a Dapper-Based Service

Because zembly is Dapper-aware, you can call a Dapp using its name and any parameters it needs. The flickrPhotoSearch Dapp is accessible, for example, as follows.

```
var mydata = Things.dapper.flickrPhotoSearch(...);
```

Let's show you how to create a service that calls this Dapp. Here's a summary of the steps you'll follow.

1. On zembly, create a service.
2. Using **Find & Use**, add template code to call your Dapp from the service.
3. Add parameter photoTags.
4. Add JavaScript code.
5. Test and publish the service.

Let's begin. From zembly, select **Create something!** and choose **Service** from the menu. Provide a name. You must provide input for each input variable you defined for your Dapp. This will typically be a parameter. For our flickrPhotoSearch Dapp, there is one input variable, SearchTerm, which is added as parameter photoTags for the service. Listing 7.2 shows the JavaScript code for service flickrPhotoSearch, which calls the Dapp (Things.dapper.flickrPhotoSearch).

Listing 7.2 flickrPhotoSearch (JavaScript)

```
var flickrSearchResults =
   Things.dapper.flickrPhotoSearch({
      SearchTerm: Parameters.photoTags
   });

return flickrSearchResults;
```

> **zembly Tip**
>
> *Note that argument* SearchTerm *must exactly match the input variable of your Dapp as shown in Figure 7.4 Otherwise, the call to* Things.dapper.flickrPhotoSearch *will fail.*

That's all there is to it. The service simply returns the same data that the Dapp generates. Test and publish the service so that you can call it from your widget.

Creating a Dapper-Based Widget

Once you've built the Dapp and published the service that invokes it, building a widget that uses your Dapp is no different than building a non-Dapp widget. The flickrPhotoSearchWidget reuses much of the same code shown in the previously built Flickr widget (see "Creating a Flickr User Slide Show Widget" on page 71). Here's a summary of the steps you'll follow to build this widget.

1. Create a new widget. Give it a name and a description.
2. Include the Prototype library.
3. Provide the HTML, CSS, and JavaScript code.
4. Use **Find & Use** to call the previously-built **zembly** service from your widget.
5. Preview and publish.
6. Embed in a web page.

Let's start with the HTML code for the flickrPhotoSearchWidget shown in Listing 7.3. You see an input field (the search term that is passed to the service and eventually to the Dapp), a button that calls the service, and a div tag to hold the results.

Listing 7.3 flickrPhotoSearchWidget (HTML)

```
<div id="FlickrSlideShowWidget">
   Enter a Flickr tag to search for photos: <br/>
```

```
    <input id="searchTags" type="text" value="blue green" />
    <button id="searchButton">Get Photos</button><br/>
    <div id="FlickrPhotoResults">
    </div>
</div>
```

Listing 7.4 shows the CSS code for the flickrPhotoSearchWidget. This code is similar to the CSS in Listing 3.12 on page 74 except for slight changes in margins and sizes (shown in bold below).

Listing 7.4 flickrPhotoSearchWidget (CSS)

```
#FlickrSlideShowWidget {
    text-align: center;
    color: #666666;
    background: #e1e1e1;
    border: 1px solid;
    padding: 5px;
}

#FlickrPhotoResults {
    padding: 5px;
}

#slideshowpic {
    height: 200px;
    max-width: 265px;
    border: 3px solid rgb(180,180,180);
    padding: 2px;
    margin-bottom: 2px;
}

#pictitle {
    font: 65% Verdana, sans-serif;
}

#slideshowDiv {
    height:240px;
}
```

This widget uses the Prototype JavaScript library. From the Resources tab, select **Libraries** (at the bottom) and choose **Prototype** from the list of libraries, as shown in Figure 7.5.

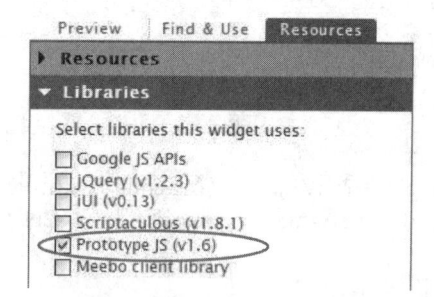

Figure 7.5 Adding the Prototype library to your widget

Listing 7.5 is the first part of the JavaScript code for the flickrPhotoSearchWidget. The code consists of support functions to build and maintain the photo slide show. You've seen these functions previously in Listing 3.3 on page 62 (function `updateSlideShow`), Listing 3.13 on page 75, or Listing 3.14 on page 76. The changes specific to this widget are in bold and pertain to the photo's title, owner, and link to the owner's home page.

Listing 7.5 flickrPhotoSearchWidget (JavaScript)—Part 1

```
var CurPic;
var ShowTimer = 3000;
var AutoRunFlag = false;
var run;

var FlickrPicArray;

function addtoSlideShow(pic) {
   FlickrPicArray.push(pic);
}

function updateSlideShow(direction) {
   CurPic = CurPic + direction;
   if (CurPic > FlickrPicArray.length - 1) CurPic = 0;
   if (CurPic < 0) CurPic = FlickrPicArray.length - 1;
   setPicture(CurPic);
}

function setPicture(picIndex) {
   document.flickrSlideShow.src = FlickrPicArray[picIndex].picurl;
   var infostr = FlickrPicArray[picIndex].title + "<br/>" +
      "<a href=\"" + FlickrPicArray[picIndex].home + "\">" +
      FlickrPicArray[picIndex].owner + "</a>";
   $("pictitle").innerHTML = infostr;
   CurPic = picIndex;
}
```

Photo Search Widget

```
function autoSlideShow() {
   if (AutoRunFlag == true) {
      AutoRunFlag = false;
      window.clearInterval(run);
      showDim();
   } else {
      AutoRunFlag = true;
      showBright();
      run = setInterval("updateSlideShow(1)", ShowTimer);
   }
}

function showDim() {
   var object = document.getElementsByName("flickrSlideShow")[0].style;
   object.opacity = .55;
}

function showBright() {
   var object = document.getElementsByName("flickrSlideShow")[0].style;
   object.opacity = 1;
}
```

Listing 7.6 shows the second part of the JavaScript code for the flickrPhotoSearchWidget. When the user clicks the search button, the event handler creates a new Array for FlickrPicArray and passes the search terms to the published flickrPhotoSearch service. The onSuccess handler is similar to Listing 3.15 on page 77, except that you access the data differently (shown in bold). You use the structure shown in the sample data in Listing 7.1 on page 241. The Prototype enumeration function each helps iterate through the photo array.

As with widget MyFlickrRandomSlideshow, the img tag includes an onClick event handler. This invokes function autoSlideShow(), which starts and stops the slide show by clicking the photo (and subsequently dimming the photo when the slide show stops).

Listing 7.6 flickrPhotoSearchWidget (JavaScript)—Part 2

```
Event.observe($("searchButton"), 'click', getflickrpics);

function getflickrpics() {
   FlickrPicArray = new Array ();
   var tags = $("searchTags").value;
   // stop the slide show if it's running
   if (AutoRunFlag) autoSlideShow();

   Things.callService("ganderson.flickrPhotoSearch",{
      "photoTags": tags},
      {onSuccess: function(data) {
```

```
            var Flickrdata = data;
            CurPic = 0;

            Flickrdata.groups.photo.each(function(photo) {
                var flickrpic = {};
                flickrpic.picurl = photo.thumbnail[0].src;
                flickrpic.title = photo.title[0].value;
                flickrpic.owner = photo.owner[0].value;
                flickrpic.home = photo.owner[0].href;
                addtoSlideShow(flickrpic);
                });

            var resultsHtml =
                " <div id=\"slideshowDiv\"> <img id=\"slideshowpic\"" +
                "src=\"\" name=\"flickrSlideShow\" "+
                " onClick=\"javascript:autoSlideShow()\"" +
                " alt=\"Waiting for photos from flickr.\"> " +
                " <div id=\"pictitle\"> </div> " + "</div> ";
            $("FlickrPhotoResults").innerHTML = resultsHtml;
            autoSlideShow();
        },
        onFailure: function(error) {
            var resultsHtml =
                "There was a problem with the call to Flickr or Dapper."
                + "<br/>" + error.errorCode + ": " + error.message ;
            $("FlickrPhotoResults").innerHTML = resultsHtml;
        }
    });
}
```

7.3 London Tube Widget

The true flexibility with Dapper is letting you build services and widgets based on arbitrary content found on the web. You don't need to rely on pre-defined adapters from zembly. If you can define web data in a reusable Dapp, then zembly lets you create a widget that presents this information. A good example is the widget in this section. A friend to London visitors and residents alike, this widget helps you travel from one point to another on the London Underground (Tube).

Widget Enhancements

A mashup using the LondonTubeWidget with Google Maps is shown in Chapter 8 (see "LondonTubeMapWidget" on page 289) and an iPhone-friendly version is shown in Chapter 9 (see "iLondonTube Widget" on page 348).

Figure 7.6 shows the widget that you'll build in this section. Arrows point to the data that the service and Dapp return.

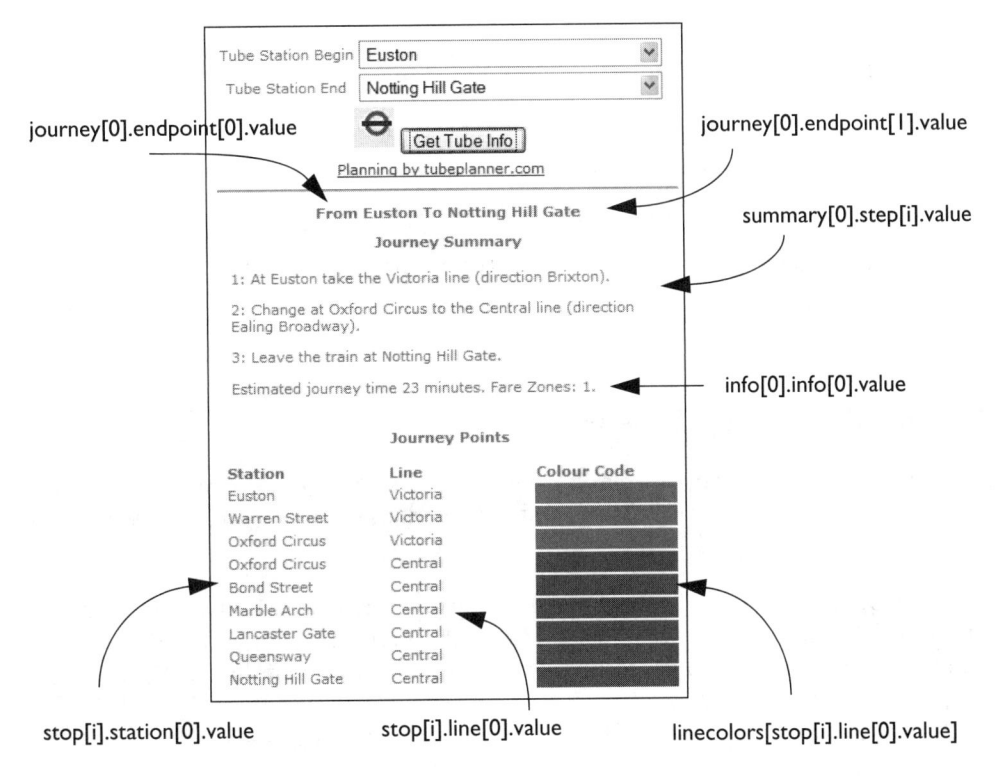

Figure 7.6 LondonTubeWidget running in a browser

Here's a summary of the steps you'll follow to build the Dapp, service, and widget.

Steps to Build the Dapp

1. Create a Dapp using source URL `tubeplanner.com`.
2. Define two input variables for each sample page.
3. Structure the data from the sample pages and publish the Dapp.

Steps to Create the Service

1. Create a service to call the London Tube Dapp. Provide a name and description.
2. Add two parameters to the service (uncheck Escape value).

3. Use **Find & Use** to call the London Tube Dapp and return data to the caller.
4. Test and publish the service.

Steps to Create the Widget

1. Create a new widget. Give it a name and a description.
2. Include the Prototype library.
3. Provide the HTML, CSS, and JavaScript code.
4. Use **Find & Use** to call the London Tube service from your widget.
5. Preview and publish.
6. Embed in a web page.

Creating the London Tube Dapp

Once again, you'll use Dapper's Dapp Factory to create the London Tube Dapp. The content comes from `tubeplanner.com`. (You may want to visit the web site to see how it works.)

Within Dapper, you'll collect sample pages, being careful to specify two input variables for each sample page: `startTube` and `endTube`. Figure 7.7 shows a sample page from the content provider marked up with the selected data that defines the Dapp.

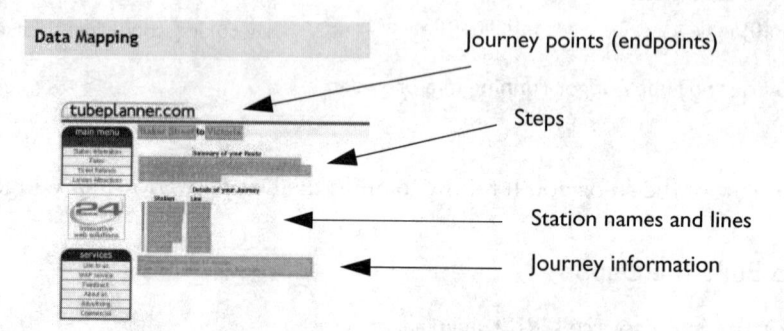

Figure 7.7 Viewing the selected data for the LondonTubeJourneyPlanner Dapp

After accumulating sample pages, you select the content you're interested in. In the London Tube example, you grab the starting and ending station names, the summary steps, and the general information (this includes the estimated travel time and the fare zones used). Finally, select the information you need for each stop. This includes the station and line names. (The station names also include links to more information about each station.) Listing 7.7 shows a sample of the JSON data that Dapper generates.

Listing 7.7 Sample of JSON Data from the LondonTubeJourneyPlanner Dapp

```
{"groups": {
  "summary": [
    {"step": [{
      "value": "1: At Baker Street take the Jubilee line (direction Stratford).",
      "originalElement": "span"
    }]},
    {        . . . omitted "steps" . . . }
  ],
  "stop": [
    {
      "station": [{
        "value": "Baker Street",
        "originalElement": "a",
        "href":
          "http://www.tubeplanner.com/cgi-bin/station/
              show_station.pl?station=Baker%20Street"
      }],
      "line": [{
        "value": "Jubilee",
        "originalElement": "span"
      }]
    },
    {        . . . omitted "stops" . . . }
  ],
  "journey": [
    {"endpoint": [{
      "value": "Baker Street",
      "originalElement": "b"
    }]},
    {"endpoint": [{
      "value": "Victoria",
      "originalElement": "b"
    }]}
  ],
  "info": [{"info": [{
    "value": "Estimated journey time 17 minutes. Fare Zones: 1.
          (See our fares page for ticket costs.)",
    "originalElement": "td"
  }]}]
}}
```

The following code accesses the endpoints of a selected journey.

```
var data = data_returned_from_service;
var start = data.groups.journey[0].endpoint[0].value;    // starting point
```

252 Chapter 7 Working with Dapper

```
var destination = data.groups.journey[1].endpoint[0].value;// destination
```

Figure 7.8 shows a preview of the LondonTubeJourneyPlanner on Dapper. Note that there are two input variables, endTube and startTube. You also see a portion of the data results: the stop array with elements station and line (station is a link).

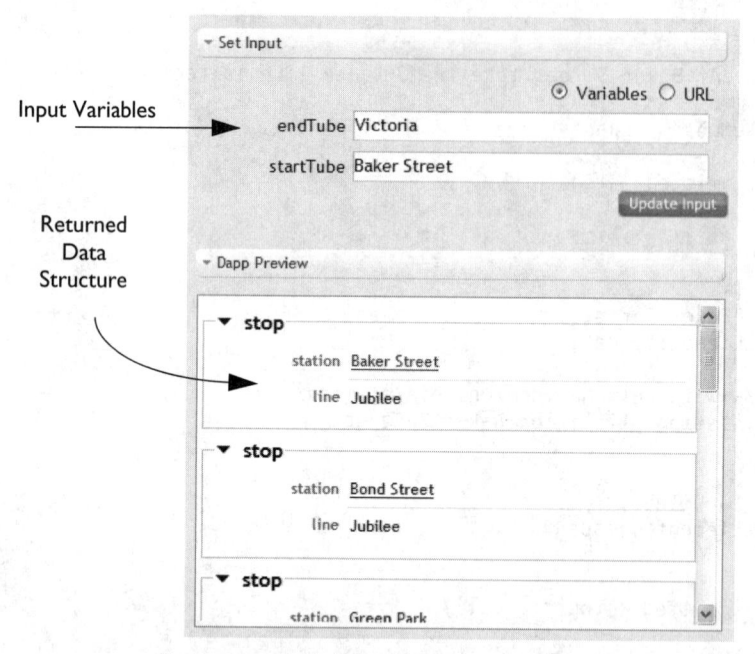

Figure 7.8 Previewing the LondonTubeJourneyPlanner Dapp

Creating Service LondonTubeJourneyPlanner

Listing 7.8 shows the JavaScript code for the LondonTubeJourneyPlanner service, which calls the LondonTubeJourneyPlanner Dapp. The two parameters (startTube and endTube) must exactly match the input variables of the Dapp. We also include error handling when you call the service.

Listing 7.8 LondonTubeJourneyPlanner (JavaScript)

```
var result = Things.dapper.LondonTubeJourneyPlanner({
    startTube: Parameters.startTube,
    endTube: Parameters.endTube});
if (result.groups) return result;
else {
    var error = { };
```

```
    error.code = 602;
    error.message = "Unknown Tube Station provided.";
    error.message += startTube + ", " + endTube;
    Log.write(error.message);
    throw error;
}
```

Creating a service from a Dapp is similar to calling a web API. However, there are several differences. For one, error handling is less than ideal. Content providers can't give you nice error messages when things go wrong. In this example, nothing is returned to the caller if there are errors with input variables. You can therefore base error handling on the value of `result.groups`. If it's empty, the input variables probably contain incorrect tube station names. Thus, we include these names in the generated error message.

Parameter Escape Value

Another difference with Dapper-based services is whether or not to escape input parameters. In this widget, several tube stations have ampersand signs (&) in their names (Elephant & Castle, Chalfont & Latimer, and Harrow & Wealdstone are examples). Note that Dapper does not unescape input variables—any escaped variables from the service are simply passed unchanged to the content provider. These escaped variables will make the widget fail because they won't match any of the options in the content provider's drop down selection component.

To get the behavior you want, uncheck the **Escape value** option when you add the parameter to the service. Figure 7.9 shows the `startTube`'s parameter dialog box with the **Escape value** option unchecked.

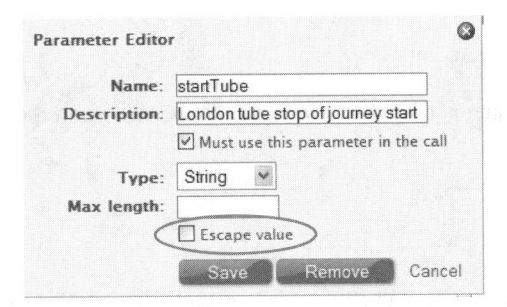

Figure 7.9 Defining parameter startTube—uncheck Escape value

Creating LondonTubeWidget

With the data accessible, you can now craft the widget that you want. Listing 7.9 shows the HTML for the LondonTubeWidget. The input fields (two drop down selection menus) appear in a table along with the button, the London Underground icon, and a link to the content-providing web site. The select tags (startTube and endTube) each have one option defined. The JavaScript code (see Listing 7.11) populates the select tags with the tube station names. Pre-defined selection options means that users will always select valid input for the Dapp. The div tag TubeResults is the placeholder to display the results.

Listing 7.9 LondonTubeWidget (HTML)

```
<div id="TubeWidgetDiv">
   <div id="stationInput">
     <table>

        <tr><td>Tube Station Begin</td>
           <td>
           <select id="startTube">
           <option>Start Tube Station</option>
        </select></td></tr>

        <tr><td>Tube Station End</td>
           <td>
           <select id="endTube">
           <option>Destination Tube Station</option>
        </select></td></tr>

        <tr><td colspan="2">
           <img src="${res('tubelogo.jpg')}">
           <button id="plannerButton">Get Tube Info</button></td>
        </tr>

      <tr><td colspan="2">
         <A href="http://www.tubeplanner.com/">Planning by tubeplanner.com</A>
      </td></tr></table><hr/>
   </div>
   <div id="TubeResults"></div>
</div>
```

Listing 7.10 shows the CSS for the LondonTubeWidget. The TubeWidgeDiv defines the style for the whole widget. The other styles define the various areas of the widget. Style stationInput applies to the table data (td) of the input components and is defined in the HTML code. The remaining styles apply to generated HTML tags in the JavaScript code.

Listing 7.10 LondonTubeWidget (CSS)

```css
#TubeWidgetDiv {
    width: 370px;
    color: #647A88;
    padding: 5px;
    font: 70% Verdana, sans-serif;
}

#stationInput td {
    font: 70% Verdana, sans-serif;
    color: #647A88;
    text-align: center;
}

#titlediv {
    padding: 5px;
    font-weight: bold;
    text-align: center;
}

#sumtitlediv {
    padding: 5px;
    text-align: center;
    font-weight: bold;
    margin-bottom: 5px;
}

#sumdatadiv {
    padding: 5px;
    margin-bottom: 5px;
    margin-left: 5px;
}

#statdiv {
    margin-left: 2px;
    padding: 1px;
}

#statdiv th {
    color: #647A88;
    font: bold 70% Verdana, sans-serf;
    text-align: left;
    width: 190px;
}

#statdiv td {
    color: #647A88;
    font: 70% Verdana, sans-serf;
    padding-bottom: 2px;
}
```

This widget uses the Prototype JavaScript library. From the Resources tab, select **Libraries** (at the bottom) and choose **Prototype** from the list of libraries, as shown in Figure 7.5 on page 246.

Listing 7.11 shows Part 1 of the JavaScript code. Function `populateSelectTags` is invoked when the widget loads. Variable `stationNames` is an Array containing all of the station names. The Prototype each function creates an `Option` object for both select tags. Variable `linecolors` is an associative array where the line name index returns the line's color code (used by the Transport for London maps of the Underground).

Listing 7.11 LondonTubeWidget (JavaScript)—Part 1

```
Event.observe(window, 'load', populateSelectTags);

function populateSelectTags() {
   var stationNames = new Array(
      "Acton Town",
      "Aldgate",
      "Aldgate East",
         . . . many station names omitted . . .
      "Woodford",
      "Woodside Park"
   );

   $("startTube").options.length = 0;
   $("endTube").options.length = 0;
   stationNames.each(function(name,i) {
      $("startTube").options[i] = new Option(name);
      $("endTube").options[i] = new Option(name);
   });
}

var linecolors = {
   "Bakerloo" : "#AE6118",
   "Central"  : "#E41F1F",
   "Circle"   : "#F8D42D",
         . . . many line colors omitted . . .
   "Foot"     : "#D2D2D2"
};
```

Listing 7.12 shows Part 2 of the JavaScript code. The `click` event handler is called when the user clicks the Get Tube Info button. First, it assigns the selected values from the select menus to the variables `startTube` and `endTube`. If the station names match, no call to the service is made. Otherwise, `startTube` and `endTube` become the parameters for the LondonTubeJourneyPlanner service.

The `onSuccess` handler extracts the data and generates the HTML tags that display the title, summary, and information portions of the output.

Listing 7.12 LondonTubeWidget (JavaScript)—Part 2

```
Event.observe($("plannerButton"), 'click', function() {
   var startTube =
      $("startTube").options[$("startTube").selectedIndex].value;
   var endTube =
      $("endTube").options[$("endTube").selectedIndex].value;
   if (startTube == endTube) {
      var resultsHtml = "<b>You're already there!</b><br/>" + startTube
            + " Station";
      $("TubeResults").innerHTML = resultsHtml;
   } else
      Things.callService("ganderson.LondonTubeJourneyPlanner",
      {
         "startTube": startTube, // London tube stop of journey start
         "endTube": endTube // London Tube stop of journey destination
      },
      {
      onSuccess: function(data) {
         var titlestr = "<div id=\"titlediv\">From " +
            data.groups.journey[0].endpoint[0].value
            + " To " + data.groups.journey[1].endpoint[0].value
            + "</div>";

         var summarystr = "<div id=\"sumtitlediv\">Journey Summary</div>" +
            "<div id=\"sumdatadiv\">";

         data.groups.summary.each(function(steps) {
            summarystr += steps.step[0].value + "<p/>";
         });
         var info = data.groups.info[0].info[0].value;

         summarystr += "<p/>" + info.substring(0,info.indexOf("(See"))
            + "</div>";
```

Listing 7.13 shows Part 3 of the JavaScript code. The Prototype each function iterates through the stop array (each stop includes a station name and line) and builds the table with the station, line, and color. The line is the index that extracts the color from the linecolors array. The handler displays the data with a generated HTML table tag. The onFailure handler displays the error message returned from the service.

Listing 7.13 LondonTubeWidget (JavaScript)—Part 3

```
      var stationstr =
         "<div id=\"sumtitlediv\">Journey Points</div><div id=\"statdiv\">" +
         "<table><tr><th>Station</th><th>Line</th><th>Colour Code</th></tr>" ;

      data.groups.stop.each(function(tube) {
         stationstr += "<tr><td>" + tube.station[0].value + "</td>";
         stationstr += "<td>" + tube.line[0].value + "</td>";
```

```
            stationstr += "<td bgcolor=\"" +linecolors[tube.line[0].value]
                + "\">" + "</td></tr>";
        });
        stationstr += "</table></div>";

        var resultsHtml = titlestr + summarystr + stationstr;
        $("TubeResults").innerHTML = resultsHtml;
    },
    onFailure: function(error) {
        var resultsHtml = "Service error: " + error.message;
        $("TubeResults").innerHTML = resultsHtml;
    }
  });
});
```

7.4 MLB Scores Widget

Aah, the crack of the bat in spring signals the beginning of a new major league baseball season. And for those aficionados who care to keep up, score feeds on the web are sorely lacking. Indeed, many baseball sites, including top news sites, offer feeds for baseball news: who's injured, who's being traded, and who will be hired and fired. But finding a feed for scores will keep you Googling all night long and coming up empty handed. Until now.

With Dapper you can create a feed for major league baseball scores. This example is a bit different from the previous ones. The content provider's site does not change with new input; instead it changes with time. When you visit the site today you'll get today's scores. Tomorrow (and throughout the day) the score reports change.

Working with content-heavy, flash-based sites on Dapper can be difficult. Sometimes there's just too much information for Dapper to handle easily. Many times the information is extraneous. For this example, the source information comes from a mobile-friendly site: http://wap.mlb.com/scores/index.jsp. This simplifies page layout and removes unwanted clutter. After experimenting a bit with other score sources (and broken Dapps), the Dapp-friendly mobile site became the content source for the Dapp, **mlbupdate**.

Dapper prefers building Dapps with multiple pages for input, but it is still possible to create a Dapp from a single page. The steps are the same; the tricky part occurs when you select content for fields. As you refine the selections by adding and removing content, Dapper eventually builds the correct data structure for you.

Here is a summary of the steps you'll follow to build Dapp mlbupdate and the service and widget that use it.

Steps to Build the Dapp

1. Initiate the Dapp Factory to create a Dapp.
2. Specify your content's source URL (http://wap.mlb.com/scores/index.jsp).
3. Select content from the sample page.
4. Group the data into a logical structure.
5. Save (publish) your Dapp.

Steps to Create the Service

1. Create a service. Provide a name and description.
2. Use **Find & Use** to call the mlbupdate Dapp from your service and return data to the caller.
3. Test and publish the service.

Steps to Create the Widget

1. Create a new widget. Give it a name and a description.
2. Include the Prototype library.
3. Provide the HTML, CSS, and JavaScript code.
4. Use **Find & Use** to call the mlbscores service from your widget.
5. Preview and publish.
6. Embed in a web page.

Building the mlbupdate Dapp

Figure 7.10 shows the mlbScoresWidget running in a browser. The widget updates scores every 30 seconds (*"Checking for scores . . . "* indicates the update is in progress). It displays the date and a table of today's games, with each row showing one game. The first column shows the opponents and their scores (if any). The second column displays the game's status, which is either the current inning, final for completed games, or the start time if the game has not yet started. The status field also contains a link to the respective game information page on mlb.com so that you can read all about your favorite team's current game. To see how you access the JSON data within the widget, the diagram includes JavaScript expressions for each item.

260   Chapter 7   Working with Dapper

groups.fields.date[0]

groups.games[0].
   game[0].value

Today's MLB Scores		
mlb.com		
Checking for scores...		
Sat, Jul 19		
OAK 1 NYY 2	Top 7	
BOS 0 LAA 0	Top 1	
CLE @ SEA	3:55 PM	
PHI @ FLA	3:55 PM	
SD 0 STL 0	Top 1	
MIL @ SF	4:05 PM	
TOR @ TB	6:10 PM	
WSH @ ATL	7:00 PM	
CHC @ HOU	7:05 PM	
DET @ BAL	7:05 PM	
KC @ CWS	7:05 PM	

Updates every 30 seconds

groups.games[0].status[0].value

groups.games[4].status[0].href

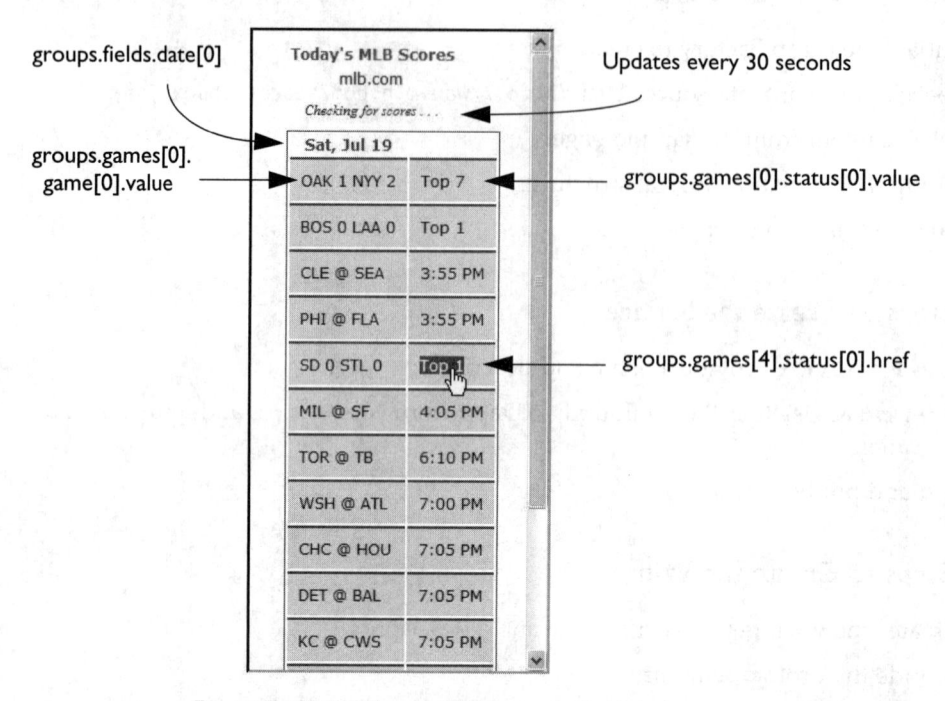

Figure 7.10 MLB Scores Widget running in a browser

Figure 7.11 shows Dapper's data mapping for the mlbupdate Dapp. The scoreboard data displays the date, status for each game, the teams that are playing, and the scores.

MLB Scores Widget

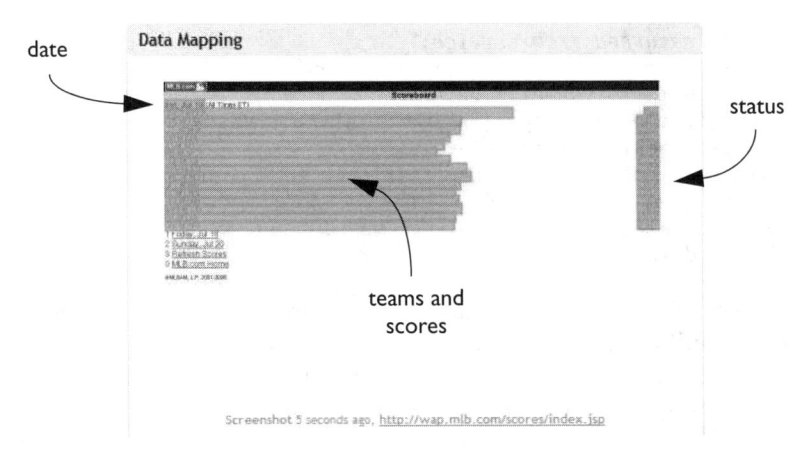

Figure 7.11 Dapper mapping of the scoreboard data

Listing 7.14 is a partial listing of the JSON data produced by the mlbupdate Dapp. It consists of a games array with game and status array objects. There is a separate ungrouped object that contains the date (shown at the end).

Listing 7.14 Sample JSON Data from the mlbupdate Dapp

```
{
  "groups": {"games": [
    {
      "status": [{
        "value": "Top 3",
        "originalElement": "a",
        "fieldName": "status",
        "href":
          "http://wap.mlb.com/scores/game.jsp?gid=2008_07_19_oakmlb_nyamlb_1"
      }],
      "game": [{
        "value": "OAK 0 NYY 2",
        "originalElement": "td",
        "fieldName": "game"
      }]
    },       . . . data omitted . . .
  ]},
  "fields": {"date": [{
    "value": "Sat, Jul 19",
    "originalElement": "span",
    "fieldName": "date"
  }]}
}
```

Here's how you access the status, teams, and date from the returned JSON object.

```
data = data_returned_from_service;
// shows teams and score (if any) of nth game
data.groups.games[n].game[0].value;
// shows status of nth game (inning or start time)
data.groups.games[n].status[0].value;
// linking URL to read more about nth game
data.groups.games[n].status[0].href;
// game information date
data.fields.date[0].value;
```

Figure 7.12 shows a preview of the mlbupdate Dapp run interactively on Dapper. You see a portion of the results: the games array with teams and scores (the game object) as well as status (Top 7, for example). The status object includes a link for more information about that game.

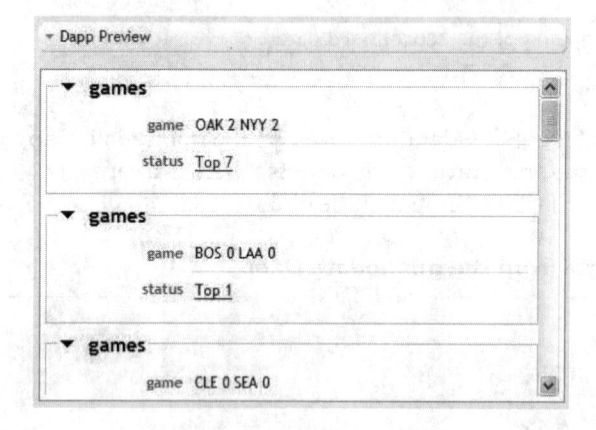

Figure 7.12 Previewing the mlbupdate Dapp

If a game hasn't started, the status field contains the game's start time.

Creating Service mlbscores

The zembly service call invokes the Dapp. There are no parameters, but we check to make sure the returned data (results) is not empty. Listing 7.15 shows the JavaScript code for the mlbscores service.

Listing 7.15 mlbscores Service (JavaScript)

```
var results = Things.dapper.mlbupdate();
if (results.groups) return results;
else {
```

```
    var error = {};
    error.code = 1;
    error.message = "No scoreboard data available.";
    throw error;
}
```

Creating mlbScoresWidget

Listing 7.16 shows the HTML code for mlbScoresWidget. We construct a table to contain the header information: the title, a link to the content provider's web site, and a placeholder (infodiv) to display messages. The div tag mlbresults is the placeholder to display the results.

Listing 7.16 mlbScoresWidget (HTML)

```html
<div id="widgetDiv">
   <div id="widgetInput">
      <table>
         <tr><th>Today's MLB Scores</th></tr>
         <tr><td><a href="http://mlb.com">mlb.com</a></td></tr>
         <tr><td><span id="infodiv"></span></td></tr>
      </table>
   </div>
   <div id="mlbresults"></div>
</div>
```

Listing 7.17 shows the CSS for the mlbScoresWidget. Styles #widgetInput and #widgetInput td control the look of the header information in the widget. Of note is the style definition for tag a (the links) which changes the background and text colors when hovering over links. Style classes .vis and .visr provide styles for the scoreboard table rows and data fields.

Listing 7.17 mlbScoresWidget (CSS)

```css
#widgetInput {
   padding-left: 20px;
}
#widgetInput td {
   text-align: center;
   padding: 2px 0 7px 0;
}
#mlbresults {
   padding-left: 20px;
}
#mlbresults table {
   border: 1px solid #696969
}
```

```css
th {
   font: bold 75% Verdana, sans-serif;
   color: #666666;
}
td {
   color: #333333;
   font: 75% Verdana, sans-serif;
   padding: 0.75em 0.75em 0.75em 0.75em;
}
a {text-decoration: none; color: #333333;}
a:hover {background: #696969; color: #fff}

#infodiv {
   color: #333333;
   font: italic 90% "Times New Roman", serif;
   text-align: center;
}

.visr {background-color: #e1e1e1;}
.vis {border-top: 2px #666 solid;}
```

This widget uses the Prototype JavaScript library. From the Resources tab, select **Libraries** (at the bottom) and choose **Prototype** from the list of libraries, as shown in Figure 7.5 on page 246.

Listing 7.18 and Listing 7.19 show the JavaScript code for the mlbScoresWidget. Listing 7.18 includes variables and functions to initialize the page. Function autoUpdate controls the periodic score updates and the Prototype Event.observe adds a listener for the window load event.

Listing 7.18 mlbScoresWidget (JavaScript)—Part I

```javascript
var UpdateTimer = 1000*30; // 30 seconds
var AutoUpdateFlag = false;
var run;

function autoUpdate() {
   if (AutoUpdateFlag == true) {
      AutoUpdateFlag = false;
      window.clearInterval(run);
   } else {
      AutoUpdateFlag = true;
      run = setInterval("updateScores()", UpdateTimer);
   }
}

Event.observe(window, 'load', function() {
   // get the scores and start the auto update timer
   updateScores();
```

```
   autoUpdate();
});
```

Listing 7.19 includes function updateScores (called when the page loads and at 30-second intervals). Function updateScores first displays a message to let the user know an update is in progress. Next, it calls service mlbscores. The onSuccess handler generates HTML with data from the service (and Dapp). It uses the Prototype each function to iterate through the games array. Lastly, the onFailure handler displays an error message from the service. That's about it: Play Ball!

Listing 7.19 mlbScoresWidget (JavaScript)—Part 2

```
function updateScores() {
   // let user know we're updating
   $("infodiv").innerHTML = "Checking for scores . . . ";
   Things.callService("panderson.mlbscores",{ },
      {
      onSuccess: function(data) {
         var resultsHtml = "<table><tr><th class='datediv'>"
            + data.fields.date[0].value + "</th></tr>";
         data.groups.games.each(function(info) {
            resultsHtml += "<tr class='visr'><td class='vis'>"
               + info.game[0].value
               + "</td><td class='vis'><a href='"
               + info.status[0].href + "'>"
               + info.status[0].value + "</a></td></tr>";
         });
         resultsHtml += "</table>";
         $("infodiv").innerHTML = "All Times Eastern";
         $("mlbresults").innerHTML = resultsHtml;
      },
      onFailure: function(error) {
         Log.write("Error: " + error.code + " : " + error.message);
         var resultsHtml = "Service error: " + error.message;
         $("mlbresults").innerHTML = resultsHtml;
      }
   });
}
```

7.5 Creating a Feed Reader

Dapper makes it very easy to build Dapps from feeds—you just provide the feed URL on the Dapp Factory page. Once you save a Dapp, you then have a way to build a *feed reader*, a widget that displays data from a feed.

In this section, you'll see how to build a feed reader from a Dapp. Figure 7.13 shows a feed reader widget running in a browser. Note that this widget takes a minimalist approach here; the feed reader provides only blog entry titles and publication dates with links to the original published post. This tack encourages users to visit the source site for additional content.

Gambits from Gail

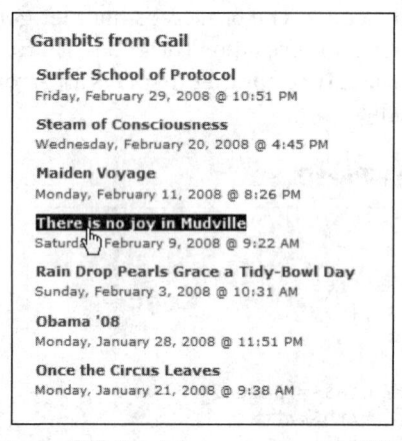

Surfer School of Protocol
Friday, February 29, 2008 @ 10:51 PM

Steam of Consciousness
Wednesday, February 20, 2008 @ 4:45 PM

Maiden Voyage
Monday, February 11, 2008 @ 8:26 PM

There is no joy in Mudville
Saturday, February 9, 2008 @ 9:22 AM

Rain Drop Pearls Grace a Tidy-Bowl Day
Sunday, February 3, 2008 @ 10:31 AM

Obama '08
Monday, January 28, 2008 @ 11:51 PM

Once the Circus Leaves
Monday, January 21, 2008 @ 9:38 AM

Figure 7.13 Feed Summary Reader Widget running in a browser

Here is a summary of the steps you'll follow to build the feed reader Dapp, service, and widget.

Steps to Build the Dapp

1. Initiate the Dapp Factory to create a Dapp.
2. Specify your content's source URL (`http://feeds.feedburner.com/GambitsFrom-Gail`).
3. Select content from the sample page.
4. Save (publish) your Dapp.

Steps to Create the Service

1. Create a service. Provide a name and description.
2. Use **Find & Use** to call the Dapp from your service and return data to the caller.
3. Test and publish the service.

Creating a Feed Reader   267

Steps to Create the Widget

1. Create a new widget. Give it a name and a description.
2. Include the Prototype library.
3. Provide the HTML, CSS, and JavaScript code.
4. Use **Find & Use** to call the mlbscores service from your widget.
5. Preview and publish.
6. Embed in a web page.

Building a Feed-Based Dapp

Figure 7.14 shows the data mapping page on Dapper for the feed content, blog *Gambits from Gail*. Three main fields appear: the title, the publication date, and the description. These fields are all provided by the RSS feed generated by www.feedburner.com.

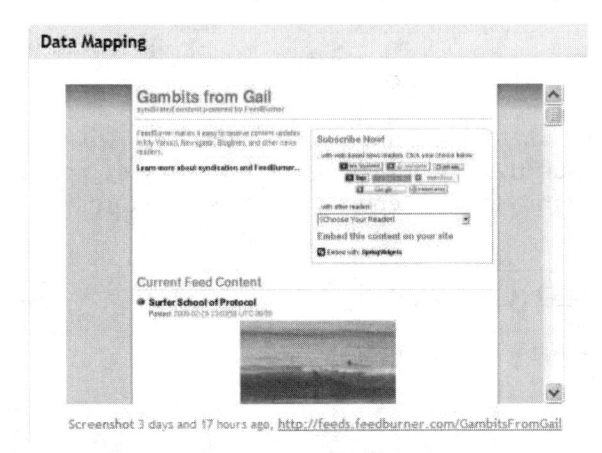

Figure 7.14 Data Mapping on Dapper

Figure 7.15 shows the results of running the Dapp interactively on Dapper's preview page. The scroll bar lets you view several entries for the feed. Each item has several date fields (the first one is the original publication date) and several link fields (the first one is the source URL for the post).

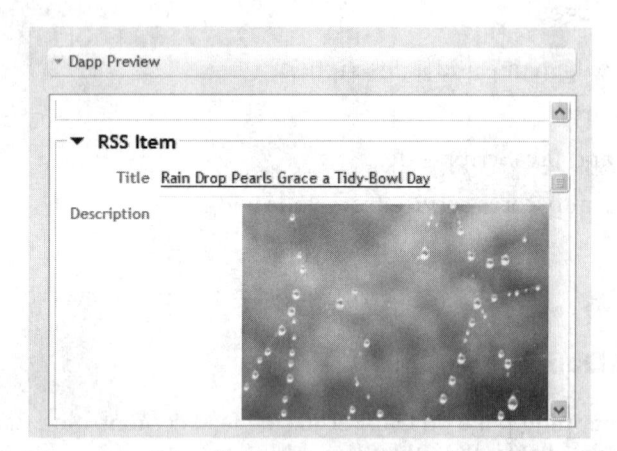

Figure 7.15 Previewing the GambitsfromGailFeed Dapp

Building Service GambitsfromGailFeed

Listing 7.20 shows the JavaScript code for the GambitsfromGailFeed service. This service checks the `results` return value to ensure it's not empty. If `results` is empty, the service builds an `error` object and throws an exception. Otherwise, it returns `results` (the feed data) to the caller.

Listing 7.20 GambitsfromGailFeed (JavaScript)

```
var results = Things.dapper.GambitsFromGailFeed();
if (results.groups) return results;
else {
   var error = {};
   error.code = 1;
   error.message = "No feed data.";
   throw error;
}
```

Building GambitsSummaryWidget

Listing 7.21 shows the HTML code for the feed reader widget. This HTML consists of a div tag (`blogFeedResults`) that serves as a placeholder for the feed content.

Listing 7.21 GambitsSummaryWidget (HTML)

```
<div id="widgetDiv">
   <div id="blogFeedResults"></div>
</div>
```

Listing 7.22 shows the CSS code for the widget. The CSS consists of three main styles: `headingdiv` for the post title, `datediv` for the entry's publication date, and `titlediv` for the blog's title. Styles for links (tag a) control background color and text color, including hover effects.

Listing 7.22 GambitsSummaryWidget (CSS)

```
a {text-decoration: none;}
a:link {color: #666666;}
a:visited {color: #666666;}
a:hover {background-color: #333333; color: #fff}

#headingdiv {
   color: #666666;
   font: bold 70% Verdana, sans-serif;
   margin: 0.5em 0 0 1em;
}

#datediv {
   color: #666666;
   font: 65% Verdana, sans-serif;
   margin: 0.3em 0 1em 1em;
}

#titlediv {
   color: #666666;
   font: bold 80% Verdana, sans-serif;
   margin: 1em 0 1em 0.5em;
}
```

This widget uses the Prototype JavaScript library. From the Resources tab, select **Libraries** (at the bottom) and choose **Prototype** from the list of libraries, as shown in Figure 7.5 on page 246.

Listing 7.23 shows Part 1 of the JavaScript code for the feed reader widget. It consists of support functions for transforming a date returned by the RSS feed into a user-friendly format.

Listing 7.23 GambitsSummaryWidget (JavaScript)—Part 1

```
var months = new Array(
   "January",
   "February",
      ...
   "December"
);

var days = new Array(
   "Sunday",
   "Monday",
      ...
   "Saturday"
);

function parseDate(datetime) {
   // 2008-02-29T22:51:00.000-08:00
   var d = datetime.substring(0,datetime.indexOf('T'));
   var t = datetime.substring(datetime.indexOf('T')+1,19);
   var z = datetime.substring(23,30);
   var zlist = z.split(":");
   var tlist = t.split(":");
   var datelist = d.split("-");
   var mydate = new Date(datelist[0],Number(datelist[1])-1,
        datelist[2],(tlist[0]), tlist[1], tlist[2]);
   //Friday, February 29, 2008 @ 10:51 PM
   var ampmstr = "";
   var hour = mydate.getHours();
   if (hour > 12) {
      hour -= 12;
      ampmstr = " PM";
   }
   else ampmstr = " AM";

   var newdate = days[mydate.getDay()] + ", " +
        months[mydate.getMonth()] + " " +
        mydate.getDate() + ", " +
        mydate.getFullYear() + " @ " +
        hour + ":" +
        mydate.getMinutes() + ampmstr;
   return newdate;
}
```

Listing 7.24 shows Part 2 of the JavaScript code for the feed reader. This code calls the service when the widget loads (Event.observe with event 'load') and pulls the first seven items of the feed. The generated HTML includes the item's title, link, and publication date. The onFailure handler generates the error message returned from the service.

Listing 7.24 GambitsSummaryWidget (JavaScript)—Part 2

```
Event.observe(window, 'load', function() {
   Things.callService("ganderson.GambitsFromGailFeed",{},
       {
       onSuccess: function(data) {
          var resultsHtml = "<div id=\"titlediv\">" +
              "<a href=\"" + "http://www.gailanderson.org" + "\">"+
              "Gambits from Gail" + "</a></div>";
          var items = data.groups.RSS_Item.length;
          if (items > 7) items = 7;
          for (var i = 0; i < items; i++) {
             var mydate = parseDate(
                       data.groups.RSS_Item[i].Publication_Date[0].value);
             var link = data.groups.RSS_Item[i].Item_Link[0].value;
             var title = data.groups.RSS_Item[i].Title[0].value;
             resultsHtml +=
                   "<div id=\"headingdiv\">" +
             "<a href=\"" + link + "\">"+ title + "</a></div>" +
                "<div id=\"datediv\">" + mydate + "</div>";
          }
          $("blogFeedResults").innerHTML = resultsHtml;
          },
       onFailure: function(error) {
          var resultsHtml = "Service error: " + error.message;
          $("blogFeedResults").innerHTML = resultsHtml;
       }
    });
});
```

8 Widget Gallery

E4X   widgets   JSON

Yahoo! Pipes   **mashups**   WeatherBug

London Tube   google maps   filtering   RSS Feeds

zembly is open-ended. There's no limit to the variety of interesting widgets and services you can construct. To that end, we've gathered together a few widgets for you in this chapter. Some of these widgets illustrate useful building techniques, some look cool on the page, and some are just fun to play with. Many of these examples build upon widgets you've seen in previous chapters.

What You Will Learn

- Using E4X in a service to extract targeted data
- Building a JSON object to return data to a caller
- Parsing JSON data in a widget
- Uploading a JavaScript script file to call from your widget
- Drawing line segments with Google Maps
- Constructing custom feeds with Yahoo! Pipes

Examples in This Chapter

All examples in this chapter are tagged **zembly-book-gallery**. To search for them, select **Search** at the top of any **zembly** page. Supply the search term **zembly-book-gallery** and click the search icon as shown in Figure 8.1.

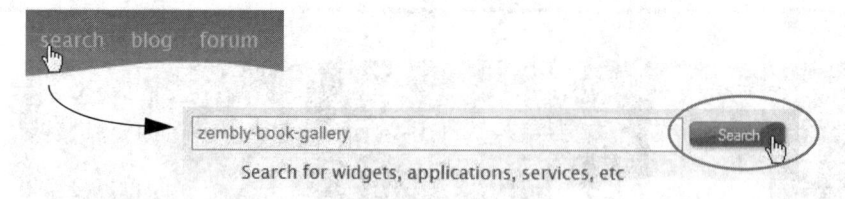

Figure 8.1 Searching for the examples in this chapter

The search results lists the widgets and services discussed in this chapter.

8.1 LiveWeatherBugWidget

The previous version of WeatherBugWidget (see "Building WeatherBugWidget" on page 51) uses "pre-packaged" HTML results from the WeatherBug service call to fashion the widget. This works fairly well, as long as the information and format are what you want. However, if you'd like to display different information (and WeatherBug gives you a quite a variety of statistical data), then you must work with the XML data that WeatherBug returns.

This new version of WeatherBugWidget (named LiveWeatherBugWidget), shows you how to grab just the data you want. In Figure 8.2 you see two different instances of this updated widget running in a browser with weather data from Fort Riley, Kansas and Kapaa, Hawaii. Note that this widget now shows you the date and time, current condition (along with a photo icon), moon phase (with an icon), current temperature, today's rain amount, today's high and low temperatures, and times for sunrise and sunset.

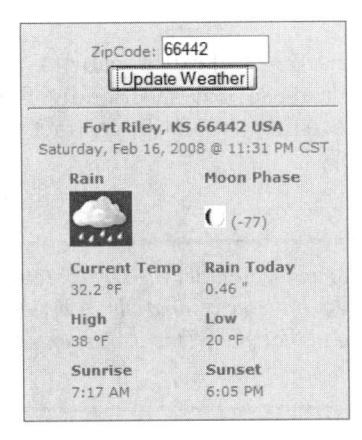

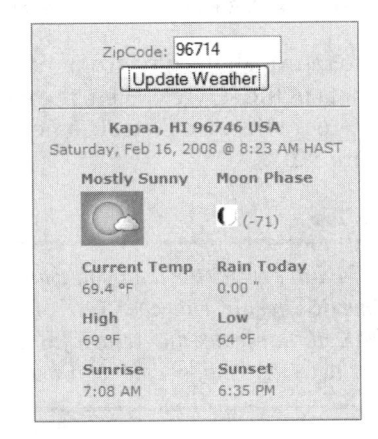

Figure 8.2 Two examples of LiveWeatherBugWidget running in a browser

This widget also makes generous use of CSS styles and relies on a modified service to provide the desired data from the WeatherBug API call. Here's a summary of the steps you'll follow to build the new WeatherBug service and widget.

Steps to Create the Service

1. Create a service to call the LiveWeather adapter. Provide a name and description.
2. Extract the XML data you want and build a JSON object to return to the caller.
3. Test and publish the service.

Steps to Create the Widget

1. Create a new widget. Give it a name and a description.
2. Include the Prototype library.
3. Provide the HTML, CSS, and JavaScript code.
4. Use **Find & Use** to call the LiveWeatherBug service from your widget.
5. Preview and publish.
6. Embed in a web page.

Using E4X to Build LiveWeatherBugService

While it's possible to return all the data from the WeatherBug API call, it's a better tack to manipulate the data in the service. Then, the widget can use browser-friendly JSON for its presentation. To do this, we'll create a new service that uses E4X to extract the data shown in Figure 8.2.

Programming Tip

It's tempting to use E4X to extract the data you want in the widget and let the service return the entire LiveWeatherRSS result. However, E4X is not cross-browser compatible. A better approach is to use E4X in the service and return JSON data to the caller. This makes your widget smaller and easier to write. And, of course, it will run in any browser.

The previous version of WeatherBugWidget (see Listing 2.10 on page 52) grabs the HTML code embedded in the [CDATA[. . .]] field of the WeatherBug response and inserts it into the document's markup. In this version, you'll extract just the data you're interested in from the XML response in the service.

Listing 8.1 shows a sample of the XML response from WeatherBug. Let's show you how to access the various nodes using JavaScript and E4X.

Listing 8.1 Sample XML Response from WeatherBug

```
<rss version="2.0">
  <channel>
    <title>Observations from Encinitas, CA - USA</title>
    <link>...</link>
    <description>...</description>
    <language>en-us</language>
    <lastBuildDate>Fri, 15 Feb 2008 01:00:00 GMT</lastBuildDate>
    <ttl>60</ttl>
    <aws:weather xmlns:aws="http://www.aws.com/aws">
      <aws:api version="2.0"/>
      <aws:WebURL>...</aws:WebURL>
      <aws:ob>
        <aws:ob-date>
          <aws:year number="2008"/>
          <aws:month abbrv="Feb" number="2" text="February"/>
          <aws:day abbrv="Thu" number="14" text="Thursday"/>
          <aws:hour hour-24="17" number="5"/>
          <aws:minute number="02"/>
          <aws:second number="01"/>
          <aws:am-pm abbrv="PM"/>
          <aws:time-zone abbrv="PST" offset="-8" text="Pacific Standard Time"/>
        </aws:ob-date>
        . . .
      </aws:ob>
```

```
    </aws:weather>
  </channel>
</rss>
```

As shown above, the weather data consists of nodes in a namespace called aws. How do you access these nodes? Here's the code.

```
// define namespace aws
var aws = new Namespace("http://www.aws.com/aws");

// The xml is stored in variable wbdata
// Here's how to access the ob-date node
var date = wbdata.channel..aws::["ob-date"];
// extract attribute number from node year in the date node
var year = date.aws::year.@number;
```

The notation *namespace::node_name* (aws::year, for example) accesses the specified node.

Programming Tip

Note that when a node name such as ob-date *contains a JavaScript character (- is the minus operator), you must quote the node name and use bracket notation to access the node data.*

WeatherBug supplies most of its data as XML node *attributes*. For example, the number data in node year is accessed using @number. Attributes provide more flexibility in representing the data. You can access node date.aws::day, for example, with attribute text ("Thursday"), attribute abbrv ("Thu"), or attribute number ("14").

Now let's look at the LiveWeatherBugService JavaScript code. Listing 8.2 shows Part 1. This service calls the LiveWeatherRSS adapter owned by WeatherBug with three parameters: the target zip code, the unit type ("0" is U.S. units such as degrees Fahrenheit and inches), and the WeatherBug API key (keys).

The rest of the code uses E4X to extract the data and return it to the caller.

Listing 8.2 LiveWeatherBugService (JavaScript)—Part I

```
var wbdata = Things.WeatherBug.LiveWeatherRSS({
    "zipcode": Parameters.zipcode, // 5-digit ZipCode, U.S. cities only
    "unittype": "0", // Optional. Default value is 1. Values are 0
    // (US customary units - miles, degrees Fahrenheit, etc.) or
    // 1 (metric units - kms, degrees Celsius, etc).
    "keys": Owner.keychain
});

var aws = new Namespace("http://www.aws.com/aws");
```

```
var date = wbdata.channel..aws::["ob-date"];
var sunrise = wbdata.channel..aws::sunrise;
var sunset = wbdata.channel..aws::sunset;

// Put the data we want in a result object
var result = new Object();
result.currentcond = { };
result.moonphase = { };
```

In JavaScript, there are two ways to build objects. You can see that object `result` has many properties (such as "citystate" and "zipcode") and a few substructures ("currentcond" and "moonphase"). Listing 8.3 contains the JavaScript code that builds object `result` using E4X notation.

Listing 8.3 LiveWeatherBugService (JavaScript)—Part 2

```
result = {
   "citystate" : wbdata.channel..aws::['city-state'] + "",
   "zipcode" : wbdata.channel..aws::['city-state'].@zipcode + "",
   "country" : wbdata.channel..aws::country + "",
   "day" : date.aws::day.@text + "",
   "month" : date.aws::month.@abbrv + "",
   "dayno" : date.aws::day.@number + "",
   "year" : date.aws::year.@number + "",
   "timestr" : date.aws::hour.@number + ":" +
      date.aws::minute.@number + " " +
      date.aws::["am-pm"].@abbrv + " " +
      date.aws::["time-zone"].@abbrv,
   "sunrisestr" : sunrise.aws::hour.@number + ":" +
      sunrise.aws::minute.@number + " " +
      sunrise.aws::["am-pm"].@abbrv,
   "sunsetstr" : sunset.aws::hour.@number + ":" +
      sunset.aws::minute.@number + " " +
      sunset.aws::["am-pm"].@abbrv,
   "currenttemp" : wbdata.channel..aws::temp + " " +
      wbdata.channel..aws::temp.@units,
   "hightemp" : wbdata.channel..aws::["temp-high"] + " " +
      wbdata.channel..aws::["temp-high"].@units,
   "lowtemp" : wbdata.channel..aws::["temp-low"] + " " +
      wbdata.channel..aws::["temp-low"].@units,
   "rain" : wbdata.channel..aws::["rain-today"] + " " +
      wbdata.channel..aws::["rain-today"].@units
};

result.currentcond = {
      "status" : wbdata.channel..aws::["current-condition"] + "",
      "icon" : wbdata.channel..aws::["current-condition"].@icon + ""
};
result.moonphase = {
```

```
        "status" : wbdata.channel..aws::["moon-phase"] + "",
        "icon"   : wbdata.channel..aws::["moon-phase"].@["moon-phase-img"] + ""
};

return result;
```

Building LiveWeatherBugWidget

Listing 8.4 shows you the HTML code for our widget, including a top-level div tag (weatherBugWidget) and an embedded div tag for the input elements (weatherInput). There's an input element for a user to supply the target zip code and a button to submit the service request to LiveWeatherBugService. Another div tag holds the results (weatherBugResults).

Listing 8.4 LiveWeatherBugWidget (HTML)

```
<div id="weatherBugWidget">
   <div id="weatherInput">
      ZipCode: <input id="zipcode" size="10" type="text" value="92024" />
      <br/><button id="weatherButton">Update Weather</button>
   </div>
   <hr/>
   <div id="weatherBugResults"></div>
</div>
```

Controlling the Look of Your Widget with CSS

The widgets in Figure 8.2 have a fixed size with a gray background and a narrow, solid border. The information is centered and the weather data appears in a table format. While the widget's JavaScript code generates the HTML to create the table, the look of the widget and the weather data's styling are all controlled by the CSS code.

Listing 8.5 shows the CSS styles for LiveWeatherBugWidget. The weatherBugWidget style includes a background color, text color, size, font, padding and border. Similarly, the weatherInput style defines user input elements, specifying centering and padding. The div tags for both these styles are defined in Listing 8.4.

The rest of the style definitions apply to tag elements generated in the JavaScript code. Listing 8.5 includes style definitions for the location information (placediv), the date and time information (datediv), and the div that holds the statistics in a table (statdiv). Note that besides definitions for statdiv, the CSS includes styles for the statdiv table headings (statdiv th) and table data (statdiv td). These styles define an indented table component (left-margin for statdiv) with a specified column width (width for statdiv th).

Listing 8.5 LiveWeatherBugWidget (CSS)

```
#weatherBugWidget {
    background: #e5e5e5;
    height: 300px;
    width: 250px;
    color: #647A88;
    border: 1px solid;
    padding: 5px;
    font: 70% Verdana, sans-serif;
}

#weatherInput {
    padding: 5px;
    text-align: center;
}

#placediv {
    padding: 2px;
    font-weight: bold;
    text-align: center;
}

#datediv {
    padding: 2px;
    text-align: center;
}

#statdiv {
    margin-left: 25px;
    padding: 5px;
}

#statdiv th {
    color: #647A88;
    font: bold 70% Verdana, sans-serf;
    text-align: left;
    width: 120px;
}

#statdiv td {
    color: #647A88;
    font: 70% Verdana, sans-serf;
    padding-bottom: 7px;
}
```

Accessing JSON Data

What does the JSON data look like that's returned from the service? Listing 8.6 shows a sample of the result object that LiveWeatherBugService builds and returns to the caller. You'll see that accessing this data is easy with JavaScript (Listing 8.7 and Listing 8.8).

Listing 8.6 Sample JSON Data from LiveWeatherBugService

```
{
  "sunrisestr": "6:28 AM",
  "lowtemp": "53 &deg;F",
  "currentcond": {
    "icon": "http://deskwx.weatherbug.com/images/Forecast/icons/cond001.gif",
    "status": "Cloudy"
  },
  "zipcode": "92024",
  "sunsetstr": "5:37 PM",
  "timestr": "11:41 AM PST",
  "country": "USA",
  "hightemp": "58 &deg;F",
  "currenttemp": "57.0 &deg;F",
  "month": "Feb",
  "dayno": "19",
  "citystate": "Encinitas,   CA",
  "year": "2008",
  "day": "Tuesday",
  "moonphase": {
    "icon": "http://api.wxbug.net/images/moonphase/mphase13.gif",
    "status": "-95"
  },
  "rain": "0.00 \""
}
```

The onSuccess handler returns the data as a JavaScript object. Here's how to access several of the fields from the sample data in Listing 8.6.

```
var currenttemp = data.currenttemp;
var month = data.month;
var today_status = data.currentcond.status;
```

LiveWeatherBugWidget JavaScript

This widget uses the Prototype JavaScript library. From the Resources tab, select **Libraries** (at the bottom) and choose **Prototype** from the list of libraries, as shown in Figure 8.3.

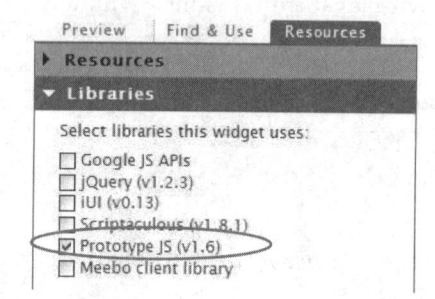

Figure 8.3 Adding the Prototype library to your widget

Listing 8.7 shows Part 1 of the widget's JavaScript code. When a user clicks the Update Weather button, the `'click'` event listener is invoked. The zip code value is extracted and supplied to the LiveWeatherBugService call. Extracting the data lets you generate the HTML to display the information.

Listing 8.7 LiveWeatherBugWidget (JavaScript)—Part 1

```
// LiveWeatherBugWidget
Event.observe($("weatherButton"), 'click', function() {
  var zipcode = $("zipcode").value;

  Things.callService("ganderson.LiveWeatherBugService", {
  zipcode: zipcode},
  {
  onSuccess: function(data) {
     var datestr = "<div id=\"datediv\">" +
        data.day + ", " +
        data.month + " " +
        data.dayno + ", " +
        data.year + " @ " +
        data.timestr + "</div>";

     var placestr = "<div id=\"placediv\">" +
        data.citystate + " " +
        data.zipcode + " " +
        data.country + "</div>";
```

First the function builds the date and time string (properties `day`, `month`, `dayno`, `year`, and `timestr`) and location information (properties `citystate`, `zipcode`, and `country`).

Listing 8.8 shows the rest of the JavaScript's generated HTML code. Variable `tablestr` holds the HTML to construct a table tag with headers (tag `th`) and data (tag `td`). Recall that these tags have styles defined in Listing 8.5. The table also includes two icon images (`data.currentcond.icon` and `data.moonphase.icon`, which tag `img` displays) along with the statistical data for the current status, moon phase, current temperature, high and low temperatures, and today's rainfall.

Listing 8.8 LiveWeatherBugWidget (JavaScript)—Part 2

```
        var tablestr = "<div id=\"statdiv\"><table>" +
          "<tr><th>" +
          data.currentcond.status +
          "</th><th>Moon Phase</th></tr><tr><td>" +
          "<img src=\"" +
          data.currentcond.icon +
          "\" alt=\"No Image\"></img></td><td><img src=\"" +
          data.moonphase.icon +
          "\" alt=\"No Image\"></img> (" +
          data.moonphase.status + ")</td></tr>";

        tablestr +=
          "<tr><th>Current Temp</th>" +
          "<th>Rain Today</th></tr>" + "<tr><td>" +
          data.currenttemp + "</td><td>" +
          data.rain +
          "</td></tr><tr><th>High</th><th>Low</th></tr>" +
          "<tr><td>" +
          data.hightemp +
          "</td><td>" +
          data.lowtemp +
          "</td></tr><tr><th>Sunrise</th><th>Sunset</th></tr>" +
          "<tr><td>" +
          data.sunrisestr +
          "</td><td>" +
          data.sunsetstr +
          "</td></tr></table></div>";
        var resultsHtml = placestr + datestr + tablestr;
        $("weatherBugResults").innerHTML = resultsHtml;
        },onFailure: function(error) {alert(error.code);}
    });
});
```

After building the table data, the code inserts the HTML (strings `placestr`, `datestr`, and `tablestr`) in the document's HTML markup with `innerHTML`.

Embedding LiveWeatherBugWidget

Since this widget has specific height and width values defined in its CSS styles (see style `#weatherBugWidget` in Listing 8.5 on page 280), you'll need to provide dimensions for the `iframe` tag to embed this widget in a web page. The height and width values below are slightly larger to accommodate the widget without scroll bars. (Select tab **Configure** to specify height and width values interactively.)

Listing 8.9 HTML to Embed Your Widget

```
<iframe width=280 height=335
   src="http://05bba928fcbf4b8ab0f9ff7126f8c59d.zembly.com/things/
   05bba928fcbf4b8ab0f9ff7126f8c59d?iframe">
</iframe>
```

Happy WeatherBugging!

8.2 LiveWeatherMapWidget

You may not be able to build a better mousetrap, but you can always build a better widget. Figure 8.4 shows another weather widget; this one includes a Google map to show the location of the target zip code. The weather statistics appear in a pop up information window attached to the map's marker.

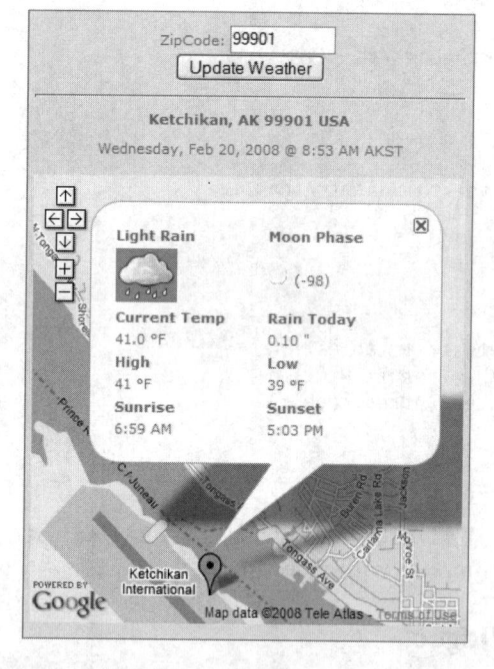

Figure 8.4 LiveWeatherMapWidget running in a browser

You'll recall from the Zillow-Google Maps mashup presented in Chapter 4 ("Building a Google Maps Mashup" on page 92) that a Google map requires a center point. As it turns out, the data from WeatherBug includes the latitude and longitude coordinates of the observation station. Before you can build a widget that includes a Google map, you'll need to add WeatherBug's latitude and longitude data to the result object returned by the service.

Fortunately, adding more data to the LiveWeatherBugService return object is easy. You simply create another property to hold the data. Furthermore, this added property does not disturb earlier widgets (such as the previously built LiveWeatherBugWidget) that use LiveWeatherBugService. The service remains backwards compatible.

Here's a summary of the steps you'll follow to build the WeatherBug mashup that includes a Google map.

1. Modify the LiveWeatherBug service to include the latitude and longitude data with the JSON return object.
2. Create a new widget (or clone the previous WeatherBug widget). Give it a name and a description.
3. Add the Google Maps script tag with your Google API key.
4. Modify the HTML, CSS, and JavaScript code to include Google maps.
5. Preview and publish.
6. Embed in a web page.

Modifying LiveWeatherBugService

Listing 8.10 shows the modified LiveWeatherBugService JavaScript code. The added code is in bold and much of the duplicate code (found in Listing 8.2 on page 277) is omitted. As you can see, only a few lines of code are required to include the coordinate data in the result object.

Listing 8.10 LiveWeatherBugService (JavaScript)

```
var data = Things.weatherbug.LiveWeatherRSS ({
    zipcode: Parameters.zipcode,
    unitType: "0",
    keys: Owner.keychain
} );

    . . . omitted code . . .
// Put the data we want in a result object
var result = new Object();
result.currentcond = { };
result.moonphase = { };
result.coordinates = { };

result = {
    . . . omitted code . . .
```

```
};
result.currentcond = {
   . . . omitted code . . .
};
result.moonphase = {
   . . . omitted code . . .
};
result.coordinates = {
   "latitude"  : data.channel..aws::latitude + "",
   "longitude" : data.channel..aws::longitude + ""
};
return result;
```

Building LiveWeatherMapWidget

Listing 8.11 shows the HTML code for the LiveWeatherMapWidget with changes from the HTML code in Listing 8.4 in bold. The `script` tag loads the Google Maps JavaScript library and the `src` attribute includes your required Google API key. (See "Exploring Google Maps API" on page 93 for information on using Google Maps in widgets.) The `div` tag with `id` attribute "`map_canvas`" provides the placeholder for the map. Its size is defined in the CSS code.

Listing 8.11 LiveWeatherMapWidget (HTML)

```
<script src="http://maps.google.com/maps?file=api&amp;v=2&amp;key=Google Key"
   type="text/javascript"></script>
<body onunload="GUnload()">

<div id="weatherBugWidget">
   <div id="weatherInput">
      ZipCode: <input id="zipcode" size="10" type="text" value="92024" />
      <br/><button id="weatherButton">Update Weather</button>
   </div>
   <hr/>
   <div id="weatherBugResults"></div>
   <div id="map_canvas"></div>
</div>
</body>
```

CSS for the Map Widget

Listing 8.12 shows the CSS code, which has modifications (shown in bold) to accommodate the different layout of the widget. For example, the table statistics (style `statdiv`) now has a smaller left margin. Likewise, style `statdiv td` has a smaller padding size. The style for `weatherBugWidget` specifies more vertical space to make room for the map. The `map_canvas` style specifies the map's view port size.

Listing 8.12 LiveWeatherMapWidget (CSS)

```css
#weatherBugWidget {
    background: #e5e5e5;
    height: 480px;
    width: 350px;
    color: #647A88;
    border: 1px solid;
    padding: 5px;
    font: 70% Verdana, sans-serif;
}

#map_canvas {
    height: 350px;
    width: 350px;
}

#weatherInput {
    padding: 5px;
    text-align: center;
}
#placediv {
    padding: 5px;
    font-weight: bold;
    text-align: center;
}
#datediv {
    padding: 5px;
    text-align: center;
    margin-bottom: 10px;
}

#statdiv {
    margin-left: 1px;
    padding: 1px;
}

#statdiv th {
    color: #647A88;
    font: bold 70% Verdana, sans-serf;
    text-align: left; width: 120px;
}

#statdiv td {
    color: #647A88;
    font: 70% Verdana, sans-serf;
    padding-bottom: 2px;
}
```

Building the LiveWeatherMapWidget Mashup

This widget uses the Prototype JavaScript library. From the Resources tab, select **Libraries** (at the bottom) and choose **Prototype** from the list of libraries, as shown in Figure 8.3 on page 282.

Listing 8.13 shows the JavaScript for LiveWeatherMapWidget. Since it's very similar to Listing 8.7 and Listing 8.8, most of the duplicate code is omitted. Note that the code now includes functions `init_map` and `add_marker` that initialize the Google map with the coordinate values returned from LiveWeatherBugService and add the marker with its pop up information window. The information window is initially opened so that users see the weather statistics without having to provide an extra mouse click. The map controls let users zoom in or out and move the view port.

The code that builds the HTML strings (`datestr`, `placestr`, and `tablestr`) is unchanged from the original LiveWeatherBugWidget presented in the previous section. Here, HTML string `tablestr` is passed to function `add_marker` so that it appears in the map's pop up information window. Once again, you see the benefit of separating HTML markup from style information, since the markup in these two widgets is unchanged.

Listing 8.13 LiveWeatherMapWidget (JavaScript)

```
var map;

function init_map(lat, lng) {
    if (GBrowserIsCompatible()) {
        map = new GMap2(document.getElementById("map_canvas"));
        map.addControl(new GSmallMapControl());
        map.setCenter(new GLatLng(lat, lng), 11);
    }
}

function add_marker(lat, lng, htmlstr) {
    var point = new GLatLng(lat, lng);
    var marker = new GMarker(point);
    GEvent.addListener(marker, "click", function() {
        marker.openInfoWindowHtml(htmlstr);
    });
    map.addOverlay(marker);
    // open information window by default
    marker.openInfoWindowHtml(htmlstr);
}

Event.observe($("weatherButton"), 'click', function() {
    var zipcode = $("zipcode").value;

    Things.callService("ganderson.LiveWeatherBugService", {
```

```
        zipcode: zipcode},
    {
    onSuccess: function(data) {
        var lat = data.coordinates.latitude;
        var lng = data.coordinates.longitude;

        init_map(lat, lng);

        var datestr  =     . . . code omitted . . .
        var placestr =     . . . code omitted . . .
        var tablestr =     . . . code omitted . . .

        add_marker(lat, lng, tablestr);
        var resultsHtml = placestr + datestr;
        $("weatherBugResults").innerHTML = resultsHtml;
    },onFailure: function(error) {alert(error.code);}
    });
});
```

Embedding LiveWeatherMapWidget

The height and width values below accommodate this new widget.

Listing 8.14 HTML to Embed Your Widget

```
<iframe width=380 height=510
     src="http://e3ee776be8b949d68f04d29f66d3dbd8.zembly.com/things/
     e3ee776be8b949d68f04d29f66d3dbd8;iframe">
</iframe>
```

8.3 LondonTubeMapWidget

In the noble quest to present engaging, visual data, let's enhance the LondonTubeWidget presented in Section 7.3 on page 248 (see "London Tube Widget"). You'll recall that the original widget lists only tube stops and line names as part of its response data. With mapping technology, you can give users a more intuitive view of the data.

To that end, this version of the widget (LondonTubeMapWidget) presents a map of London that users may consult to identify tube starting points and destinations. Users make tube stop selections from the options in the selection menu. Figure 8.5 shows LondonTubeMapWidget running in a browser with starting point Oxford Circus and destination Angel.

290   Chapter 8   Widget Gallery

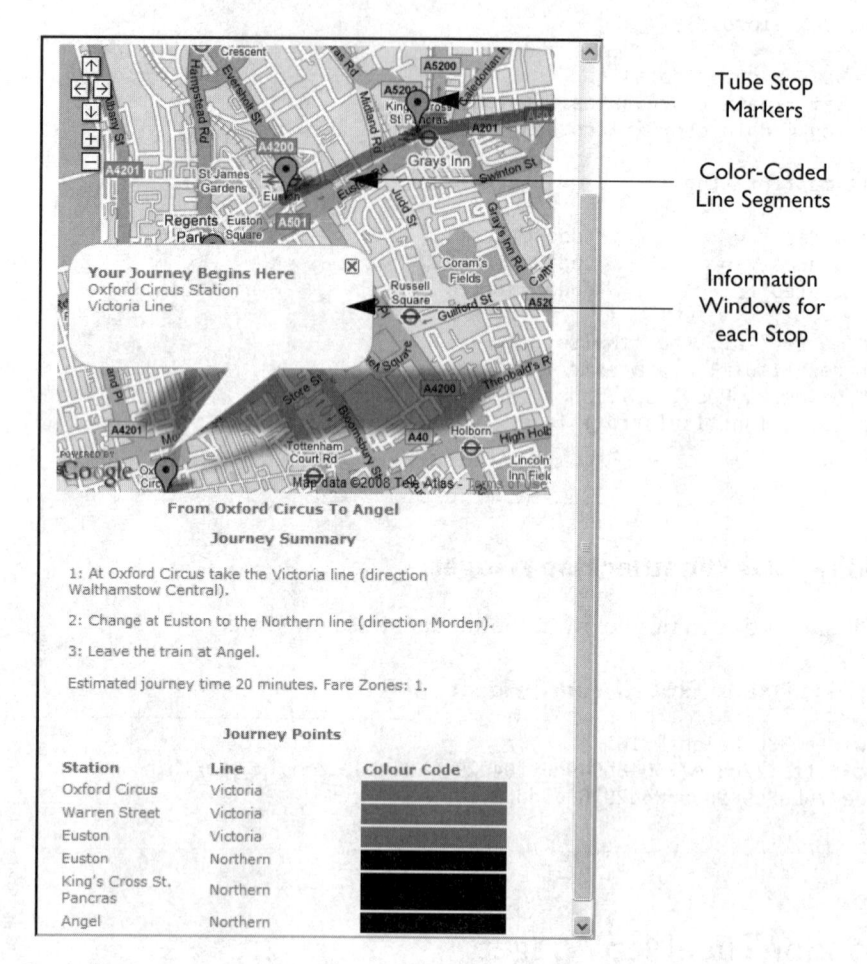

Figure 8.5 LondonTubeMapWidget running in a browser

The widget marks each stop on the map with a marker and information window. The stops are connected with Google Maps "polylines," color-coded with the London Underground line colors. Information windows include the journey's start and end points and indicate where the traveler changes tube lines.

Here's a summary of the steps you'll follow to build the LondonTubeMap widget.

1. Create a new blank widget (or clone the previous LondonTube widget). Give it a name and a description.
2. Add the Google Maps script tag with your Google API key.

3. Upload JavaScript file `stations_data.js` using the Resources tab.
4. Modify the HTML, CSS, and JavaScript code to include Google maps.
5. Preview and publish.
6. Embed in a web page.

Building LondonTubeMapWidget

No changes are required to the Dapp or service, since we're only changing the widget's presentation. Listing 8.15 shows the HTML code for the LondonTubeMapWidget with changes in the HTML code indicated in bold.

Listing 8.15 LondonTubeMapWidget (HTML)

```
<script src="${res('stations_data.js')}"
   type="text/javascript"></script>
<script src="http://maps.google.com/maps?file=api&amp;v=2&amp;key=Google Key"
   type="text/javascript"></script>
<body onunload="GUnload()">

<div id="TubeWidgetDiv">
   <div id="stationInput">
      <table>

         <tr><td>Tube Station Begin</td>
            <td>
            <select id="startTube">
            <option>Start Tube Station</option>
         </select></td></tr>

         <tr><td>Tube Station End</td>
            <td>
            <select id="endTube">
            <option>Destination Tube Station</option>
         </select></td></tr>

         <tr><td colspan="2">
            <img src="${res('tubelogo.jpg')}">
            <button id="plannerButton">Get Tube Info</button></td>
         </tr>

      <tr><td colspan="2">
         <A href="http://www.tubeplanner.com/">Planning by tubeplanner.com</A>
      </td></tr></table><hr/>
   </div>
   <div id="map_canvas"></div>
   <div id="TubeResults"></div>
</div>
</body>
```

Listing 8.15 includes two `script` tags. The first one loads JavaScript file `stations_data.js`.

File `stations_data.js` instantiates array `stations`, containing geocode data for each station. We describe its format in the next section. Figure 8.6 shows how you upload an arbitrary resource to the `zembly` server, making it available for use in your widget. After you click Upload (as shown in Figure 8.6), `zembly` adds the following code to your widget's HTML.

```
<script src="${res('stations_data.js')}" type="text/javascript">
</script>
```

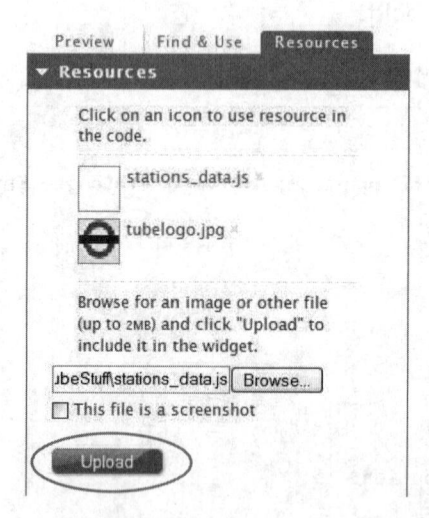

Figure 8.6 Uploading file stations_data.js to the `zembly` server

The second `script` tag loads the Google Maps JavaScript library. Attribute `src` includes your required Google API key. (See "Exploring Google Maps API" on page 93 for information on using Google Maps in widgets.) The `div` tag with `id` attribute `"map_canvas"` provides the placeholder for the map. Its size is defined in the CSS code.

Adding Geocode Data for Stations

All geocode data for London Underground stations are publicly available at http://wiki.openstreetmap.org/index.php/Tube_Stations. Collecting the data (with a simple cut and paste) and converting values to a JavaScript data object turned into an exercise in regular expressions search and replace. Listing 8.16 shows a portion of the `stations_data.js` file, which instantiates array `stations` with the `name` and `geocode` data for each station. Each `geocode` object consists of `latitude` and `longitude` values.

Listing 8.16 Sample Geocode Data for Stations

```
stations = [
   { name: "Acton Town", geocode:
        { latitude: " 51.502500", longitude: " -0.278126" }},
   { name: "Aldgate", geocode:
        { latitude: "51.51394", longitude: "-0.07537" }},
   { name: "Aldgate East", geocode:
        { latitude: "51.51514", longitude: "-0.07178" }},
   { name: "All Saints", geocode:
        { latitude: "51.510301", longitude: "-0.012832" }},

        . . . many stations omitted . . .

   { name: "Woodford", geocode:
        { latitude: "51.60582", longitude: "+0.03328" }},
   { name: "Woodside Park", geocode:
        { latitude: "51.6181717295887", longitude: "-0.185578887883903" }}
];
```

Once the global stations array is initialized, you can access station name and geocode information as follows.

```
var name = stations[tubestopindex].name;            // get name
var lat = stations[tubestopindex].geocode.latitude; // get latitude
var lng = stations[tubestopindex].geocode.longitude; // get longitude
```

Using CSS for the Map Widget

Listing 8.17 shows the CSS code. The code includes the single addition of the map_canvas style, which specifies the map's view port size. (See Listing 7.10 on page 255 for the omitted styles.)

Listing 8.17 LondonTubeMapWidget (CSS)

```
#TubeWidgetDiv {
    width: 370px;
    color: #647A88;
    padding: 5px;
    font: 70% Verdana, sans-serif;
}

#map_canvas {
    height: 350px;
    width: 400px;
}

        . . . omitted styles . . .
```

Building Mashup LondonTubeMapWidget

Listing 8.18 through Listing 8.21 show the JavaScript for the LondonTubeMapWidget. The code for this widget is very similar to Listing 7.11 through Listing 7.13 described in "London Tube Widget" on page 248 through page 258. Note that Listing 8.18 now includes several new functions. Function init_map initializes the Google map, add_marker adds a marker with a pop up information window to the map, and draw_segment draws a line of a specified color between two map points. These support functions enable the widget to show station stops and draw lines between two stops on the map. The map control lets users zoom in or out and move the view port.

Listing 8.18 LondonTubeMapWidget (JavaScript)—Part 1

```
var map;
var stations;

function init_map(lat, lng) {
    if (GBrowserIsCompatible()) {
        map = new GMap2(document.getElementById("map_canvas"));
        map.addControl(new GSmallMapControl());
        map.setCenter(new GLatLng(lat, lng), 14);
    }
}

function draw_segment(g1, g2, color) {
    var polyline = new GPolyline([
        new GLatLng(g1.latitude, g1.longitude),
        new GLatLng(g2.latitude, g2.longitude)
    ], color, 10);
    map.addOverlay(polyline);
}

function add_marker(lat, lng, htmlstr) {
    var point = new GLatLng(lat, lng);
    var marker = new GMarker(point);
    GEvent.addListener(marker, "click", function() {
        marker.openInfoWindowHtml(htmlstr);
    });
    map.addOverlay(marker);
}
```

Listing 8.19 shows Part 2 of the JavaScript code for this widget. Function init_app calls populateSelectTags to populate select tags with the station names. Function init_app also initializes Google maps, using Baker Street tube station as its center. Function populateSelectTags calls init_station_data to initialize the stations array with the stations names and respective geocode values. After stations is initialized, populateSelectTags builds the select tags options arrays.

Function `findstation` returns the index value of a given station name from the `stations` array. Array `linecolors` is unchanged from Listing 7.11 on page 256.

Listing 8.19 LondonTubeMapWidget (JavaScript)—Part 2

```
Event.observe(window, 'load', init_app);

function init_app() {
   populateSelectTags();
   var i = findstation("Baker Street");
   init_map(stations[i].geocode.latitude, stations[i].geocode.longitude);
}
function populateSelectTags() {
   stations = init_station_data();
   $("startTube").options.length = 0;
   $("endTube").options.length = 0;
   stations.each(function(tube,i) {
      $("startTube").options[i] = new Option(tube.name);
      $("endTube").options[i] = new Option(tube.name);
   });
}

function findstation(name) {
   for (i = 0; i < stations.length; i++) {
      if (stations[i].name == name) {
         return i;
      }
   }
   return -1;     // station name not found
}
var linecolors = {
   "Bakerloo" : "#AE6118",
         . . . code omitted . . .
};
```

Listing 8.20 shows the 'click' event handler (invoked when users click the Get Tube Info button). If the start and ending destination are the same, the code re-initializes the map with the selected station at its center. Otherwise, the handler calls the LondonTubeJourneyPlanner service with the requested journey endpoints. The onSuccess handler interprets the return data to build the table and map the station stops.

Listing 8.20 LondonTubeMapWidget (JavaScript)—Part 3

```
Event.observe($("plannerButton"), 'click', function() {
   var startTube =
      $("startTube").options[$("startTube").selectedIndex].value;
```

```
      var endTube =
         $("endTube").options[$("endTube").selectedIndex].value;
      if (startTube == endTube) {
         var i = findstation(startTube);
         init_map(stations[i].geocode.latitude, stations[i].geocode.longitude);
         var resultsHtml = "<b>You're already there!</b><br/>" + startTube
             + " Station";
         $("TubeResults").innerHTML = resultsHtml;
         add_marker(stations[i].geocode.latitude,
             stations[i].geocode.longitude, resultsHtml);
      } else
         Things.callService("ganderson.LondonTubeJourneyPlanner",
         {
             "startTube": startTube, // London tube stop of journey start
             "endTube": endTube
             // London Tube stop of journey destination
         },
         {
         onSuccess: function(data) {
             var titlestr = "<div id=\"titlediv\">From " +
                 data.groups.journey[0].endpoint[0].value
                 + " To " + data.groups.journey[1].endpoint[0].value
                 + "</div>";

                    . . . omitted code is the same
            (see Listing 7.12 on page 257 and Listing 7.13 on page 257)
                           . . .

             stationstr += "</table></div>";
```

Listing 8.21 includes the added code to map the results. First, the code calls `init_map` with the geocode values for the starting tube station. The for loop iterates through each stop, creating the markers and drawing the line segments between the current station and the next station. The loop includes several tests. If the current stop is the same as the next stop, this indicates a line change. If the station name doesn't match any known stations, we skip the stop since it can't be mapped. Or, if this is the last station, we're done drawing line segments. Upon completion, the map includes markers (and information windows) for all stations including color-coded line segments that the user can follow from starting point to final destination. The `onFailure` handler displays the error message received from the service.

Listing 8.21 LondonTubeMapWidget (JavaScript)—Part 4

```
          // Build the map
          var stops = data.groups.stop;
          var startindex = findstation(startTube);
          init_map(stations[startindex].geocode.latitude,
              stations[startindex].geocode.longitude);
          var markerflag = stops.length;
```

LondonTubeMapWidget

```
            var save_starting_point = -1;

            for (var i = 0; i < stops.length; i++) {
               var index = findstation(stops[i].station[0].value);
               var htmlstr = "";
               if (index >= 0) {
                  if (i == 0) htmlstr = "<b>Your Journey Begins Here</b><br/>";
                  else if (i == stops.length-1)
                       htmlstr = "<b>This is your destination</b><br/>";
                  htmlstr += stations[index].name + " Station<br/>"
                     + stops[i].line[0].value +" Line<br/>";
               }
               if (i < stops.length-1) {
                  var next = findstation(stops[i+1].station[0].value);
                  if (next >= 0) {
                     if (index == next) {
                        htmlstr += "Change to " + stops[i+1].line[0].value
                           + " Line<br/>";
                        markerflag = i+1;
                     } else {
                        if (save_starting_point >= 0) {
                           draw_segment(stations[save_starting_point].geocode,
                              stations[next].geocode,
                              linecolors[stops[i].line[0].value]);
                           save_starting_point = -1;
                        } else
                           draw_segment(
                              stations[index].geocode,
                              stations[next].geocode,
                              linecolors[stops[i].line[0].value]);
                     }
                  } else {// next is -1
                     if (index >= 0) save_starting_point = index;
                  }
               }

               if (markerflag != i && index >= 0) {
                  add_marker(stations[index].geocode.latitude,
                     stations[index].geocode.longitude, htmlstr);
               } else markerflag = stops.length;
            }

            var resultsHtml = titlestr + summarystr + stationstr;
            $("TubeResults").innerHTML = resultsHtml;
         },
         onFailure: function(error) {
            var resultsHtml = "Service error: " + error.message;
            $("TubeResults").innerHTML = resultsHtml;
         }
      });
});
```

Embedding LondonTubeMapWidget

Listing 8.22 gives you the height and width values that best accommodate this widget.

Listing 8.22 HTML to Embed Your Widget

```
<iframe height=700 width=450
   src="http://a8e3f4d1f1e4475aa2c0a7e2b4fc3c3d.zembly.com/things/
   a8e3f4d1f1e4475aa2c0a7e2b4fc3c3d;iframe">
</iframe>
```

"Mind the gap!"

8.4 Yahoo! Pipes

A long time ago[1] in a land far, far away,[2] Ken Thompson and Doug McIlroy thought about creating a set of utilities that would all share a common way to read input and produce output. The utilities operated on text and did things like sort, find and filter using search strings, transform, combine, format, and limit the amount of output. This common approach allowed users to combine commands in arbitrary ways. Creating new utilities was simply a matter of picking the operations you want and stringing together the commands. The connection that allowed you to combine commands was the Unix pipe mechanism (described as connecting data streams together with garden hoses).

Fast forward to the present and Yahoo! has created a similar mechanism that manipulates RSS feeds: Pipes. Yahoo! Pipes are similar in concept to Unix pipes, but Yahoo! has created a graphical user interface for building pipes (yes, pipes look like blue garden hoses). You can create your own pipes by defining RSS feed sources (and other data sources as well) and specifying operations graphically (no programming required!). Once you save and publish your pipe, it is public. This means you can use it to build a widget in **zembly**.

Figure 8.7 shows a widget running in a browser built with **zembly** based on a published Yahoo! Pipes. In this section, you'll see how to build a "service" using Yahoo! Pipes and call it from a widget on **zembly**.

---

1. 1973
2. Bell Labs Computing Research Department

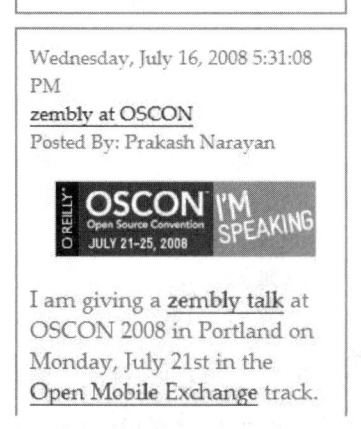

Figure 8.7 Widget zemblyrumblings running in a browser

Here's a summary of the steps you'll follow to build the zemblyblog pipe and zemblyrumblings widget.

Steps to Build a Pipe

1. Create a pipe on Yahoo! Pipes.
2. Specify the pipe data sources and operators.
3. Save and publish the pipe.

Steps to Create a Widget

1. Create a widget on zembly. Give it a name and a description.
2. Use **Find & Use** to call the zemblyblog pipe from your widget.
3. Include the Prototype library.
4. Provide the HTML, CSS, and JavaScript code to present the data from your pipe.
5. Preview and publish.
6. Embed in a web page.

Creating a Pipe

Figure 8.8 shows the Yahoo! Pipes **zemblyblog** we built for this example. The first step, then, is to sign on to Yahoo! Pipes and show you how to build a pipe.

Figure 8.8 Creating a data service with Yahoo! Pipes

Here is a summary of what the **zemblyblog** pipes does:
- Gathers RSS feeds for some blogs
- Combines the feeds into a single feed
- Filters the feed so that we only keep entries that reference "**zembly**"
- Sorts the entries so that the most recently published entry is first

Figure 8.9 shows the Yahoo! Pipes home page. Start by selecting menu item **Create a pipe**.

Figure 8.9 Creating a pipe

The zemblyblog pipe is based on RSS feeds from multiple blogs. The pipe uses a Fetch Feed object to gather input, a Union object to combine them, a Filter object to select a subset of entries, and finally, a Sort object to arrange the entries in reverse chronological order (most recent first).

Fetch Feed Source

The first object you'll need in your pipe is a Fetch Feed object, as shown in Figure 8.10. From the left-hand tool bar, select **Fetch Feed** under Sources. Fetch Feeds require a URL that corresponds to a web page or blog RSS feed. Usually, a web page or blog provides links for the RSS feed. Grab the RSS feed URL and paste it into the Fetch

Yahoo! Pipes 301

Feed URL field. You can add more URLs to the Fetch Feed object (click the plus sign next to the URL). You can also add more Fetch Feed objects (or other Source objects).

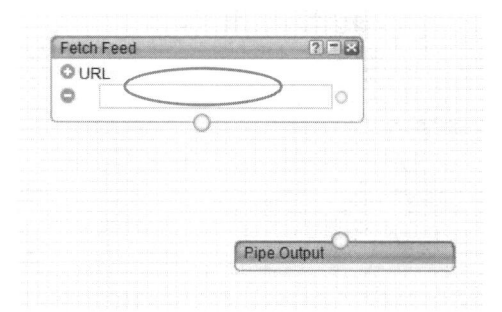

Figure 8.10 Using a Fetch Feed object to get RSS data

Union Operator

This zemblyblog Pipes example gathers blog entries from six different RSS feeds. You can combine multiple data sources into a single data stream using a Union object. From the left-hand tool bar on the Pipes editing page, open the Operators menu and select **Union**, as shown in Figure 8.11.

Connect the output of the Fetch Feed to the input of the Union object. This is a very intuitive operation that results in a nice visual "pipe" connecting your data source to the Union object.

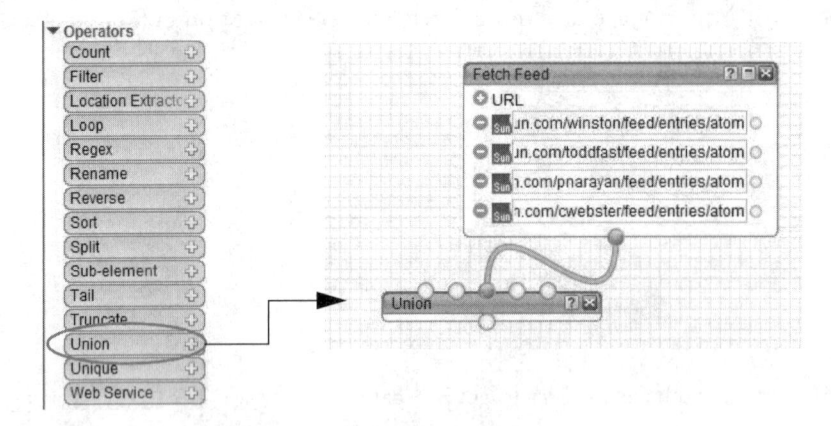

Figure 8.11 Connecting a Fetch Feed object to a Union operator

Figure 8.12 shows two Fetch Feed objects (six data sources in all) that feed into the Union operator. The Pipes editor displays the connections visually.

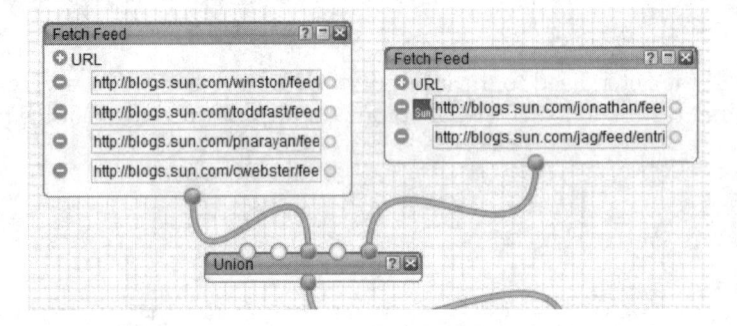

Figure 8.12 Adding more sources to Fetch Feed URLs

Filter Operator

After feeding the data sources into the Union operator, you'll now specify a Filter object (this is also under the Operators menu). Filter objects let you limit the data by specifying rules. Only when the input satisfies the rule, will it proceed to the next pipe object. You can use multiple Filter objects if required. Here, you use one Filter object with two rules: RSS feed items are selected if either RSS field `item.title` or `item.description` contains the text "**zembly.**"

After defining the Filter, connect it to the output of the Union operator and feed it into the Pipes Output object, as shown in Figure 8.13.

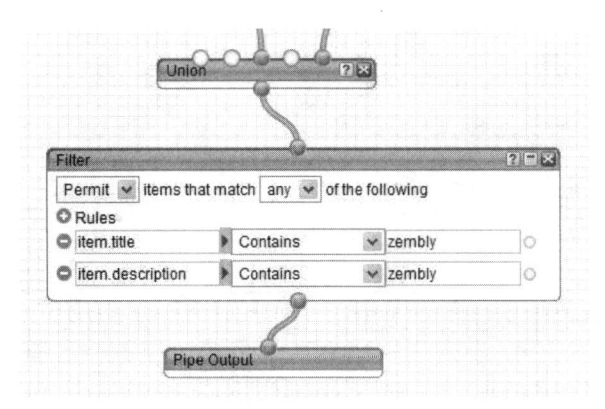

Figure 8.13 Specifying a Filter object

Sort Operator

Remember, the widget should display the blog entries in reverse chronological order. Easy! Select **Sort** (under Operators) and drag it to your editing page. In the **Sort by** field, select the RSS field that determines the sort order you want and specify ascending or descending. Here, we select RSS field item.pubDate and descending order. You can add more Sort by rules to further define ordering if required.

After defining the Sort object, connect it to the output of the Filter operator and feed it into the Pipes Output object, as shown in Figure 8.14.

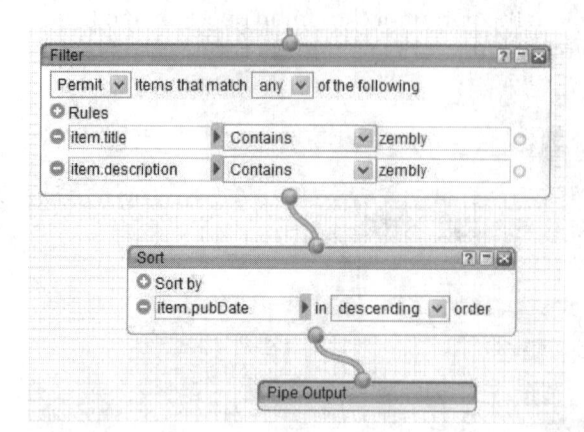

Figure 8.14 Adding a Sort operator to your pipe

Saving and Publishing Your Pipe

When you're finished editing your pipe, save it (select **Save**) and publish it (select **Publish** or **Re-publish**), as shown in Figure 8.15. Once your pipe is published, you can use zembly's Find & Use search mechanism to easily add code to a zembly service or widget that calls the pipe.

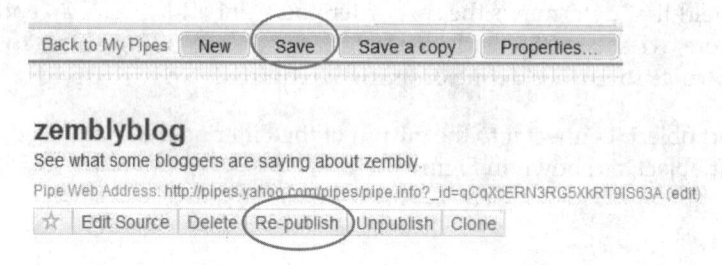

Figure 8.15 Saving your pipe and publishing (or re-publishing)

Building Widget zemblyrumblings

From zembly, create a new blank widget (call the widget **zemblyrumblings**). From the widget development page, select the **Find & Use** tab and specify **zemblyblog** in the Search field. Click **Search**. Figure 8.16 shows the results.

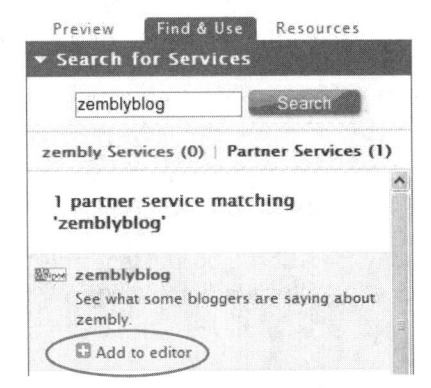

Figure 8.16 Using zembly's Find & Use to add calling code to editor

Select the JavaScript tab in the widget's editor window and select the **Add to editor** link from the search results window. This adds the code you need to call pipe zemblyblog from your widget.

This widget uses the Prototype JavaScript library. From the Resources tab, select **Libraries** (at the bottom) and choose **Prototype** from the list of libraries, as shown in Figure 8.3 on page 282.

The zemblyrumblings widget is very simple. We want to format the data that Yahoo! Pipes provides so that it looks good. The response format is a JSON representation of an extended RSS schema. The RSS items array is a child of the value object. Each item has the RSS fields title, link, description, and publication date (pubDate). Listing 8.23 shows the format of the response.

Listing 8.23 Format of Response from Yahoo! Pipes call

```
{
    "count": "Number of items contained in this result",
    "value": {
      "pubDate": "Data publication date",
      "title": "Channel title",
      "items": [{ "pubDate": "Item creation Date",
          "title": "Item title",
          "description": "Item description",
          "link": "Item URL"
      }],
      "description": "Channel description",
      "link": "URL for this channel"
    }
}
```

Listing 8.24 shows the HTML source code for widget **zembly**rumblings. It consists of a single div element as a placeholder for markup generated in the JavaScript code.

Listing 8.24 Widget zemblyrumblings (HTML)

```
<div id="widgetDiv">
</div>
```

Listing 8.25 shows the CSS code. It provides some padding, a border, and specifies the color and background. Each blog entry is enclosed in its own display box.

Listing 8.25 Widget zemblyrumblings (CSS)

```
.entry {
   color: #787878;
   background-color: #fff;
   border: 2px solid #99AC55;
   margin: 10px;
   padding: 10px;
}
.title {
   font-size: 120%; font-weight: bold;
}
```

Listing 8.26 shows the JavaScript code. First, Things.CallService invokes a call to "yahoo.pipes" with the id that corresponds to the Yahoo! Pipes we built. After a successful response, a call is made to format_bloginfo, which provides the formatting we want.

Since publication dates are provided in two different formats, functions formatDate and normalizeDate put the date information in a consistent format. Note that the author's name is available in field author.name (in the items array).

Listing 8.26 Widget zemblyrumblings (JavaScript)

```
Things.callService("yahoo.pipes",
   {
   _id: "qCqXcERN3RG5XkRT9IS63A" // Pipe ID for "zemblyblog"
   },
   {
      onSuccess: function(data) {
         Log.write(data);
         format_bloginfo(data);
      },

      onFailure: function(error) {
         Log.write("Error: " + error.code + " : " + error.message);
```

```
    }
  });
function formatDate(date) {
   var d = new Date(Date.parse(date));
   if (d == "Invalid Date") d = normalizeDate(date);
   return d.toLocaleString();
}

function normalizeDate(datestr) {
   var s = datestr.split('T');
   var d = s[0].split('-');
   var t = s[1].split(':');
   var nd = new Date(d[0], Number(d[1])-1, d[2], t[0], t[1], t[2].sub-
string(0,2));
   return nd;
}

function format_bloginfo(data) {
   htmlstr = "<div class='entry'><span class='title'>"
      + data.value.title + "</span><br/>There are "
      + data.count + " blog entries as of <br/>"
      + formatDate(data.value.pubDate) + "<br/>"
      + data.value.description
      + "</div>";
   var entrystr = "";
   data.value.items.each(function(entry) {
      entrystr += "<div class='entry'>" + formatDate(entry.pubDate) + "<br/>"
         + "<a href='"
         + entry.link + "'>"
         + entry.title + "</a><br/>"
         + "Posted By: " + entry.author.name + "<br/>"
         + entry.description
         + "</div>";
   });
   $("widgetDiv").innerHTML = htmlstr + entrystr;
}
```

Doing More with Yahoo! Pipes

This example only scratches the surface of what you can do with Pipes. For example, you can select a User Input object that lets you specify arguments. You can then supply input (for example) for terms for the Filter object or RSS fields for the Sort object. This lets you control behavior by providing input through a widget.

Yahoo! Pipes also lets you specify many different sources of data input, including CSV (comma separated values) data, arbitrary web pages, Flickr data, Yahoo! search results, and more. And, anything you can build with Yahoo! Pipes, you can then use in a *zembly* widget or service.

9 Building for the iPhone

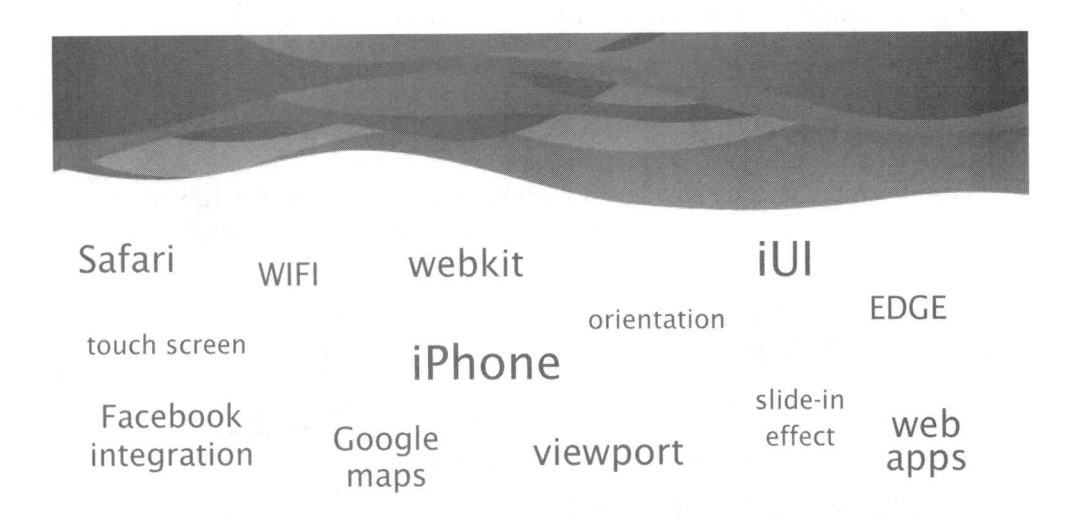

Safari   WIFI   webkit   iUI
                        orientation   EDGE
touch screen   iPhone
Facebook   slide-in   web
integration   Google   viewport   effect   apps
              maps

Apple's iPhone has only been available since June 2007, yet people have come to perceive the iPhone as a mobile computer—not just a mobile phone. With access to the internet and a Safari web browser optimized for the iPhone, web pages and iPhone-friendly widgets, or "web apps," help expand the number of applications for iPhone users. Now with **zembly**, building an iPhone web application just got easier. With a few tricks and nods to usability issues, you can deliver a delightful iPhone web application.

What You Will Learn

- An overview of the Apple iPhone and iPod Touch
- Working with the iPhone form factor and touch screen
- Using the iPhone virtual key pads
- Using the iUI CSS and JavaScript bundle
- Adding an icon to the iPhone Home Screen

- Accessing Google Maps
- Bringing up the numeric key pad by default
- Building iPhone-friendly buttons and controls
- Accessing the Safari webkit
- Integrating an iPhone-friendly web application with Facebook
- Adding iPhone-friendly custom map controls for Google Maps

Examples in This Chapter

All examples in this chapter are tagged **zembly-book-iphone**. To search for them, select **Search** at the top of any zembly page. Supply the search term **zembly-book-iphone** and click the search icon as shown in Figure 9.1.

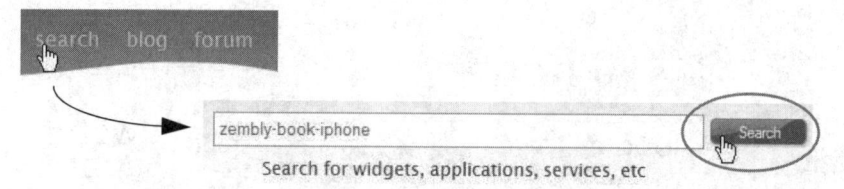

Figure 9.1 Searching for the examples in this chapter

9.1 Targeting the iPhone

The iPhone is both a mobile phone and a mobile computer. It runs iPhone OS, which is a Linux-like operating system based on Mac OS X. The iPhone comes with several default applications, including an iPhone-optimized version of Google Maps, as well as Photos, Camera, Calculator, and other applications. These applications run natively on the device. The iPhone also includes main functional applications such as Phone, Mail, Safari, and iPod. Safari is an iPhone-specific web browser that handles markup display and the multi-touch screen input for maximum usability.

The iPhone connects to the internet using local area wireless network (wifi) if it is available. You can save access passwords and the iPhone will switch networks as you move around. High connection speeds make this connection mode preferable. As a backup, the iPhone uses the wide-area EDGE network, a much slower connection alternative. The EDGE is a cellular network. Thus, phone functions are disabled while you're accessing the internet over EDGE.

Apple has also released the iPod Touch, which is not a phone. However, the iPod Touch still connects to the internet using local area wireless. It includes the same multi-touch screen as the iPhone and provides the same native version of Safari. Since it is not a phone, the iPod Touch cannot connect to the internet with EDGE. Furthermore, it does not include a camera and lacks all of the phone hardware. However, with the internet and Safari, you can run web applications on the iPod Touch with the same user experience as the iPhone.

iPhone Applications

Apple has recently released (still in beta as of this writing) an SDK that allows third-party developers to write applications that run directly (natively) on the iPhone or iPod Touch. Third-party applications will be available through Apple's Application Store at a price set by the developer (Apple keeps a percentage of the fee).

Alternatively, you can also develop web applications for the iPhone and iPod Touch. These applications are available now (and have been possible since the iPhone became available). You simply access them using Safari on the internet. Web applications run on Safari and use standard HTML, CSS, and JavaScript. In the world of **zembly**, an iPhone web application is nothing more than a widget. In this chapter, you'll see how to develop widgets for the iPhone. Besides the standard markup and JavaScript, you'll see how the form factor and the specialized user interface affects your designs. Let's start with the iPhone form factor so you can better appreciate your target device.

A Closer Look at the iPhone

If you have an iPhone, you know that the user experience is completely different than the way you interact with a computer, even a small laptop. The mantra on Apple's web site is "The finger is not a mouse" and, indeed, you will need to rethink how to manage user input for iPhone web applications.

The iPhone supports a multi-touch screen; you use your finger (or fingers) for input. For example, within Safari or Google Maps, a double tap zooms and centers the tapped area. Moving a finger across the screen causes a pan in the direction of movement. A flick up or down induces scrolling. A "pinch in" zooms in and a "pinch out" zooms out. A touch on a link or button is equivalent to a mouse click.

iPhone Tip

At this writing, you can not write JavaScript that detects any touch event except click. However, Safari on the 2.x iPhone will let you detect all gesture events.

A consequence of using your finger as an input device means that you should not create links, buttons, or other input fields that are rendered closely together. Compared to a mouse, a "fat finger" cannot easily select a small button or link. Fingers also leave the screen or touch area, whereas a mouse moves and remains on the screen. Consequently, traditional web pages that detect hover or mouseover events don't work. Cut and paste operations as well as text selection are also not supported.

For keyboard input, the iPhone uses a virtual key pad. The virtual key pad has several varieties: a phone key pad used for "dialing" phone numbers, an alpha key pad for alpha characters, a numeric key pad for numbers and common symbols, a symbol key pad for lesser-used symbols, and a URL key pad that is displayed when the iPhone expects a URL.

Figure 9.2 shows the iPhone's alpha and numeric virtual key pads. When you specify an input tag element in HTML, Safari gives you the alpha key pad by default. You can force the numeric key pad instead, but currently there isn't a way to force the URL key pad. (See "iLoanPayment Widget" on page 314 for an example of how to specify the numeric key pad.)

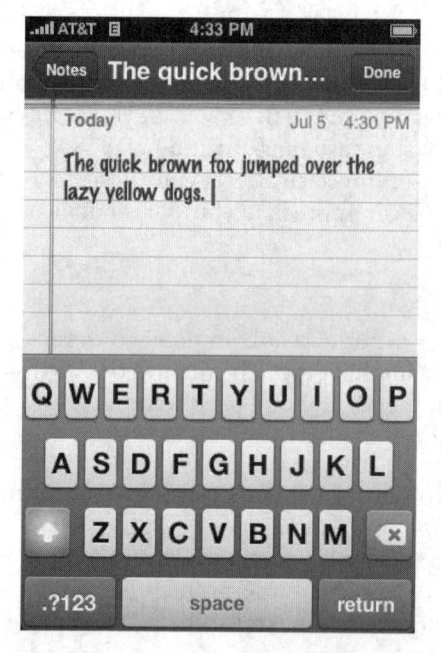

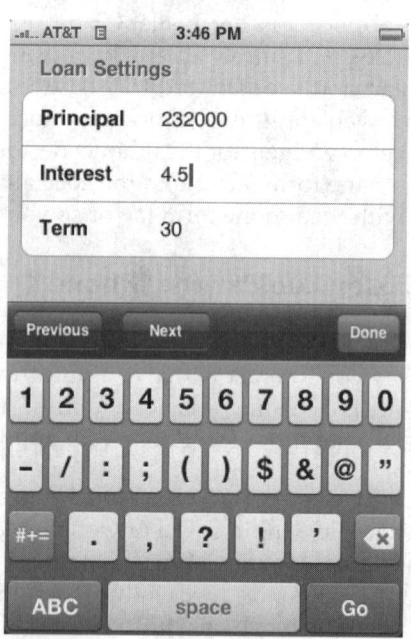

Figure 9.2 The iPhone virtual key pad: alpha (left) and numeric

The key pad takes some getting used to. When you touch a letter, your finger obscures the target letter. However, a larger, bubble version of the selected letter pops up above your finger. You can then move your finger to other letters if the initial selection is wrong. Selection, then, occurs when you *remove* your finger from the screen.

Output on the iPhone is a 320 by 480 pixel screen in portrait mode. You can rotate the iPhone so that it displays in landscape mode, which makes the screen 480 pixels wide. Changes in orientation are detected by applications (including Safari), and the screen contents are redisplayed in the new orientation. (Web applications can detect changes in orientation and mimic Safari's ability to automatically rotate and redisplay contents.)

Safari automatically scales web pages so that more of it will fit in the viewport (the viewable area) of the iPhone. Usually, you will then double-tap or pinch in to zoom and center the portion you want to see. Web pages that are not designed for mobile devices are tedious to view unless care has been taken to display content in columns.

Furthermore, when Safari runs on the iPhone, it includes a "chrome." This is the upper address bar (which you can hide) and a lower bar that includes back and forward page buttons, a plus symbol to add bookmarks, a bookmark access symbol, and a windows symbol that lets you access other Safari windows.

Now that you have a better understanding of the iPhone, let's look at a JavaScript library that makes writing web applications for the iPhone a whole lot easier.

The iUI Library

Native iPhone applications exhibit a certain look and feel. Screens slide in and out and input choices are wide selection areas to accommodate fingers. Each screen view displays a small amount of information and each step in an application typically brings up a new screen—smoothly sliding in a new interaction segment of a program. Developers who write web applications would naturally like to mimic the look and feel of native iPhone applications as much as possible. Fortunately, Joe Hewitt (www.joehewitt.com) has created a JavaScript/CSS bundle called **iUI** that helps you create iPhone web applications that do just that.

There are a few basic principles that iUI follows. First, iUI encourages single page navigation; that is, multiple use-cases exist on the same page, but each use case is displayed by itself as if it were a separate page. This keeps the web application moving because new views load instantly. Secondly, iUI uses Ajax to load content when you link to an external URL. Thirdly, iUI is set up so that your application has a hierarchical navigation system. iUI requires that you use standard HTML; it takes care of the JavaScript that produces the Ajax loading and the smooth sliding among views. Furthermore, iUI detects phone orientation changes. To use iUI with your **zembly** widget, select library iUI under Resources as shown in Figure 9.8 on page 318.

9.2 iLoanPayment Widget

The best way to show you how to use iUI is with an example. Our first example re-implements the Loan Payment widget (see "Creating Your First Widget: LoanPaymentWidget" on page 34) as an iPhone web application.

Figure 9.3 shows widget iLoanPayment as it first comes up and a second screen after you tap the **Set Loan Parameters** menu item. After setting values for one or more of the loan parameters, press the Loan Payment "back" button to return to the initial screen.

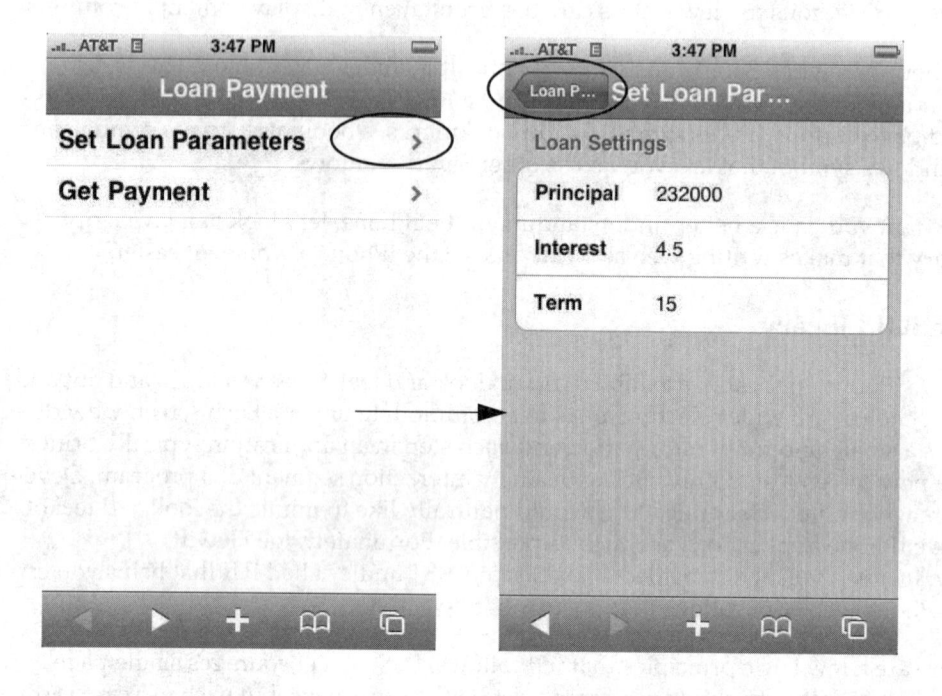

Figure 9.3 Loan Payment widget (iLoanPayment) running on the iPhone

Tapping **Get Payment** then produces the monthly payment amount as shown in Figure 9.4.

Figure 9.4 iLoanPayment displaying results

Here's a summary of the steps you'll follow to build and run the iLoanPayment widget.

1. Create a new widget (or clone LoanPaymentWidget). Provide a name and description.
2. Include both the iUI and Prototype JavaScript libraries.
3. Upload any PNG file resources to your widget.
4. Modify/provide the HTML, CSS, and JavaScript code.
5. Preview and publish.
6. Text or email the "Share This Widget" URL to your iPhone to run.
7. Add the run icon to your iPhone Home Screen (optional).

Running iLoanPayment on Your iPhone

Here are the steps to run the iLoanPayment widget on your iPhone. Because the URLs that access **zembly** widgets are long, you don't want to type them in by hand (especially on the iPhone where typing skills are handicapped by the iPhone form factor). Instead, from **zembly**, select **search** from the top of the page and provide search target **iLoanPayment**, as shown in Figure 9.5.

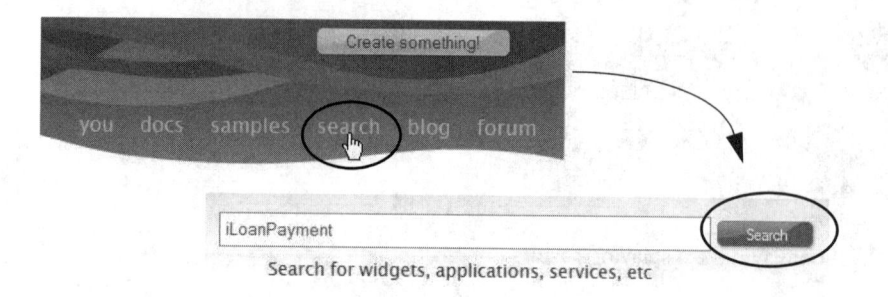

Figure 9.5 Finding widget iLoanPayment using the zembly search feature

Select the iLoanPayment widget from the results and zembly displays the widget's page. Scroll down to the section "Share This Widget." Select the *src attribute text only* of the URL (copy and paste) and email (or text message) this URL to your iPhone. When you tap the link from your message or email content, the widget will run on your iPhone. For example, here is the URL to execute iLoanPayment on your iPhone.

```
http://25631ef6dd1c4e249779b30ed11390ff.zembly.com/things/
            25631ef6dd1c4e249779b30ed11390ff;iframe
```

Figure 9.6 shows the URL displayed in an email message and the corresponding iPhone screen with widget iLoanPayment running.

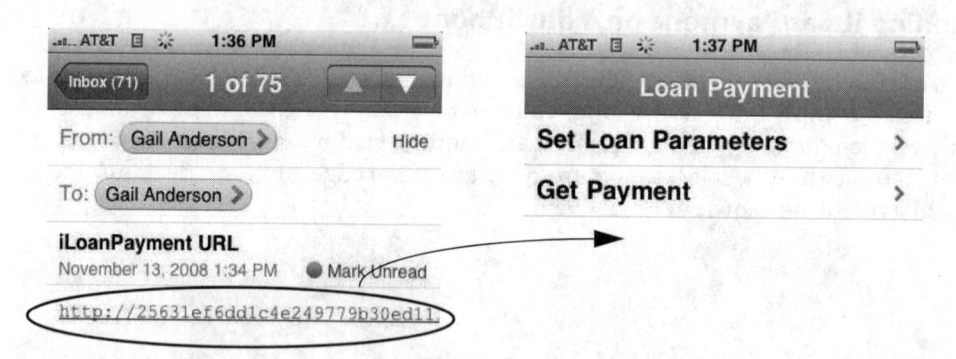

Figure 9.6 Emailing the iLoanPayment URL to yourself

iLoanPayment Widget 317

> **iPhone Tip**
>
> An alternative testing environment is the iPhone simulator at http://www.testiPhone.com. Copy and paste the URL into the simulator's address bar and hit <Enter>, as shown in Figure 9.7.

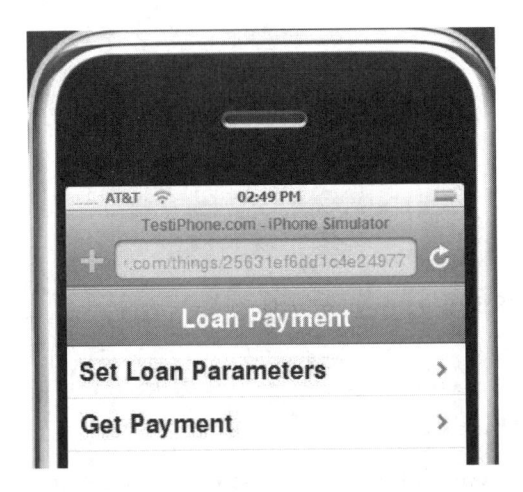

Figure 9.7 iLoanPayment running in the simulator at www.testiPhone.com

Adding an Icon to Home Screen

Widget iLoanPayment specifies an icon that you can add to your Home Screen for easy call up. While iLoanPayment is running on your iPhone, select the plus sign on the bottom chrome. Safari pops up a selection menu that lets you add a bookmark, add an icon to the home screen, or mail a link to this page. Select **Add to Home Screen**.

Safari now displays a screen that includes an icon (a House) and an input field to supply a title. When you select **Add**, Safari adds an icon to your home screen so you can quickly access this page. The HTML code that gives you a customized icon is shown in Listing 9.1 on page 320.

318   Chapter 9   Building for the iPhone

Including the iUI and Prototype Libraries

The iLoanPayment widget uses the iUI and Prototype libraries. (The iUI library does not require the Prototype library, but we use it for the syntactic shortcuts with '$'.) To use the iPhone iUI library in your **zembly** widget, simply select it under the widget's Resources / Libraries tab, as shown in Figure 9.8.

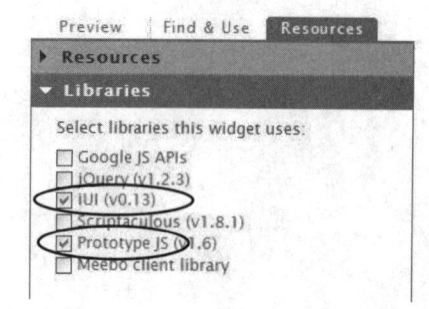

Figure 9.8 Adding the iUI and Prototype JS libraries to your widget

Widgets on the iPhone Dashboard

In order to provide a custom icon to place your iPhone widget on the Home Screen (or iPhone dashboard), upload a PNG image file (it should be 57 by 57 pixels) to your widget's resources on **zembly**, as shown in Figure 9.9.

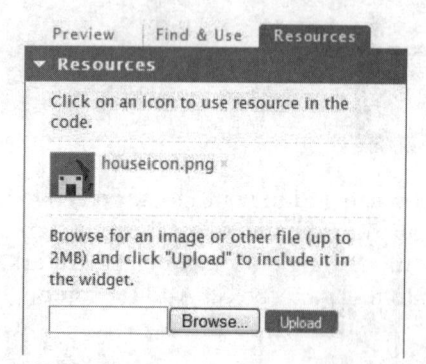

Figure 9.9 Uploading the house icon

Then, use the following `link` tag in your widget's HTML markup. The `href` attribute should include the **zembly**-generated URL to point to the image resource (in this case image `houseicon.png`).

```
<link rel=\"apple-touch-icon\"
    href=\"${res(\'houseicon.png\')}\"/>
```

Building the iLoanPayment Widget

Although the iLoanPayment widget gives the appearance of three separate pages, the HTML is actually a single page. For standard "iUI" type widgets, you should provide the following HTML components.

- Icon link—A PNG image URL within a `link` tag with attribute `rel` set to `apple-touch-icon`.

- Viewport—A `meta` tag with attribute `name` set to `viewport` and attribute `content` as shown in Listing 9.1. The viewport will be set to 320 pixels wide and set to 1.0 scale (no scaling).

- Title—A `title` tag for the URL chrome.

- Page toolbar—A `div` tag (`class="toolbar"`) as shown in Listing 9.1. Tags `h1` and `a` provide programmatically set titles and back button behavior for all your navigation changes.

- Menus using tags `ul` and `li`—A hierarchical menu using tags `ul` and `li`. When a menu choice brings up different markup, provide an anchor name (such as `#settings`) that points to an element `id` further down your page. The iUI Library loads the page fragment using a horizontal slide effect. When the menu choice processes a click event executing JavaScript code, use the `target="xhr"` attribute.

- Placeholders to display results—A `div` or `span` element to display results. These results are rendered using iUI functions `update` and `showPage` in your JavaScript code.

- Tags `form` and `fieldset` for input—Tag `fieldset` lets you gather input for one or more fields. By default, Safari uses the alpha virtual key pad for input. If an element `name` attribute includes the word "zip" or "phone", you'll see the numeric key pad. Safari automatically handles multiple input fields in a fieldset, allowing users to select buttons Next and Done to process all fields.

Listing 9.1 shows the HTML source code for widget iLoanPayment. Tags `link`, `meta`, `title`, and the "toolbar" `div` set up the page as described above. The top-level menu (`id="home"`) provides the two menu items (Set Loan Parameters and Get Payment) as shown in Figure 9.3 on page 314. Note that menu item Set Loan Parameters uses an anchor in attribute `href`. This displays the page fragment that includes the form element (`id="settings"`). Menu item Get Payment, on the other hand, executes JavaScript code via the `'click'` event handler set in the JavaScript. Attribute `target="xhr"` tells iUI not to do anything (except let the JavaScript code event handler execute).

320 Chapter 9 Building for the iPhone

The empty `div` with `id="results"` is a placeholder for the monthly payment returned from the service call.

The `form` markup sets a title and specifies `class="panel"` for an iPhone-native look. Each input tag has its own `div` (`class="row"`) and label. The input tag `id` attribute is used in the JavaScript to access the tag's value. Each input tag's `name` attribute is set to a value that includes the text "zip" (such as `principal_zip`). This tells Safari to bring up the numeric key pad instead of the default alpha key pad.

The `div` with `id="messagePanel"` is a placeholder for any error messages generated by the service call.

Listing 9.1 Widget iLoanPayment (HTML)

```
<link rel="apple-touch-icon" href="${res('houseicon.png')}"/>
<meta name="viewport"
    content="width=320; initial-scale=1.0; maximum-scale=1.0; user-scal-
able=0;" />
<title>zembly Loan Payment</title>
<div class="toolbar">
    <h1 id="pageTitle"></h1>
    <a id="backButton" class="button" href="#"></a>
</div>
<ul id="home" title="Loan Payment" selected="true">
    <li><a href="#settings">Set Loan Parameters</a></li>
    <li><a id="myloanlink" target="xhr">Get Payment</a></li>
</ul>

<div id="results" title="Monthly Payment" class="panel">
</div>

<form id="settings" title="Set Loan Parameters" class="panel">
    <h2>Loan Settings</h2>
    <fieldset>
        <div class="row">
            <label>Principal</label>
            <input type="text" name="principal_zip" id="principal" />
        </div>

        <div class="row">
            <label>Interest</label>
            <input type="text" name="interest_zip" id="interest" />
        </div>

        <div class="row">
            <label>Term</label>
            <input type="text" name="years_zip" id="years" />
        </div>

    </fieldset>
```

```
</form>

<div class="panel" id="messagePanel">
   <div class="message" id="messagePanelMessage"></div>
</div>
```

Most of the widget's CSS is specified by iUI CSS code. However, we customize the results div with centering, padding, and increasing the font size, as shown Listing 9.2.

Listing 9.2 Widget iLoanPayment (CSS)

```
#results {
    text-align: center; padding: 10px; font-size: 150%;
}
```

Listing 9.3 shows the JavaScript code for widget iLoanPayment. It is very similar to the JavaScript for LoanPaymentWidget (see Listing 2.5 on page 41). Function onLoanGet grabs the values from the input elements and calls LoanPaymentService (see "Creating Your First Service: LoanPaymentService" on page 25). The results element is updated with the return data and is displayed using the iUI function showPage. This provides the iPhone "slide in" effect. Similarly, any error messages are added to element messagePanelMessage and displayed with the same function showPage.

Listing 9.3 Widget iLoanPayment (JavaScript)

```
// set some default values for the loan parameters
$("principal").value = 300000;
$("interest").value = 6;
$("years").value = 30;
var markup = null;

// Hook up handler
Event.observe($("myloanlink"), "click", onLoanGet);

function onLoanGet(event) {
   var principal = $("principal").value;
   var interest = $("interest").value;
   var years = $("years").value;
   Things.callService("ganderson.LoanPaymentService",
   {
      principal: principal, // The principal of the loan (in dollars)
      interest: interest, // The interest rate (per cent) (e.g., 6.5)
      years: years // How long your loan will endure (in years)
   },
   {
      onSuccess: function(data) {
         Log.write(data);
```

```
            $("results").update(data);
            iui.showPage($("results"));
            return;
        },
        onFailure: function(error) {
            Log.write("Error: " + error.code + " : " + error.message);
            markup = "Error calling service: " + error.message;
            $("messagePanelMessage").update(markup);
            iui.showPage($("messagePanel"));
            return;
        }
    });
}
```

9.3 iLiveWeather Widget

The iPhone already has a native Weather application, but it doesn't necessarily show you all the weather data you might want to see. Let's use the LiveWeather service adapter available through **zembly** and build a custom widget. You've already seen a basic widget that provides weather data (see "Putting It All Together—Using the WeatherBug API" on page 45) and we also show several weather widgets in the Widget Gallery (see "LiveWeatherBugWidget" on page 274 and "LiveWeatherMapWidget" on page 284). This iPhone weather application (iLiveWeather) is based on LiveWeatherMapWidget (it includes mapping), with modifications made to make it iPhone friendly.

Here is a summary of the steps you'll follow to build widget iLiveWeather.

1. Create a new widget (or clone the LiveWeatherMap widget). Provide a name and description.
2. Include both the iUI and Prototype JavaScript libraries.
3. Upload any PNG file resources to your widget.
4. Modify/provide the HTML, CSS, and JavaScript code.
5. Preview and publish.
6. Text or email the "Share This Widget" URL to your iPhone to run.
7. Add the run icon to your iPhone Home Screen (optional).

Figure 9.10 shows the top-level Live Weather web application. Selecting Set Zipcode brings up the Set Zipcode page where you can change the default zip code. Your new value is saved on the iPhone using cookies. The Get Weather menu item displays weather information (as shown in Figure 9.11).

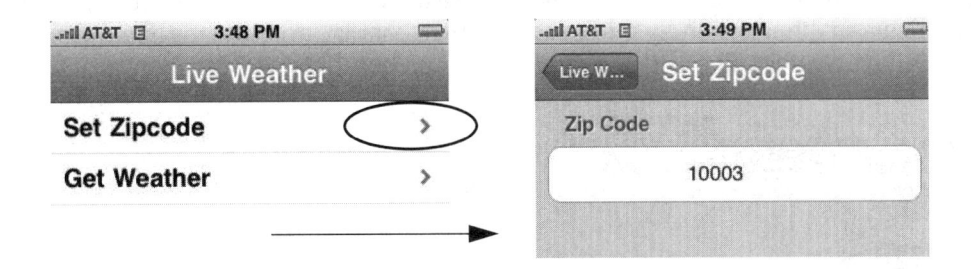

Figure 9.10 Live Weather widget (iLiveWeather) running on the iPhone

Figure 9.11 shows the Weather Info results, as well as the Google Maps displayed after selecting the Get Map button. The Google Maps is the native application. Instead of using the Google Maps API, the iLiveWeather widget links to maps.google.com, which iPhone intercepts to bring up the native application. This provides iPhone-friendly mapping, as long as you are able to make your map request using Google's recognized query parameters.

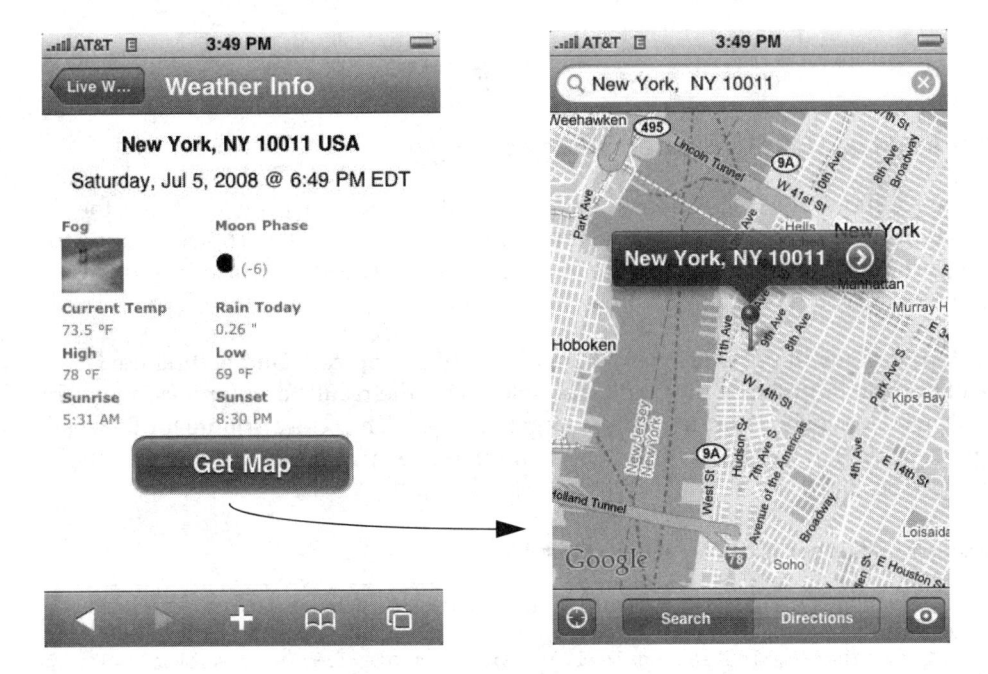

Figure 9.11 iLiveWeather results and map running on the iPhone

324　Chapter 9　Building for the iPhone

Figure 9.12 shows the resources used by iLiveWeather widget. File `blueButton.png` implements an iPhone-friendly button and `weathericon.png` provides the home screen icon for iLiveWeather. These files were uploaded on **zembly** using the Resources tab.

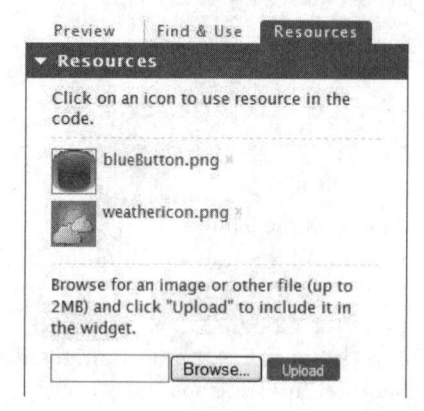

Figure 9.12 Resources used by the iLiveWeather widget

Building the iLiveWeather Widget

Listing 9.4 shows the HTML source for iLiveWeather. Because this widget uses the iUI library, the first part looks very similar to iLoanPayment. The iUI artifacts include the viewport (tag `meta`), the title, and the toolbar (tag `div`). The widget also includes a home screen icon (tag `link`).

The top-level menu provides menu items for setting a zip code and getting the weather data. Empty tags provide place holders for the results and for messages. The `form` tag includes the `input` tag for the target zip code. The `name` attribute for the `input` tag ("zipcode") makes Safari bring up the numeric key pad because it includes the string "zipcode."

Listing 9.4　Widget iLiveWeather (HTML)

```
<link rel="apple-touch-icon" href="${res('weathericon.png')}"/>
<meta name="viewport"
content="width=320; initial-scale=1.0; maximum-scale=1.0; user-scalable=0;" />
<title>zembly Live Weather</title>

<div class="toolbar">
    <h1 id="pageTitle"></h1>
```

```
      <a id="backButton" class="button" href="#"></a>
   </div>
   <ul id="home" title="Live Weather" selected="true">
      <li><a href="#settings">Set Zipcode</a></li>
      <li><a id="myweatherlink" target="xhr">Get Weather</a></li>
   </ul>

   <div id="results" title="Weather Info" class="panel"></div>
   <form id="settings" title="Set Zipcode" class="panel">
      <h2>Zip Code</h2>
      <fieldset>
      <div class="row">
      <input type="text" name="zipcode" id="zipcode" />
      </div>
      </fieldset>
   </form>
   <div class="panel" id="messagePanel">
      <div class="message" id="messagePanelMessage"></div>
   </div>
```

iLiveWeather CSS Code

Listing 9.5 shows the CSS code for iLiveWeather. Most of the styles format the weather data. (You'll note very similar output with the widgets in Figure 8.2 on page 275.) The CSS code also includes styles for class `applebutton` and `blue`, which provide an image-based blue button that depends on the Safari display engine (`-webkit`) for correct rendering. Using `-webkit` in CSS code prevents markup from displaying in non-Safari browsers, but with iPhone-only widgets this is not a concern.

Programming Tip

You can run a Windows or Mac OS version of Safari on your development system to test the widget before running it on your iPhone. Or, use the iPhone simulator at www.testiPhone.com.

The `.blue` class references the image resource URL with `../resources/blueButton.png`. This alternate form for the resource is required (instead of `${res('blueButton.png')}`, which can't be used in CSS or JavaScript code).

Listing 9.5 Widget iLiveWeather (CSS)

```
#messagePanelMessage {
   color: #a00;
}

#placediv {
   padding: 5px;
```

```css
    font-weight: bold;
    text-align: center;
}

#datediv {
    padding: 5px;
    text-align: center;
    margin-bottom: 10px;
}

#statdiv {
    margin-left: 1px;
    padding: 1px;
}

#statdiv th {
    color: #647A88;
    font: bold 70% Verdana, sans-serif;
    text-align: left;
    width: 120px;
}

#statdiv td {
    color: #647A88;
    font: 70% Verdana, sans-serif;
    padding-bottom: 2px;
}

// Code to render a nice iPhone blue button
// (taken from Web App Samples on Apple's web site)
/* The button class defines properties for buttons
   that are either 30px or 46px high */
.applebutton
{
/* Set a button to be a block so its height and width can be adjusted */
    display: block;

/* Use the highest button height to ensure that text will
   vertically align on all buttons */
    line-height: 46px;

/* A button will expand to the width of its parent cell if no width is specified
*/
    width: 150px;

    font-size: 20px;
    font-weight: bold;
    font-family: Helvetica, sans-serif;
    color: #fff;

    text-decoration: none;
    text-align: center;
```

```
}

/* Builds a button using a 29x46 image */
.blue
{
   margin: 3px auto;
   color: #fff;
/* Put a 1 pixel blur black shadow below the button's text */
   text-shadow: #000 0px 1px 1px;

/* The right and left borders are 14 pixels wide */
   border-width: 0px 14px 0px 14px;

/* The leftButton image is split into three.
   Both left and right sides are 14 pixels wide. */
/* The remaining 1 pixel is used for the middle part of the image. */
/* The left and right sides will remain fixed
   while the middle part is scaling horizontally. */
   -webkit-border-image: url(../resources/blueButton.png) 0 14 0 14;
}
```

iLiveWeather JavaScript Code

The iLiveWeather JavaScript is presented in three parts. Part 1 includes the global variables, initialization code, and code to hook up the event handlers. Part 2 calls the LiveWeatherBugService and formats the weather data and Part 3 includes the functions that support cookies.

Listing 9.6 includes the global variables and function `initapp`, which initializes the application. When you set the zip code, its value is stored in a cookie. The initialization function checks to see if a "zip code" cookie has been set and, if so, stores it in the markup. Part 1 also includes code to tie the `"click"` event for element `"myweatherlink"` to function `onWeather` and to create a cookie if the element `"zipcode"` changes value.

Listing 9.6 Widget iLiveWeather (JavaScript)—Part 1

```
var zipcode = null;
var latitude = null;
var longitude = null;
var markup = null;
var datestr = null;
var tablestr = null;
var placestr = null;
var ZIPCODE_KEY = "zipcode";
var COOKIES_DAYS = 365*100;
var DEFAULT_ZIPCODE = 92024;

function initapp() {
   // see if the zipcode is stored in a cookie
```

```
   zipcode = readCookie(ZIPCODE_KEY);
   if (zipcode == null) zipcode = DEFAULT_ZIPCODE;

   // put default into markup
   $("zipcode").value = zipcode;
}

initapp();

// Hook up handlers

Event.observe($("myweatherlink"), "click", onWeather);

Event.observe($("zipcode"), "change", function() {
   zipcode = $("zipcode").value;
   createCookie(ZIPCODE_KEY, zipcode, COOKIES_DAYS);
});
```

Listing 9.7 includes function onWeather, which calls the LiveWeatherBugService and formats the returned data. This code is the same as Listing 8.7 on page 282 and Listing 8.8 on page 283, except here we include a link to maps.google.com with query parameters z=11 (zoom level 11) and q=city_state_zipcode (search for location based on city, state, and zip code). The iPhone intercepts this call to Google and invokes the native Google Maps application.

iPhone Tip

To return to the web application from the Google Maps application, click the Home Screen circle below the iPhone screen and then select the Safari icon from the Home Screen. The iLiveWeather application will continue in its current state (it will not reload).

Listing 9.7 Widget iLiveWeather (JavaScript)—Part 2

```
function onWeather(event) {
   Things.callService("ganderson.LiveWeatherBugService", {
   zipcode: zipcode},
   {
   onSuccess: function(data) {

      latitude = data.coordinates.latitude;
      longitude = data.coordinates.longitude;

      datestr = "<div id=\"datediv\">" +
      data.day + ", " +
      data.month + " " +
      data.dayno + ", " +
      data.year + " @ " +
      data.timestr + "</div>";
```

```
    placestr = "<div id=\"placediv\">" +
    data.citystate + " " +
    data.zipcode + " " +
    data.country + "</div>";


    tablestr = "<div id=\"statdiv\"><table>" +
       "<tr><th>" +
       data.currentcond.status +
       "</th><th>Moon Phase</th></tr><tr><td>" +
       "<img src=\"" +
       data.currentcond.icon +
       "\" alt=\"No Image\"></img></td><td><img src=\"" +
       data.moonphase.icon +
       "\" alt=\"No Image\"></img> (" +
       data.moonphase.status + ")</td></tr>";

    tablestr +=
       "<tr><th>Current Temp</th>" +
       "<th>Rain Today</th></tr>" + "<tr><td>" +
       data.currenttemp + "</td><td>" +
       data.rain +
       "</td></tr><tr><th>High</th><th>Low</th></tr>" +
       "<tr><td>" +
       data.hightemp +
       "</td><td>" +
       data.lowtemp +
       "</td></tr><tr><th>Sunrise</th><th>Sunset</th></tr>" +
       "<tr><td>" +
       data.sunrisestr +
       "</td><td>" +
       data.sunsetstr +
       "</td></tr></table>";

    var marker = "&q=" +
       data.citystate + " " + data.zipcode + "";
    tablestr +=
       "<a class='blue applebutton' href='http://maps.google.com/maps?z=11"
       + marker + "' target='_blank'>Get Map</a> </div>";

    markup = placestr + datestr + tablestr;
    $("results").update(markup);
    iui.showPage($("results"));
    return;
 },
 onFailure: function(error) {
    Log.write("Error: " + error.code + " : " + error.message);
    markup = "Error calling service: " + error.message;
    $("messagePanelMessage").update(markup);
    iui.showPage($("messagePanel"));
    return;
```

```
    }
  });
}
```

Listing 9.8 includes functions to create, read, and erase cookies. This allows your favorite zip code to be saved so that you don't have to provide it each time you run iLiveWeather.

Listing 9.8 Widget iLiveWeather (JavaScript)—Part 3

```
///////////////////
// Cookie helper functions
// This free code is from:
// http://www.quirksmode.org/js/cookies.html
///////////////////
function createCookie(name,value,days) {
    if (days) {
        var date = new Date();
        date.setTime(date.getTime()+(days*24*60*60*1000));
        var expires = "; expires="+date.toGMTString();
    }
    else var expires = "";
    document.cookie = name+"="+value+expires+"; path=/";
}
function readCookie(name) {
    var nameEQ = name + "=";
    var ca = document.cookie.split(';');
    for(var i=0;i < ca.length;i++) {
        var c = ca[i];
        while (c.charAt(0)==' ') c = c.substring(1,c.length);

        if (c.indexOf(nameEQ) == 0) {
            return c.substring(nameEQ.length);
        }
    }
    return null;
}

function eraseCookie(name) {
    createCookie(name,"",-1);
}
```

9.4 iCapitalPunishment Widget

Capital Punishment (see "Capital Punishment—A Challenging Facebook Application" on page 162) runs under Facebook. This application relies on the Facebook infrastructure to update your profile, send invitations to your friends, record scores, and see your friends' scores. But the basic function of the application—the world capitals quiz widget—is a good fit for the iPhone form factor. With just a few changes to the user interface, iCapitalPunishment is an entertaining distraction when you're out and about and would like a few minutes to shut out the world. Of course, you can also integrate the Facebook features as well, which we'll show you how to do in the next section. For now, let's concentrate on adapting the Capital Punishment quiz to the iPhone.

Here is a summary of the steps you'll follow the build widget iCapitalPunishment.

1. Create a new blank widget (or clone the Home widget from the Capital Punishment application). Provide a name and description.
2. Include both the iUI and Prototype JavaScript libraries.
3. Upload any PNG file resources to your widget.
4. Modify/provide the HTML, CSS, and JavaScript code.
5. Preview and publish.
6. Text or email the "Share This Widget" URL to your iPhone to run.
7. Add the run icon to your iPhone Home Screen (optional).

In a phone application, less is more. We use iUI to help make the radio button layout iPhone-friendly. Google Maps no longer comes up automatically, but is an option (a Get Map button). Using the Apple "blue button" markup helps make the button option stand out. And, as with iLiveWeather, this widget does not use the Google Maps API. Instead, it calls maps.google.com with query parameters to set the coordinates and create the marker. This makes the iPhone-native Google application execute.

Figure 9.13 shows the iCapitalPunishment main screen and Google Maps after choosing a capital and selecting the Get Map button. The Start Over button lets you restart the game and the About button provides information about the application.

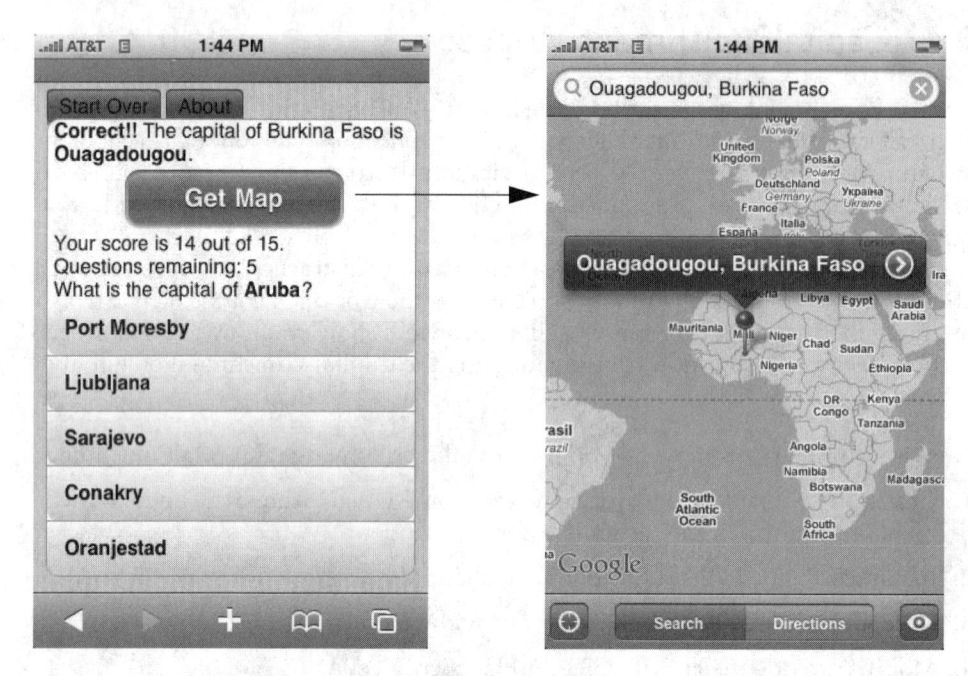

Figure 9.13 Capital Punishment running on the iPhone

iPhone Tip

To return to the web application from the Google Maps application, click the Home Screen circle below the iPhone screen and then select the Safari icon from the Home Screen. The iCapitalPunishment application will continue in its current state (it will not reload).

Figure 9.14 shows the widget's Resources tab in **zembly** for iCapitalPunishment. JavaScript file countrydata.js contains the country and capital cities data (unchanged from the original version). Image globeicon.png provides the home screen icon and image blueButton.png provides the button image for the Get Map button.

iCapitalPunishment Widget 333

Figure 9.14 Resources used by widget iCapitalPunishment

Building the iCapitalPunishment Widget

Listing 9.9 shows the HTML code for widget iCapitalPunishment. By now you'll recognize the structure you use with the iUI JavaScript library. The main user interaction area includes five radio buttons that let you select a capital city. Three div tags ("answerDiv", "scoreDiv", and "questionDiv") provide the feedback, current score, and next question. Two buttons ("startOver" and "aboutCap") use iUI's blueButton class for the look. Attribute target="xhr" allows smooth sliding-in of the markup generated by the JavaScript functions that these buttons call. Note that the script tag references resource countrydata.js.

Listing 9.9 Widget iCapitalPunishment (HTML)

```
<link rel="apple-touch-icon" href="${res('globeicon.png')}"/>
<meta name="viewport"
content="width=320; initial-scale=1.0; maximum-scale=1.0; user-scalable=0;" />
<title>iCapital Punishment</title>
<script src="${res('countrydata.js')}"
   type="text/javascript"></script>

<div class="toolbar">
   <h1 id="pageTitle"></h1>
   <a id="backButton" class="button" href="#"></a>
</div>

<form id="cities" title="Capital Punishment" class="panel" selected="true">
   <div class="dialog">
      <a id="startOver" class="blueButton" target="xhr">Start Over</a>
      <a id="aboutCap" class="blueButton" target="xhr">About</a>
   </div>
```

```
    <fieldset>
        <div id="answerDiv"></div>
        <div id="scoreDiv"></div>
        <div id="questionDiv"></div>
        <div class="row">
            <label id="radio0"></label>
            <input type="radio" name="capital" id="r0" />
        </div>
        <div class="row">
            <label id="radio1"></label>
            <input type="radio" name="capital" id="r1" />
        </div>
        <div class="row">
            <label id="radio2"></label>
            <input type="radio" name="capital" id="r2" />
        </div>
        <div class="row">
            <label id="radio3"></label>
            <input type="radio" name="capital" id="r3" />
        </div>
        <div class="row">
            <label id="radio4"></label>
            <input type="radio" name="capital" id="r4" />
        </div>
    </fieldset>
</form>
<div class="panel" id="messagePanel">
    <div class="message" id="messagePanelMessage"></div>
</div>
```

iCapitalPunishment CSS Code

Listing 9.10 shows the CSS code for iCapitalPunishment. The CSS for classes .apple-button and .blue are omitted since the code is the same as that shown in listing Listing 9.5 on page 325. The pageTitle's font is reduced so that the title Capital Punishment fits on the iPhone's screen easily without being shortened.

Listing 9.10 Widget iCapitalPunishment (CSS)

```
#scoreDiv, #questionDiv, #answerDiv {
    text-align: center;
}

.blueButton { padding: 5px; }

#pageTitle { font-size: 85%; }

// Code to render a nice iPhone blue button
// (taken from Web App Samples on Apple's web site)
```

```
// Styles for class applebutton and blue (duplicate code removed)
.applebutton { }
.blue { }
```

iCapitalPunishment JavaScript Code

Listing 9.11 includes the JavaScript code for iCapitalPunishment. Code that is unchanged from the original widget (see Listing 6.5 on page 170 through Listing 6.9 on page 179) is omitted. Note that code that supports updating the profile, publishing and saving scores, and challenging friends has been removed. Most of the modifications here link the Get Map button to maps.google.com and implement function doHelp. Minor changes in formatting the feedback were made to accommodate the iPhone screen.

Listing 9.11 Widget iCapitalPunishment (JavaScript)

```
var countries;
var myscore = { };
var countrydata = { };
var mycountries = { };
var usedcountries;
var choicesArray;
var QuizTotal = 20;
var rank = "Lackey";

function parsecoord(geo) {
   // code unchanged
}

function displayScore() {
   // code unchanged
}

function quizend() {
   if (myscore.score >= 20) rank = "Top Diplomat";
   else if (myscore.score >= 15) rank = "Senior Diplomat";
   else if (myscore.score >= 10) rank = "Career Diplomat";
   else if (myscore.score >= 5) rank = "Junior Diplomat";
   else rank = "Lackey";
   alert("Congratulations! \n\nYou have completed the Quiz. "
      + "\n\nYour score is "
      + myscore.score + " out of " + myscore.total
      + ".\n\nYou have achieved the rank of " + rank
      + ".\n\n");

   startover();
}
```

```
function getNextQuestion() {
   // code unchanged
}

function fillchoices() {
   // code unchanged
}

function reset_score() {
   myscore.score = 0;
   myscore.total = 0;
   mycountries.codestring = "";
   mycountries.namestring = "";
   $("answerDiv").innerHTML = "";
   usedcountries = new Array();
   displayScore();
   getNextQuestion();
}

function init_app() {
   countries = init_country_data();
   reset_score();
}

function processAnswer() {
   // code unchanged
}

Event.observe(window, 'load', function() {
   init_app();
});

Event.observe($("startOver"), "click", startclean);
Event.observe($("aboutCap"), "click", doHelp);
Event.observe($("r0"), "change", getGeo);
Event.observe($("r1"), "change", getGeo);
Event.observe($("r2"), "change", getGeo);
Event.observe($("r3"), "change", getGeo);
Event.observe($("r4"), "change", getGeo);

function doHelp() {
   var markup = "Welcome to Capital Punishment. " +
      "By Gail and Paul Anderson.<p/>" +
      "This is an iPhone-friendly version of the Facebook App " +
      "by the same name.<p/> " +
      "To return to the game after getting a map, " +
      "press the circle button, then select Safari.";
   $("messagePanelMessage").update(markup);
   iui.showPage($("messagePanel"));
   return;
}
```

```
function startclean() {
   if (myscore.score) {
      if (confirm("Okay to wipe out your current score?")) {
         startover();
      }
   }
   else {
      startover();
   }
}

function startover() {
   reset_score();
}

function getGeo() {
   myscore.total++;
   var feedback = "";
   if (processAnswer()) {
      feedback = "<b>Correct!!</b> ";
      myscore.score++;
   } else {
      feedback = "<b>Sorry . . .</b> ";
   }
   feedback += "The capital of " + countrydata.name + " is <b>" +
      countrydata.capital +
      "</b>.<br/>(" +
      countrydata.latitude + "," +
      countrydata.longitude + ")";
   var marker = "&ll=" +
      parsecoord(countrydata.latitude) + "," +
      parsecoord(countrydata.longitude) + "&q=" +
      countrydata.capital + ", " + countrydata.name + "";
   feedback +=
      " <a class='blue applebutton' href='http://maps.google.com/maps?z=3" +
      marker + "' target='_blank'>Get Map</a>";
   $("answerDiv").innerHTML = feedback;
   displayScore();
   if (myscore.total >= QuizTotal) quizend();
   else getNextQuestion();
}
```

9.5 Facebook Integration—iPhoneHome Widget

A stand-alone widget like iCapitalPunishment is great, but what if you want to run an iPhone friendly version under Facebook? What if you want to update your profile and publish a story touting your amazing world capital city knowledge using an iPhone version of Capital Punishment?

Great ideas, but access to Facebook (and all of its required authorization) results in additional challenges. For one, you don't want the "Facebook skin" (the blue top dashboard and left navigation area) to gobble up precious real estate from your iPhone application. However, as soon as you run "outside" the Facebook box, you'll lack the context that lets you access all of Facebook's (and your Facebook application's) features.

Happily, there is a solution. Using a combination of Facebook and **zembly** features (and a bit of JavaScript), you can give your loyal application users a great iPhone experience. With Capital Punishment, for instance, users can save their scores (silently behind the scenes), update their profiles, and publish their world geography prowess in their news feed right from an iPhone (or iPod Touch).

To do this, you'll build widget iPhoneHome inside the Capital Punishment Facebook application. You'll start with the iCapitalPunishment widget from Section 9.4 on page 331. Then you'll add JavaScript code that handles the Facebook session authorization. There's a bit of tweaking that's necessary for some Capital Punishment services, but all changes will be backward compatible to the standard Capital Punishment widget (Home).

zembly Tip

If you cloned Capital Punishment previously, your cloned application includes widget iPhoneHome, the iPhone-friendly version.

Here's a summary of the steps you'll follow to provide an iPhone-friendly, Facebook-aware widget for the Capital Punishment Facebook application.

1. Create a new widget within the Capital Punishment Facebook application. Provide a name (iPhoneHome) and description.
2. Include both the iUI and Prototype JavaScript libraries.
3. Upload any PNG file resources to your widget.
4. Modify/provide the HTML, CSS, and JavaScript code with the functions to save the user's score, update the profile, and publish the score to the news feed. Add the functions to get a Facebook session.
5. Create service getSessionKey inside the Capital Punishment application.
6. Modify Capital Punishment services SaveScore, UpdateProfileBox, and PublishScore.
7. Preview and publish the iPhoneHome widget.
8. Text or email the "Share This Widget" URL to your iPhone to run.
9. Add the run icon to your iPhone Home Screen (optional).

Executing a Facebook Application Widget

First of all, how do you call your Facebook application iPhoneHome widget from your iPhone?

Use the following URL that references **zembly**:

```
http://application-number.zembly.com/things/widget-number;iframe
```

The URL parts are defined as follows.

- `application-number` is the **zembly** artifact number you see when you're inside the Capital Punishment Facebook application development page on **zembly**.
- `widget-number` is the **zembly** artifact number of the iPhoneHome widget inside the Capital Punishment Facebook application.
- `;iframe` is the URL ending necessary to execute the widget. Without it, you'll end up on **zembly**'s widget development page for iPhoneHome instead.

iPhone Tip

*The URL for widget iPhoneHome is included in the widget's description on **zembly**. Do not type this long URL into your iPhone Safari address line. Instead, email or send yourself a text message with the URL so that you can simply touch it.*

Facebook Session Authorization

Normally, **zembly** takes care of acquiring a valid Facebook session for you. Since you'll be calling the iPhoneHome widget outside a Facebook session, you'll have to establish a valid session within the widget's code. Let's step through this process before we show you the actual JavaScript code.

Figure 9.15 shows an Activity Diagram with numbers to help describe the different scenarios.

You'll invoke an iPhone web application the first time using a link on your iPhone that has either been emailed to you or sent in a text message. When you select this link, you'll begin the authorization process at Start, shown in Figure 9.15. There will be no query parameters nor any session key cookies, so you'll transition to label 1 (see the diagram). The iPhoneHome web application displays a Log In button, which redirects you to a Facebook login procedure (label 2). If you're not currently logged into Facebook (or Facebook doesn't recognize the source of the login), you'll be presented with a login sequence (label 3). When the login sequence is complete (or if Facebook recognizes you), Facebook redirects you back to the iPhoneHome widget. The redirect URL includes an authorization token in a query parameter (label 4).

iPhone Tip

Orient your iPhone to landscape mode if you need to log into Facebook. This makes the virtual key pad wider, giving more space between keys. You can rotate the iPhone back to portrait mode when the login is complete.

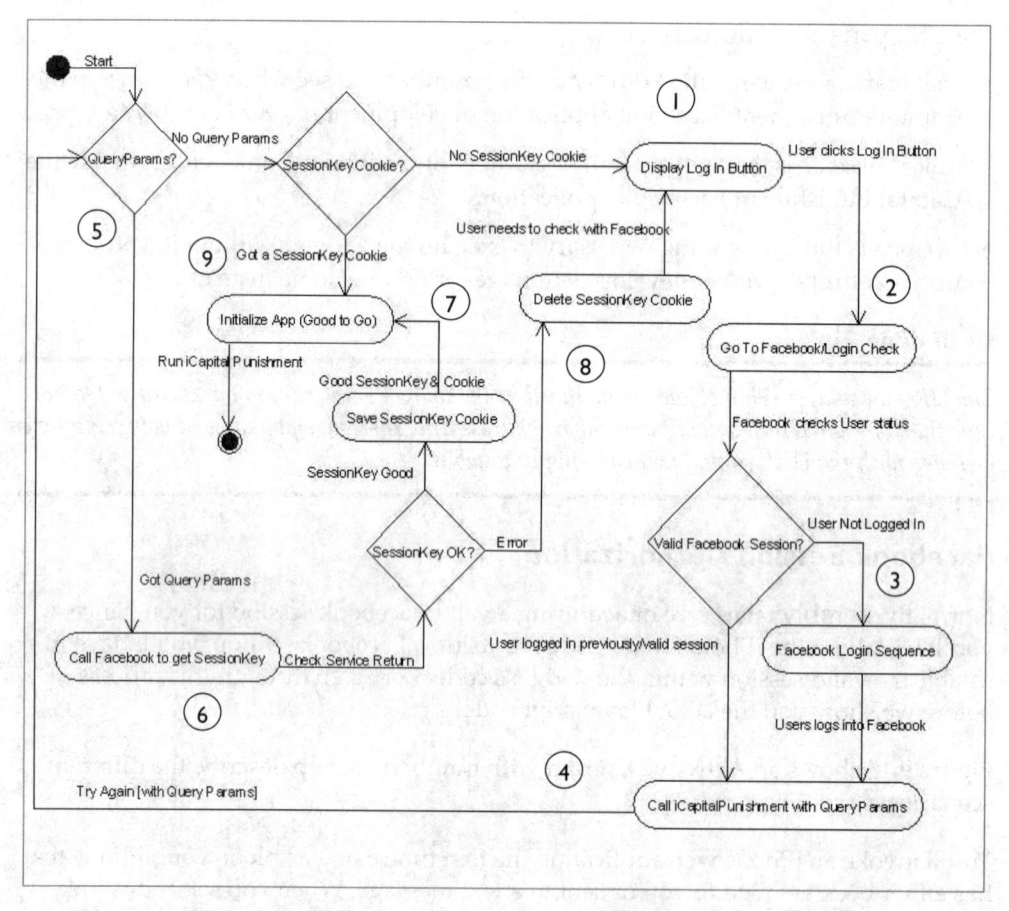

Figure 9.15 Activity Diagram showing the sequence of possible events during session authorization

You're at Start once again, but this time the web application sees an authorization token in the query parameters (label 5). The widget authorization code calls service getSessionKey (which calls the Facebook API) using the authorization token (label 6).

This service returns a Facebook session key which is saved for future use in a cookie and the application is initialized (label 7).

If service getSessionKey returns an error, any saved cookie is deleted (label 8) and you must return to the Facebook login procedure to get a new authorization token (label 1).

The next time you run the widget you begin (as usual) with Start. Although there are no query parameters this time, there will be a cookie with the saved Facebook session key (label 9). The widget's authorization code can now proceed with initializing the application.

Building the iPhoneHome Widget

Let's look at the changes you'll make to the iCapitalPunishment widget to build widget iPhoneHome. Figure 9.16 includes two different screens shown when running widget iPhoneHome from your iPhone. The first screen shows the quiz. The second screen shows the results from a completed quiz.

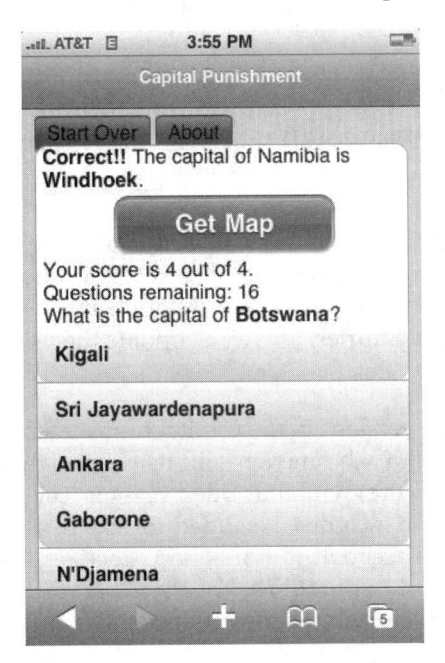

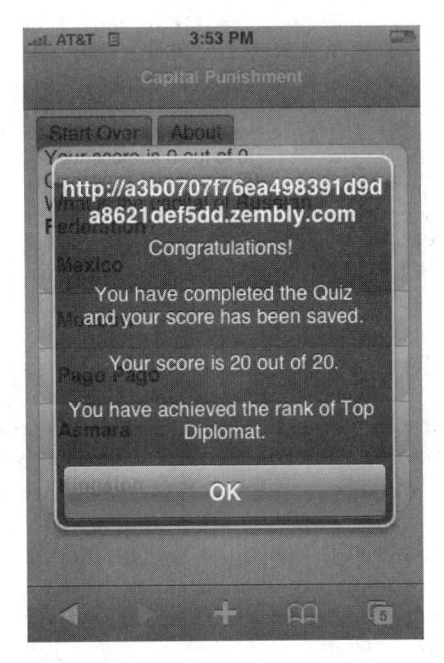

Figure 9.16 iPhoneHome during the quiz and at completion running on the iPhone

Listing 9.12 shows the HTML for widget iPhoneHome. Some of the unchanged code is omitted. The only change here is to add a div tag (id="login") that holds the markup to login to Facebook (marked in bold). The display is unaffected when the empty div tag doesn't contain any text or elements.

Listing 9.12 Widget iPhoneHome (HTML)—Capital Punishment

```html
<link rel="apple-touch-icon" href="${res('globeicon.png')}"/>
<meta name="viewport" content="width=320; initial-scale1.0; maximum-scale=1.0;
   user-scalable=0;"/>
<title>iPhone/Facebook Capital Punishment</title>
<script src="${res('countrydata.js')}" type="text/javascript"></script>

<div class="toolbar">
   <h1 id="pageTitle"></h1>
   <a id="backButton" class="button" href="#"></a>
</div>

<form id="cities" title="Capital Punishment" selected="true" class="panel" >
   <div id="login">
   </div>
   <div class="dialog">

   . . . omitted identical code (see Listing 9.9 on page 333) . . .

</form>
<div class="panel" id="messagePanel">
   <div class="message" id="messagePanelMessage"></div>
</div>
```

There are no changes to the CSS code. Listing 9.13 contains Part 1 of the JavaScript code for widget iPhoneHome. Function quizend now calls functions saveScore (to store the user's score in Facebook's data store), and publishScore (to publish a news feed story with the score and correctly named countries, as well as update the profile with doprofile).

These functions are modified slightly from the versions in the Capital Punishment Home widget code (see Listing 6.9 on page 179). Each function calls its respective service (SaveScore, UpdateProfileBox, or PublishScore) with the added session_key parameter. Furthermore, function saveScore also includes the added fb_userid parameter. These values are obtained from the Facebook authorization process, which stores them in global variables fbSessionKey and fbUserID. These service parameters are optional so that the Capital Punishment Home widget does not need to supply them.

Listing 9.13 Widget iPhoneHome (JavaScript)—Capital Punishment Part 1

```javascript
function quizend() {
   if (myscore.score >= 20) rank = "Top Diplomat";
   else if (myscore.score >= 15) rank = "Senior Diplomat";
```

```
      else if (myscore.score >= 10) rank = "Career Diplomat";
      else if (myscore.score >= 5) rank = "Junior Diplomat";
      else rank = "Lackey";

      // Add code for saveScore(), doprofile(), and publishScore()
      saveScore();
      publishScore();

      alert("Congratulations! \n\n"
         + "You have completed the Quiz\n and your score has been saved. "
         + "\n\nYour score is "
         + myscore.score + " out of " + myscore.total
         + ".\n\nYou have achieved the rank of " + rank + ".");
   }

   function saveScore() {
      Things.callService("ganderson.CapitalPunishment.SaveScore",
      {
         score: myscore.score, // user's capital punishment score
         session_key: fbSessionKey, // Facebook session key
         fb_userid: fbUserID // facebook user id
      },
      {
         onSuccess: function(data) {
            Log.write(data);
         },
      onFailure: function(error) {
         eraseCookie(SESSION_KEY);
         Log.write("Error: " + error.code + " : " + error.message);
         }
      });
   }

   function doprofile() {
      var nameinfo = "<fb:name uid='" + fbUserID
         + "' firstnameonly='true' useyou='false' />";

      var fbtext = " played <a "
      + "href=\"http://www.facebook.com/apps/application.php?id=12659122390\">"
         + "Capital Punishment</a> from the iPhone and achieved the rank of "
         + rank + ", scoring "
         + myscore.score + " correct answers out of "
         + myscore.total + "! <br/><br/>";

      var maptextb =
         "<a href=\"http://www.world66.com/myworld66/visitedCountries\">" +
         "<img width=\"385px\" " +
      "src=\"http://www.world66.com/myworld66/visitedCountries/worldmap?visited="
         + mycountries.codestring + "\"></a><br/><br/>"
         + "Correctly named capitals of countries shown in red:<br/>" +
         mycountries.namestring + ".<br/><br/>";
```

```javascript
    var maptext_main =
    "<a href=\"http://www.world66.com/myworld66/visitedCountries\">" +
    "<img width=\"190px\" " +
    "src=\"http://www.world66.com/myworld66/visitedCountries/worldmap?visited="
    + mycountries.codestring + "\"></a><br/><br/>";

    var name2info = "<b>Can you beat "
    + "<fb:name uid='" + fbUserID
    + "' firstnameonly='true' useyou='false' possessive='true' /> score?</b>";
    Things.callService("ganderson.CapitalPunishment.UpdateProfileBox",
    {
        text: nameinfo + fbtext + maptextb + name2info,
        session_key: fbSessionKey, // Facebook session key
        text_main: nameinfo + fbtext + maptext_main + name2info
    },
    {
        onSuccess: function(data) {
            startover();
        },
        onFailure: function(error) {
            Log.write("Error: " + error.code + " : " + error.message);
            eraseCookie(SESSION_KEY);
        }
    });
}

function publishScore() {
    Things.callService("ganderson.CapitalPunishment.PublishScore",
    {
        score: myscore.score, // the score earned by the user
        total: myscore.total, // possible total number correct
        countries: mycountries.namestring, // correct answer country names.
        session_key: fbSessionKey, // Facebook session key
        codes: mycountries.codestring , // Country codes to produce map
        rank: rank // Rank achieved by user
    },
    {
        onSuccess: function(data) {
            Log.write(data);
            doprofile();

        },
        onFailure: function(error) {
            Log.write("Error: " + error.code + " : " + error.message);
            eraseCookie(SESSION_KEY);
        }
    });
}
```

Listing 9.14 contains the JavaScript code that acquires a Facebook session. Figure 9.15 on page 340 details the steps in an Activity Diagram; here you see how the steps are implemented.

The first step checks to see if a query parameter for the authorization token exists. If the token exists, function `acquireSessionKey` calls service `getSessionKey` to get a Facebook session key. If there isn't an authorization token, the next step is to see if a `SESSION_KEY` cookie exists. (The code to create, read, and delete cookies is presented in Listing 9.8 on page 330. This same code is reused here.) The `SESSION_KEY` cookie not only contains the valid Facebook session key, but also the user's Facebook user id is embedded in the session key. The user id is extracted from the session key and stored in variable `fbUserID`. The session key is stored in variable `fbSessionKey`.

If there's no query parameter and no session key cookie, the user must access the Facebook web site for validation. On the Facebook site, you will need to login if Facebook determines that you are not already logged in. After login verification, Facebook generates an authorization token and redirects you back to the iPhoneHome widget sending the authorization token in the query parameter.

Note that this authorization process gets a Facebook session key either from a stored cookie or a service call that returns a session key. Only then can the application begin its initialization process (calling function `init_app`). The session key stored in `fbSessionKey` allows the widget to access the Facebook API through the Capital Punishment services.

Facebook Tip

Even if we have a stored session key in a cookie, we make sure that it's still good (session keys expire) by calling service CheckSessionKey. CheckSessionKey simply makes a Facebook API call that requires a valid session. We call function `facebook_login` *if CheckSessionKey fails.*

Facebook Tip

Note that function `facebook_login` *calls the same Facebook utility login.php to get a valid session that you call when authorizing an application (see "Controlling the Allow Access Process" on page 136). If the user has already authorized the application, Facebook will not redirect, but will re-invoke widget iPhoneHome with the authorization tokens.*

Listing 9.14 Widget iPhoneHome (JavaScript)—Capital Punishment Part 2

```
// Begin the Facebook authorization process here:
// Look for auth_token and process it if present
var queryParams = parseQueryParams(document.location.search);
if (queryParams["auth_token"] != null) {
```

```
      acquireSessionKey(queryParams);
   }
   // If there is no auth_token, look for Facebook session key
   // in a cookie
   else {
      fbSessionKey = readCookie(SESSION_KEY);

      // If we don't have one, point to FB login
      if (fbSessionKey == null) {
         facebook_login();
      } else {
      // Is the sessionkey good?
      Things.callService("ganderson.CapitalPunishment.CheckSessionKey",
      {
         session_key: fbSessionKey // Check to see if this session key is valid
      },
      {
         onSuccess: function(data) {
            Log.write(data);
            // extract the Facebook UserId from the session key
            var pair = fbSessionKey.split("-");
            fbUserID = pair[1];
            // We're good to go
            init_app();
         },
         onFailure: function(error) {
            Log.write("Error: " + error.code + " : " + error.message);
            facebook_login();
         }
      });
      }
   }
}

///////////////////////////////////////////////
// Query parameters helpers
///////////////////////////////////////////////
function parseQueryParams(query) {
   if ((query == null) || (query.length == 0)) {
      return {};
   }

   if (query.charAt(0) != "?")
      return {};

   // Remove initial question mark
   query = query.substring(1);

   var pairs = query.split("&");
   var params = {};
   for (var i = 0; i < pairs.length; i++) {
      var pair = pairs[i].split("=");
      var key = pair[0];
```

Facebook Integration—iPhoneHome Widget

```
         var value = pair[1];
         params[key] = value;
      }

      return params;
   }

   /////////////////////////////////////////////////////
   // Facebook functionality
   /////////////////////////////////////////////////////

   // Configuration / constants
   var SESSION_KEY = "fbSessionKey";
   var COOKIES_DAYS = 365*100;
   var API_KEY = "cb9b1e3b1decd6566f005425d44fee61";// Look this up in Facebook

   var fbSessionKey = null;
   var fbUserID = null;

   function acquireSessionKey(queryParams) {
      Things.callService("ganderson.CapitalPunishment.getSessionKey",
      {
         auth_token: queryParams["auth_token"]
      },
      {
         onSuccess: function(data) {
            createCookie(SESSION_KEY, data.session_key, COOKIES_DAYS);
            fbSessionKey = data.session_key;
            fbUserID = data.uid;
            init_app();
         },
         onFailure: function(error) {
            alert("Error: There was a problem acquiring session key. "
               + "Please try logging into Facebook again.");
            eraseCookie(SESSION_KEY);
            facebook_login();
         }
      });
   }

   function facebook_login() {
      // Go to login URL
      eraseCookie(SESSION_KEY);
      var url =
         "http://www.facebook.com/login.php?api_key="
            + API_KEY + "&v=1.0"
            + "&next=iPhoneHome;iframe";
      alert("In order to use this application,"
         + " you need to login to Facebook. Going to Login");
      document.location = url;
   }
```

Building the iPhoneHome Services

Widget iPhoneHome requires a new service to get a session key from Facebook using the authorization token. Listing 9.15 shows the JavaScript code for service getSessionKey.

Listing 9.15 Service getSessionKey (JavaScript)—Capital Punishment

```
return Things.facebook.auth.getSession({
   auth_token: Parameters.auth_token,
   keys: Application.keychain
});
```

The iPhoneHome widget makes several calls to services within the Capital Punishment application. These services require the Facebook session key, which is normally available through the application context. Because iPhoneHome runs outside the Facebook context, this widget must pass a session key to services that access the Facebook API. These services were all presented previously with the optional session key or user id. When the caller doesn't supply the parameter, the service gets the session key or user id from the application context.

Listing 6.17 on page 199 shows the JavaScript code for service SaveScore, Listing 6.10 on page 182 shows the JavaScript code for service UpdateProfileBox, and Listing 6.12 on page 186 shows the JavaScript code for service PublishScore.

9.6 iLondonTube Widget

Adapting the London Tube widget (see "LondonTubeMapWidget" on page 289) for the iPhone is a perfect target. You're out and about in London and your iPhone tells you how to get from point A to point B. The iPhone widget has both instructions and a map to show you tube stops and connections.

The biggest problem you're faced with in adapting this widget is that you can't use the native Google Maps application here. Why not? You need the Google Maps API to draw line segments and place markers at each tube stop. However, using Google Maps from the internet means that you no longer have the iPhone-friendly map controls. Panning with your finger doesn't work (it just moves the viewport around); neither does double tap to zoom in and center or pinch in and pinch out.

To get around these inconveniences, you can build your own map controls using image-based buttons. Image-based buttons help make button controls large enough for fingers. You'll provide controls to pan the map in all four directions and to zoom in and out.

The rest of the web application is the same as the London Tube Map Widget. Figure 9.17 shows the application running on an iPhone. The top-level menu lets you select the tube stops (start/end) and get the tube information.

Safari on the iPhone renders an option selection component as a spinning dial. You can spin either forward (down) or backwards (up) using a flick motion with your finger. Tap the option to select it. Figure 9.17 shows tube stop Angel selected for the destination.

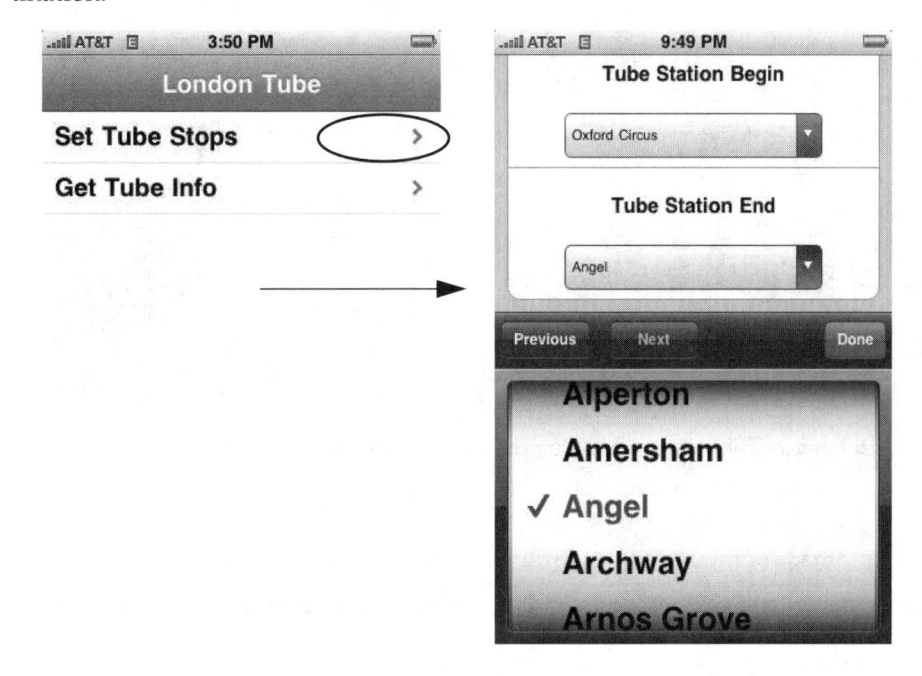

Figure 9.17 London Tube widget running on the iPhone: setting the tube stops

After selecting the tube stops, return to the top menu and select Get Tube Info. Figure 9.18 shows the results from selecting Oxford Circus as a starting point and Angel as the destination. The second screen in Figure 9.18 includes the Journey Summary and Journey Points, which are visible when you scroll down from the map. The map shows the starting point marker and color-coded lines connecting the tube stops.

Figure 9.18 London Tube widget showing the custom Google Maps control buttons

Here is a summary of the steps you'll follow to implement the iLondonTube widget.

1. Create a new blank widget (or clone LondonTubeMapWidget). Provide a name and description.
2. Include both the iUI and Prototype JavaScript libraries.
3. Upload any PNG file resources to your widget.
4. Modify/provide the HTML, CSS, and JavaScript code to comply with iUI widgets. Include code to implement the Google map controls.
5. Preview and publish the widget.
6. Text or email the "Share This Widget" URL to your iPhone to run.
7. Add the run icon to your iPhone Home Screen (optional).

iLondonTube Resources

Figure 9.19 shows the iLondonTube widget Resources tab on **zembly** (partial list). Each button has a PNG image file (there are six), as well as the Home Screen icon (`tubeicon.png`) and the JavaScript file that contains the station data (`station_data.js`).

Figure 9.19 Resources used by the iLondonTube widget

Building the iLondonTube Widget

The original London Tube widget presented in the Dapper chapter (Chapter 7) gets its routing information from the Dapp based on data from web site tubeplanner.com. (See "London Tube Widget" on page 248 for details on how to create the Dapp and construct the original widget.) Then, in Chapter 8 we built an enhanced widget that makes use of Google Maps to display routing and tube stop information. (See "LondonTubeMapWidget" on page 289 for details on using the Google Maps API to place markers and draw line segments.) With this enhanced widget as a beginning point, you'll use the iUI CSS and JavaScript bundle to construct the HTML that is iPhone-friendly. You'll then build your own Google Maps control buttons and use the iUI functions to update the markup. We've omitted CSS and JavaScript that is unchanged to help clarify the presentation.

Listing 9.16 shows the HTML markup for widget iLondonTube. Its structure reflects the usual iUI web application that includes tags for the Home Screen icon (link), the iPhone viewport (meta), the title, and the top-level toolbar.

The menu item to set the tube stops is anchor #settings and the menu item to get the tube information results from the 'click' event handler for element "plannerButton."

Tag element div with id "map_canvas" is a placeholder for the Google Maps.

The six map control buttons have PNG images and invoke 'click' event handlers (in the JavaScript code). These functions issue Google Maps API calls that update the map.

Tag div with id "TubeResults" is a placeholder for the markup generated in the JavaScript to display the journey information.

Listing 9.16 iLondonTube (HTML)

```html
<link rel="apple-touch-icon" href="${res('tubeicon.png')}" />
<meta name="viewport"
   content="width=320; initial-scale=1.0; maximum-scale=1.0; user-scal-
able=0;" />
<title>London Tube</title>
<script src="${res('stations_data.js')}"
   type="text/javascript"></script>
<script src="http://maps.google.com/maps?file=api&amp;v=2&amp;key=Your Google Key"
   type="text/javascript"></script>
<body onunload="GUnload()">
<div class="toolbar">
   <h1 id="pageTitle"></h1>
   <a id="backButton" class="button" href="#"></a>
</div>
<ul id="home" title="London Tube" selected="true">
   <li><a href="#settings">Set Tube Stops</a></li>
   <li><a id="plannerButton" target="xhr">Get Tube Info</a></li>
</ul>

<form id="settings" title="Set Tube Stops" class="panel">
   <fieldset>
      <h4>Tube Station Begin</h4>
      <div class="row">
         <select id="startTube">
            <option>Start Tube Station</option>
         </select>
      </div>
      <h4>Tube Station End</h4>
      <div class="row">
         <select id="endTube">
            <option>Destination Tube Station</option>
         </select>
      </div>
   </fieldset>
</form>

<div class="panel" id="LondonPage">
   <div id="map_canvas"></div>
   <div id="mapcontrols">
      <span id="panleft"><a id="fpanleft" target="xhr" >
         <img src="${res('panleft.png')}" alt="pan left" width="53" height="36"
```

```
            border="0" /></a></span>
        <span id="panright"><a id="fpanright" target="xhr" >
            <img src="${res('panright.png')}" alt="pan right" width="53"
            height="36" border="0" /></a></span>
        <span id="panup"><a id="fpanup" target="xhr" >
            <img src="${res('panup.png')}" alt="pan up" width="36" height="54"
            border="0" /></a></span>
        <span id="pandown"><a id="fpandown" target="xhr" >
            <img src="${res('pandown.png')}" alt="pan down" width="36" height="54"
            border="0" /></a></span>
        <span id="zoomin"><a id="fzoomin" target="xhr" >
            <img src="${res('zoomin.png')}" alt="zoom in" width="50" height="51"
            border="0" /></a></span>
        <span id="zoomout"><a id="fzoomout" target="xhr" >
            <img src="${res('zoomout.png')}" alt="zoom out" width="50" height="51"
            border="0" /></a></span>
    </div>
    <div id="TubeResults"></div>
</div>
```

Listing 9.17 shows the CSS for widget iLondonTube. The map_canvas style is reduced to fit the iPhone viewport. There are additional styles for the map control buttons (pandown, panup, panleft, panright, zoomin, and zoomout). The remaining styles are unchanged (see Listing 7.10 on page 255 for the omitted styles).

Listing 9.17 iLondonTube (CSS)

```
h4, .row { text-align: center; }
#startTube, #endTube { height: 35px; }

#map_canvas {
    width: 320px;
    height: 340px;
}
#pandown, #panup {
    height:54px;
    width:36px;
}

#panleft, #panright {
    height:36px;
    width:53px;
}

#zoomin, #zoomout {
    height:54px;
    width:36px;
}
          . . . omitted styles . . .   (see Listing 7.10 on page 255)
```

354 Chapter 9 Building for the iPhone

The JavaScript code for widget iLondonTube is presented in two parts. Listing 9.18 shows Part 1. Function `init_map` initializes Google maps. Note that the code to include the map controls is omitted, since you'll use the customized buttons instead. The 'click' event handlers for these custom controls call Google maps functions panDirection (for the panning changes) and zoomIn and zoomOut (for the zoom level changes).

Listing 9.18 iLondonTube (JavaScript)—Part 1

```
var map;
var stations;

function init_map(lat, lng) {
    if (GBrowserIsCompatible()) {
        map = new GMap2(document.getElementById("map_canvas"));
        map.setCenter(new GLatLng(lat, lng), 14);
    }
}

function draw_segment(g1, g2, color) {
    // Code unchanged
}

function add_marker(lat, lng, htmlstr, isfirst) {
    // Code unchanged
}

// Custom map controls
Event.observe($("fpanleft"), 'click', function() {
    map.panDirection(+1, 0);
});
Event.observe($("fpanright"), 'click', function() {
    map.panDirection(-1, 0);
});
Event.observe($("fpanup"), 'click', function() {
    map.panDirection(0, +1);
});
Event.observe($("fpandown"), 'click', function() {
    map.panDirection(0, -1);
});
Event.observe($("fzoomin"), 'click', function() {
    map.zoomIn();
});
Event.observe($("fzoomout"), 'click', function() {
    map.zoomOut();
});

Event.observe(window, 'load', init_app);

function init_app() {
    populateSelectTags();
```

```
}
function populateSelectTags() {
   // Code unchanged
}
function findstation(name) {
   // Code unchanged
}
var linecolors = {
   "Bakerloo" : "#AE6118",
   . . . code omitted . . .
   "Foot" : "#D2D2D2"
};
```

Listing 9.19 shows Part 2 of the iLondonTube JavaScript code. The entire listing consists of the 'click' event handler for the plannerButton element. Much of the code is identical to previously shown JavaScript for the London Tube widget. Note that instead of using innerHTML to update the markup, we use function update followed by iUI function showPage (marked in bold). Otherwise, the same code is reused.

Listing 9.19 iLondonTube (JavaScript)—Part 2

```
Event.observe($("plannerButton"), 'click', function() {
   var startTube =
      $("startTube").options[$("startTube").selectedIndex].value;
   var endTube =
      $("endTube").options[$("endTube").selectedIndex].value;
   if (startTube == endTube) {
      var i = findstation(startTube);
      init_map(stations[i].geocode.latitude, stations[i].geocode.longitude);
      var resultsHtml = "<b>You're already there!</b><br/>" +
         startTube + " Station";
      $("TubeResults").update(resultsHtml);
      iui.showPage($("LondonPage"));
      add_marker(stations[i].geocode.latitude, stations[i].geocode.longitude,
         resultsHtml, true);
      return;
   } else
      Things.callService("ganderson.LondonTubeJourneyPlanner",
      {
         "startTube": startTube, // London tube stop of journey start
         "endTube": endTube // London Tube stop of journey destination
      },
      {
      onSuccess: function(data) {
         var titlestr = "<div id=\"titlediv\">From " +
            data.groups.journey[0].endpoint[0].value
            + " To " + data.groups.journey[1].endpoint[0].value
```

```
            + "</div>";

        . . . omitted code . . .
        (see Listing 7.12 on page 257 and Listing 7.13 on page 257)
              . . .

        stationstr += "</table></div>";

        // Build the map

        . . . omitted code . . .
        (see Listing 8.21 on page 296)
              . . .

        var resultsHtml = titlestr + summarystr + stationstr;
        $("TubeResults").update(resultsHtml);
        iui.showPage($("LondonPage"));
        return;
        },
    onFailure: function(error) {
        var resultsHtml = "Service error: " + error.message;
        $("TubeResults").update(resultsHtml);
        iui.showPage($("LondonPage"));
        return;
        }
    });
});
```

9.7 iCandy—Samples from Apple

While the iUI library gives your web applications the look and feel of native applications, you can certainly build widgets without iUI. Candidates for not using iUI include widgets that have few, if any, navigational links and can execute as a single-page display. To offer a few tidbits of what's possible, we'll show you a couple of samples from the Apple iPhone Developer's page (https://developer.apple.com/webapps/index.php). This may inspire you to incorporate similar visual elements in your web applications. Note that these examples all depend on the Safari display engine (webkit) so they won't run on non-Safari browsers.

iLeaves Widget

Widget iLeaves is a `zembly` port of an iPhone web application that demonstrates some Safari webkit features. The original web application is featured on Apple's Developer Connection site at https://developer.apple.com/webapps/docs_iphone/samplecode/Leaves/ (you may have to log in to access the site). The application shows falling leaves in an animation sequence. Figure 9.20 shows the widget running on an iPhone (except, of course, the animation is frozen).

There are actually two versions of this sample application on the iPhone site. One version uses CSS extensions available with the iPhone 2.0 software. The version we show here does not rely on the CSS extensions but performs all the animation with JavaScript.

Figure 9.20 Widget iLeaves running on the iPhone

We're not going to display the complete code to implement this web application. Instead, we'll tell you the modifications that were made to run this widget on **zembly**.

Upload the PNG Images

The first step is to upload the four PNG images to your widget page on **zembly**. Figure 9.21 shows the four images uploaded to widget iLeaves.

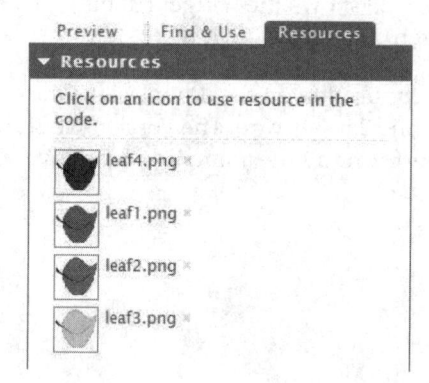

Figure 9.21 Image resources for widget iLeaves

Import and Update HTML, CSS, and JavaScript Code

When you download and import the sample code from the Apple Developer's site, there are just a few modifications to make. Because you must upload image resources required by zembly widgets, you must make sure that references to the resources are consistent in your code. In this example (see Listing 9.20) we've added four img elements with id attributes that can be referred to in the JavaScript code. We set the style attribute to 'display:none' so that these images aren't rendered.

Listing 9.20 Widget iLeaves (HTML)

```
<!DOCTYPE HTML PUBLIC "-//W3C//DTD HTML 4.01//EN"
"http://www.w3.org/TR/html4/strict.dtd">
<link rel="apple-touch-icon" href="${res('leaf1.png')}" />
<title>Falling Leaves &mdash; Not Using CSS Animations and Transforms</title>
<meta http-equiv="Content-type" content="text/html; charset=utf-8"/>
<meta name="viewport" content="width=device-width, initial-scale=0.64"/>

   . . . omitted code unchanged from Apple Developer's Site . . .

<img id='image1' src="${res('leaf1.png')}" style='display:none' />
<img id='image2' src="${res('leaf2.png')}" style='display:none' />
<img id='image3' src="${res('leaf3.png')}" style='display:none' />
<img id='image4' src="${res('leaf4.png')}" style='display:none' />
```

There are no changes to the CSS code. Listing 9.21 shows function CreateALeaf from the JavaScript code. This is the only function that was modified (changed code is shown in bold). To create a leaf from one of the images, a new img element takes on the src attribute from one of the non-displayed static images in Listing 9.20.

Listing 9.21 Widget iLeaves (JavaScript)

```
. . . omitted JavaScript code unchanged from Apple Developer's Site . . .

/*
Uses an img element to create each leaf of the animation.
Function CreateALeaf modified to handle zembly resource syntax.
*/
function CreateALeaf(container)
{
   /* Start by creating an empty img element */
   var image = document.createElement('img');

   /* Randomly choose a leaf image and assign it to the newly created element
*/
   var t = document.getElementById('image' + randomInteger(1, 5) + "");
   image.src = t.src;

   /* Figure out the random start and end y-axis positions of the image */
   var startPositionOnYAxis = randomInteger(-300, 0);
   var endPositionOnYAxis = randomInteger(600, 700);

   /* Compute a random duration for the animation */
   var duration = randomFloat(5, 11);

   /* Position the leaf at a random start location within the screen */
   image.style.top = pixelValue(startPositionOnYAxis);
   image.style.left = pixelValue(randomInteger(0, 500));
   /* Now that the image is set up, add it to the container */
   container.appendChild(image);
   /* Finally, create and start an animation using Dropper */
   new Dropper(image, startPositionOnYAxis, endPositionOnYAxis,
      duration).start();
}
```

iButtons Widget

The iButtons widget illustrates some image-based buttons that you can use in your web applications. In fact, iLiveWeather and iCapitalPunishment both use the blue button shown in Figure 9.22 (see Listing 9.5 on page 325 for the complete CSS for the blue button). The button renders in a nice size (a good target for fingers) and expands horizontally to fit the text. The text has a drop-shadow effect and stands out with white against the blue background.

Other buttons include black on white, white on black left and right arrow buttons, and a white on gray button.

360   Chapter 9   Building for the iPhone

Figure 9.22 Widget iButtons running on the iPhone

This sample is adapted from the iPhoneButtons sample application on the Apple Developer's web site.

Figure 9.23 shows the zembly Resources tab with the images for widget iButtons.

Figure 9.23 Image resources for widget iButtons

The only change required was to modify the CSS webkit image url to point to the resources directory (../resources) for the iButtons widget, as shown in Listing 9.22.

Listing 9.22 Widget iButtons (CSS)

```
     . . . CSS code omitted that is unchanged in each class . . .
/* Builds a button using a 29x46 image */
.blue
{
     -webkit-border-image: url(../resources/blueButton.png) 0 14 0 14;
}

/* Builds a button using a 29x46 image */
.white
{
     -webkit-border-image: url(../resources/whiteButton.png) 0 14 0 14;
}

/* Builds a button using a 29x46 image */
.black
{
     -webkit-border-image: url(../resources/grayButton.png) 0 14 0 14;
}

/* Creates a button using a 18x30 image */
.blackLeft
{
     -webkit-border-image: url(../resources/leftButton.png) 0 5 0 12;
}

/* Creates a button using a 18x30 image */
.blackRight
{
     -webkit-border-image: url(../resources/rightButton.png) 0 12 0 5;
}
```

Index

Symbols

$("element_id") Prototype notation 41

A

About Page, Facebook 125
acquire Facebook session, zembly testing 155
actions, zembly 16
{*actor*} token 183
adapters, zembly 24
Add to editor, Find & Use Tab 40
Add to Home Screen, iPhone icons 317
Add to Info button, Facebook 114, 212
Add to Profile button, Facebook 141, 144, 176
  with HTML 166
addOverlay function, Google Maps 97
admin tool, Facebook data store model 193
Ajax.FBML, FBJS (responseType) 143, 150
Ajax.JSON, FBJS (responseType) 217
allow access, Facebook applications 111, 136
Amazon AWS services 25
AmazonProductSearch sample service 13
AmazonProductSearchWidget 17–20
animation library, Facebook 151
API calls, zembly 24
API key, Facebook 118
Apple iPhone Developer 356
application context, Facebook 134
Application Directory, Facebook 130
Application Info section, Facebook 212, 219
Application object, zembly 134
Application Tabs, Facebook 110, 223
applications
  See also Facebook applications
  create Facebook 114–120
  favorites 16
  score 15
Applications menu bar, Facebook 106
arrays with FBJS 158
associations, Facebook data store model 192
attributes, XML node 277

B

Binary parameter type for services 28
bookmark, Facebook applications 107, 108
Boolean parameter type for services 28
Boxes tab, Facebook 108

BuddyMugs Facebook application, HTML 160
BuddyPics Facebook application 137–158
  Home Widget (JavaScript) 148
  service GetFriendInfo 153
  service UpdateProfileBox 157

C

call service, zembly 32
Call tab, zembly 30
canvas page URL, Facebook 117
canvas page, Facebook 104
Capital Punishment Facebook application 163–190
  countrydata.js file 165
  data store model 193
  DeleteScore service 204
  detecting users who have authorized 172
  FBMLGetFriendScores service 201
  FBMLGetMyScores service 201
  feed stories 182–186
  getSessionKey service 348
  Home Widget (JavaScript) 170
  iPhoneHome widget 337–348
  PublishChallenge service 190
  PublishScore service 186
  SeeScores widget 205
  SendInvitation widget 187
capture example, zembly 30
clearInterval JavaScript function 63
Clearspring widget sharing 18, 66
clearTimeout JavaScript function
  with FBJS 147
clone, zembly 15
  Facebook applications 142
code name, zembly 22
code testing tools, Facebook 133
collaboration requests, zembly 21
comma formatted numbers, JavaScript 90
contacts, zembly 21, 22–24
  search 23
context data, Facebook applications (table) 135
cookie helper functions, JavaScript 330
count-down timer, JavaScript 170
CreateDataStore service, Facebook data store
  model 196
CSS styles 35, 59
  hover events 60
  opacity 62

363

D

Dapp 238
    create 240–243
    feed reader 266
    flickrPhotoSearch 240–243
    GambitsfromGailFeed 267
    LondonTubeJourneyPlanner 250–252
    mlbupdate 259–262
Dapper 239
    flickrPhotoSearch service 243
    flickrPhotoSearchWidget 244–248
    GambitsfromGailFeed service 268
    GambitsSummaryWidget 268–271
    LondonTubeJourneyPlanner service 252–253
    LondonTubeMapWidget 289–298
    LondonTubeWidget 254–258
    mlbscores service 262
    mlbScoresWidget 263–265
`dapper.net` 238
data extraction 239
data store model, Facebook 192
Developer, Facebook application 116
`Dialog` FBJS object 159
directional controls, Google Maps 94
drafts, `zembly` 31, 42–45
    Erase and start over 43
    saving new 43

E

E4X notation 48, 84, 276
    namespace 277
`each` Prototype function 63
ECMAScript for XML 84
EDGE network, iPhone 310
editor commands, `zembly` 31
Email parameter type for services 28
email, Facebook 112
embed a widget 14
enumeration with Prototype 63
Erase and start over (all drafts) 43
Error Codes, services 29
Escape value 49
`Event.observe` Prototype function 64
examples
    BuddyPics Facebook application 137–158
    Capital Punishment Facebook application 163–190
    Chapter Building Flickr Widgets 56
    Chapter Building for the iPhone 310
    Chapter Building Zillow Widgets 80
    Chapter Facebook Basics 102
    Chapter Facebook Integration 162
    Chapter Widget Gallery 274
    Chapter Working with Dapper 238
    Chapter `zembly` Basics 12
    FlickrPeopleService 68–71
    flickrPhotoSearch Dapp 240–243
    flickrPhotoSearch service 243
    flickrPhotoSearchWidget 244–248
    FlickrSlideShow 57–67
    GambitsfromGailFeed Dapp 267
    GambitsfromGailFeed service 268
    GambitsSummaryWidget 268–271
    iButtons widget 359–361
    iCapital Punishment widget 331–337
    iLeaves widget 356–359
    iLiveWeather widget 322–330
    iLoanPayment widget 314–322
    iLondonTube widget 348–356
    iPhoneHome widget 337–348
    LiveWeatherBugService 276–279
    LiveWeatherBugWidget 279–283
    LiveWeatherMapWidget 284–289
    Loan Calculator Facebook application 121–125
    LoanPaymentService 25–34
    LoanPaymentWidget 34–42
    LondonTubeJourneyPlanner Dapp 250–252
    LondonTubeJourneyPlanner service 252–253
    LondonTubeMapWidget 289–298
    LondonTubeWidget 254–258
    mlbscores service 262
    mlbScoresWidget 263–265
    mlbupdate Dapp 259–262
    Mood Pix Facebook application 208–231
    MyFlickrRandomSlideshow 71–77
    RecentSalesMashup 92–99
    RecentSalesService 82–88
    RecentSalesWidget 88–92
    WeatherBugService 45–51
    WeatherBugWidget 51–54
    zemblyblog pipe 299–304
    zemblyConnectDemo Facebook application 232–235
    zemblyrumblings widget 304–307

F

Facebook
    background 103–114
    acquire session 155
    Add to Info button 114, 212
    Add to Profile button 141, 166, 176
    allow access dialog 111
    animation library 151
    API 131
    API key 118
    API test console 133
    application context 134
    Application Directory 130
    Application Tabs 110
    Applications menu bar 106
    Boxes tab 108
    canvas page 104
    canvas page URL 117
    code testing tools 133
    Connect facility 231–235
    create applications 114–120
    Data Store API 191–208
    data store model 192
    detecting users who have authorized 172
    Developer application 116
    email 112
    `fb_sig_added` 134, 216
    `fb_sig_canvas_user` 134, 217
    `fb_sig_friends` 134, 147
    `fb_sig_user` 134, 217
    FBJS 120
    FBML 120

overview 138
   dynamic content 142–143
   test console 133
`fbSessionKey` 134
`fbUserID` 134, 177
features and integration points *(table)* 104
feed forms 211
feed preview console 133
feed story types 183
`feed.publishUserAction` 186
FQL 199
friend 105
Home link 113
Info section 212
Info tab 114
invite friends widget 187
iPhoneHome widget 337–348
JavaScript Client Library 233
left-hand column 109
locked services and widgets 120
news feed 112
notices 112
preview widget 124
profile 105
profile boxes 108, 180
profile publisher 113
`profile.getInfo` adapter 221
`profile.setInfo` adapter 221
publishing feed stories 182–186
Registered Template Bundles Console 182
registered templates console 133
secret key 118
session authorization 136, 339
template bundles 182
tokens, feed templates 183
user 105
XFBML 233
Facebook applications
   About Page 125
   Add to Profile button 144
   allow access and login techniques 136
   bookmark 107, 108
   BuddyPics 137–158
   Capital Punishment 163–190
   clone 142
   context data *(table)* 135
   developer mode 129
   FriendChooser 191
   Help widget 126
   Home widget 124
   HTML widgets 121
   icon 128
   Loan Calculator 121–125
   logo 129
   Make it public button 129
   Mood Pix 208–231
   permissions 108
   private installation 129
   PublishScore service 186
   registered template bundles 189
   RegisterTemplates service 184
   `requireLogin`, FBJS 137, 206
   `responseType`, FBJS 143, 150
   template widgets and services 126
   Terms of Service widget 126

UpdateProfileBox service 126, 181
   ways to enhance 127–129
   zemblyConnectDemo 232–235
Facebook Connect 231–235
   zemblyConnectDemo application 232–235
Facebook data store admin tool 193
Facebook Data Store API 191–208
Facebook data store model 192
   associations 192
   CreateDataStore service 196
   delete object 204
   FQL 199
   object types 193
   properties 192
   SaveScore service 198
Facebook Developer application 116
Facebook Developers Wiki 133
Facebook JavaScript, *See* FBJS
Facebook Markup Language, *See* FBML
Facebook Query Language, *See* FQL
Facebook services
   acquire Facebook session 155
   testing 155
   UpdateProfileBox 157
favorites, zembly 16
`fb:action` FBML tag 187
`fb:add-section-button` FBML tag 144, 214
`fb:board` FBML tag 139
`fb:dashboard` FBML tag 144
`fb:else` FBML tag 139
`fb:friend-selector` FBML tag 139, 227
`fb:help` FBML tag 187
`fb:if` FBML tag 139
`fb:if-is-app-user` FBML tag 138
`fb:multi-friend-selector` FBML tag 187
`fb:name` FBML tag 138
`fb:profile-pic` FBML tag 138
`fb:pronoun` FBML tag 138
`fb:request-form` FBML tag 187
`fb:rock-the-vote` FBML tag 139, 144
`fb:user` FBML tag 138
`fb_sig_added`, Facebook 134, 216
`fb_sig_canvas_user`, Facebook 134, 217
`fb_sig_friends`, Facebook 134, 147
`fb_sig_user`, Facebook 134, 217
FBJS 120
   differences with JavaScript 158
   arrays 158
   `clearTimeout` function 147
   `Dialog` object 159
   `setInnerFBML` function 143
   `setTimeout` function 147
   vs JavaScript 120
FBML 120
   overview 138
   dynamic content 142–143
   `fb:action` 187
   `fb:add-section-button` 214
   `fb:board` 139
   `fb:dashboard` 144
   `fb:else` 139
   `fb:friend-selector` 139, 227
   `fb:help` 187
   `fb:if` 139
   `fb:if-is-app-user` 138
   `fb:multi-friend-selector` 187

Index

fb:name 138
fb:profile-pic 138
fb:pronoun 138
fb:request-form 187
fb:rock-the-vote 139, 144
fb:user 138
   feed forms 215
   test console 133
   vs HTML 120
FBML widgets 144
FBMLGetFriendScores service, Facebook 201
FBMLGetMyScores service, Facebook 201
fbSessionKey, Facebook 134
fbUserID, Facebook 134, 177
feed forms, Facebook 211, 215
   FeedHandlerService 218
feed reader Dapp 266
feed stories, Facebook 182–186
feed.publishUserAction Facebook adapter 186
www.feedburner.com 267
FeedHandlerService, Facebook feed forms 218
Fetch Feed object, Yahoo! Pipes 300
fieldset tag, iUI Library 319
Filter operator, Yahoo! Pipes 302
Find & Use tab, zembly 39, 49, 69
   search Facebook adapters 131
   Yahoo! Pipes 304
Firebug debugger 33
Flickr
   FlickrPeopleService 68–71
   flickrPhotoSearchWidget 244–248
   FlickrSlideShow widget 57–67
   MyFlickrRandomSlideshow widget 71–77
Flickr API
   key 68
   photo source URL 64
   sample JSON data 65
flickr.interestingness.getList adapter 56
flickr.people.findByUsername adapter 56, 68
flickr.people.getInfo adapter 56
flickr.people.getPublicPhotos adapter 56, 68
flickr.photos.addTags adapter 57
flickr.photos.comments.addComment adapter 57
flickr.photos.geo.getLocation adapter 57
flickr.photos.search adapter 57
flickr.photosets.getList adapter 57
flickr.photosets.getPhotos adapter 57
FlickrPeopleService 68–71
flickrPhotoSearch Dapp 240–243
flickrPhotoSearch service 243
FlickrPhotoSearchService sample service 13
flickrPhotoSearchWidget (Dapp-based) 244–248
FlickrSlideShow widget 57–67
   (JavaScript) 62
FQL 191–208
fql.query Facebook adapter 154, 202
friend, Facebook 105
FriendChooser Facebook application 191
full story type, Facebook 112, 183

G

GambitsfromGailFeed Dapp 267
GambitsfromGailFeed service 268

GambitsSummaryWidget 268–271
geocodes 92
   conversion from degrees 171
   tube station data 292
gesture events, iPhone 311
getSessionKey service, Facebook integration 348
GMap2 Google Maps function 93, 288
Google, iGoogle Home page widgets 19–20
Google Maps
   addOverlay function 97
   API key 93
   Capital Punishment Home widget 171
   directional controls 94
   geocodes 92
   GMap2 function 93, 288
   GPolyline function 294
   information window 288
   iPhone 323, 348
   latitude 92
   LiveWeatherMapWidget 284–289
   load JavaScript client script file 93
   LondonTubeMapWidget 289–298
   longitude 92
   map type control 94
   markers 97, 288
   obtaining API key 95
   panDirection function 354
   polylines 294
   RecentSalesMashup, Zillow 92–99
   setCenter function 94
   zoom control 94
   zoomIn function 354
   zoomOut function 354
GoogleGeocodeSampleService sample service 13

H

HelloWorld sample service 13
HelloWorldWidget sample widget 14
Help widget, Facebook application 126
Hewitt, Joe 313
Home link, Facebook 113
home page, zembly 20
Home widget, Facebook 124
   configure 124
hover events
   and CSS styles 60
HTML
   Facebook friend invite widget 191
   Facebook widgets 121
   page markup 35
   radio buttons 167
   select tag options array 294
   vs FBML 120
HTTP, call service 33

I

iButtons widget 359–361
iCapital Punishment widget 331–337
icon, Facebook applications 128
iframe 14
iGoogle Home page 19–20
iLeaves widget 356–359

iLiveWeather widget 322–330
iLoanPayment widget 314–322
iLondonTube widget 348–356
image, upload an 36
`img` tag 36
   `src` attribute 77
Inbox tab, zembly 21
Info section, Facebook 212
Info tab, Facebook 114
information window, Google Maps 288
`innerHTML` 40
instant publishing, Facebook 113
invite friends, Facebook widget 187
iPhone
   overview 310–314
   EDGE network 310
   Facebook integration 337–348
   Facebook session authorization 339
   getSessionKey service 348
   Google Maps 323
   iButtons widget 359–361
   iCapital Punishment widget 331–337
   icons to Home Screen 317
   iLeaves widget 356–359
   iLiveWeather widget 322–330
   iLoanPayment widget 314–322
   iLondonTube widget 348–356
   iPhoneHome widget 337–348
   iUI Library 313
   multi-touch screen 311
   numeric key pad 324
   orientation changes 313
   run widgets 315
   screen 313
   simulator 317
   URL for Facebook application widget 339
   URLs 316
   virtual key pad 312
   web applications 311
iPhoneHome widget 337–348
iPod Touch 311
iUI Library, iPhone 313
   `fieldset` tag 319

J

JavaScript 35
   differences with FBJS 158
   arrays with FBJS 158
   cookie helper functions 330
   Facebook Client Library 233
   formatting numbers 90
   `Number` function 98
   regular expressions 150
   vs FBJS 120
JavaScript Editor
   code completion 131
   Facebook API 131
JavaScript Editor, zembly 31
`joehewitt.com` 313
JSON notation 52, 281
   and portability 87, 276
   Facebook adapters 156
   Flickr API data 64
   sample response from Yahoo! Pipes 305

JSON parameter type for services 28

K

Key parameter type for services 28
keychain
   Flickr API 68
keychain, zembly 24–25, 46

L

latitude, Google Maps 92
left-hand column, Facebook 109
Libraries
   Prototype JS 37
   Resources tab 37
LiveWeatherBugService 276–279
   add geocode data 285
   sample JSON data 281
LiveWeatherBugWidget 279–283
LiveWeatherMapWidget 284–289
LiveWeatherRSS adapter 47–50, 277
Loan Calculator Facebook application 121–125
LoanPaymentService 25–34
   (JavaScript) 27
LoanPaymentWidget 34–42
   (JavaScript) 38
lock badge, Facebook services and widgets 120
`Log.write` 33
logo, Facebook applications 129
LondonTubeJourneyPlanner Dapp 250–252
LondonTubeJourneyPlanner service 252–253
LondonTubeMapWidget 289–298
   `stations_data.js` file 293
LondonTubeWidget 254–258
longitude, Google Maps 92

M

main profile page, Facebook 109
Manage your Keychain, zembly 46
map type control, Google Maps 94
markers, Google Maps 97
mashups
   Capital Punishment Home widget 171
   LiveWeatherMapWidget 284–289
   LondonTubeMapWidget 289–298
   RecentSalesMashup 92–99
`Math.random` JavaScript function 75
`max-width` style attribute 60
McIlroy, Doug 298
messages, zembly contacts 21
mlbscores service 262
mlbScoresWidget 263–265
mlbupdate Dapp 259–262
Mood Pix Facebook application 208–231
   application Info section 219
   application tabs 223
   Info section 213
   profile publisher 224
   PublisherFriend service 227
   PublisherSelf service 226
   SeeMessages widget 231

SendMoodPix widget 227
SetInfoOptions service 222
Mood Pix Home Widget, *(JavaScript)* 217
multi-touch screen, iPhone 311
MyFlickrRandomSlideshow 71–77
    (JavaScript) 75

N

namespace, XML notation 277
news feed story types, Facebook 112, 183
news feed, Facebook 112
notices, Facebook 112
`Number` JavaScript function 98
Number parameter type for services 28
numeric key pad, iPhone input 324

O

object types, Facebook data store model 193
one-line story type, Facebook 112, 183
`onFailure` service call condition 66
online/offline status, zembly 44
`onMouseout` JavaScript event 65
`onMouseover` JavaScript event 65
opacity style attribute 62
`openInfoWindowHtml` Google Maps function 288
orientation changes, iPhone 313
`Owner.keychain`, zembly 46

P

`panDirection` Google Maps function 354
Parameter Editor, zembly 28, 70
parameters
    add a new 70
    escape value 49
    extracting in a widget 75
    in widgets 72
    required 29
    services 27
    types for services *(table)* 28
    validation 30
People tab, zembly 21, 23
permissions, Facebook applications 108
Pipes, *See* Yahoo! Pipes
PNG image file, iPhone 318
polyline, Google Maps feature 294
Preview tab, zembly 41
preview widget, Facebook 124
preview widgets, zembly 17
profile boxes 180
    main 109, 180
profile boxes, Facebook 108
`profile` parameter, `setFBML` adapter 157
profile publisher, Facebook 113, 224
profile, Facebook 105
profile, zembly 21–22
`profile.getInfo` Facebook adapter 221
`profile.setFBML` Facebook adapter 157
`profile.setInfo` Facebook adapter 221
`profile_main` parameter, `setFBML` adapter 157
properties, Facebook data store model 192

Prototype JS library 37
    `$("element_id")` 41
    `each` function 63
    enumeration 63
    `Event.observe` function 64
Publish action, Yahoo! Pipes 304
publish, zembly 32, 41
PublishChallenge service, Facebook application 190
PublisherFriend service, Facebook 227
PublisherSelf service, Facebook 226
PublishScore service, Facebook 186

R

radio buttons, HTML 167
    JavaScript event handlers 173
random number, generate in JavaScript 75
real estate service, Zillow 80
RecentSalesMashup 92–99
    (JavaScript) 97
RecentSalesService 82–88
    (JavaScript) 86
RecentSalesWidget 88–92
    (JavaScript) 90
registered template bundle, Facebook application 189
Registered Template Bundles Console, Facebook 182
registered templates, Facebook 133
RegisterTemplates service, Facebook application 184
regular expressions, JavaScript 150
required parameters, zembly 29
`requireLogin`, FBJS 137, 206
Resources tab, zembly 36
    Libraries 37
`responseType: Ajax.FBML`, FBJS 143, 150
`responseType: Ajax.JSON`, FBJS 217
RSS feed 267

S

Safari, webkit 356
sample data from LiveWeatherBugService 281
samples, on zembly 13
Save action, Yahoo! Pipes 304
save current draft, zembly 31
SaveScore service, Facebook data store model 198
scores, zembly Things 15
screen name, zembly 22
screen, iPhone 313
search for contacts, zembly 23
secret key, Facebook 118
SeeScores widget, Facebook 205
select tag options array, JavaScript 294
SendInvitation widget, Facebook 187
SendMoodPix widget, Facebook 227
service providers, zembly 24
services
    call 32
    Call tab 30
    capture example 30
    creating 25

Index

drafts 42–45
E4X notation 276
Erase and start over (all drafts) 43
Error Codes 29
favorites 16
Find & Use tab 49, 69
FlickrPeopleService 68–71
flickrPhotoSearch (Dapp-based) 243
GambitsfromGailFeed 268
getSessionKey, iPhone/Facebook integration 348
LiveWeatherBugService 276–279
LoanPaymentService 25–34
LondonTubeJourneyPlanner 252–253
mlbscores 262
online/offline status 44
parameter types *(table)* 28
parameter validation 30
parameters 27
publish 32
published versions 42
RecentSalesService 82–88
score 15
search for using Find & Use tab 39
test drive now 30
timeline 44
viewing versions 44
watch action 16
WeatherBugService 45–51
Yahoo! Pipes 306
session authorization, Facebook 136
`setCenter` Google Maps function 94
SetInfoOptions service, Facebook 222
`setInnerFBML` FBJS function 143
`setInterval` JavaScript function 62
`setStyle` FBJS function 144
`setTimeout` JavaScript function with FBJS 147
short story type, Facebook 112, 183
slide show widget 57–67
   BuddyPics Facebook application 137–158
Sort operator, Yahoo! Pipes 303
`src` attribute, `img` tag 77
`stations_data.js` file, LondonTubeMapWidget 293
story types, Facebook news feed 112
String parameter type for services 28

T

tags, Flickr photo search 63
tags, zembly 16
`{*target*}` token, Facebook feed story 183
template bundles, Facebook 182
template services and widgets, Facebook applications 126
templates, widgets 35
Terms of Service widget, Facebook application 126
test services, zembly 30
`www.testiPhone.com` simulator 317
Things tab, zembly 20
Thompson, Ken 298
timeline, zembly 44
timer code, JavaScript 170
tokens, Facebook feed story 183
touch events, iPhone 311

U

Union operator, Yahoo! Pipes 301
Unix pipe mechanism 298
UpdateProfileBox service, Facebook applications 181
UpdateProfileBox, Facebook applications 126
upload an image, zembly 36
URI parameter type for services 28
URL
   Facebook canvas page 117
   Flickr photo source 64
   iPhone widgets 316
user, Facebook 105

V

versions, zembly
   published widgets and services 42
   timeline 44
virtual key pad, iPhone 312

W

watch a service or widget, zembly 16
WeatherBug API 45
   sample XML data 276
WeatherBugService 45–51
   (JavaScript) 50
WeatherBugWidget 51–54
   (JavaScript) 52
WeatherTodayService sample service 13
web applications, iPhone 311
webkit, Safari display engine 356
What's happening tab, zembly 21, 24
widgets
   actions 16
   adding to iGoogle Home page 19–20
   clone 15
   create 35
   drafts 42–45
   embed 14
   Erase and start over (all drafts) 43
   execute on iPhone 315
   favorites 16
   flickrPhotoSearchWidget 244–248
   FlickrSlideShow 57–67
   GambitsSummaryWidget 268–271
   HTML and Facebook 121
   iButtons 359–361
   iCapital Punishment 331–337
   iLeaves 356–359
   iLiveWeather 322–330
   iLoanPayment 314–322
   iLondonTube 348–356
   iPhone simulator 317
   iPhoneHome 337–348
   Libraries 37
   LiveWeatherBugWidget 279–283
   LiveWeatherMapWidget 284–289
   LoanPaymentWidget 34–42
   LondonTubeMapWidget 289–298
   LondonTubeWidget 254–258
   mlbScoresWidget 263–265

MyFlickrRandomSlideshow 71–77
   online/offline status 44
   parameters 72
   preview 17
   Preview tab 41
   publish 41
   published versions 42
   RecentSalesMashup 92–99
   RecentSalesWidget 88–92
   Resources tab 37
   score 15
   sharing with Clearspring 18, 66
   templates 35
   timeline 44
   viewing versions 44
   watch action 16
   WeatherBugWidget 51–54
   zemblyrumblings 304–307

X

XFBML, Facebook 233
   server tags 234
(X)HTML, page markup 35
XML data 48, 84, 276
   namespace 277
   node attributes 277
XML parameter type for services 28

Y

Yahoo! Pipes 298
   Fetch Feed object 300
   Filter operator 302
   format of service call 306
   JSON notation response 305
   Publish action 304
   Save action 304
   Sort operator 303
   Union operator 301
   zemblyblog pipe 299–304
   zemblyrumblings widget 304–307
YahooTripSearchService sample service 13
You tab, `zembly` 20
YouTubeSampleService sample service 13

Z

`zembly`
   actions 16
   adapters 24
   Add to editor 40
   API calls 24
   `Application` object 134
   Call tab 30
   capture example 30
   clone 15
   code name 22
   collaboration requests 21
   contacts 22–24
   create a service 25
   create a widget 35
   create Facebook applications 114–120
   drafts for services and widgets 42–45
   editor commands 31
   Erase and start over action 43
   favorites 16
   Find & Use tab 39, 49
   home page 20
   Inbox tab 21
   keychain 24–25, 46
   Manage your Keychain 46
   messages 21
   online/offline status 44
   `Owner.keychain` 46
   Parameter Editor 28
   parameter validation 30
   People tab 21, 23
   Preview tab 41
   preview widgets 17
   profile 21–22
   publish 32, 41
   Resources tab 36, 37
   save current draft 31
   scores 15
   screen name 22
   search for contacts 23
   service providers 24
   tags 16
   test services 30
   Things tab 20
   timeline 44
   upload resources 36
   watch a service or widget 16
   What's happening tab 21, 24
   You tab 20
zemblyblog pipe 299–304
zemblyConnectDemo Facebook application 232–235
zemblyrumblings widget 304–307
Zillow
   RecentSalesMashup 92–99
   RecentSalesService 82–88
   RecentSalesWidget 88–92
   sample XML data 84
   `zpid` 82
Zillow real estate service 80
zillow.homevaluation.GetChart adapter 80
zillow.homevaluation.GetComps adapter 80
zillow.homevaluation.GetDemographics adapter 81
zillow.homevaluation.GetRegionChart adapter 81
zillow.homevaluation.GetRegionChildren adapter 81
zillow.homevaluation.GetSearchResults adapter 81, 83
zillow.homevaluation.GetZestimate adapter 81
zillow.propertydetails.GetDeepComps adapter 81, 85
zillow.propertydetails.GetDeepSearchResults adapter 81
ZillowSampleService sample service 13
zoom control, Google Maps 94
`zoomIn` Google Maps function 354
`zoomOut` Google Maps function 354
`zpid`, Zillow property ID 82
zventsSearchService sample service 14

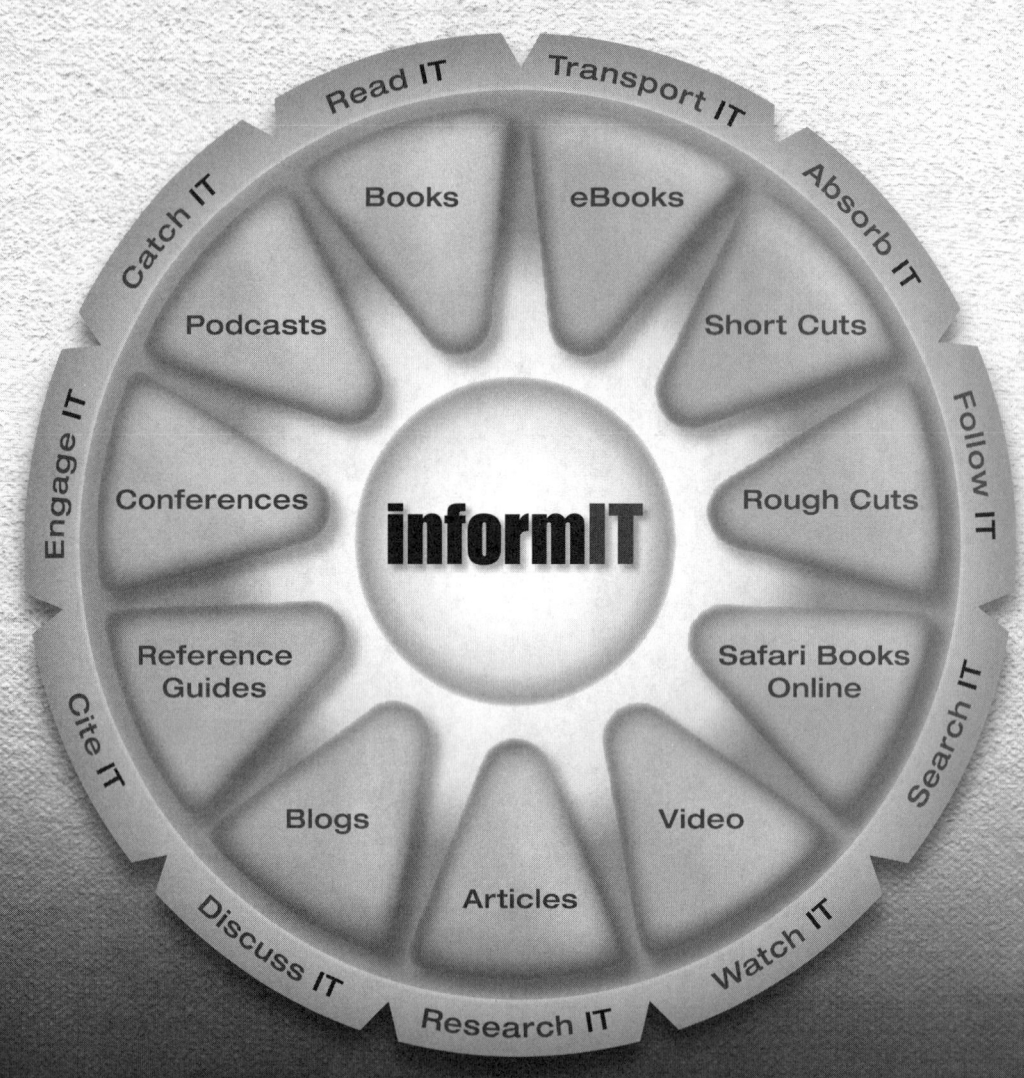

Try Safari Books Online FREE

Get online access to 5,000+ Books and Videos

Safari Books Online

FREE TRIAL—GET STARTED TODAY!
www.informit.com/safaritrial

Find trusted answers, fast
Only Safari lets you search across thousands of best-selling books from the top technology publishers, including Addison-Wesley Professional, Cisco Press, O'Reilly, Prentice Hall, Que, and Sams.

Master the latest tools and techniques
In addition to gaining access to an incredible inventory of technical books, Safari's extensive collection of video tutorials lets you learn from the leading video training experts.

WAIT, THERE'S MORE!

Keep your competitive edge
With Rough Cuts, get access to the developing manuscript and be among the first to learn the newest technologies.

Stay current with emerging technologies
Short Cuts and Quick Reference Sheets are short, concise, focused content created to get you up-to-speed quickly on new and cutting-edge technologies.

FREE Online Edition

Your purchase of **Assemble the Social Web with zembly** includes access to a free online edition for 45 days through the Safari Books Online subscription service. Nearly every Prentice Hall book is available online through Safari Books Online, along with more than 5,000 other technical books and videos from publishers such as Addison-Wesley Professional, Cisco Press, Exam Cram, IBM Press, O'Reilly, Que, and Sams.

SAFARI BOOKS ONLINE allows you to search for a specific answer, cut and paste code, download chapters, and stay current with emerging technologies.

Activate your FREE Online Edition at www.informit.com/safarifree

> **STEP 1:** Enter the coupon code: NDNJIXA.

> **STEP 2:** New Safari users, complete the brief registration form. Safari subscribers, just log in.

If you have difficulty registering on Safari or accessing the online edition, please e-mail customer-service@safaribooksonline.com